Public Order

Law and Practice

Public Order
Law and Practice

John Beggs QC

George Thomas

and

Susanna Rickard

OXFORD
UNIVERSITY PRESS

OXFORD

UNIVERSITY PRESS

Great Clarendon Street, Oxford OX2 6DP
United Kingdom

Oxford University Press is a department of the University of Oxford.
It furthers the University's objective of excellence in research, scholarship,
and education by publishing worldwide. Oxford is a registered trade mark of
Oxford University Press in the UK and in certain other countries

First published 2012
Reprinted 2013

British Library Cataloguing in Publication Data
Data available

Library of Congress Cataloging in Publication Data
Data available

ISBN 978-0-19-922797-6

Foreword

The police response to incidents of protest, events such as football, and public disorder has always been subject to scrutiny by the public. Historically, the breaching of the peace was the point when action was taken. However, as society and the law have changed, it is important that there is a clear understanding of the legal framework that underpins the options for action at all command levels and by staff on the ground. As the Association of Chief Police Officers lead for Public Order and Public Safety, I welcome this book, which provides a single reference source for the various pieces of legislation in what has become an increasingly complex arena.

I have known of John Beggs by reputation for many years. An often heard description of him as 'outstanding' and 'providing clear and concise views' is clearly merited not only from the cases he has been involved in but also from personal knowledge in more recent times. *Public Order: Law and Practice* is readily understandable and provides an illustration of the breadth of areas that can result in disorder and how the legislation should be interpreted. The more recent increase in protest, whether in relation to the use of land or single issue, is covered by separate chapters. These chapters not only outline the relevant legislation, but also include the practical interpretation by citing examples and case studies. Whilst some legislation is utilised on a regular basis by officers, this book also covers that which clearly isn't: for example, Section 9(2) Criminal Law Act 1977, concerning trespassing on land such as a foreign embassy. *Public Order: Law and Practice* provides a 'one stop shop' as a guide on public order legislation and should prove to be an invaluable tool for practitioners at all levels.

Sue Sim
Chief Constable, Northumbria Police
ACPO Lead for Public Order and Public Safety
November 2011

Preface

The purpose of this book is to provide police officers with a legal 'ready reckoner' for public order situations. The aim is to help the uniformed constable responding to a pub fight or domestic fracas, just as much as the police commander acting as bronze or silver commander on a major public protest. We hope it will also be of use to the lawyer, regardless of role, background or experience, seeking an accessible and reasonably thorough guide to the myriad powers available to the police.

Policing public disorder is inevitably complex, due to the chaos, the danger to officers and the public and the risk of escalation. Every year in the UK these challenges mutate unpredictably. A sound grasp of the basic legal powers available for combating and reducing disorder is now a fundamental requirement for almost all police officers.

The book starts with the general themes of human rights, breach of the peace and common public order offences, before moving on to address scenarios that have led to specific legal problems and policing powers. In each chapter, we have sought to identify the key features of the law. We have not attempted an academic treatise, but have done our best to provide practical, relevant advice. Plainly this book can never be a substitute for police officers taking legal advice in any given situation—and we commend the notion of police officers taking legal advice *before* rather than *after* a particular operation.

In many situations, the powers available to prevent a breach of the peace will be the most appropriate and effective 'first line' response. Breach of the peace has a chapter of its own, but this flexible application of these common law powers is a theme that runs through the whole of the book. Once the threat to the peace has been averted or the disorder quelled, the 'second line' response may include arrests for substantive offences, warnings to those threatening the peace, containment, or even simply an ongoing monitoring of the situation. It is at this point that specific offences and powers may come to the fore in the officer's mind.

The key police objective must always be to prevent death or serious injury. This in turn means preventing the escalation of disorder: reimposing order is always a much more difficult and dangerous task. However, the timing and nature of pre-emptive police action requires careful consideration, particularly when Article 10 (freedom of expression) or 11 (freedom of assembly) rights are engaged. When human rights are engaged, and the police have the delicate task of balancing competing rights, priority must *always* be given to preventing death or serious injury.

As a rule of thumb, police officers will rarely be criticized if they act to pre-serve life and limb, and do so in good faith based upon the information reason-ably known to them at the time. While such an approach may sometimes lead to legal error, such errors will not generally result in career-ending litigation or media excoriation. 'Doing the right thing' remains an appropriate mantra for police officers facing the threat of, or actual, public disorder. In modern life, doing the right thing must include recording what was done, and the reason for it. Police officers must remain mindful that every time they use a coercive power, they may—quite properly—be called to account.

Our profound thanks go to our consulting editor, Mick Messinger. The corner-stone of public order policing in London for many years, he embraced the arrival of the European Convention on Human Rights in domestic law. His commitment to the aim in every policing operation to *facilitate* peaceful public events remains the standard to which everyone in the police service should aspire. His guidance has been invaluable. Our thanks also to Amy Street, whose input was so crucial at the beginning of this project, particularly in the drafting of chapters 2 and 3.

Our colleagues in chambers have been generous with their support and advice throughout the book's long, and at times painful, gestation. Helena White con-ducted assiduous research on hate crime. Our thanks also go to OUP for their support and patience, in particular our editors, Lucy Alexander and Emma Hawes. Hopefully the book will justify their enduring faith in us. Last, but by no means least, we must acknowledge the unstinting support, and calmness and cajoling, of our partners and families, with particular thanks to Sarah and Sara, who have lived with the book from its inception and without whom it would almost certainly remain uncompleted.

Despite the expert input from friends and colleagues, any legal errors are our own. We have attempted to state the law as of 1 October 2011.

John Beggs QC
George Thomas
Susanna Rickard

Serjeants' Inn Chambers (formerly 3 Serjeants' Inn)
October 2011

Contents

Contents

Contents

Special Features

This book contains several special features that it is hoped will make it more helpful to the reader. These are defined and explained below.

Point to Note/Key points

Information requiring particular emphasis is summarized in key points.

Definitions

Definitions of specific terms are provided where this is useful.

Case studies

Where these are appropriate, the material in the text will be related to case study examples to give an indication of how the issue relates to the practical business of policing.

Scenarios

To illustrate some of the issues discussed in the chapters, example scenarios are presented.

Tables

Some information or concepts have been tabulated for ease of illustration and presentation.

Further information and reading

These boxes provide the reader with additional information and direct the reader towards additional reading that will elaborate upon points discussed in the text.

Table of Cases

Table of Legislation

Statutory Instruments

List of Abbreviations

AC	Appeal Court
ACPO	Association of Chief Police Officers
AFO	Authorised Firearms Officer
AGM	Annual General Meeting
All ER	All England Law Reports
ASBA	Anti-social Behaviour Act 2003
CAD	computer aided dispatch
CCTV	Closed Circuit Television
CDA	Crime and Disorder Act 1998
CJA	Criminal Justice Act 2003
CJPA	Criminal Justice and Police Act 2001
CJPOA	Criminal Justice and Public Order Act 1994
CPS	Crown Prosecution Service
Cr App R	Criminal Appeals Reports
Crim LR	Criminal Law Review
DBO	Drinking Banning Order
DPP	designated public place
DPP	Director of Public Prosecutions
DPPO	Designated Public Places Order
ECHR	European Convention on Human Rights
ECtHR	European Court of Human Rights
FA	Football Association
FBO	Football Banning Order
FBOA	Football Banning Orders Authority
FIFA	Fédération Internationale de Football Association
FIT	Forward Intelligence Team
FIU	Football Intelligence Unit
FSA	Football Spectators Act 1989
GBH	grievous bodily harm
Hansard HC	Official Record of the House of Commons
Hansard HL	Official Record of the House of Lords
HRA	Human Rights Act 1998
IRB	incident report book
PACE	Police and Criminal Evidence Act 1984
PCSO	Police Community Support Officer
PHA	Protection from Harassment Act 1997
POA	Public Order Act 1986
POCA	Proceeds of Crime Act 2005

RIPA	Regulation of Investigatory Powers Act 2000
RPA	Representation of the People Act 1983
SECAA	Sporting Events (Control of Alcohol etc) Act 1985
SOCPA	Serious Organised Crime and Police Act 2005
TULRCA	Trade Union and Labour Relations (Consolidation) Act 1992
UEFA	Union of European Football Associations
VCRA	Violent Crime Reduction Act 2006

1

Getting It Right

1.1 **Introduction**

Public order policing is difficult. It involves chaos and confusion. It involves police commanders making decisions under pressure where the consequences of those decisions may be very serious, including death or serious injury to members of the public or police officers. Furthermore, frontline officers often have to maintain their cool under extreme provocation and violence.

Those causing disorder are sometimes drunk, or very violent or intent on injuring police officers. Some are politically motivated and intelligent. The challenge of keeping the peace, while upholding a person's rights under the European Convention of Human Rights, often in the face of deliberate provocation, is difficult to meet. A solid grasp of the important public order powers is absolutely fundamental because it is at these times that it is hardest to recall accurately the range of legal powers available to the police and the restrictions placed upon them.

Police commanders of public disorder sometimes struggle to record coherent notes of what decisions they took and why—both during the planning and operational stages of a public order event. Their subsequent memories play them false—unsurprisingly.

Frontline officers struggle to recall and record, coherently, what has just happened. This is because they are tired or confused or suffer from perceptual distortions derived from stress.

In the artificially calm and critical atmosphere of the courtroom, differences in the notebook entries of frontline officers are often pounced upon by defence lawyers as indicative of error—when they are as often as not indicative of nothing more than differing perceptions of the same stressful event. Indeed, differences may often be indicative of *greater* accuracy and honesty than pocket notebooks curiously identical in wording.

How then, can police officers engaged in public order policing maximize their prospects of ensuring they are acting lawfully, securing proper criminal convictions, avoiding civil claims and, perhaps most importantly, maintaining the Queen's peace and the good reputation of British policing? The answers lie in the following five principles of public order policing:

- Planning
- Briefing
- Conduct of the operation
- Post-incident
- Giving evidence.

These principles that cover the planning of major events can equally be speedily and practically applied (with the exception of the briefing phase) to even the minor, spontaneous public order scenario. These situations have at least as much potential to test an officer's knowledge and application of public order law as a major incident.

As he or she approaches the front door of a house in response to a report of a disturbance, an officer should train him or herself to consider, out of habit, issues such as, 'What do I know about this situation? What are the likely powers I might need to use, and in what circumstances? How am I going to conduct myself?' After the event, recording an accurate account with an eye on ultimately giving evidence in court is important, whatever the nature of the incident that has occurred.

1.2 Planning

Any major pre-planned public order event requires detailed planning. That much is obvious. But certain features of planning are less obvious.

1.2.1 Intelligence

First, what is the quality of your intelligence? There are many examples of public order events where the police intelligence has been good but poorly interpreted, or poor intelligence has been over-interpreted as if it were of a good quality.

Indeed, one might go further and suggest that often the police service has an institutional tendency to 'sex up' the intelligence (a characteristic not unique to policing) and thereby to overexaggerate the expectant risks. Those in charge of the intelligence side of a pre-planned operation have a particular duty to check, and continue to check, right up until the last available opportunity, the accuracy and true meaning of the intelligence to ensure that the police tendency to get overexcited about the risks does not creep in.

Indeed, a simple but valuable intelligence question always to ask is: what more can reasonably be done to confirm the intelligence? If the answer is 'plenty', then the next question is 'so why isn't that work being done?'

The risk of hyping the intelligence is particularly acute in the planning of the policing of political protest. This is because often the intelligence cells will be populated with police officers (sometimes from Special Branch) who may not have a true understanding of the protest group or who harbour a jaundiced attitude to all protestors—that is, seeing all green protestors as extremists, all anti-globalization campaigners as anarchists, or all animal rights campaigners as members of, or sympathizers with, militant animal rights organizations.

Political groups often exaggerate the extent of their support and likely attendance. Open source material on the internet is often of dubious accuracy. The job of the intelligence cell is soberly to assess, in respect of the protestors the likely:

- numbers
- disposition

- objectives
- tactics
- leadership.

The more that the police planners can demonstrate earnest and professional attempts to discern an accurate intelligence picture, the more likely it is that any court reviewing the policing of the protest will be sympathetic—especially if the event goes badly wrong.

The fruits of intelligence previously gathered remains vital. The Court of Appeal in *Wood v Commissioner of Police for the Metropolis* [2010] 1 WLR 123 held that where the police visibly and with no obvious cause chose to take and retain photographs of an individual going about his lawful business in the street, that was a sufficient intrusion by the state into the individual's privacy as to amount to a prima facie violation of his rights under Article 8(1) (see section 2.6.2). The decision has been misunderstood. It remains lawful both to gather intelligence by video or photograph and to retain it, provided there is a genuine, significant intelligence need. What is not permitted is to retain the images that were initially gathered for the purpose of subsequent identification of crime/suspects, where it later emerges is there is no policing need for it to be retained. Thus forward intelligence teams continue to play an important role in planning for major public order events.

Key questions will always be:

- what more could the police have done to ascertain the true intelligence picture?
- did the police soberly and sensibly analyse the intelligence received?
- did the police react (ie plan) appropriately to that intelligence assessment?

1.2.2 **Legal advice**

At the planning stage, it is far better to get legal advice on the legality of proposed police tactics *before* rather than (more expensively and potentially disastrously) *after* the event. Nevertheless, legion are the examples of police forces deploying a particular tactic or arrest power only to discover—after checking with a lawyer after the event—that the tactic is probably unlawful or that the arrest power did not in fact exist; or that a much better power existed.

1.2.3 **Clarity of purpose**

Clarity and rationality of police objectives are two key building blocks to successful planning.

The planning of resource allocation must be specific and tailored to the intelligence, likely activity and police objectives. Generic, unfocused resource planning is inefficient and ineffective. An over-reliance on plans that have previously 'worked' is also dangerous. Groups, particularly protestors, will change their activities if their perception is that a previous event was over-policed or policed too well.

Recent years have seen a significant move from the tactic of dispersing a troublesome assembly towards containment of it. It is unfortunate that containment is regularly perceived or reported as an infringement of protestors' rights. Provided there is competent planning, the correct criteria for its implementation are applied (necessity) and appropriate measures taken for the welfare of the crowd and their swiftest possible release, then the total impact on the rights of the protestors and the community in which the protest is taking place should be lessened. ('Kettling' is an inaccurate word with negative connotations of heat, pressure and letting off steam, none of which are helpful in public order policing.)

Containment is to be regarded as a tactic of last resort and the conditions to be satisfied are stringent. In *Austin v Commission of Police for the Metropolis* [2009] 1 AC 564 Lord Neuberger stated at paragraph 60 that containment could be lawful 'provided, and it is a very important proviso, that the actions of the police are proportionate and reasonable, and any confinement is restricted to a reasonable minimum, as to discomfort and as to time, as is necessary for the relevant purpose, namely the prevention of serious public disorder and violence'.

In *Moos v Commission of Police for the Metropolis* [2011] EWHC 957 at paragraph 56, the Court stated that, in relation to containment:

> *There have to be proper advanced preparations.* It is only when the police reasonably believe that there is no other means whatsoever to prevent an imminent breach of the peace that they can as a matter of necessity curtail the lawful exercise of their rights by third parties.
>
> [emphasis added]

In *R (Castle) v Commissioner of Police for the Metropolis* [2011] EWHC 2317 the High Court observed that an *entirely innocent* person, caught up in a containment that was necessary only due to a failure in planning, might have a civil remedy.

If there is a risk of police containment, then this trend in recent case law underscores the need for specific consideration by the police of how the protestors will manage toileting or refreshments and the like. The police are not expected to provide Starbucks-type facilities, but basic needs should, if at all possible, be catered for, especially if the event is a pre-planned one and the containment reasonably envisaged.

It is vital that the planning meetings and decisions are properly recorded. It is essential that the minutes of planning meetings record the date of the meeting, together with who was present. Police records do not have to be lengthy— just intelligent, recording the key rationale for the key decisions, together with reference to the key evidence or intelligence relied upon.

1.3 **The Briefing**

> In some cases [the protestors] describe the officers whom they spoke to as pleasant and giving optimistic assurances about when releases would take place. In other cases the witnesses complain that the officers either did not respond at all, or responded in a way that was unhelpful, giving no reasons or explanation. Some officers said that they did not know when releases would be allowed or that they were following orders.
>
> Tugendhat J, in the first instance decision in
> *Austin and Saxby v Commissioner of Police for the Metropolis* in 2005.

Just as communication with protestors is critically important, so accurate and professional briefings to the police 'troops' carrying out the plans is essential. It is now over ten years since the containment at Oxford Circus, challenged in the case of *Austin*. The courts now demand a higher standard of briefing for a major public order event where containment is anticipated.

In *Moos* in 2011 the Court said at paragraph 62:

> . . . it is evident that there were instances of unduly inflexible release and instances of unnecessary and, we think, unjustified force in the pushing operation. The evidence as to instructions in these respects is not satisfactory. No doubt instructions of the kind which [Silver commander] described were given, but they were very general and imprecise and may not have been fully conveyed to individual officers, some of whom appear not to have been trained for crowd control operations of this kind. It is not for us to be prescriptive in detail as to how such matters should be dealt with. But no doubt it is necessary to have a combination of training and on the spot instruction.

Communicating to the frontline officers precisely what the objectives of the police operation are must be done in clear and simple terms—it would be as well for briefings to confirm that the frontline officers understand their briefings.

Very often the objectives will include matters such as:

- facilitating peaceful protest
- keeping rival protestors apart
- blocking certain roads or pathways
- protecting certain sensitive venues
- keeping people moving.

Clarity of objectives is essential. The 'Chinese whisper' is a dangerous phenomenon in modern policing. If Gold is going to delegate briefing to Silver superintendents and Silver to Bronze, and the Bronze superintendents to frontline inspectors, will the key messages be lost or distorted along the way?

An obvious way to minimize losses in translation is to reduce the core elements of the briefing to writing and to distribute the same to the frontline officers. But any such documents should be short—ideally no more than a page or two of A4—and should be reinforced by clear oral messages in live briefings.

Best practice is to record the briefing on video and to make it available on the intranet to officers who were unable to attend the briefing. This also shows police transparency and confidence in any legal review of the event.

How does the senior commander ensure that the ethos of the frontline troops is appropriate? It is easy for commanders to forget that generally it is not they being goaded, or spat at, or having to retreat under a barrage of missiles. Nonetheless, reminding officers of their duties, (i) to keep the peace using (ii) a minimum of force whilst (iii) respecting the right to protest, is a key requirement.

So too is the need to remind police officers that protestors are not that different from them; indeed, many officers may have friends and family attending the instant or similar protests. But the tendency for a 'them and us' climate to develop is inevitable and such a mindset militates against restrained and professional policing, in favour of more aggressive and thus more dangerous policing.

Where containment is a potential tactic, the commanders of the operation need carefully and clearly to explain to the frontline officers how their discretion—for example to release certain protestors from the cordon—should be exercised. Often this is no more complicated than inviting officers to exercise their common sense: the obvious Japanese tourist caught up with his wife in a protesting crowd should, if at all possible, be released from any police containment to avoid offending or upsetting the tourists and to avoid falsely imprisoning them. So too the obviously distressed or injured or 'I've had enough' protester, if at all possible.

Courteous crowd communication is now expected from officers on public order duties. Encouraging frontline officers to maintain, where appropriate, a dialogue with protestors is good practice. Once protestors start talking with police officers, tensions tend to reduce and a rapport can be developed. Frontline officers need to learn and/or display the art of chatting with people who may well have extreme or unpleasant views—but dialogue is better than a standoff. Furthermore, intelligent dialogue may bear fruit.

Any intelligent public order commander will want an unassailable record of his or her briefings so that there can be no dispute after the event as to the good faith or lawfulness of the police intentions. The fact that those in command have done their best, in planning and briefing, to reduce recourse to police use of force is a key ingredient to successful public order policing.

> Against this background, in determining whether the force used was compatible with Article 2, the Court must carefully scrutinise . . . not only whether the force used by the soldiers was strictly proportionate to the aim of protecting persons against unlawful violence but also whether the anti-terrorist operation was *planned and controlled by the authorities* so as to minimise, to the greatest extent possible, recourse to lethal force.
>
> Judgment of the European Court of Human Rights, in *McCann v UK*, Application No. 18984/91; emphasis added.

Conversely, if it becomes plain to any reviewing court that the command and control of an operation has been sub-optimal, then the criminal and civil, to say nothing of professional, consequences may be significant. The attempt to get it right is a powerful mitigation even if things in fact went badly wrong. That the police attempts were sound, in good faith and lawful is evidently a major benefit to any officer who becomes the subject of media excoriation.

Almost every protestor now carries a video camera with them on their mobile telephone. Many know how to use both the camera and the internet to maximum effect. Of the thousands of video clips taken during the day, the two or three showing frontline officers at their stoniest, if not rudest, will be the footage most widely publicized. It is too easy to react with despair or anger. In contrast, the following message delivered at the briefing is both more balanced and less demoralizing:

> Filming of the police on camera phones is now inevitable. Rather than worry about whether or not they are being filmed, it is safe and realistic for officers to assume that they are being filmed at all times, and modify their behaviour accordingly:
>
> - Evidence of good practice: tactful communication with crowd members is (contrary to the cynical view) frequently uploaded by people at public order events.
> - If dealing with an unreasonable member of the public, an officer who maintains courteous conversation with that person can highlight that person's unreasonable attitude.
> - Sometimes, surprisingly, other members of the public will join a patient officer in his efforts to calm down an excitable or rude crowd member.
> - If the same officer has been standing in the same cordon for an hour, that officer is allowed to acknowledge that a protestor is bored and even confess that they are bored too, or that they don't know when either they, or the protestor, are going to be allowed home.

1.3.1 Powers of arrest

One particularly important topic for all police briefings is identification of the optimal powers of arrest. Whilst certain types of operation may lend themselves to certain statutory powers to arrest (such as outside a nuclear power station) it is never to be forgotten that the most effective power that the police have to prevent violence or damage to property is the common law one to arrest to *prevent* a breach of the peace.

It would be as well to reiterate the ingredients of the lawful use of this common law power to all frontline officers—reasonable apprehension of imminent violence such that intervention is necessary—and to underscore for them that it is essentially a preventive power to be used only for so long as necessary to prevent violence.

Officers can be reminded that upon restoring the peace it will be open to them to release the 'arrestee' or to formally arrest them for a substantive offence. Continuing detention would be unlawful, if detention were no longer necessary either to prevent a breach of the peace or to bring the arrested person before the magistrates. Officers can be reminded that performing arrests requiring escort to police stations may be inimical to the success of the policing operation if it unduly depletes the frontline establishment of officers.

Officers should also be reminded that the power of arrest generally requires only reasonable suspicion of the offence being committed, about to be committed, or just been committed. In many sections of this book, potential defences to specific offences are discussed. However, in the majority of cases the officer must focus on the prima facie evidence giving rise to reasonable suspicion. It is not generally the role or duty of the public order officer to stop and ask themselves, in the heat of the moment, whether there might be a defence to the offence apparently being committed in front of them.

1.3.2 During the public order operation

Plainly communication between police officers and between police officers and protestors is another critical ingredient to good public order policing.

As between police officers, many are the examples where the 'Silver' commander loses touch of what is happening on the front line and/or is unable properly to get his message to the front line. Such situations can become a recipe for disaster. So what has been done in planning to facilitate communications will be all-important.

So, too, will be communication with protestors. If the police are going to form a blockade of a street, then tell the protestors via loudspeaker or personally; if the police are forming a cordon because serious violence is anticipated, then, once it can be done safely and without thwarting the very objective, the protestors should be told that they are being contained and why. This message should be repeated, clearly, as frequently as necessary. Keeping protestors in the dark about police intentions, or repeating a formulaic, generic explanation, is rarely conducive to good police/protestor relations (anymore than it is between rail travellers and train operators).

Plainly if protestors can be pre-warned as to the likely unpleasant consequences of their continued behaviour, then they should be. Protestors should always, where possible, be given the opportunity to change their course or objectives so as to avoid confrontation or arrest. That is the essence of policing by consent. But any such warnings must be delivered in a timely and clear fashion so that the scope for misunderstanding or manipulation by a hardcore minority is reduced. Most police public order commanders will be well aware of the propensity of well-organized extremist groups hijacking otherwise peaceful protests for their own political ends. This has been a regular feature of certain radical political groups. Distinguishing the hardcore from the peaceable majority is seldom easy and sometimes impossible, but genuine attempts need to be made. This is no more than the exercise of common sense, which is a key ingredient to all aspects of policing, even if a plethora of manuals and doctrines sometimes obscures this fact.

Commanders need to be decisive in the heat of what may become a battle. Indecision or lack of clarity in communication of objectives may be just as dangerous as 'gung-ho' decision making. Very serious consideration should be given to a continuous dictaphone recording of the analysis and decisions of the Silver commander for the duration of a major or controversial event.

However carefully regimented the public order planning and organization, the individual constable retains the discretion vested in him as to the exercise of his powers. The bread and butter powers are all available to him. For example, the officer's power under s 1 of the Police and Criminal Evidence Act 1984 to stop and search a member of the public (where he has reasonable grounds for suspecting that he will find stolen or prohibited articles) will remain of great potential assistance in almost all large and small-scale public order scenarios.

In the public order context, an officer also has a further specific power relating to anti-social behaviour: under s 50 of the Police Reform Act 2002, an officer in uniform may require a person to give his name and address, if the officer has reason to believe that the person has been acting, or is acting, in an anti-social manner. A person who refuses to give his name and address (or gives false details) is guilty of an offence and thus liable to be arrested.

This is a significant exception to the normal position where an officer cannot compel a person to provide their personal details unless they are suspected of having committed an offence or a breach of the peace. It requires considerable discretion on the part of the police officer, particularly in the context of freedom of expression. For example, a protestor that commits what would normally be regarded as a very low level degree of as anti-social behaviour, but is entirely normal behaviour in the context of an otherwise peaceful protest, such as shouting loudly in the street, should not be subjected to a s 50 request. The briefing is an opportunity to remind officers of the need to police such incidents proportionally.

1.3.3 **Doing the 'right' thing**

Sometimes the police commander or frontline officer faced with an emergency will have no realistic chance of considering what the law may or may not permit. In such situations the sensible operational rule of thumb for the officer is to *do the right thing*. This 'right thing' is that which minimizes the risk of death or serious injury to persons, or damage to property, always according protection of life the highest priority.

The law is increasingly complex. The superimposition of human rights principles on top of the common law can make things more difficult still.

Police officers should never forget that if, in the heat of a moment of emergency, they do that which they honestly and reasonably believe to be most likely to protect life and limb then the courts will be reluctant to criticize them.

Furthermore, despite the hyperbolic language of some tabloid newspapers, doing the right thing in public disorder often equates with acting according to the law. The common law defence of necessity (both in relation to criminal and tort) will apply if:

- the aim was to preserve life or limb, or to prevent serious disorder or damage to property;
- there was no other practical alternative but to act in that, or a very similar way (though lack of pre-operation planning will expose the police when claiming necessity; see for example *Rigby v Chief Constable of Northamptonshire* [1985] 1 WLR 1242).

Both the common law and European law attempts to strike a balance between individual freedom and the interests of society. Neither the law nor the courts attempt to make a fool of the law.

So, if in doubt, officers should act boldly in defence of life and limb and let the lawyers sort out any litigation that ensues.

1.4 **Post-incident**

The law on post-incident procedures is gathering pace, as is the guidance provided in police manuals.

There are several key aspects to post-incident procedure:

- Preservation of evidence
- Achieving independence of investigation
- Compilation of first accounts

1.4.1 **Preservation of evidence**

It is a truism that as soon as a public order disaster occurs, evidence will start to be dissipated by time, contamination, loss of witnesses, and so forth.

Thus the priority for the police after a public order incident which has degenerated into violence or serious criminality is to erect forensic cordons and to bring in those whose task it is to identify seize and 'bag' the exhibits, as soon as possible. Ideally, such personnel should be independent of those police personnel who are primary witnesses, though this will not always be possible.

Those who wish to traduce the police service will always look for evidence of conspiracy and cover-up. The quicker the forensic scenes can be preserved and the exhibits (whether petrol bombs, CCTV or police note batons) seized, the better.

Consideration must be given prior to the event to the types of documentary evidence it may be necessary to collate after the event. This may well include:

- minutes of planning meetings, or meetings with organizers;
- publicity generated prior to the briefing and between the briefing and the event;
- correspondence with, evidence of attempts to contact, and the responses of organizers;
- operation planning documents;
- intelligence and material collated from the public domain as to threat levels prior to the incident;
- pocket notebooks, incident report books, etc;
- Forward Intelligence Team (FIT) video evidence, evidence gathering transcripts, relevant camcorder footage;
- officers' notebooks/incident report books (IRBs);
- computer aided despatch (CAD) logs and, potentially, the audio recording of the CAD radio channel;
- decision logs, as to the commander and the tactical advisor (see above);
- deployment records of the police serials ordered to attend.

Again, the importance of ensuring these documents are accurately dated, and the author identified, is crucial.

1.4.2 Independence

Where death or serious injury has occurred, the likelihood is that there will be a professional standards or IPCC investigation. In such situations, where Articles 2 or 3 may be engaged, securing the independence of the investigation is all-important.

The quicker operatives who are not connected with the police officers who participated in the public order event are introduced to take over the investigation, the better.

1.4.3 First accounts

The importance of officers' first accounts after violent or traumatic public order situations cannot be underestimated. Should those accounts be based upon post-incident collaboration?

It is recognized that operational police officers should record, usually within their pocket notebook, evidence and details of any material incident that may result in criminal, civil or other significant proceedings. Many force policies on notebooks reflect that they should be used by officers:

- as the first record of evidence, recording the key points of any incident and any other details they feel may assist them to recall the circumstances of the event at a later date, in particular when they are giving evidence in court;

- to record information about an occurrence or event which the officer considers to be significant;
- as an aid to memory to assist officers to recall the circumstances surrounding events.

This rehearses the obligation to ensure timely, effective and accurate post-incident note-making. Further, the making of notes which are thorough, accurate and capable of withstanding scrutiny has been rendered all the more important by the Criminal Justice Act 2003, which prescribes that in circumstances where previous statements were once admissible just in relation to issues of credibility, they are now admissible as to the truth of their contents: see, for example, s 120.

Crucially, this new regime includes previous statements which are used to rebut a suggestion of recent fabrication and those used by witnesses as memory refreshing documents (provided, in the case of the latter category, that the witness has been cross-examined on that statement and as a consequence it is received as evidence in the proceedings).

This means that post-incident notes will inevitably become important evidence to be weighed by juries in criminal, as well as civil and coronial, cases.

There is an understanding in some quarters within the police service that there is some sort of 'right' enshrined within the case law for officers to confer in the making of their notes following an incident which they have witnessed together and before they make their notes. There is no such right, as any careful analysis of the case law shows.

The dangers of post-incident collaboration are obvious: officers may innocently contaminate their own account by hearing the accounts of their fellow officers. As academic commentators have observed, the courts are not so naive as to be unable to distinguish between a discrepancy which materially affects the reliability of the evidence concerned and one which can safely be dismissed as insignificant and the product of nothing more significant than different perspectives of different witnesses. But the convention of pre-note-making collaboration by police officers has never been explicitly approved by the Court of Appeal. It is a convention and decidedly not any kind of 'right'.

Furthermore, in the context of a public order incident where violence and death has occurred, there is now a risk arising from post-incident collaboration by police officers. In *Ramsahai v the Netherlands* (15 May 2007) the ECtHR said the following about police officers who had shot a suspect at paragraph 330:

> Although there was no evidence that they had colluded with each other or with their colleagues . . . *the mere fact that appropriate steps had not been taken to reduce the risk of such collusion had amounted to a significant shortcoming.*
>
> [emphasis added]

The Court concluded that there had been 'a violation of Article 2 of the Convention in that the investigation into the circumstances surrounding the death of Moravia Ramsahai was inadequate' and cited the opportunity for collusion as one of a number of bases for this conclusion.

In *R (Saunders & another) v IPCC* [2008] EWHC 2372 Underhill J did *not* support the convention of officers conferring before making their notes. He decided that the IPCC had not acted incompatibly with Convention rights in not giving a direction to chief officers to prohibit conferring between officers following a fatal shooting by police officers. Underhill J's judgment provides the fullest judicial analysis available from a domestic court on the topic of post-incident conferring in modern times. His characterization of the practice of post-incident conferring as 'highly vulnerable to challenge' seems to be a clear warning that if its legality were to be directly questioned now, it would probably be found wanting. In the firearms arena, the Association of Chief Police Officers (ACPO) has taken the necessary steps to protect the police service and Authorised Firearms Officers (AFOs) from such challenges by issuing new guidance.

1.5 **Giving Evidence**

Many police officers have little experience in giving evidence in court. Furthermore, not all police forces invest in training their officers in this skill. Giving evidence can be a difficult and lonely experience. There are, however, some golden rules which if deployed by police witnesses will at least minimize the risk of unforced errors and assist officers to present themselves to the best of their abilities. Of course, telling the truth is the major obligation. Taking that as read, together with the assumption that the officer has prepared themselves adequately, the authors' '10 Golden Rules' for giving evidence in a court are as follows:

1. **Listen to the question.** Without this, officers tend to answer a question that has not been asked.
2. **Make sure you understand the question.** If not, ask for it to be repeated or explained.
3. **Think before speaking.** There are no brownie points for speed, and giving evidence is not easy. So think carefully about what your answer actually is.
4. **Answer the question.** Many witnesses fail to answer the question, which is both irritating to the court and looks evasive.
5. **Keep answers short and to the point.** A 'yes' or 'no' may well suffice.
6. **Don't be evasive.** There is no point avoiding a question or appearing to do so. It simply draws attention to your evidence and makes you look defensive.
7. **Be reasonable.** Officers should not fear making reasonable concessions. It makes them look more, rather than less, impressive.

8. **Be courteous at all times**. Getting personal with the advocate is unwarranted and counterproductive.
9. **Admit your mistakes**. Police officers are only human. Admission of mistakes doesn't necessarily undermine your evidence; indeed, it may enhance it.
10. **Tell it like it is**. Avoid police jargon, or long-winded or 'politically correct' answers.

NOTES

NOTES

2

Human Rights

2.1 **Introduction**

Consideration of human rights must be part of all aspects of policing, with public order policing being one of the most obvious examples of this proposition. Some human rights arguments come to the fore in this very context. The rights of one group, such as protestors, frequently conflict with those of another group, such as residents, workers or shoppers, who want to get on with their daily lives; or the rights of one group of protestors may clash with those seeking to hold a counter-demonstration.

In these situations, it is not enough for the police to seek to protect one group's human rights. The role of the police requires them to strike a lawful balance between competing interests, both of which may involve Convention rights.

POINT TO NOTE

The concept of

balance

is key to upholding principles of human rights.

2.1.1 **Sources of human rights**

There are many international instruments that set out sources of human rights. In domestic law, the only directly applicable document is the European Convention on Human Rights and Fundamental Freedoms ('the Convention'). This has been incorporated into domestic law by the Human Rights Act 1998 ('HRA'). The HRA makes it unlawful for a public body (which includes the police) to act in breach of these incorporated rights.

KEY POINTS—THE RIGHTS MOST RELEVANT TO PUBLIC ORDER POLICING

THE RIGHT TO . . .	RELEVANT CONVENTION ARTICLE
Life	Article 2
Freedom from torture, inhuman or degrading treatment	Article 3
Liberty	Article 5
Privacy and family life, including the right to be free from injury	Article 8
Freedom of thought, conscience and religion	Article 9
Freedom of expression	Article 10
Freedom of association	Article 11

| Peaceful enjoyment of property | Article 1 of Protocol 1 |
| Non-discrimination in enjoyment and protection of Convention rights | Article 14 |

2.1.2 **Why an understanding of human rights is important**

Police officers need to have an understanding of human rights law so that they can identify what rights may be affected in any given situation and take the appropriate steps to uphold human rights. They need to understand the general thrust of each of the Convention articles, and how each impacts on their daily work and the powers they as police are likely to use.

If the police act in breach of a person's Convention rights, that person can bring a free-standing human rights claim in the courts of England and Wales. If the court finds the breach proved, it can award damages to the person whose rights were breached, although damages under the HRA tend to be very modest when compared to ordinary common law damages. The point of such claims may be as much political or about 'principle' as anything else (as the *Laporte* litigation showed).

Quite apart from the question of damages, a person can also use human rights as part of his or her arguments to show that a particular action or omission was or will be unlawful. Human rights should be considered, explicitly, as a matter of course when planning police actions in relation to public order.

- Human rights considerations may mean that the police simply *cannot* lawfully do something. For example, the police cannot lawfully ban a controversial public procession under s 13 Public Order Act 1986 because of a fear of serious public disorder, if proper policing (and the imposition of conditions under s 12 if necessary) would allow it to occur peacefully.
- The other side of the coin, human rights considerations may mean that the police *have* to take positive action, such as by providing a presence at a small counter-demonstration along the course of the procession so that it will not be overcome by the main demonstrators.
- In addition, if particular steps are in principle lawful, or required, human rights considerations may continue to have a bearing on the way things are done. For example, in the case of a procession, any conditions imposed must strike a proper balance between the rights of the people taking part in the procession, the people who live, work and shop on its route, and any counter-demonstrators.

2.1.3 **How to go about considering human rights**

In the planning stages, or early on during an incident, officers should assess whether there are any risks which mean that human rights need to be given particular thought. For example, is there a risk of any of the following:

- injury or death
- damage to property

19

- people not being allowed to express their views or manifest their beliefs as they would like to, whether individually or in a group
- people being kept in one place for a long time
- people being prevented from moving or going home.

The police should assess these risks from two perspectives.

First, what is the risk that the police themselves will cause these things to happen? Human rights mean that the police may have an obligation *not to do certain things*, in other words, a negative obligation. Second, what is the risk that other people will cause these things to happen? Human rights also mean that the police sometimes have to take *positive action to protect people's rights* from interference by others, in other words, a positive obligation.

Once officers have identified the types of issues that might arise, they need to consider the specific articles of the Convention that might be relevant. In relation to each Convention right, officers first need to work out whether what they plan to do might interfere with (or 'engage') the right. There may not be a clear answer to this and it is generally appropriate to err on the side of caution. If in doubt, assume that someone's rights will be interfered with and that you will need to justify your actions under the Convention, by showing that they are lawful, in pursuance of a legitimate aim and proportionate to achieving that legitimate aim. If there is time to plan, and you are in doubt about a human rights issue, consider whether you need to seek legal advice in advance. It is generally better to seek legal advice before a problem crystallizes than afterwards—for obvious reasons of cost and reputation or public trust, as well as to protect the rights of the individual.

Officers then need to work out whether any interference (or 'engagement') might be justified because it falls within a legitimate exception. Each article sets out the exceptions (if any) which apply to it.

Some rights do not allow for any exceptions at all, or only allow for specified exceptions. These are sometimes called 'absolute rights', but this name is potentially a little misleading: even some absolute rights do allow closely defined exceptions. For example, Article 5 protects the individual's right to liberty, but one of the exceptions allowed is for lawful arrest or detention undertaken 'to secure the fulfilment of any obligation prescribed by law'.

Absolute rights contrast with 'qualified rights', which are rights that allow for general exceptions for specified aims, as set out in the relevant article.

The main rights which are relevant in the public order field and which allow specified exceptions only (ie what lawyers would call 'absolute rights') are those protected by Articles 2, 3 and 5.

The main rights which are relevant in the public order field and which allow for general exceptions for specified aims (ie what lawyers would call 'qualified rights') are Articles 8, 9, 10 and 11, and Article 1 of Protocol 1.

Incorporation of Human Rights Considerations into Planning

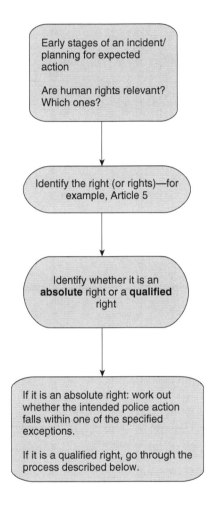

Early stages of an incident/ planning for expected action

Are human rights relevant? Which ones?

Identify the right (or rights)—for example, Article 5

Identify whether it is an **absolute** right or a **qualified** right

If it is an absolute right: work out whether the intended police action falls within one of the specified exceptions.

If it is a qualified right, go through the process described below.

Article 5 (an absolute right):

'Nobody shall be deprived of his liberty save in the following cases and in accordance with a procedure prescribed by law . . .

(b) the lawful arrest or detention of a person . . . in order to secure the fulfilment of any obligation prescribed by law;

(c) the lawful arrest or detention of a person . . . when it is reasonably considered necessary to prevent his committing an offence or fleeing after having done so. . .'

2.1.4 Qualified rights: the approach to take

All 'qualified rights' have the same structure. The first paragraph sets out the relevant right, and the second paragraph the grounds on which interference with the right may be justified.

The wording of the second paragraph differs between the various articles, but there are three essential elements to the justifications which are allowed. The action must be

- in accordance with, or prescribed by, law;
- pursuant to a legitimate aim set out within the second paragraph of the relevant article;
- necessary.

There is an obligation on the police, as agents of the State to provide reasons for the interference which are both relevant and sufficient. While this explanation may often be given after the event, for a pre-planned policing operation, the obligation may require the police to demonstrate that the impact of Convention rights were considered *prior* to its execution.

The first element: is the intervention in accordance with, or prescribed by, law?

The intervention must have a sound legal basis. Even if the intervention is pursuant to a legitimate aim (such as protecting the safety of the public), it will amount to an infringement or violation of a person's rights if there is no legal authority to act under UK law. This authority may arise from the common law, statute, secondary legislation (including procedural rules) or by-laws. In each case, the basis must be clear and precise, and accessible to the public. In other words, the police must have a legal basis for each intervention they wish to take.

The need for clarity and precision does not mean that legal powers cannot be discretionary, or flexible; nor that the law needs to prescribe an exact method or procedure for the police to use to carry out each power. For example, the claimants in *Steel v United Kingdom* (1998) 28 EHRR 603 argued that the common law concept of 'breach of the peace', and the attendant powers of arrest, were insufficiently certain under English law. The government argued against this, submitting that the powers were 'well established'. The European Court considered the fact that the concept of breach of the peace had been clarified in English courts over two decades, and decided that it was sufficiently clear to members of the public when a breach of the peace would be committed, and that a person may be arrested for it.

In essence, the law will look to whether the police action is reasonably predictable.

POINT TO NOTE

Steel v UK

[These phrases] '. . . stipulate not only full compliance with the procedural and substantive rules of national law, but also that any deprivation of liberty be consistent with the purpose of [the Convention Article] and not arbitrary. In addition, given the importance of personal liberty, it is essential that the applicable national law meet the standard of 'lawfulness' set by the Convention, which requires that all law, whether written or unwritten, be sufficiently precise to allow the citizen—if need be, with appropriate advice—to foresee, to a degree that is reasonable in the circumstances, the consequences which a given action may entail . . .'

The second element: do the police have a 'legitimate aim'?

Each article sets out the particular aims which may provide a justification for interfering with that right—the 'legitimate' aims. With the exception of Article 2, each of the qualified rights specifically allows for intervention if it is necessary for

- public safety
- the protection of public order/prevention of disorder or crime
- the protection of rights and freedoms of others.

However legitimate in it may be in everyday terms, an aim will not be regarded as legitimate unless it falls within one of the specific categories in the exceptions. For example, an intervention to prevent a breach of the peace may engage, *inter alia*, a person's Article 10 rights, but is potentially in pursuit of a legitimate aim, the protection of public order.

The third element: is the action necessary?

Once one or more legitimate aims such as the prevention of disorder, or the protection of public safety have been established, the interference with the right for that purpose must be 'necessary in a democratic society'; in the pursuit of the identified aim(s).

The meaning of 'necessary' does not go as far as 'indispensable', but certainly implies more than just reasonable, useful or desirable. It means meeting a 'pressing social need'. This is not likely to come into question where action is taken for the purposes of protecting the public.

'Proportionality'

Another essential ingredient within the concept of necessity is that of proportionality. Although the word proportionality is not included in any of the stated qualifications to the Convention rights, it is at the heart of every evaluation of the necessity of interference with a Convention right. When taking action that might interfere with someone's Convention rights, police should consider whether that action is a proportionate response to the situation on the ground. For example, in *Steel*, the European Court considered that the arrest (for breach of the peace) of protestors, whose actions carried an inherent risk of danger and disorder, was proportionate. Some of those protestors had been standing in front of members of a grouse shoot who were about to fire their weapons. Others were climbing into trees and onto construction machinery on a building site, and one stood underneath a JCB digger. In contrast, the arrest (also for breach of the peace) of claimants who had been peacefully handing out leaflets and holding up banners was not proportionate.

The Court's approach to the issue of balance and proportionality was succinctly described by Dyson LJ in *Wood v Commissioner of Police for the*

Metropolis [2010] 1 WLR 123 at paragraph 84. The same considerations as those applied by the Court after the event should guide the planning and execution of police actions that will (or may) infringe a person's rights under the ECHR:

> . . . the court is required to carry out a careful exercise of weighing the legitimate aim to be pursued, the importance of the right which is the subject of the interference and the extent of the interference. Thus an interference whose object is to protect the community from the danger of terrorism is more readily justified as proportionate than an interference whose object is to protect the community from the risk of low-level crime and disorder.

If an alternative action, involving a significantly lesser degree of interference with a Convention right, is likely to be as effective, then there is a risk that the intervention may be found to be disproportionate, and therefore unnecessary. In the case of *Moos v Commissioner of Police for the Metropolis* [2011] EWHC 957 (Admin), the containment of 'climate camp' protesters, when the concern of police was that their protest might be infiltrated by members of a less peaceful nearby protest, was found be disproportionate, because the police could instead have used cordons (a less intrusive tactic) to block off potential infiltration routes.

The European Court will allow a 'margin of appreciation' to member states as to how they operate. Domestic courts in the UK will often allow a corresponding degree of deference, either to the expertise of the police, or in recognition of the fact that decisions are sometimes taken in an instant, whereas the Court has the luxury of hours (if not days) in which to analyse alternatives. However, such deference cannot be relied upon in advance: whenever action is contemplated which may engage a Convention right, reasonable effort must be taken by the police officers planning the event to ensure the policing intervention is proportionate to its aim.

Tying the elements together

What the whole phrase 'necessary in a democratic society' really means is that the interference with the right must be proportionate to the (legitimate) aim of the police. The police must, in summary:

- identify what they want to achieve and why
- identify which rights will be engaged
- show how the interference with the right in question is logically going to help them achieve a legitimate aim, within the relevant second paragraph of the Convention right
- work out what action constitutes the minimum interference with the right necessary to achieve that aim effectively
- decide whether that would strike an appropriate balance between all the interests involved.

2.2 **Article 14: Prohibition of Discrimination**

Article 14 states that there must be no discrimination in relation to the *other* rights in the Convention, on *any* ground. A large number of examples are given in Article 14: sex, race, colour, language, religion, political or other opinion, national or social origin, association with a national minority, property, birth or other status. These include some characteristics not protected by domestic legislation (such as political affiliation), and—probably reflecting the date of the Convention—does not expressly refer to age, disability or sexual orientation. However, these characteristics have just as much protection as the ones expressly listed, for the purposes of this anti-discrimination safeguard.

Article 14 does not provide a free-standing right to be free from discrimination. It says that there shall be no discrimination in the protection of the other Convention rights. It therefore only applies where a person seeks to assert or rely on another of the rights recognized and protected by the Convention.

A concrete effect of this anti-discrimination provision is that the police must not get involved in the merits of any arguments about politics or religion. They should not decide which groups will be allowed to protest based on the merits of their religious or political views. While this may be an obvious point, it is particularly relevant when the exercise of rights is likely to engage the rights of others, or provoke a reaction from them.

If the police learn that members of a far-right political party intend to hold a counter-demonstration on the day of an anti-fascist rally, the police must not be influenced by any opinions held favouring one group or the other; they must take steps to allow *both* groups to express their views lawfully. Faced with the two counter-demonstrations, Article 14 puts the police under an obligation not to discriminate when protecting the Article 9, 10 and 11 rights of each group.

2.3 **Article 2: The Right to Life**

2.3.1 **The negative obligation**

There is an obligation on the police not to take life: the 'negative obligation'.

In the countries such as the UK, which do not have the death penalty, the right to life is absolute, ie has no built-in exceptions. But Article 2's scope is defined in order to limit the situations in which a breach of the right can be alleged. Article 2(2) states:

> Deprivation of life shall not be regarded as inflicted in contravention of this article when it results from the use of force which is no more than absolutely necessary:
>
> (a) in defence of any person from unlawful violence;

   (b) in order to effect a lawful arrest or to prevent the escape of a person lawfully detained;

   (c) in action lawfully taken for the purpose of quelling a riot or insurrection.

In order for the limitation to apply, the force used must be no more than 'absolutely necessary'. This is a very strict test; but no stricter than the common law test for the use of lethal force in self-defence: *R (On the application of Bennett) v HM Coroner for Inner South London* [2006] HRLR 22, paras 24–27.

The following measures, as usual, will be critical.

• Planning
• Risk assessment
• Detailed record-keeping, decision logs, etc.
• Prior and ongoing consideration of alternatives
• Warnings.

Subparagraph (c) in Article 2(2) has direct and explicit application to public order situations.

'Riot' is not defined, and will not necessarily have the same meaning as in s 1 of the Public Order Act 1986. For example, in the context of the use of lethal force by the state against its own people, it would seem unlikely that Article 2 would normally apply to disturbances involving as few as twelve people. The European Court of Human Rights (ECtHR) has considered the following to be examples of 'riots':

• an assembly of 150 persons throwing missiles at a patrol of soldiers, to the point that they risked serious injury: *Stewart v United Kingdom*, App. No. 10044/82; 39 DR 162;
• a crowd of several thousand people, throwing projectiles at members of the security forces so that the latter were at risk of being injured, and breaking the windows of public buildings: *Güleç v Turkey* (1998) 28 EHRR 121 (Comm. Rep. para 232, Court judgment para 71).

Even if the Court considers that there was a riot situation, it will look critically at the degree of threat the rioters posed. The European Court in *Güleç* noted that there was no evidence to support the assertion that there were armed terrorists among the demonstrators. This highlights the importance of the police providing good (ie accurate and reliable) evidence to support their choices and actions.

The Court will also look critically at whether the use of lethal force to deal with the situation was justified. The police may be unable to rely on the exception in Article 2(2)(c) if they were at fault in allowing a situation to develop where they then had no alternative but to use lethal force. For example, in *Güleç*, the Court found that the use of lethal weapons to deal with a riot breached Article 2, even though no other weapons were available to the security forces. The court criticized the lack of proper riot-prevention equipment.

POINT TO NOTE

'The Court, like the Commission, accepts that the use of force may be justified in the present case under paragraph 2 (c) of Article 2, but it goes without saying that a balance must be struck between the aim pursued and the means employed to achieve it. The gendarmes used a very powerful weapon because they apparently did not have truncheons, riot shields, water cannon, rubber bullets or tear gas. The lack of such equipment is all the more incomprehensible and unacceptable because the province of Sirnak, as the Government pointed out, is in a region in which a state of emergency has been declared, where at the material time disorder could have been expected.'

Paragraph 71 of the judgment of the European Court of Human Rights, *Güleç v Turkey* (1998)

This principle also applies in UK law. The police may not be able to rely on the defence of necessity if they negligently caused the situation to develop in the first place. In the case of *Rigby v Chief Constable of Northamptonshire Police* [1985] 1 WLR 1242, the police had fired CS gas canisters into a shop, in order to arrest an intruder, after their fire-fighting equipment had been taken elsewhere. The CS gas caused a fire. As they had not replaced the fire-fighting equipment following its removal, more damage was caused than needed to have been. In an action against the police for, *inter alia*, trespass and negligence, the court held that they were not entitled to rely on the necessity defence.

2.3.2 **The positive obligation**

There is also a positive obligation to protect life. The police are under a duty to take reasonable steps to avoid a real and immediate risk to life of which they are or should reasonably be aware: *Osman v United Kingdom* (1998) 29 EHRR 245.

POINT TO NOTE

Osman v United Kingdom, **paragraphs 115–116**

'. . . The Court notes that the first sentence of Article 2(1) enjoins the State not only to refrain from the intentional and unlawful taking of life, but also to take appropriate steps to **safeguard** the lives of those within its jurisdiction . . . It is common ground that the State's obligation in this respect extends beyond its primary duty to secure the right to life by putting in place effective criminal-law provisions to deter the commission of offences against the person backed up by law-enforcement machinery for the prevention, suppression and sanctioning of breaches of such provisions. **It is thus accepted by those appearing before the Court that Article 2 of the Convention may also imply in certain well-defined circumstances a positive obligation on the authorities to**

> **take preventive operational measures to protect an individual whose life is at risk from the criminal acts of another individual . . .**
>
> For the Court, and bearing in mind the difficulties involved in policing modern societies, the unpredictability of human conduct and the operational choices which must be made in terms of priorities and resources, such an obligation must be interpreted in a way which does not impose an impossible or disproportionate burden on the authorities. Accordingly, not every claimed risk to life can entail for the authorities a Convention requirement to take operational measures to prevent that risk from materializing. Another relevant consideration is the need to ensure that the police exercise their powers to control and prevent crime in a manner which fully respects the due process and other guarantees which legitimately place restraints on the scope of their action to investigate crime and bring offenders to justice, including the guarantees contained in Articles 5 and 8 of the Convention . . .'

This positive duty to protect life is always in the background of public order policing. It is one of the human rights reasons why the police need to manage demonstrations properly and to avoid things getting out of control, such that a risk to life is threatened.

This obligation could provide the legal basis for interference with other rights. For example, for the purpose of protecting life appropriately the police may impose conditions on a procession. This may interfere with the rights to freedom of expression and freedom of assembly under Articles 10 and 11 of those taking part, but such interference may be justified by the need to protect life.

The negative and positive limbs of the Article 2 obligation may appear to come into conflict. For example, police officers may shoot a suspected suicide bomber reasonably believing it is absolutely necessary to do so in order to save the lives of members of the public. But this is not really a conflict at all, because of the limitation of the scope of Article 2 in Article 2(2)(a) which states that a killing will not be a breach of Article 2 if it is strictly necessary 'in defence of any person from unlawful violence'. A suicide bomber threatens unlawful violence.

Officers should take Article 2 into account at the planning stage of operations where life realistically could be threatened, and should record having done so.

2.4 **Article 3: Prohibition of Torture, Inhuman, or Degrading Treatment**

At first glance, it might seem unlikely that this right would have any real relevance to the policing of public order. Nevertheless, two specific situations arise where public order policing has been found to engage, thereby potentially to infringe, people's Article 3 rights:

- where a member of the public suffers injuries, or is subjected to ill treatment, during the policing of public order
- where a victim alleges that the police have failed to prevent them from suffering such treatment by a third party.

It has become common for a breach of Article 3 to be alleged in claims of assault against the police. However, the European Court of Human Rights has said that ill treatment must reach a *minimum level of severity* before it falls within the scope of Article 3: *Ireland v United Kingdom* (1978) 2 EHRR 25 para 162. The unnecessary (therefore unlawful) handcuffing of an individual is unlikely, without more, to amount to degrading treatment—see *Raninen v Finland* 1997 26 EHRR 563.

Nevertheless, where even minor injuries have been sustained following the unnecessary or disproportionate use of force by the police against members of the public, the European Court has found that Article 3 has been breached. One such case is *Balçik v Turkey* App. No. 25/02 29 November 2007. In *Balçik,* two of the applicants suffered minor injuries ('bruises on both arms and a swelling on the left foot') following the use by the Turkish police of tear gas and batons to disperse a peaceful, albeit unlawful, assembly, only 30 minutes after it had begun. The Court found that the use of force was disproportionate, concluding that the Turkish government had 'failed to furnish convincing or credible arguments which would provide a basis to explain or to justify the degree of force used against the applicants'. Where applicants could prove they had been injured by the police, the European Court found a violation of Article 3.

There is also a positive obligation to prevent the degrading treatment of a person by others. In *E v Chief Constable of the Royal Ulster Constabulary* [2009] 1 AC 536 the claimant (a child) and her schoolmates were repeatedly subjected to a barrage of insults, abuse and offensive missiles from a hostile crowd of protestors as they tried to walk to school. The protests, a manifestation of sectarianism, continued for several weeks while the police tried to reach a political solution. The claimant alleged that she had been subjected to degrading treatment by the protestors, and that the respondent police force had failed to protect her from it.

The respondent agreed that the treatment potentially breached Article 3, but stated that he had fulfilled his Article 3 obligations as he had done what was reasonable in all the circumstances to protect the claimant. The House of Lords (now the Supreme Court) agreed that the fact that the police might possibly have adopted more robust action was insufficient to establish that the course adopted was misguided, let alone unreasonable, and confirmed that the respondent had fulfilled his Article 3 obligations. This is a fairly unusual case, but demonstrates the potential of Article 3 to impact on public order policing.

2.5 **Article 5: Right to Liberty and Security**

Article 5 is 'absolute' and therefore not subject to any general exceptions. However, its scope is limited, as it allows for deprivation of liberty in the defined circumstances set out in Article 5(1)(a)–(e).

Article 5 is likely to be engaged in many public order situations where there is police intervention. The most common scenarios are:

- arrest
- stop and search
- non-arrest detention, such as containment.

2.5.1 **Arrest**

If an arrest is valid under domestic law, it is likely to comply with Article 5. Section 24(6) of the Police and Criminal Evidence Act (PACE) was amended from 2006 so as to require the arrest to be *necessary* to achieve one of the aims in s 24(6).

Breach of the peace, whilst not an offence under English law, is deemed to be an offence for the purposes of Article 5 (*Steel*, paragraph 46). This means that under Article 5(1)(c) a person who is suspected to have committed a breach of the peace can lawfully be detained and taken to court.

2.5.2 **Stop and search**

In *Gillan v Commissioner of Police for the Metropolis* [2006] 2 AC 307, the House of Lords decided that, in the absence of special circumstances, a person who is stopped and searched under sections 44 and 45 of the Terrorism Act 2000 should not be regarded as being deprived of his liberty. What happens to him would be better described as being kept from proceeding, or kept waiting. The House of Lords also decided that even if a stop and search did amount to a deprivation of liberty, it could be justified under the second limb of Article 5(1)(b), namely 'to secure the fulfilment of any obligation prescribed by law', because the public have a clear obligation not to obstruct a constable exercising a lawful power to stop and search for articles which could be used for terrorism, and any detention is in order to secure effective fulfilment of that obligation.

However, when the case went to the European Court of Human Rights the Court passed comment, without making an actual finding, that it probably *was* a deprivation of liberty.

POINT TO NOTE

'Although the length of time during which each applicant was stopped and searched did not in either case exceed 30 minutes, during this period the applicants were entirely deprived of any freedom of movement. They were

---

obliged to remain where they were and submit to the search and if they had refused they would have been liable to arrest, detention at a police station and criminal charges. This element of coercion is indicative of a deprivation of liberty within the meaning of Article 5 . . .'

The European Court of Human Rights in
Gillan and Quinton v United Kingdom (2010) 50 EHRR 45

2.5.3 **Detention short of arrest**

Other public order situations may arise in which the police need to keep an individual or a group in one place, in order to avert a threat to public safety. One example is what happened on May Day 2001 in Central London when about 3,000 people were 'contained' by the Metropolitan Police at Oxford Circus. (The current term used by the media of 'kettling' to describe this tactic should be avoided by all of those dealing in public order, particularly police officers. It is both pejorative and imprecise.)

Police intelligence for May Day 2001 suggested that hard core anti-capitalist demonstrators would cause violence and disorder. When a crowd of demonstrators marched into Oxford Circus, the police decided the only way to prevent serious violence and disorder was to contain them within cordons of police officers, in order to carry out a controlled dispersal away from the area. Prolonged disorder inside and outside the cordon meant many people were not released for over seven hours. When two of the people who were contained brought a claim against the Metropolitan Police, one of the questions for the Court was whether they had been deprived of their liberty under Article 5 and, if so, whether this was justified.

'Necessity' is not one of the circumstances in which a deprivation of liberty is permitted. In the House of Lords decision in *Austin v Commissioner of Police for the Metropolis* [2009] AC 564), the Court was tasked with deciding whether the 2001 May Day containment had amounted to a deprivation of liberty, or whether it had been a mere 'restriction'. When the case had been in the Court of Appeal the Metropolitan Police had made legal arguments about the interpretation and application of Articles 5(1)(c) and 5(1)(b) in those circumstances. The Court of Appeal had commented on what it thought the European Court of Human Rights would be likely to do if it decided that there was a deprivation of liberty in such circumstances—where the judge had decided that the police had no real alternative other than to use containment. The Court of Appeal said it thought that the European Court of Human Rights would be likely to decide that the justification in either paragraph (b) or (c) applied, in order to ensure that the proper balance was maintained, see paragraphs 91, 93 and 94.

The Court of Appeal in fact dealt with the matter by deciding that keeping the crowd at Oxford Circus was not a deprivation of liberty under Article 5(1), and therefore did not need to be brought within one of the subparagraphs. They drew analogies with situations in which a football crowd is contained for what may turn out to be quite long periods, partly for the protection of individuals in the crowd and partly (in some cases) to avoid crowd violence, perhaps between groups of opposing supporters; or where motorists are unable to leave a motorway, perhaps for many hours, because of police action following an accident. The Court of Appeal noted that in such cases it may be necessary for police to confine individuals in particular areas for what may be much longer than originally intended, and did not think that these types of cases should be regarded as arbitrary detention which amounts to a deprivation of liberty under Article 5, see paragraphs 102–103.

The claimants appealed and the case went to the House of Lords, which reviewed case law from the European Court of Human Rights on deprivations and restrictions of liberty. The House of Lords dismissed the appeal. They held that even in the case of Article 5, there was room for a pragmatic approach which took account of all the circumstances. They said that the key purpose of Article 5 was to prevent arbitrary or unjustified deprivations of liberty, and in deciding whether Article 5 was engaged at all, the court could consider the *purpose* for which the containment measures had been taken.

POINT TO NOTE

'The ambit that is given to Article 5 as to measures of crowd control must, of course, take account of the rights of the individual as well as the interests of the community. So any steps that are taken must be resorted to in good faith and must be proportionate to the situation which has made the measures necessary. This is essential to preserve the fundamental principle that anything which is done which affects a person's right to liberty must not be arbitrary. If these requirements are met, however, it will be proper to conclude that measures of crowd control which are undertaken in the interests of the community will not infringe the Article 5 rights of individual members of the crowd whose freedom of movement is restricted by them'.

Lord Hope giving the leading judgment in the House of Lords,
in *Austin*, paragraph 34

The ECtHR has been asked to consider whether Ms Austin suffered a deprivation of liberty within the meaning of Article 5. At the time of writing, the decision in *Austin v United Kingdom* is awaited. Pending this decision, the key point to take from *Austin* is that if containment is used, it needs to be necessary and justified. Subsequent challenges to the tactic of containment confirm that the necessity test sets a high threshold.

One such challenge followed the G20 protests in London in April 2009. The legality of a containment imposed on protestors forming a 'climate camp' in the City of London was considered by the High Court in the case of *Moos*. The judgment confirms that while containment can be lawful if a breach of the peace is reasonably apprehended, mass containment in this way will only be justifiable in a 'very exceptional case'. In *Moos*, the Court held that the use of cordons would have been an alternative to containment and therefore the containment had been unlawful.

> It is only when the police reasonably believe that there is no other means whatsoever to prevent an imminent breach of the peace that they can as a matter of necessity curtail the lawful exercise of their rights by third parties.
>
> [*Moos* paragraph 56]

At the time of writing, it is understood that *Moos* is also subject to appeal.

The different outcomes in *Austin* and *Moos* arose because while in *Austin* the Court was convinced that there was no other practical means by which a serious breach of the peace could be prevented other than by an absolute containment, in *Moos* the defendant was unable to show that simple cordons would have been ineffective. This emphasizes the importance of both considering, and recording, the alternative responses as an unpredictable public order situation develops. If, despite such considerations, there is a subsequent legal challenge, such a decision-making process ought also to be able to demonstrate that the police:

- **planned properly**, taking into account all relevant factors
- **responded appropriately to events on the day**
- **made an appropriate assessment of the risks**, and
- had **no reasonable alternative** to what they did, if they were to avoid a risk of serious injury or death.

Other points to consider are as follows:

- All reasonable steps should be taken to minimize the length of time for which any containment is maintained.
- Good practice in containment situations will often entail briefing officers to use discretion, to allow out members of the crowd who are clearly distressed or not intent on causing disorder.
- Officers should make clear in planning and their decision logs and notebooks etc what the ultimate aim of their operation is. For example, if the ultimate aim is to disperse crowds safely, rather than simply to keep people detained, this should be recorded explicitly.
- Good communication with the crowd and ensuring that the conditions are as comfortable as possible may not in the end make the difference as to whether the containment engages Article 5, but are nevertheless important.

The question whether police action amounts to a deprivation of liberty under Article 5, or merely restricts people's freedom of movement, is one of degree. Various police actions that do not amount to deprivations of liberty would still amount to a restriction on freedom of movement, such as directing a procession down a specified route rather than the route the group desires.

Freedom of movement is governed by Article 2 of Protocol 4, which unlike the other rights discussed here, has not been incorporated into our domestic law. This means a person cannot bring a claim under the Human Rights Act 1998 for breach of it. However, this does not mean that the police do not need to justify restrictions on freedom of movement: they do, for at least two reasons. First, the restriction on freedom of movement may also interfere with other rights (such as a demonstrator's right to freedom of expression). Second, the restriction must be justified under domestic law. If the police use reasonable force trying to prevent the person from breaking through a cordon, and are sued for assault, the police will need to establish that the imposition of the cordon was lawful under domestic law.

2.6 Article 8: Right to Respect for Private and Family Life

This is a qualified right. In the context of public order policing, it might be thought that Article 8 has little, if any, application. A claim for a breach of Article 8 is sometimes tagged on to Article 5, 9, 10 or 11 claims if someone is arrested, or a public event or incident is halted by police action. However, there are two situations in which the individual's right to a private life is directly relevant to public order policing:

- the exercise of stop and search powers
- evidence gathering—particularly photographing and filming.

2.6.1 Stop and search

Stopping and searching a person, and requiring them to reveal their personal details, clearly engages their Article 8 rights. The stop and search powers exercisable under s 1 of PACE are exercisable only when a constable has reasonable grounds to suspect that stolen or prohibited articles (and in the case of the Misuse of Drugs Act, controlled substances) may be in the person's possession. If exercised properly, such powers are in accordance with the law, for the purposes of preventing crime or disorder, and are proportionate.

However, once an authorization had been given, the powers previously exercisable under ss 44–46 of the Terrorism Act 2000 could be exercised without either suspicion or specific purpose. In *Gillan and Quinton v UK* [2010] ECHR 28, (2010) 50 EHRR 45 the European Court declared that the powers of authorization and confirmation, as well as those of stop and search under sections 44 and 45, were neither sufficiently circumscribed nor subject to adequate legal safeguards against abuse. Therefore they were not 'in accordance with the law', so were incompatible with the UK's obligations under the treaty, and their use amounted a violation of Article 8 of the Convention.

The government has subsequently issued the Terrorism Act 2000 (Remedial) Order 2011. This provides that, pending the passing of an amendment to the Terrorism Act 2000, it is to have effect as if new sections 47A–47C had been substituted: see section 8.5.3.

2.6.2 Evidence gathering

One of the principal tools in anticipating and planning major public order situations that has been developed over the last 15 years is the gathering of intelligence by filming/photographing public order events and the activities of those who attend. Overt surveillance in public does not require Regulation of Investigatory Powers Act (RIPA) authorization. However, going hand in hand with the increased use (and utility) of these methods have been concerns about both the impact on people's privacy and the chilling effect on people's right to protest.

In *Wood v Commissioner of Police for the Metropolis* [2010] 1 WLR 123 the claimant, a man of good character, who was not associated with unlawful protest activity, challenged the actions of the defendant. The defendant's officers had overtly filmed him attending the Annual General Meeting (AGM) of a public company which organized arms fairs. The Commissioner stated that the original purpose in taking the photographs was in case the claimant was involved in criminal activity at the AGM. However, the images were then retained pending a forthcoming arms fair, and had not been destroyed after the arms fair, although they had not been added to the Public Order Branch's database of known or suspected activists.

The Court of Appeal held that the taking of photographs, even overtly in a public place, may engage Article 8 depending on the activities photographed, the reason for taking photographs, the use to which the photograph is put, and whether the photograph is stored, published or destroyed. On the facts in *Wood*, the Court found that Article 8 was engaged, and the taking of the photographs would have been justified under Article 8(2) in order to obtain evidence if offences were committed at the AGM. However, the long term retention of the photographs thereafter rendered the police activity disproportionate, and therefore a breach of Article 8.

This decision probably affects the legality of the retention of photographs to a much greater extent than the initial filming at a protest (at which time it will not be known whether or not there will be disorder or who will be involved). The retention of personal data following the decisions in *Wood* and *Marper v United Kingdom* [2008] ECHR 1581 is beyond the scope of this book.

Article 8 has also been interpreted to say that people have the right to be free from injury. This is therefore the human rights basis for the police taking action in a public order setting to minimize the risk of injury to members of the public.

2.7 Articles 9, 10, & 11: Right to Freedom of Religion, Thought, Expression, and Assembly

Articles 9, 10 and 11 are highly significant for policing protests. They are all 'qualified', ie are subject to general exceptions for specified legitimate aims. As well as restraining the state from certain actions, they all impose positive obligations on the state to take positive steps in some circumstances. They all give rise to the possibility that the state may have to balance the competing rights of different individuals or groups.

2.7.1 Article 9: Freedom of thought, conscience and religion

Article 9 provides broad protection to the holding of beliefs and manifestation of them. The beliefs do not need to be religious or philosophical: the scope of thought or belief is much wider than 'religious belief' as defined in domestic hate crime legislation. The European Court has recognized that, while religious freedom is primarily a matter of individual conscience, it also implies a freedom to manifest one's religion (see *Kokkinakis v Greece* [1993] ECHR 20). 'Bearing witness' in words and deeds is bound up with the existence of religious convictions, and it is in the context of this type of conduct that public order situations will often develop. It follows that in such cases the rights or freedoms of assembly and expression will also be engaged.

The protection of the freedom to manifest one's belief does not extend to acts done in pursuance of whatever beliefs a person may hold, such as attacking places where experiments are conducted on animals (see *R v DPP ex p Pretty* [2002] 1 AC at paragraph 163).

The freedom of thought and religion is a qualified rather than an absolute right. However, the qualifications under Article 9(2) are significantly narrower than for Articles 10(2) and 11(2). They are confined to those which are 'prescribed by law and are necessary in a democratic society in the interests of public safety, for the protection of public order, health or morals, or the protection of the rights and freedoms of others'. These are the very exceptions that are likely to apply in public order scenarios.

Under s 13(1) of the HRA, where a question arises for the Court's determination, particular regard must be paid to the importance of freedom of thought, conscience or religion. It was argued in *Connolly v DPP* [2007] EWHC 237 (Admin) that where freedom of expression is concerned, priority must also be attached to the protection of religious expression, However, in that case the High Court declined to find that freedom of religious expression was of a higher order, or was regarded by the ECtHR as more worthy of protection than the freedom of secular expression enshrined in Article 10 (see section 4.6.2 for a detailed consideration of *Connolly* in relation to s 5 of the Public Order Act (POA)).

This is potentially an important factor to bear in mind in a public order scenario: where a balance has to be struck between the protection of the manifestation of religious belief under Article 9 and a non-religious freedom of expression under Article 10, the rights are to be accorded equal weight.

The qualifications in Article 9(2) are therefore likely to be applied in a very similar way to the corresponding qualifications under Article 10(2), as was the case in *Connolly*.

2.7.2 **Article 10: Freedom of expression**

Article 10 provides:

1. Everyone has the right to freedom of expression. This right shall include freedom to hold opinions and to receive and impart information and ideas without interference by public authority and regardless of frontiers. This article shall not prevent States from requiring the licensing of broadcasting, television or cinema enterprises.

2. The exercise of these freedoms, since it carries with it duties and responsibilities, may be subject to such formalities, conditions, restrictions or penalties as are prescribed by law and are necessary in a democratic society, in the interests of national security, territorial integrity or public safety, for the prevention of disorder or crime, for the protection of health or morals, for the protection of the reputation or the rights of others, for preventing the disclosure of information received in confidence, or for maintaining the authority and impartiality of the judiciary.

Article 10 is closely related to Article 9. The right to freedom of expression is interpreted broadly. It covers not just speech, but all other forms of expression, such as waving (even burning) flags, holding placards, distributing leaflets, and setting up peace or climate camps. It is difficult to find an 'expression' which does not at least potentially fall within its scope. For example, in *Redmond-Bate v DPP* [1999] EWHC Admin 732, Sedley LJ made the following now well known and very important observation:

> Free speech includes not only the inoffensive but the irritating, the contentious, the eccentric, the heretical, the unwelcome and the provocative provided it does not tend to provoke violence. Freedom only to speak inoffensively is not worth having.

Section 12 of the HRA provides that where a court is considering whether to grant any relief which, if granted, might affect the exercise of freedom of expression, particular regard must be had to the importance of the Convention right to freedom of expression. The wording of this section indicates that it relates primarily to injunctions against media reporting, rather than public order scenarios. In the context of public order, Article 10 rights enjoy no specific priority over other ECHR rights.

Article 10(2) specifically allows for restrictions on the exercise of free speech, provided that they are prescribed by law and necessary in a democratic society for one of the following six specific reasons:

- in the interests of national security, territorial integrity or public safety;
- for the prevention of disorder or crime;
- for the protection of health or morals;
- for the protection of the reputation or the rights of others;
- for preventing the disclosure of information received in confidence;
- or for maintaining the authority and impartiality of the judiciary.

The threshold of unlawful or unreasonable conduct justifying interference in a person's freedom of expression may be relatively low, particularly where a balance is to be struck with the rights of others (who are not acting unlawfully).

In *Lucas v UK* 37 EHRR CD 86, Dr Lucas (anti-nuclear campaigner, and at the time of writing Green Party MP for Brighton) participated in a sit-down protest in the road near Faslane Naval Base in Scotland. She was warned by the police that if she did not move, she would be arrested. She did not move, was arrested, later convicted for a breach of the peace (a criminal offence in Scotland, unlike in England and Wales) and fined £150. Mrs Lucas appealed against her conviction to the ECtHR, claiming the conviction was a breach of her Article 10 rights. The European Court found Mrs Lucas's application to be inadmissible: her conduct either caused, or could have caused, disruption to traffic on the road, and could have posed a threat to the safety of the protesters and other road users. The interference with her rights was justified under Article 10(2) as it was proportionate to a legitimate aim, given the dangers posed by the applicant's conduct in sitting in a public road and the interest in maintaining public order (as well as the relatively minor penalty that was imposed). In England and Wales, sit-down protests may still result in convictions for obstruction of the highway, see section 5.6.3.

When police are considering arrest in response to somebody whose words are causing harassment, alarm or distress, they should consider whether the person's conduct poses such a threat to public order that use of the criminal law is justified. In *Dehal v CPS* [2005] EWHC 2154 (Admin) the Court reminded itself of the important words of Sedley LJ in *Redmond-Bate*: irritating, contentious and provocative will not be enough to justify the invocation of the criminal law, unless those words are tending to provoke violence. If a person is exercising their freedom of expression, and there is no likelihood of violence being provoked, then this will often provide a defence to an offence under s 5 POA, see section 4.7.5.

In *Abdul v DPP* [2011] EWHC 247 (Admin) the appellants, protesting against the return of a regiment of soldiers from Afghanistan and Iraq, chanted words such as 'British soldiers murderers', 'British soldiers go to hell', 'baby killers', and 'rapists all of you'. On appeal from their convictions under s 5 POA, the High Court had little hesitation in confirming that the prosecution and conviction was proportionate in pursuit of a legitimate aim, not only of the prevention of disorder, but also of the protection of the reputation or rights of others. See further section 4.7.5 in relation to s 5 of the Public Order Act.

There comes a point at which at which the expression of particularly danger-ous ideas, such as speech inciting hatred or violence, or support for terrorism, can become so extreme that it may no longer fall within the protection of Article 10 at all. Article 17 prevents reliance on Convention rights if the acts are aimed at the destruction of any of the rights and freedoms of others. For example, in *Norwood v United Kingdom (Admissibility Decision)* Application No. 00023131/03, the display of strongly anti-Muslim sentiment was held by the ECtHR not to be protected:

> Such a general, vehement attack against a religious group, linking the group as a whole with a grave act of terrorism, is incompatible with the values pro-claimed and guaranteed by the Convention, notably tolerance, social peace and non-discrimination. The applicant's display of the poster in his window constituted an act within the meaning of Article 17, *which did not, therefore, enjoy the protection of Articles 10 or 14* . . .

> [emphasis added]

It may be a difficult task to decide whether or not a particular form of expression continues to attract the protection of Article 10. For the purpose of practical public order policing, officers should assume that the freedom of expression is to be protected, unless at least one of the following apply to the person's conduct:

- It is a clear breach of the criminal law—including s 5 POA and the hate crime offences under Parts III and IIIA of the POA (see section 7.2–7.3); or
- It is likely to cause a breach of the peace or disorder, is unreasonable and/or is interfering with the rights of others: see section 3.6.2–3.6.3.

2.7.3 Article 11: Freedom of assembly and association

Article 11 contains two related rights: freedom of peaceful assembly, and free-dom of association with others. Freedom of peaceful assembly is clearly relevant to public order policing. Freedom of association (eg the right to form or join groups or organizations) is of less direct relevance.

The state has both positive and negative obligations, and the police are required not only to facilitate lawful public assemblies, but also to take reason-able steps to protect a person's right to freedom of assembly if others seek to prevent it.

'Assembly' in Article 11 has a broader meaning than the word 'assembly' in the Public Order Act 1986, covering groupings of people with some kind of common intention. A procession by the definition of the Public Order Act 1986 would count as an 'assembly' under Article 11. However, assembling of people that takes place for purely social or recreational purposes is not protected by Article 11. In *R (Countryside Alliance) v Attorney General* [2008] 1 AC 719, Lord Hope stated at paragraph 58:

> The essence of the freedom of assembly that Article 11 guarantees is that it is a fundamental right in a democracy and, like the right to freedom of expression, is one of the foundations of such a society . . . the situations to which it applies must relate to activities which are of that character, of which the right to form and join a trade union . . . is an example . . . it does not guarantee a right to assemble for purely social purposes.

Thus, in the *Countryside Alliance* case, the right of the hunt to gather publicly to demonstrate in favour of their sport, even by riding over the land, was protected by Article 11. But the right to simply hunt, ie to chase and kill the pursued animal, was not.

From a policing perspective, this means that disorderly situations caused by purely social assemblies (such as an unruly gathering of friends in a park) are not likely to require consideration of Article 11 rights; whereas any assembling of people linked to political, religious, trade union or other activity linked to the functioning of our democratic society is likely to fall within the scope of Article 11.

The Article 11 right to public assembly does not apply to private land: see *Appleby v UK* [2003] 37 EHRR 38. There are a number of apparently public spaces in the UK that are actually privately owned, such as (as in *Appleby*) a privately owned shopping mall in a town centre that had previously been a public space. If the private landowner bans people from holding any assembly, or handing out leaflets, or singing carols, those who wish to do so have no legal remedy (except, in limited circumstances not relevant to this book, a potential private law claim for discrimination).

The negative obligation requires the state not to place excessive burdens on demonstrators. These organizational burdens could include notification requirements or excessive stewarding levels.

Whilst Article 11 expressly protects only *peaceful* assemblies, police should bear the following in mind:

- If some people engage in violence at an assembly, this does not mean that everyone else loses the protection of Article 11 (*Ezelin v France* (1991) 14 EHRR 362).
- If a group intends to assemble peacefully, but violence develops, this can be taken into account in deciding whether it is appropriate to restrict the assembly under Article 11(2).

- Even if an assembly is technically unlawful, those assembling do not automatically lose the protection of Article 11, as measures taken to control the assembly must still be proportionate (*Oya Ataman v Turkey* Application No. 74552/01).
- Where an unlawful assembly had been allowed to continue for several hours before being dispersed by the police, the European Court found that the police had shown the necessary tolerance to the demonstration, although they had no prior knowledge of it (*Molnar v Hungary*, Application No. 10346/05). The principle that, as long as protestors have had a fair opportunity to protest, the police are not required to allow an otherwise unlawful event to continue indefinitely has also been applied in the UK. In *Moos* the Court found that: 'The demonstration had lasted the best part of 12 hours—quite long enough to take full advantage of rights under Articles 10 and 11 of the Convention'.

The positive obligation to protect a person's freedom of assembly will most frequently be put under pressure when the person's rights conflict (or may conflict) with the rights of others. Freedom of peaceful assembly includes the right to protection against counter-demonstrators, where this should reasonably be provided.

The police cannot of course guarantee that a protest will be free from interference by counter-protestors. In *Plattform Ärtze für das Leben v Austria* (1988) 13 EHRR 204 the Court stated (in paragraph 34):

> While it is the duty of Contracting States to take reasonable and appropriate measures to enable lawful demonstrations to proceed peacefully, they cannot guarantee this absolutely and they have a wide discretion in the choice of the means to be used . . . In this area the obligation they enter into under Article 11 of the Convention is an obligation as to measures to be taken and not as to results to be achieved.

Guidance as to the approach to take when striking the balance between protest and counter-protest was set out in the House of Lords in *R (Laporte) v Chief Constable of Gloucestershire* [2007] 2 AC 105:

- Under normal circumstances, it will be the group threatening or provoking violence or disorder who will be the primary focus of police intervention.
- Even where someone does not actually intend to provoke others into a violent reaction, but behaves in an outrageous way which is liable to produce such a reaction, intervention should be concentrated on that person, or group.
- Sometimes, lawful and proper conduct by A may be liable to result in a violent reaction from B, even though it is not directed against B. If B's resort to violence can be regarded as the natural consequence of A's conduct, *provided there is no other way of preserving the peace*, a police officer may order A to stop, even though his conduct is both lawful and reasonable.
- The action or degree of restriction, placed on either party, must be proportionate.

There is no automatic principle that the 'first' group has priority. If in a particular case it appears that the primary purpose of the counter-protest is to disrupt the protest originally planned, or to provoke its participants to violence, then either the first or second bullet point above would apply. However, the need for the intervention to be proportionate would apply even if one of the groups was obviously acting less reasonably than the other. Allowing both protests to continue, albeit with conditions, would in many scenarios be a more proportionate response than refusing permission to and/or dispersing one of the groups.

The blanket-banning of assemblies may be proportionate—and therefore justified under Article 11(2)—but only if it can be shown that there is a real risk of their resulting in disorder which cannot be prevented by other less stringent means (*Christians Against Racism and Facism v UK* 21 DR 138). The limitations on the banning of processions or assemblies in domestic law are discussed in chapter 5.

2.8 Article 1 of Protocol 1: Right to Property

This article guarantees the right of property, stating, 'Every natural or legal person is entitled to the peaceful enjoyment of his possessions'. It is a qualified right that gives rise to both negative and positive obligations. In the public order context, the positive obligation to protect property may on occasion require the police to interfere with the rights of others. For example, the need to protect commercial premises from criminal damage by violent anti-capitalist protestors may in principle provide grounds for the police to place some restrictions on the way that the protest is carried out.

The right enshrined in Article 1 to Protocol 1 is not inherently less important than the rights in the main body of the Convention. However, there are limited occasions when it will be necessary to disturb a person enjoyment of their own possessions. The article states, 'No one shall be deprived of his possessions except in the public interest and subject to the conditions provided for by law and by the general principles of international law.' This is a broader qualification than any of Articles 8–12. However, although the wording of the qualification is broad, any action taken must still be proportionate to the nature and degree of the public interest.

2.9 Conclusion: How Should the Police 'Use' Human Rights in the Context of Public Order?

1. At the planning stage, the aims of the police operation should be identified. This is good practice quite independently from human rights, but will also help demonstrate compliance with the principles of the Convention. If one of the

aims of the exercise is to protect the human rights of a person or a group of people, this should be noted specifically, identifying the particular article(s) of the Convention at stake.

Identification of the aims serves two purposes. First, included in the identified aims should be the human rights which need protecting. This is with a view to the police fulfilling their positive human rights duties. Second, also included in the aims should be the protection of any other, competing legitimate interests which potentially provide a justification for interference with any rights. This is with a view to the police fulfilling their negative human rights duties. For example, political protest requires a particularly careful consideration of whether interference in the freedom of expression/assembly is both justifiable and proportionate.

2. Those planning the operation should then decide what action is or might be needed to satisfy each aim.

Consideration must then be given to whether the proposed action risks interfering with the human rights of a person or a group of people. This may be a subtle question, and legal advice may be required. Not all restrictions on what people want to do will be an interference with their human rights.

If there may be an interference, consider what potential justification(s) there may be, by reference to the specific wording of that article.

If there is a justification, consider whether it in fact applies, eg whether the interference is logically connected to, and proportionate to, the aim to be achieved; and state why.

3. Officers may have identified action which they think is necessary to achieve one of their aims but which also risks interfering with someone else's human rights. In that situation, a balancing exercise will need to be carried out. In an exercise like that, police need to consider the effect on each group of the proposed course of action—what is at stake—and what the alternatives are.

KEY POINTS—PRACTICAL ISSUES

- *Showing* that you have considered human rights: good record-keeping.
- Erring on the side of caution: if in doubt, assume that someone's rights will be interfered with and that you need to justify your actions under the Convention.
- If there is time to plan and you are in doubt about a human rights issue, consider whether you need to consult a lawyer in advance.
- In fast-moving situations, particularly where there is a risk of injury or death if you do not act, do not be afraid of doing what seems right at the time— common sense—as long as you have tried your best to think of all possible alternatives and have interfered with people's liberties to the least extent necessary.

Further reading

- *Steel v United Kingdom* [1998] ECHR 95
- Hare, I. and Weinstein, J. (eds), *Extreme Speech and Democracy* (Oxford: OUP, 2010)
- Joint Committee on Human Rights Seventh Report of 2008–2009: *Demonstrating respect for rights? A human rights approach to policing protest*
- Joint Committee on Human Rights Twenty-Second Report of 2008–2009: *Demonstrating Respect for Rights? Follow–up*
- Joint Committee on Human Rights Sixth Report of 2009–2010: *Demonstrating Respect for Rights? Follow Up: Government Response to the Committee's Twenty-second Report of Session 2008–09*

NOTES

NOTES

NOTES

Breach of the Peace

3.1 **Introduction**

The duty to keep the peace is the foundation of a police officer's public order functions. Despite parliament's increasing expansion and modification of other areas of police power, the powers to deal with and prevent a breach of the peace still come from the common law. They were expressly preserved by both the Public Order Act 1986, s 40(4) and the Police and Criminal Evidence Act (PACE) 1984, ss 17(6) and 25(6).

The scope of this power—indeed *duty*—to intervene has been challenged in the domestic courts and tested in the European Court of Human Rights (ECtHR). The principles that govern this all-important aspect of policing have therefore been (and will continue to be) developed by the case law of the courts of England and Wales and the European Court of Human Rights.

This chapter sets out the common law powers available to police officers to deal with and prevent a breach of the peace. The numerous statutory powers to prevent disorder are addressed in later chapters, in the context of specific public order situations, such as professional protestors or weekend drink-related disorder.

The power and duty of a police officer to prevent a breach of the peace is one of the most useful in any situation of public disorder, from minor street confrontation to major confrontation at a football match or political protest. It is a simple power that is easy to understand and can be used to deal with immediate crises, with the officer able to reflect later on appropriate charges, if any, when the demands of duty permit.

A breach of the peace can occur in public or in private: *McConnell v Chief Constable of Greater Manchester Police* [1990] 1 WLR 364. Breach of the peace powers can therefore properly be used in relation to domestic disputes, and a discussion of the particular problems this can raise is contained below.

The main questions that arise in relation to the exercise of powers to prevent a breach of the peace are as follows:

- What is a breach of the peace?
- What powers are there to deal with a past, present or future breach of the peace?
- When can the police intervene to prevent a breach of the peace?
- What type of action can the police take?
- Against whom can or should the duty to prevent a breach of the peace be taken?
- What duty, if any, does the citizen have to assist when asked to prevent a breach of the peace, and how can the police make use of it?
- What is a bind over order and when should it be used?

There is a duty on all citizens to take reasonable steps to prevent a breach of the peace occurring, as confirmed in *Albert v Lavin* [1982] AC 546. However, for a private citizen, in the absence of an express request from a constable this is not a duty giving rise to liability for a failure to act (see section 3.7). All the legal powers available to police officers to intervene to prevent a breach of the peace are also available to all members of the public. Like police officers, members of the public are entitled to use reasonable force when preventing a breach of the peace.

Someone who commits a breach of the peace and/or who is likely to do so again may be taken before the magistrates' court to be bound over to be of good behaviour. However, breach of the peace is *not* a criminal offence in the domestic law of England and Wales (although for the purposes of the European Convention on Human Rights (ECHR), it is classified as one, see *Steel v United Kingdom* (1998) 28 EHRR 603). Note that the term 'breach of the peace' has a different meaning in Scotland, where it is a criminal offence.

Except where otherwise stated, the rest of this chapter assumes that it is *police officers* who are taking the action to prevent a breach of the peace rather than members of the public.

3.2 **What is a Breach of the Peace?**

Historically, the courts resisted setting down a formal definition of what constitutes a breach of the peace. The view was that the 'Queen's peace' was the normal state of society; any interruption of that peace and good order which ought to prevail in a civilized country was a breach of the peace. This was noted by Lord Scarman in his report on the Red Lion Square disorders (Cmd 5919). This approach categorized 'breach of the peace' negatively, by what it is not: the normal state of society.

Over time, it has come to be recognized that a clear and positive definition of what *does* constitute a breach of the peace is not only useful, but necessary.

The concept of breach of the peace now used universally by the domestic courts is that set out by the Court of Appeal in *R v Howell* [1982] QB 416:

> . . . there is a breach of the peace whenever harm is actually done or is likely to be done to a person or in his presence to his property or a person is in fear of being so harmed through an assault, an affray, a riot, unlawful assembly or other disturbance.

This definition has been approved by the European Court of Human Rights in *Steel v United Kingdom* (1998) 28 EHRR 603 and by the House of Lords in *R (Laporte) v Chief Constable of Gloucestershire Police* [2007] 2 AC 105 at paragraphs 27–28. Thus the *Howell* definition can be taken as definitive.

As can be seen, the essence of a breach of the peace is actual or threatened violence or damage to someone's property. Mere irritation, provocation, disorder, noise or disruption to the life of the community is not sufficient, (though other offences may be committed by such conduct, such as public nuisance or breaches of environmental noise pollution restrictions). Even insulting or offensive behaviour would not necessarily amount to a breach of the peace.

The essence of a breach of the peace is actual or threatened violence, or damage to property.

Although the ECtHR in *Steel* stated that the definition of a breach of the peace was as set out in *R v Howell*, the Court in fact provided its own definition that is slightly wider. It stated at paragraph 55: 'a breach of the peace is committed only when an individual causes harm, or appears likely to cause harm, to persons or property or acts in a manner the natural consequence of which would be to provoke others to violence'.

On this basis it would theoretically be respectable to consider that a breach of the peace has occurred if property is 'merely' damaged (ie no risk of harm to people) in the absence of its owner. However, though this view is respectable, the authors' view is that the domestic courts may not accept such a wide definition, as it would cover minor acts of graffiti or the unlawful removal of a wheel clamp—behaviour which, without more, might not sensibly be said to be a breach of the peace. So whilst *Steel* might allow for future legal argument, the current position is probably that damage to property, whatever its value, *if in the absence of its owner*, is not necessarily a breach of the peace.

However, where someone is present when their property is being threatened or actually damaged, it is likely that 'owner' would not be interpreted overly strictly by the courts. It would almost certainly include the bailee or guardian of the property, such as a controlled keeper of a motor vehicle or any other property on loan or hire. Moreover, in many cases, even if the owner/guardian were not present, it is likely to be difficult to rule out the prospect of such a person returning to the scene in the immediate future. Damage caused to property in a violent manner would also be a breach of the peace if it were likely to put people nearby in fear of harm.

Definition of breach of the peace

A breach of the peace is conduct which either amounts to:

- actual harm or the threat of harm to a person;
- actual harm or the threat of harm to property in the presence of its owner;

or, in relation to either a person or their property, conduct which is likely to:

- cause such harm; or
- put a person in fear of such harm being done.

Many more serious offences such as grievous bodily harm (GBH) or affray would, of course, also fall into the above categories. However, provided the conduct also amounts to a breach of the peace, then the common law power means that a police officer does not have to have a specific offence in mind if the immediate purpose of the arrest is to prevent a breach of the peace.

The common law power to prevent a breach of the peace is an excellent and flexible legal power—and thus operational tool—for a police officer to use in a heated or difficult situation when the peace is threatened and the officer is unable immediately to work out who is doing what or precisely what the offences being committed are or might be. The power enables the officer to take immediate preventive action to preserve the peace, and then *later* to work out who, if anyone, needs to be more formally 'arrested' and taken to a police station.

Thus the officer can physically intervene to prevent the breach of the peace without the need to be aware of the background to the problem, such as who might have thrown the first punch in a fight, or the legitimacy of a dispute between a passenger and a taxi driver. An exercise of the officer's power in such a situation would obviously not be lawful if the officer knew who was the proper party to arrest. An officer who goes to the assistance of a colleague who turns out to be acting unlawfully cannot subsequently rely on his powers to prevent a breach of the peace unless there is also a breach of the peace occurring which is not directly linked to his colleagues unlawful conduct—see section 4.8.1 in relation to when a constable is acting in the execution of his duty.

Any person contemplating taking action in relation to a breach of the peace must be aware whether they are dealing with an *actual* breach of the peace, or conduct that gives rise to the belief a breach of the peace is imminent. This may make a difference as to what action would be reasonable: see 3.3.

Once the officer or officers have restored the peace—or prevented a breach of it— then he or she must immediately 'de-arrest' anyone in respect of whom there are not valid grounds for arrest (as to which see PACE s 24). This is because the essence of the common law power is *preventive*: once the peace has been restored, there must be some other ground for holding any person detained under the power.

3.3 **What Powers are There to Deal with a Past, Present, or Future Breach of the Peace?**

The common law power to prevent a breach of the peace is just that: *preventive*. It is a power to take reasonable steps to prevent actual or threatened violence or damage to property. If intervention short of formal arrest is likely to be effective, then arrest should not be used. Where an arrest has been necessary, once the threat has been dissipated due to an arrest for breach of the peace, the officer has three options:

1. release the person who has been detained

2. arrest the person who has been detained for a substantive offence, provided sufficient facts have been established to amount to reasonable grounds for an arrest

3. take the person who has been detained to a court to be bound over to keep the peace, if there are proper grounds for believing that this is reasonably necessary: see section 3.8.

The powers available to an officer in relation to a breach of the peace will depend on whether the breach is past, current or anticipated.

3.3.1 **Past**

A past breach of the peace is not an offence. If a breach of the peace has occurred in the past and is well and truly over then there would be no basis for arresting the person who breached the peace. However, a past breach of the peace may also have involved the commission of a criminal offence and thus the officer can revert to consideration of the powers of arrest under s 24 of PACE.

If the breach of the peace has finished, and no imminent threat remains, then the officer has no power at common law to take action, and if there is no continuing threat to the peace, then the person must be released (see *Williamson v Chief Constable of the West Midlands* [2004] 1 WLR 14 at paragraph 29). If his previous conduct warrants a bind over, then he could be taken or summoned to court (see section 3.8).

However, if the breach of the peace has finished but looks about to restart, then the power to intervene is a power to prevent a future, imminent, breach of the peace.

3.3.2 **Present**

If a breach of the peace is occurring in the presence of a police officer, he or she has the power and duty to take action to bring an end to the breach of the peace.

It does not really matter whether one calls that action restraint, arrest or detention because *in every case the duration of the action must be limited to the time necessary to bring the breach of the peace to an end*: thus in some cases, formal arrest and transport to a police station will be necessary (eg major disturbances, ongoing protests or drunken confrontations) whilst in other cases—such as a minor fracas between school children over a mobile telephone—action very much short of formal arrest may suffice.

Where an officer is exercising common law powers (rather than s 24 of PACE), there is no clear dividing line between the temporary detention of a person and a formal non-PACE arrest. The traditional approach was that an officer arrests a person when he:

- states in terms that he is arresting the person, or
- uses force to restrain the individual concerned, or

- by words or conduct he makes it clear that he will, if necessary, use force to prevent the individual from going where he may want to go.

(See *Hussien v Chong Fook Kam* 1970 AC 942 at 947B.)

Thus even the temporary, compulsory detention of a person for a few minutes in the street may constitute both an arrest and 'imprisonment' at common law, even though it is not an arrest under s 24 of PACE. At common law, it would still constitute a non-PACE arrest.

The House of Lords in *Austin v Commissioner of Police for the Metropolis* [2009] 1 AC 564 decided that the *purpose* of the deprivation of a person's liberty may be a factor in whether or not Article 5 of the ECHR is engaged—along with factors such as the type, duration, effects and manner of implementation of the measure in question. This is of particular significance in action taken against 'innocent' people.

Temporary restraint of a particular person to prevent a further breach of the peace by (or provoked by) that person is likely to constitute a potentially valid basis for detention under Article 5 of the ECHR, provided it is necessary.

Whatever the legal basis for an officer's intervention, it is *vital* that the person stopped receives an explanation for their treatment. If it is subsequently determined that the person has been deprived of their liberty, Article 5.2 requires that in every case the person is informed of the reasons for his arrest.

If a breach of the peace is being committed, a substantive criminal offence may also be taking place, such as under the Public Order Act 1986, s 4 or s 5. But even if a substantive criminal offence *is* also taking place, the power to take action in relation to the breach of the peace may have tactical and procedural advantages over the power to arrest for specific offences, most particularly the advantage of simplicity for the officer: restore the peace first and then work out who, if anyone, should be arrested, and for what.

If, having initially detained a person under the broad breach of the peace powers, an officer decides they are to be arrested for a substantive criminal offence, it is vital that the person is immediately informed that they are under arrest for that offence, in accordance with the usual s 28 PACE requirements.

POINT TO NOTE

In every case where an officer intervenes in an existing breach of the peace, the duration of the intervention must be limited to the time necessary to bring the breach of the peace to an end.

3.3.3 Future

There is power to arrest, restrain or take other action short of arrest in order to prevent an imminent breach of the peace from occurring or recurring. Whether or not there has been a breach of the peace in the past, *imminence* is the key threshold test that must be satisfied before any preventative action can be taken.

It is in the context of anticipated, future breaches of the peace that most problems arise. The difficult question of when the opportunity to intervene lawfully arises is addressed in detail in 3.4.

3.4 **When can the Police Intervene to Prevent an Anticipated Breach of the Peace?**

It is essential to understand that *imminence* is the threshold which must be passed before any preventive action (ie action to *prevent* a breach of the peace) may be taken. This was confirmed in *R (Laporte) v Chief Constable of Gloucestershire* [2006] UKHL 55.

Of course, whether a risk to the peace is imminent is a question of judgement for the individual officer. Provided he or she honestly believes in the imminence of the breach of the peace, and does so on reasonable grounds, then any necessary and proportionate intervention will be lawful even if it were subsequently to be shown that the threat to the peace was neither imminent nor real. The law recognizes that officers can only act upon what they hear and see, or are told (for example by other officers or intelligence records).

'Imminent' simply means that the breach of the peace is 'about to happen'. The proximity needs to be both by reference to time and place. The test of imminence is flexible because of the very different and unpredictable circumstances in which threats to the peace arise. The following guidance can be taken from the case of *Laporte*:

- Imminence depends on the particular context and cannot be measured in a fixed number of minutes.
- The absence of any further opportunity to take preventive action may be relevant; in other words, if it is believed that this is the last opportunity to take effective action—ie the officer is of the view that by not taking action now he or she may subsequently be unable to quell the imminent outbreak— then he or she may intervene earlier rather than later.
- The event must be *about to happen* in the near future. But that does not mean that the officer must be able to say that the breach is going to happen in the next few seconds or next few minutes. That would be an impossible standard for an officer to meet, since a police officer will rarely be able to predict precisely when violence will break out. The protagonists may take longer than expected to resort to violence or it may flare up quicker than anticipated.
- A breach of the peace will be imminent at a stage before it is instantaneous. There is no need for the police officer to wait until an opposing group comes into sight before taking action. That would be to turn every intervention

into an exercise in crisis management—an officer is allowed to act earlier to prevent the crisis, provided he or she acts when the anticipated crisis is imminent.

• Where events are building up inevitably to a breach of the peace it may be possible to regard it as imminent at an earlier stage than in the case of other more spontaneous breaches. Large-scale events may justify intervention many minutes before, and a significant distance from, the anticipated breach of the peace.

KEY POINT—KEY CONSIDERATIONS IN RELATION TO IMMINENCE, FOLLOWING *LAPORTE*:

• What amounts to 'imminence' depends on the context.
• An officer does not need to be able to predict exactly when or where a breach may occur.
• The absence of any further opportunity to take effective preventive action is relevant.
• An obvious, inevitable build up towards a breach of the peace may justify earlier intervention on the grounds of imminence.

3.5 What Type of Action can the Police Take when they Intervene to Prevent a Breach of the Peace?

Once the threshold test of imminence is passed, the police can *only* take action which is *reasonable* and *necessary* to prevent the breach of the peace.

There are no artificial limits on the type of action which might be reasonable and necessary to prevent a breach of the peace except that the action must be proportionate. Everything will depend on the context. Examples of reasonable and proportionate action to prevent a breach of the peace include:

• arrest: confirmed in *Laporte*
• using physical force: *Albert v Lavin*
• entering premises: expressly preserved by s 17(6) of PACE, and confirmed in *McLeod v Commissioner of Police for the Metropolis* [1994] 4 All ER 553
• ordering a person not to hold a meeting at which a breach of the peace is likely to occur: *Duncan v Jones* [1936] 1 KB 218
• requiring a political meeting to be stopped and dispersed: *O'Kelly v Harvey* (1883) 15 Cox CC 435
• restraining freedom of movement within premises: *DPP v Meaden* [2004] 1 WLR 945 (not a public order case, but it was found to be lawful to detain temporarily a person in one room of a house to allow a search of the property to take place)

- seizing a person's property: *Minto v The Police* (1987) 1 NZLR 374
- instructing a person to desist from conduct which is likely to result in a breach of the peace. If the person continues he may be arrested for obstructing a police officer in the execution of his duty under section 89(2) of the Police Act 1996: *Laporte*
- escorting demonstrators and others away from a protest: *Austin & Saxby v Commissioner of Police for the Metropolis* [2008] 1 QB 660 at paragraph 69 (Court of Appeal decision)
- blocking access to a place (ie establishing a cordon to keep people out): *DPP v Morrison* [2003] EWHC 683 (Admin) at paragraphs 4 and 25
- erecting a cordon of police officers and detaining those inside the cordon: *Austin* (Court of Appeal decision)
- preventing a person from joining a picket line: *Piddington v Bates* [1961] 1 WLR 162.

What action will be reasonable and necessary *depends on all the circumstances* in each individual case. Thus it is crucial that police officers make proper notebook or MG11 statements to explain the circumstances that were prevailing and why they took the action that they did. Those circumstances may include factors such as the resources available to the police, the likely impact of the feared breach of the peace on the community, experience of similar situations in the past (particularly if involving the same participants or locality), or the degree of disorder anticipated.

The action taken by the police must be proportionate. This means nothing more than that the action taken by the police must be the minimum reasonably necessary to achieve the aim of preventing the breach of the peace, and must be in proportion to the magnitude of the risk the officer faces.

What is reasonable and necessary will of course depend on the circumstances, such that greater intervention may be justified in separating several hundred angry rival football fans than in separating two teenage boys arguing over a girlfriend. The first situation may justify corralling the opposing fans for 30 minutes at different ends of the ground whilst the 'away' fans are funnelled down the road towards the tube station to take them away, whereas in the second situation it may only be necessary simply to split the teenagers up whilst officers speak to them individually and calm them down. They might then reasonably be allowed to go on their way once calm has been restored.

Taking proportionate action involves achieving an appropriate balance between the rights of those who are threatening a breach of the peace and those who might be affected by a breach of the peace. This can be a difficult balance to strike, particularly if action is being considered against persons not themselves directly posing a threat to the peace.

An officer should consider firstly what *type* of action should be taken (eg separation, corralling, arrest), and secondly what degree of action (eg for how long, where) is the minimum necessary in the circumstances. Some practical guidance was given by the House of Lords in *Laporte* (per Lord Rodger at paragraph 73):

> In many straightforward cases the steps which are reasonably necessary will be obvious. Where the officer believes, for instance, that an individual is about to punch someone else, then it may well be necessary for the officer to restrain and arrest the potential aggressor. But, sometimes, all that may be required is to advise the potential aggressor or the potential victim to leave as quickly as possible.

In other cases, perhaps involving rival gangs or rival groups of football supporters, the police officer may see that the members of one gang or group are making offensive remarks with the intention of provoking the other side to a fight. Then the officer may prevent the breach of the peace by ordering the first group to desist and, if they fail to do so, arresting them for obstructing a police officer in the execution of his duty under section 89(2) of the Police Act 1996.

The best way to establish the legality of any intervention, not least so that officers can protect themselves, is to record contemporaneously all the factors relied upon in supporting their belief that a breach of the peace was imminent and why they took the particular preventive measures they did.

In many circumstances, the earlier that intervention takes place, the less intrusive such intervention might need to be. This is the 'nipping in the bud' concept—but remember, you can't nip the bud before it is even appearing to flower. Imminence is always the key test.

In most cases, it is open to an officer to attempt to achieve with persuasion something that he does not have the power to *force* a member of the public to do. (It should be noted that PACE Code of Practice A paragraph 1.5 states that officer should not search a person, even with his or her consent, where there is no power to search. As a statement of good practice this may be sensible, but the authors struggle to see that it could be an accurate statement of law.) Therefore, while a police officer could request members of the public to do a great many things, the potential power to *coerce* them to do so only arises if a breach of the peace is reasonably apprehended to be imminent.

KEY POINT—REASONABLENESS, PROPORTIONALITY AND NECESSITY OF INTERVENTION

- Think flexibly—consider the full range of tactical options.
- The intervention should be the minimum reasonably necessary to achieve the aim of preventing a breach of the peace.
- The intervention should be in proportion to the magnitude/seriousness of the risk. Try to balance the legitimate rights of those who are threatening a breach of the peace and the rights of those who might be affected by it.
- In most cases persuasion may be attempted before coercion is justified or necessary.
- Record your reasoning!

3.6 **Against Whom can Action be Taken?**

The remainder of this section assumes that the preventive police action envisaged is some form of restraint by the police, which may include arrest.

In general terms the following types of people/situation need to be considered:

1. Those acting unlawfully.
2. Those acting lawfully but by their conduct provoking an unreasonable reaction in others.
3. Those acting lawfully but deliberately interfering with others' rights and so provoking them to react reasonably.
4. Innocent bystanders caught up in a violent or volatile situation.

Points 2 and 3 are sometimes known as 'hostile audience' situations.

3.6.1 **Those acting unlawfully**

Where people are threatening or provoking a breach of the peace and are acting in an unlawful manner, then police action should be targeted at them. In such cases there is clearly a power to intervene against the persons acting unlawfully, provided they are actually breaching the peace or imminently threatening to do so.

3.6.2 **Hostile audience 1: Those acting lawfully but by their conduct provoking other *unreasonable* persons**

An example of this might be evangelical Christians preaching (perhaps proselytizing) in a shopping centre in a predominantly Muslim area who are confronted by angry Muslim youths who take offence for purely religious reasons. The Christian preachers may be doing no more than exercising their freedom to assemble and expressing their religious beliefs and not saying anything which could reasonably be construed as racist or outrageous. They are threatened by the Muslim youths who object to their presence.

In such a situation the police would be duty bound to protect the rights of the Christian preachers and to take any preventive action against the youths.

This type of situation, involving someone acting lawfully but provoking an unreasonable third party, has found expression in three important English cases, *Foulkes*—domestic violence, *Redmond-Bate*—evangelical preachers, and *Bibby*—a bailiff. The facts of these cases are set out in detail to provide a clear picture of the types of problems that have actually arisen.

Case study

Foulkes v Merseyside Police [1998] 4 All ER 248

In the early hours of December 1994, Trevor Foulkes had an argument with his family at the house which he owned jointly with his wife of 22 years. His two teenage children, Karl (18) and Lindsay (19), were playing music loudly and would not leave the house when he told them to. Mrs Foulkes was also involved and there had been general abuse. Four police officers went to the house. They escorted Karl and Lindsay away from the house and told them to go back to Lindsay's flat. As Lindsay was leaving, she stubbed a cigarette out on her father's jumper.

Later that morning Mr Foulkes found that his children had returned for breakfast. There was a heated family discussion. Mr Foulkes told the children to leave immediately. Mrs Foulkes took the children's side and asked her husband to go out for a walk or stay with one of his brothers or friends. Mrs Foulkes herself then went out. The argument between Mr Foulkes and his children carried on. He tried to use the phone to call the police but his son stopped him from doing so. Just before 9am he went to a public phone box and called the police. In the meantime, Mrs Foulkes returned home. She and her son arranged quickly for the lock to be changed with the replacement lock they had standing by.

When two officers arrived they found Mr Foulkes sitting on his doorstep, locked out of his house. Mr Foulkes appeared to the police as slightly unkempt, very nervous, jittery and not completely coherent. His hands were shaking but otherwise he seemed calm. Mr Foulkes told one police officer that he had had arguments, that his son had locked him out of the house and he wanted to get back in. A second police officer went inside the house and spoke to Mrs Foulkes, Karl and Lindsay. The second police officer then came outside and told Mr Foulkes that his wife and children did not want him to go back into the house and that if he went back there would be arguments. The officer suggested that Mr Foulkes should go and have a cup of tea or go to a relative until tempers had cooled. Mr Foulkes did not like this suggestion. He said that he had called the police, it was his house, and he wanted to go back inside.

The officers suggested several times that he leave the front of the house to cool down but he refused. An officer cautioned him and told him that if he did not go away until tempers had cooled he would be arrested to prevent a breach of the peace. He refused again and an officer arrested him, fearing that it was Mr Foulkes's actions outside the property that were going to cause a breach of the peace. The officer thought that if he left Mr Foulkes outside the house he would keep trying to get in. If he got in, there would be an argument and violence. It did not matter to the officer whether the violence would be to him or to other members of the family. The officer thought that a breach of the peace would occur because of his actions. He thought that arresting him was the last resort.

Mr Foulkes was taken to a police station and detained there. Mrs Foulkes was asked to go to the station to make a statement. She did this and completed her statement shortly before 2pm. In her statement she said she wanted her husband bound over to keep the peace. By this time it was too late for Mr Foulkes to be taken before a magistrate so he was kept in custody until the following morning. The following morning Mrs Foulkes withdrew her suggestion that she wanted her husband to be taken before a magistrate and bound over to keep the peace. Mr Foulkes was released.

Mr Foulkes brought a false imprisonment claim against the police. He said that he should not have been arrested and that he had been detained for too long. The county court judge decided that the arresting officer had an honest belief that if he did not arrest Mr Foulkes there would be a breach of the peace, and that he had reasonable grounds for that belief.

The Court of Appeal disagreed: it decided that although the police officer had acted with the best of intentions, he did not have enough evidence to conclude that a breach of the peace was about to happen. There must be a sufficiently *real and present* threat to the peace to justify the extreme step of depriving a person of his liberty when that person is not at the time acting unlawfully.

The case raises issues about using breach of the peace powers in the context of family or matrimonial disputes. The Court of Appeal pointed out that Mr Foulkes had a legal right not to be locked out of the matrimonial home. The officer should have first pointed out to Mrs Foulkes that she was not entitled to resolve the dispute as to the presence of the children by locking out her husband. It expressed the hope that only in the rarest of cases would breach of the peace powers be used in the context of domestic disputes and the rights of occupation of the matrimonial home. Lord Justice Thorpe said he found it hard to envisage a situation in which the power of arrest for an apprehended breach of the peace would be an appropriate management of a dispute between husband and wife within the matrimonial home. However, with respect to the Court of Appeal, if one party to a matrimonial argument is threatening violence, it is very difficult to see why breach of the peace powers cannot be invoked.

Indeed, the first High Court decision after *Foulkes*, namely *Wragg v DPP* [2005] EWHC 1389 (Admin), demonstrated that, despite the words of the Court of Appeal in *Foulkes*, there will continue to be situations where it is necessary and lawful to use breach of the peace in the context of matrimonial disputes.

Wragg concerned the lawfulness of the defendant's arrest to prevent a breach of the peace following a domestic incident. Mr Wragg, who was refusing to leave his home, had been drinking, appeared to be rather intimidating (unlike Mr Foulkes), and his partner had told the police that she and the children feared violence were he to remain at the property. The Divisional Court held, despite

Foulkes, that there had been an imminent risk of a breach of the peace and the defendant's arrest was accordingly lawful.

Although the facts of the two cases are superficially similar, the crucial distinction is that in *Wragg* the arrest was lawful because the husband appeared to be intimidating, and his wife and children told the police they feared violence. It reinforces the importance of keeping in mind not only whether a breach of the peace is imminent, but *who* is posing a risk to the peace.

Case study

Redmond-Bate v DPP (1999) 163 JP 789; [1999] Crim LR 998

Ms Redmond-Bate was one of three Christian fundamentalist women who were preaching from the steps of Wakefield Cathedral in October 1997 just after midday. They belonged to a small organization called Faith Ministries who, among other things, preached to passers-by in the street. They had agreed with the police that on this occasion they would do so from the steps of Wakefield Cathedral. When they were preaching, an unidentified couple complained about them to a police officer who was on uniformed foot patrol. The officer went to the cathedral steps. No crowd had gathered. The officer warned the women not to stop people. They were not doing so. The officer left.

Twenty minutes later the officer returned to find a crowd of more than 100 had gathered. Another of the women was now preaching and some of the crowd were showing hostility to them. The message of the preaching was about morality, God and the Bible. The officer asked the women to stop preaching, because he feared (probably reasonably) a breach of the peace. When they refused to do so he arrested them all for breach of the peace.

Ms Redmond-Bate was charged with obstructing a police officer in the execution of his duty and the question came up in court whether it was reasonable for the officer to believe that she was about to cause a breach of the peace.

The High Court stated that if the officer thought there was a threat of violence, because Ms Redmond-Bate and the other preachers were being so provocative that someone in the crowd, without behaving wholly unreasonably, might be violent, he was entitled to ask them to stop, and to arrest them if they did not. If the officer thought a threat of disorder was coming from passers-by who were taking the opportunity to react so as to cause trouble, then the passers-by and not the preachers should have been asked to desist and arrested if they would not.

On the facts of the case, the High Court said that it was not lawful to arrest the preachers. No one had to stop and listen to the preachers. If they did, they could express their views. The officer had previously had to move on a group of youths who were chanting and swearing, and this was exactly the right thing to do. If there are two alternative sources of trouble, the police can choose to take steps against either, but only if both are threatening violence or behaving in a manner that might provoke violence. Freedom to speak includes the right to say offensive and unwelcome things, provided it does not provoke violence. It was illiberal and illogical to say that preaching about morality, God and the Bible was going to provoke violence.

The officer was therefore *not* acting in the execution of his duty when he required the women to stop preaching and Ms Redmond-Bate was therefore not guilty of obstructing him in the execution of his duty.

It is important to note that in this case Redmond-Bate was exercising her rights under Articles 9 (religion) and 10 (expression) and this imposed an even greater obligation on the police to do what they could to protect her rights to preach, provided she acted lawfully and not outrageously. Furthermore, unlike in section 3.6.3 below, Redmond-Bate was not substantially interfering with the rights of others.

After *Laporte* and *Austin*, there arises the question as to whether the police officers present could have required Ms Redmond-Bate's assistance in preventing a breach of the peace. If asked to assist by stopping preaching temporarily while the police controlled or dispersed the hostile crowd, she would have been obliged to do so. The citizen's duty to assist is addressed in more detail at 3.7.

Case study

Bibby v Chief Constable of Essex (2000) 164 JP 297

Mr Bibby was a bailiff. Mr Brannan was a businessman who had fallen behind in the payment of his rates. Chelmsford Borough Council obtained a liability order against him. There was an agreement between Mr Brannan and Mr Bibby's firm that gave a list of personal property at the premises.

Mr Bibby went to Mr Brannan's shop, told him that money was due and that he needed cash or he would have to take goods. Mr Brannan forcefully told him to leave saying that they would call friends to prevent the goods being taken, as they had done before. Both Mr Bibby and Mr Brannan called the police.

When the police arrived they went to a room in the shop where Mr Bibby and Mr Brannan were. The circumstances were that Mr Bibby was a large man who was being forthright and short-tempered, and was at the end of his tether. There were five people in their 50s in a small room, including a woman.

Mr Bibby was asked by the police to leave but did not do so, even when he was told that if he did not leave he would be arrested to prevent a breach of the peace. The police thought that there would be a breach of the peace, told Mr Bibby to go, and when he refused they arrested him. They released him about an hour later, taking the view that there was no longer any risk of a breach of the peace.

Mr Bibby sued the police for assault and wrongful imprisonment. The arresting officer noted at the time the circumstances above—that Mr Bibby was a large man who was being intimidating, forthright, short-tempered, appearing to be at the end of his tether, and noted the people present, and Mr Bibby's refusal to leave despite being told by police that if he did not leave he would be arrested to prevent a breach of the peace.

The judge decided that Mr Bibby had been arrested lawfully because he was acting provocatively (albeit lawfully) and his provocation was likely to cause a breach of the peace, by violence either by Mr Brannan on Mr Bibby, or the other way round, or both. It was *reasonable* of the officer to ask Mr Bibby to go and *unreasonable* of Mr Bibby to insist on staying until he had either the money or the goods.

The Court of Appeal disagreed with the judge's decision. It was Mr Brannan, not Mr Bibby, who was acting unreasonably. To say otherwise would mean there was a charter for violence. The Court gave the example of a policeman about to arrest a man who threatens violence to the policeman if the policeman touches him. A passer-by tells the policeman to go away because otherwise there will be a breach of the peace. The policeman is not bound to obey. He can carry out his lawful actions despite the fact that they may cause violence from someone who does not want to be arrested.

Like in *Redmond-Bate*, the officer had not properly considered *where* the threat was coming from. The threat of violence should have been perceived as coming from Mr Brannan and not Mr Bibby. Mr Brannan was not threatening violence, but he was threatening to prevent Mr Bibby from doing what he could lawfully do.

In *Bibby* the Court of Appeal set out some useful and important guidance on dealing with persons not acting unlawfully but who are confronted by a so-called 'hostile audience'. The Court was of the view that:

1. There must be the clearest of circumstances and a sufficiently real and present threat to the peace to justify the extreme step of depriving of the liberty of a citizen who is not at the time acting unlawfully.
2. The threat must be coming from the person who is to be arrested.
3. The conduct must clearly interfere with the rights of others.
4. The natural consequence of the conduct must be violence from a third party.
5. The violence in (4) must not be *wholly* unreasonable.
6. The conduct of the person to be arrested must be unreasonable.

In point 4, the phrase 'wholly unreasonable' is not explained further in the decision. It is suggested that, to satisfy point 4, the person's reaction would need to be understandable, and the sort of response that a reasonable person, moved to anger or exasperation, might display—even if it is what a calm person might think was an overreaction.

Indeed, these six guidelines are apposite to the very next section which concerns those acting lawfully but deliberatively provocatively.

KEY POINT—DEALING WITH THE 'HOSTILE AUDIENCE' AFTER *BIBBY*

- The threat must be coming from the person who is to be arrested.
- The conduct must clearly interfere with the rights of others.
- The natural consequence of the conduct must be violence from a third party.
- The violence from the third party must not be wholly unreasonable.
- The conduct of the person to be arrested must be unreasonable.

3.6.3 Hostile audience 2: Those acting lawfully but deliberately provoking others whose 'lawful activity' they may be disrupting

This is a difficult example of the police duty to prevent a breach of the peace. Where someone is behaving lawfully, but deliberately provocatively, the task for the police involves making judgements as to: *who* is behaving reasonably or unreasonably; the activities each party is seeking to undertake; whether ECHR rights are engaged; and how the balance between competing rights should be struck.

Should the police arrest the provocateur or the person being provoked? The answer will often depend upon the following considerations:

- whether the provocateur has the protection of Articles 10 or 11 (eg the protestor or evangelist)
- whether those provoked are having their rights interfered with (eg the anglers in the case of *Nicol and Salvanayagam*—see the case study in this chapter)
- whether those provoked react reasonably (the anglers trying to remove the anti-anglers), or unreasonably (the Muslim youths trying to evict Christians they simply disagree with).

An example of this sort of situation might be Christian evangelical preachers who picket a Mosque at Friday prayers and harangue the Muslims attending. If they do so provocatively but peacefully, the police must do their best to hold the line between the two religious groups, via appropriate directions as to the location and timing of gatherings.

But what if the Christian evangelical preachers deploy lurid placards and chanting? The placards might equate *all* Muslims with suicide bombers (something self-evidently both inaccurate and liable to be very offensive). If the placards are melodramatic and contain bloody or violent images, and the chanting does likewise, thus putting some of the Mosque-goers in fear of attack, such that some of their number threaten to respond physically to the Christians, the police might have to intervene to corral or limit the place and *nature* of the Christians' protest. As a first step, the most provocative banners might have to be removed from the protestors.

This sort of situation was recognized by Lord Rodger in *Laporte* at paragraph 75:

> Even where someone does not actually intend to provoke others into a violent reaction but behaves in an outrageous way which is liable to produce such a reaction, he can be stopped. That was the position in *Wise v Dunning* [1902] 1 KB 167. When addressing meetings in a public place in Liverpool the appellant used gestures and language which were highly insulting to the Roman Catholic population. His actions had caused, and were liable to cause, breaches of the peace by his opponents and supporters. The Divisional Court held that the magistrate's decision to bind him over to keep the peace had been fully justified. In doing so, the court rejected his argument that he could not be held responsible for any breaches of the peace that occurred since an unlawful act could not be regarded as the natural consequence of his insulting or abusive language or conduct.

Another example is that of anti-bloodsports campaigners throwing sticks or pebbles into the water of a river where an angling competition is taking place. The campaigners are not, of themselves, doing anything unlawful but are, of course, *deliberately* provoking the anglers. This very situation arose in the case of *Nicol*.

Case study
Nicol and Selvanayagam v DPP (1996) 160 JP 155; [1996] Crim LR 318

In May 1994 an angling competition took place at a lake in Middlesbrough. About 40 anglers were taking part. Ms Nicol and Ms Selvanayagam believed that angling was cruel. Between 11:00 and 11:30am they went to the lake as part of a group of 6–10 people. They tried to dissuade the anglers from doing what they were doing and to disrupt the competition. The group threw sticks and twigs at the anglers' lines and into the water where the anglers were fishing, sounded air horns and sought verbally to persuade the anglers to stop fishing. There was no violence and no threat of violence.

Someone contacted the police. Between 12:15 and 12:25pm, three police officers arrived. They warned Ms Nicol and Ms Selvanayagam, and other protestors about their behaviour and told them to stop it. But Ms Nicol and Ms Selvanayagam carried on as before. They were arrested.

The police took them to a magistrates' court and made an application that they should be bound over. The magistrates' court found that they had behaved in a way which made a breach of the peace likely. The court found that:

- their conduct would have disrupted and interfered with the lawful activities of the anglers;

- their conduct was intended to prevent the anglers getting on with their lawful activities;
- the consequence of their conduct would almost certainly have been a breach of the peace, in that some or all of the anglers would forcefully remove or restrain them;
- the resulting confrontation would almost certainly have resulted in acts of violence or disorder, provoked by them from the anglers. (At least two anglers had commented to the police that they would shortly take violent action to remove the protestors.)

The Court ordered Ms Nicol and Ms Selvanayagam to agree to be bound over. Both refused to be bound over and were sent into custody for 21 days.

The High Court decided that the magistrates had been correct to order Ms Nicol and Ms Selvanayagam to be bound over. They were not threatening violence themselves. But violence from the anglers was the natural consequence of what they were doing (*Bibby*, point 4). Ms Nicol and Ms Selvanayagam were also acting unreasonably because they were trying to stop the anglers' lawful conduct (*Bibby*, point 6). In contrast, the anglers would not have been acting wholly unreasonably if they had responded violently (*Bibby*, point 5) because the protestors were trying to interfere with their lawful activity (*Bibby*, point 3).

It would have been different if the protestors were not trying to interfere with any lawful activity. For example, had the protesters simply held up anti-angling banners and chanted anti-angling slogans.

An example of this different position is provided by three of the five protestors (Andrea Needham, David Polden and Christopher Cole) in the *Steel* cases, who had simply been handing out anti-war leaflets at a military conference. The ECtHR in *Steel v United Kingdom* (1999) 28 EHRR 603 considered three cases concerning five people who had protested against different issues in three different ways.

Case study

Case 1: Helen Steel—Shoot saboteuse

On Saturday 22 August 1992, Helen Steel took part in a protest against a grouse shoot in Yorkshire. During the morning the protestors tried to get in the way of the people taking part in the shoot and distract them. In the afternoon the police arrived and warned the protestors to stop their behaviour. The protestors ignored these requests and the police arrested 13 people, including Ms Steel, who was arrested for breach of the peace at about 2pm. The police said that she intentionally got in the way of one of the people taking part in the shoot in that she walked in front of him as he lifted his shotgun to take aim such that he could not fire.

After she was arrested, Ms Steel was detained in a police vehicle. At about 3:45pm she was transferred to a prison van. At about 7:15pm she was taken to a police station. At 11:00pm the police authorized her continued detention at the police station to prevent a further breach of the peace. The case police decided to apply for a bind over order. At 9:40am on 24 August, Steel was charged with an offence under s 5 Public Order Act 1986. That morning she was also taken to court and released on bail on the condition that she did not attend any game shoot in North Yorkshire. She had been detained for a total of 44 hours.

At trial, Ms Steel was acquitted of a s 5 charge relating to the morning of 22 August, but convicted of a charge relating to the afternoon. The court also found that she had committed a breach of the peace but did not say what behaviour they based this conclusion on, and whether it happened in the morning or the afternoon. Ms Steel appealed to the Crown Court. The Crown Court upheld the magistrates' findings. Because of the breach of the peace, the Court ordered that Ms Steel agree to be bound over to keep the peace and be of good behaviour for 12 months in the sum of £100. She refused to be bound over and was committed to prison for 28 days.

Case study
Case 2: Rebecca Lush—Construction obstruction

On 15 September 1993, Rebecca Lush took part in a protest against an extension to the M1 motorway in Wanstead. During the day a group of 20–25 protestors repeatedly broke into a construction site. They climbed into trees which were going to be cut down. They climbed onto some of the stationary machinery. Each time they were removed by security guards. The protestors did not resist being removed.

At about 4:15pm Ms Lush was standing under the bucket of a JCB digger. She was arrested for conduct likely to provoke a disturbance of the peace. She was taken to a police station where she was 'charged'. The charge sheet states that she had been arrested as a person whose conduct was likely to provoke a disturbance of the peace, and that she was to be brought before a court. She was kept in custody until 9:40 the following morning, approximately 17 hours later, on the grounds that if she were released she would cause a further breach of the peace. She appeared at a magistrates' court on the morning of 16 September 1993 to answer an allegation that she had engaged in conduct likely to provoke a disturbance of the peace. The case was adjourned and she was released. Three months later the case came back to court. The allegation of conduct likely to cause a breach of the peace was proved. Ms Lush was ordered to agree to be bound over to keep the peace and be of good behaviour, in the sum of £100. She refused to be bound over and was committed to prison for 7 days.

The European Court pointed out that English courts had found that both Ms Steel and Ms Lush had actually caused, or had been likely to cause, a breach of the peace. The European Court said there was no reason to doubt that the police were justified in fearing that their behaviour, if it carried out, might provoke others to violence. Therefore their arrests and initial detention were *lawful* under English law.

The European Court thought that the natural consequence of the behaviour of Ms Steel and Ms Lush was to provoke others to violence and that the English courts were justified in ordering them to agree to be bound over. The European Court decided that the imprisonment of Ms Steel and Ms Lush when they refused to be bound over could potentially be justified because they had not complied with the order of a court.

Ms Steel and Ms Lush argued that they had not been given sufficient details of the charges against them. They argued that 'breach of the peace' was too general, and that the charge sheets should have given specific details about what they were said to have done. The European Court disagreed. They had both been given charge sheets which said that they had committed a breach of the peace on a stated date in a stated place.

Ms Steel and Ms Lush argued that their arrests and detention were in breach of their right to freedom of expression under Article 10. The European Court found that their arrests and detention were proportionate. The European Court noted that Ms Steel had been detained for a long time and her right to freedom of expression had been interfered with. However, it thought that the interference was proportionate because of the dangers of what Ms Steel was doing and the risk of disorder which could have been caused by the persistent obstruction of the grouse shoot. The European Court then considered the 44 hours' detention and decided that this was proportionate too. It acknowledged that this was a long time, but also considered that Ms Steel's behaviour risked injury to herself and others, and that the protest risked ending in disorder and violence. The European Court recognized that if released she could simply go back to the kind of protests which she had carried out before, possibly with serious consequences. It was also proportionate for Ms Steel to be ordered to be bound over.

The European Court made similar findings in relation to Ms Lush. Although the risk of disorder which she created was less serious than that created by Ms Steel, the Court had no reason to doubt the conclusion of the magistrates' court that she had acted in a way which was likely to cause a breach of the peace.

Case study

Case 3: Needham, Polden and Cole—The three leafleteers

On 20 January 1994, Ms Needham, Mr Polden and Mr Cole went to the Queen Elizabeth Conference Centre in Westminster, London, where the Fighter Helicopter II Conference was being held. They went there to protest against the sale of fighter helicopters. They protested by handing out leaflets and holding up banners saying 'Work for Peace and not War'.

At about 8:25am, Ms Needham was holding a banner and Mr Polden and Mr Cole were giving out leaflets. They were arrested and taken to a police station. The custody record stated that they had committed a breach of the peace or had acted in a way which was likely to cause one, and that they were to be brought before a court. At about 10:40am they were taken to a magistrates' court. At court they were detained in a cell. They had a seven-hour wait and finally went before the magistrates at 3:45pm. The magistrates adjourned the case because of lack of time. Ms Needham, Mr Polden and Mr Cole were released.

The cases came back to court about a month later on 25 February 1994. The prosecution decided not to call any evidence and the cases were dismissed.

The European Court decided that their protest was entirely peaceful. They did not try to get in the way of the people attending the conference. They did not do anything which was likely to provoke other people to be violent. They had not done anything which justified the fear of the police that they were likely to cause a breach of the peace. The European Court therefore decided that their arrests were unlawful under English law.

Ms Needham, Mr Polden and Mr Cole claimed that their right to freedom of expression under Article 10 had been breached. The European Court upheld this claim for two reasons. First, there had been no legal authority for their detention. Interferences with Article 10 which are not lawful under English law can never be justified. Second, the police had acted disproportionately in arresting them. The United Kingdom was ordered to pay £500 compensation to each of them.

As can be seen from these three decisions in *Steel*, where persons are acting lawfully, peacefully and pursuant to their Article 10 and 11 rights, the police will rarely have any justification for arresting them because of an associated fear of a breach of the peace occurring. On the contrary, the police will have to exercise care to protect the protest and expression rights of persons behaving lawfully and peacefully.

3.6.4 Innocent bystanders caught up in a violent or volatile situation

There may be exceptional circumstances where the police are entitled to detain everyone involved, including innocent bystanders, if there is no other reasonable way to prevent a breach of the peace.

This was the situation on 1 May 2001 at Oxford Circus, London, where the police 'contained' up to 3,000 protestors for over seven hours, many of whom were plainly not intent on causing any trouble or violence. The High Court (*Austin v Commissioner of Police for the Metropolis* [2005] EWHC 480 (QB)) found that, in all the prevailing circumstances, there was nothing else that the police could reasonably have done that would have been effective to prevent serious rioting breaking out in the target rich environment of Oxford Street.

The Court of Appeal (*Austin v Commissioner of Police for the Metropolis* [2008] 1 QB 660) agreed with this assessment, and the Court's central findings on these factual issues were not challenged in the House of Lords.

The Court of Appeal considered the rights of the innocent protestors both at common law and under Article 5 of the ECHR.

Common Law

- Where a breach of the peace was taking place or reasonably thought to be imminent, the police could not interfere with or curtail the lawful exercise of rights by innocent third parties unless they had taken all other possible steps to prevent the breach or imminent breach of the peace and to protect the rights of third parties.
- The taking of all other possible steps included, but was not limited to, making proper advance preparations to deal with such a breach, the absence of which would render the interference with the rights of innocent third parties unjustified or unjustifiable.
- Only where the police reasonably believed that there were no other means whatsoever to prevent a breach or imminent breach of the peace could they—as a matter of *necessity*—curtail the lawful exercise of their rights by third parties.
- The necessity test would be met only in truly extreme and exceptional circumstances *and* the action taken had to be both reasonably necessary and proportionate.
- The policy of leaving to police officers discretion to release individuals within the crowd was rational, sensible and necessary.

The Court of Appeal concluded that, although the claimants had been imprisoned, for the purposes of the tort of false imprisonment, that imprisonment had been lawful.

Article 5

- The protection of the rights of demonstrators pursuant to Article 5 was subject to permitting preventive action against an innocent third person where it was reasonably apprehended that there was no other possible means of avoiding an imminent breach of the peace.
- Whether there had been a deprivation of liberty in any particular case depended on a number of factors which had to be weighed in the balance.
- In the exceptional circumstances, the approach adopted by the police in imposing and then maintaining the cordon had struck a fair balance between the general interests of the community, and the interests of those contained within the cordon, including their protection from the consequences of violence.

Although the claimants' containment within the cordon had been an interference with their liberty of movement, it had not amounted to the kind of arbitrary deprivation of liberty contemplated by Article 5 of the Convention.

The House of Lords (*Austin v Commissioner of Police for the Metropolis* [2007] 2 AC 205) was asked to consider only the allegation of a breach of Article 5. There was no challenge to the finding that, faced with the unusually challenging set of circumstances at Oxford Circus on 1 May 2001, there was no viable alternative to wide-scale containment over a period of several hours if serious disorder was to be prevented.

In its decision, the House of Lords had to tangle with the central problem that the wording of Article 5 does not, on the face of it, permit the deprivation of an innocent person's liberty where to do so is necessary in order to prevent serious public disorder.

The House of Lords dealt with this problem by finding that necessary, reasonable and proportionate temporary crowd control measures did not *engage* the Article 5 rights of the innocent participant within the crowd.

Commenting on the ambit of Article 5, Lord Hope stated [37]:

> In my opinion measures of crowd control will fall outside the area of its application, so long as they are not arbitrary. This means that they must be resorted to in good faith, that they must be proportionate and that they are enforced for no longer than is reasonably necessary.

Lord Neuberger emphasized that this was an exceptional step for the police to take, noting that in the case of *Austin*:

- The cordon was imposed purely for crowd control purposes, to protect people and property from injury.
- The cordon was necessary as many of the demonstrators were bent on violence and impeding the police.
- The need for the cordon was not attributable to policing failures.
- The purpose and reason for imposing the cordon were at all times plain to those constrained within it.
- The cordon lasted for as short a time as possible: during its imposition, the police attempted to raise it on a number of occasions, but decided that it was impractical.
- The inclusion of the appellant and the demonstrators constrained with her within the cordon was unavoidable.

Those who were not demonstrators, or were seriously affected by being confined, were promptly permitted to leave.

3.6.5 Containment decisions after *Austin*

KEY POINTS—*AUSTIN V COMMISSIONER OF POLICE*: THE CIRCUMSTANCES IN WHICH AN INNOCENT MEMBER OF A CROWD CAN BE DETAINED

- Exceptional cases (last resort).
- Purely for crowd control purposes, to protect people and property from injury.

- Resorted to only in good faith.
- Must be reasonable and proportionate.
- Imposed for no longer than is reasonably necessary.
- Not to be used as a consequence of prior policing/planning failures.
- Obvious non-demonstrators must be allowed to leave.

The exceptional circumstances that are required to be present before it can be lawful to impose mass containment over a significant number of hours to prevent a breach of the peace were amply demonstrated in the recent first instance decision in *Moos v Commissioner of Police for the Metropolis* [2011] EWHC 957. This case involved a challenge by way of judicial review to the policing of the G20 'climate camp' in the City of London on 1 April 2009. The case bore a number of superficial similarities to *Austin*. There had been an earlier protest at the Royal Exchange, approximately one quarter of a mile away, at which there had been an escalation in disorder. The climate camp was a significantly more peaceful event, but it was anticipated that protestors from the Royal Exchange would try to join it. The police anticipated an imminent breach of the peace and imposed an absolute cordon around the climate camp which lasted for approximately four hours.

The High Court confirmed that [56]:

> It is only when the police reasonably believe that there is no other means whatsoever to prevent an imminent breach of the peace that they can as a matter of necessity curtail the lawful exercise of their rights by third parties. The test of necessity is met only in truly extreme and exceptional circumstances. The action taken has to be both reasonably necessary and proportionate and taken in good faith. The case of *Austin*, where the containment was held to be lawful, was a very exceptional case.

The Court went on to find that, at the time the absolute containment was imposed there was no reasonably apprehended breach of the peace within the climate camp itself sufficient to justify containment. There *was* a risk of a breach of the peace but it was at that stage only a future risk, rather than a risk of *imminent* breaches of the peace sufficient to justify full containment at the climate camp. Although the Court recognized the flexibility within the concept of 'imminence', it could not extend to the particular facts of that case.

It is relevant to note that although the decision to turn filter cordons into an absolute containment was found to have been unlawful, the decision to terminate the demonstration and clear the climate camp, by force if necessary with the aid of section 14 of the Public Order Act 1986, was fully justified.

It should be noted that both of these cases are subject to appeals: *Moos* to the Court of Appeal and *Austin* to the European Court of Human Rights.

Although the innocent bystander or attendee has limited protection if they are caught up in a containment deemed to be necessary to prevent a breach of the peace, the Court has returned the importance of planning so as to minimize the impact on the innocent or vulnerable bystander in *R (Castle) v Commissioner of Police for the Metropolis* [2011] EWHC 2317. In *Castle* the claimants, who were both children, challenged the imposition of a containment during a student demonstration in Central London on 24 November 2010. The demonstration took place two weeks after serious disorder had erupted at a previous student demonstration. The claimants were peaceful participants in the demonstration, who found themselves in a containment where they were kept for about six hours. The necessity to impose a containment to prevent a breach of the peace was not challenged. However, it was alleged that the containment was unlawful, insofar as it related to children, because the Commissioner had failed to take account of his obligation under s 11 of the Children Act 2004 to ensure that policing functions are discharged having regard to the need to safeguard and promote the welfare of children.

The Divisional Court reminded itself of paragraph 35 of the Court of Appeal decision in *Austin*: see the bullet points under 'Common Law' at section 3.6.4. It stated that:

- An improper failure to anticipate the need to take action to prevent a breach of the peace, and a failure to take other practicable steps to prevent it, will render containment unjustified with regard to those innocent third parties who may be affected by it.
- Even if, in breach of the requirements as to planning, advance preparation has not taken place, it will remain the positive obligation of the police to intervene to prevent a breach of the peace—if necessary by containment. However, if innocent parties are affected, the action taken may be unjustified so far as they are concerned.

The Divisional Court agreed that, when planning for or imposing a containment, the police must ensure that regard is paid to the need to safeguard and promote the welfare of children, although it was satisfied that the Commissioner of Police had fulfilled this obligation. Nevertheless, the Court's judgment in *Castle* confirms that where an innocent person is caught up in a containment that might have been avoidable with better planning, they have a potential cause of action against the relevant chief of police.

3.7 The Citizen's Duty to Assist when Asked to Prevent a Breach of the Peace

It is the duty of every citizen to take reasonable steps to prevent a breach of the peace (*Albert v Lavin*). However, under normal circumstances, should a member of the public fail to take such action, he or she is not liable to any civil or criminal penalty.

The situation is different where a member of the public is asked by a police officer to assist in preventing a breach of the peace. Provided it is necessary, a police officer is entitled to call on *any* able-bodied bystanders for their active assistance in suppressing a breach of the peace. If, without any lawful excuse, they refuse to give it, they are guilty of an offence.

A colourful example of a conviction following such a refusal is found in *R v Brown* (1841) C & Mar 314, where the constable chanced upon an illegal prize fight, attended by numerous spectators. The constable's attempts to stop the fight led to a riot, and the defendant was one of a number of people the constable could have asked to assist him. When asked, the defendant refused, and later argued in his defence to the charge of refusing to assist, that his assistance would not have helped. The court found that whether the aid of the defendant, if given, would have proved sufficient or useful, was not the criterion. If it were, any individual might give the same excuse. The defendant may have been able to help, and his refusal to lend assistance may have led, and perhaps did lead, to others also refusing. It was observed that 'Every man is bound to set a good example to others by doing his duty in preserving the public peace'.

This is an aspect of breach of the peace powers that—if it were ever a common occurrence—seems to have fallen into relative disuse in recent years. However, both *Laporte* (in the House of Lords) and *Austin* (at first instance) confirmed that it remains a valid component of public order policing. As it was put in *Laporte* by Lord Rodger at paragraph 83, 'In the eyes of the law therefore innocent bystanders caught up in a breach of the peace are to be regarded as potential allies of the police officers who are trying to suppress the violence'.

This has the potential to affect substantially the policing of difficult public order situations. Suppose a breach of the peace were imminent and a person were to be acting lawfully, but nevertheless were contributing to the problem. Rather than taking direct action against that person, a constable could request their assistance in preventing a breach of the peace. This assistance could include both stopping doing an act, or a more positive step such as leaving the area. Provided this action was necessary to prevent or suppress a breach of the peace, the request would be lawful, and the member of the public legally obliged to comply, and could be arrested if they did not so assist.

Used appropriately, this common law duty could provide an answer for some of the most difficult and sensitive situations. For example, in the case of Ms Redmond-Bate, set out earlier in this chapter, rather than simply requesting Ms Redmond-Bate to stop, it may have been possible to resolve the matter by requesting her assistance in preventing a breach of the peace. Her assistance could have taken the form of temporarily desisting from making her speech while the police officers present dealt with the hostile crowd that was gathering. In extreme circumstances, had Ms Redmond-Bate refused, she could have been lawfully arrested for refusing to assist the constable, provided the request was indeed necessary. Necessity in this context would mean that such a request was the only practical way the imminent breach of the peace could be avoided. It would only be if it could be shown that the alternative option of taking action against the hostile crowd was not practical that the request would be justified.

KEY POINTS—REFUSAL TO ASSIST A CONSTABLE TO PREVENT A BREACH OF THE PEACE

- A constable may require a member of the public to assist him in preventing a breach of the peace—current or imminent.
- The assistance must be necessary, ie the only practical way to prevent the breach of the peace is to seek that person's assistance.
- A person who refuses to assist is guilty of an offence at common law.
- It is no defence that the person's help would not have assisted the constable.

This power to enlist the assistance of members of the public is clearly something that should only be employed where absolutely necessary. It should not be a substitute for lazy or timid policing. In most circumstances the appropriate person against whom to take action will remain the person acting unlawfully or threatening the peace. In cases of public protests, the rights of the protestor (particularly freedom of expression) would be engaged as soon as they were requested to cease protesting, even temporarily. An officer must bear in mind that if he were to arrest for a failure to assist a constable, that officer might well have to establish at a later date that it was truly necessary to make the request in the first place.

3.8 **The Binding Over Order**

The magistrates' court and Crown Court have powers to 'bind over' someone to keep the peace. The powers derive from the common law, the Justices of the Peace Act 1361, the Justices of the Peace Act 1968 and the Magistrates' Courts Act 1980, s 115.

An order binding a person over to keep the peace is not a criminal conviction, but a preventive measure, imposed by the court, with the purpose of avoiding further breaches of the peace. Binding over orders are worthwhile against prolific or repeat 'offenders', ie people who might well be deterred by the knowledge that if they behave in breach of the order they may then be taken back before the court by the police and, if the breach is proven, fined for the breach.

They also, of course, commonly act as a compromise between prosecution and defence, where the CPS is happy not to proceed with a prosecution and the defendant agrees to be bound over.

A binding over order requires the person bound over to enter into a 'recognizance', or undertaking secured by a sum of money fixed by the court, to keep the peace for a specified period of time. The Magistrates' Courts Act s 115 provides means of bringing someone before the magistrates' court for an application to bind over to be made. Such an application is made by way of complaint.

For the purpose of English law, a binding over order is not a criminal conviction and a breach of the peace is not a criminal offence (although it is considered to be an 'offence' for the purpose of Article 5 of the Convention). This means that an arrest for breach of the peace is not carried out under PACE. PACE does not apply directly, but it is good practice to operate the PACE custody system insofar as it is consistent with the common law powers of the police (see *Williamson v Chief Constable of the West Midlands* [2004] 1 WLR 14 at paragraph 23).

In the past, it may have been common practice for police forces to purport to exercise a power of common law detention to bring a person before the court to be bound over. However, there appears to be no direct legal authority for this. Such a power is not necessary for the police to get someone to court to be bound over, now that a summons can be issued on the making of a complaint under the Magistrates' Courts Act 1980, s 115. Provided the threat to the peace has passed, such people should be brought before the court immediately, or if the person's name and address can be verified, served with a summons and released.

A Law Commission report recommended that the power to bind over be abolished, but this has not been implemented. However, two European Court judgments have caused domestic courts to modify the practice relating to binding over orders. Both challenges were in part based on the vague language of such an order. Firstly, in *Steel*, the European Court was concerned (in the cases of *Steel* and *Lush*) with applicants who had been found to have committed a breach of the peace. The European Court stated that the expression 'to be of good behaviour' was particularly imprecise, and offered little guidance to the person bound over as to the type of conduct which would amount to a breach of the order. However, because in each case the binding over order was imposed after a finding that she had committed a breach of the peace, it was sufficiently clear that the applicants were being requested to agree to refrain from causing further, similar, breaches of the peace during the ensuing 12 months.

In the second case of *Hashman and Harrup v United Kingdom* (2000) 30 EHRR 241, the applicants were hunt saboteurs who had disrupted a foxhunt.

An application for a binding over order was made by way of complaint, pursuant to the Justices of the Peace Act 1361. The applicants appealed against a binding over order to keep the peace and be of good behaviour. The Crown Court found that the applicants had not caused or been likely to occasion a breach of the peace. However, their conduct had been *contra bonos mores*, described as 'conduct which has the property of being wrong rather than right in the judgment of the majority of contemporary fellow citizens' in *Hughes v Holley* [1988] 86 Cr App R 130. This was a wider concept than a mere breach of the peace, and justified the making of an order to be of good behaviour.

The ECHR repeated the criticism expressed in *Steel* of the vagueness of the phrase 'to be of good behaviour'. In this case, as the applicants had not been found to have breached the peace in a particular way, there was no specific similar conduct that they could avoid in future. The Court disagreed that it must have been evident to the applicants what they were being ordered not do. Therefore the binding over order to keep the peace and not to behave *contra bonos mores* was not 'prescribed by law' and so did not comply with Article 10(2).

The consequence of this is that:

• Following a finding that a person has caused, or been likely to cause, or contributed to a breach of the peace, the power to bind over to keep the peace under s 1(7) of the Justices of the Peace Act 1968 remains.
• A general order to keep the peace, be of good behaviour or not to behave *contra bonos mores* would not be lawful if made purely preventatively, where no past breach of the peace (or threat to the peace) was established.
• Rather than binding an individual over to 'keep the peace' in general terms, the court should identify the specific conduct or activity from which the individual must refrain.
• The phrase *contra bonos mores* should be avoided altogether in any order sought or made.

KEY POINTS—INTERVENING WHERE A BREACH OF THE PEACE IS IMMINENT

In order for preventative action to be lawful:

• The officer must honestly apprehend a breach of the peace, ie violence.
• That apprehension must be based on objectively reasonable grounds.
• The apprehended breach of the peace must be imminent.
• The action taken must be reasonably necessary and proportionate to the nature of the anticipated breach.
• In the absence of *exceptional* circumstances, the target of the intervention should be the person who is threatening unlawful violence.

Further reading

There are a great many cases concerning the common law powers to intervene to prevent a breach of the peace. The judgments in the two House of Lords cases of *Laporte* and *Austin* contain detailed analyses of many of the principles and cases outlined in this chapter. *Steel v UK* provides a good introduction to the approach taken by the ECtHR:

- *Steel v United Kingdom* (1998) 28 EHRR 603
- *R (Laporte) v Chief Constable of Gloucestershire Police* [2007] 2 AC 205
- *Austin & Saxby v Commissioner of Police for the Metropolis* [2009] 1 AC 564
- *The ACPO Manual of Guidance on Keeping the Peace*, accessible in its up-to-date edition via the ACPO website at <http://www.acpo.police.uk/>

NOTES

NOTES

NOTES

Offences Against
Public Order

4.1 **Introduction**

Part 1 of the Public Order Act 1986 (in this chapter, 'the Act' or the POA) was designed to be a single piece of legislation for public order offences, covering individual incidents of abusive behaviour to large scale riots. Since 1986, a bewildering number of Acts have been passed which have added to or altered this legislation. Nonetheless, Part 1 of the Act remains the foundation of (and the starting point for consideration of) public order offences.

This book is a guide to the practical application, by the police, of the law surrounding public order incidents. It is not a textbook on criminal law. Nonetheless, the basic legal concepts behind the offences in Part 1 of the Act need to be considered.

Part 1 of the Act creates two groups of offences. The first group contains the generally more serious offences of riot (s 1), violent disorder (s 2) and affray (s 3). These are triable on indictment or either way. They involve violence, or the threat of violence. They *generally* require the participation of more than one person. These are dealt with in sections 4.2–4.5 of this chapter.

The second group of offences are triable only summarily, and can always be committed by an individual. They are intentionally causing the fear or provocation of violence (s 4), intentionally causing harassment, alarm or distress (s 4A), and behaviour likely to cause harassment alarm or distress (s 5). There is often a degree of confusion about the different mental elements of these offences. These offences are dealt with in sections 4.6–4.7.

Between them, these two groups of offences will constitute the majority of an officer's typical involvement with public order offences. Many officers will regularly attend at scenes where offences are being committed under this Act. But in unusual situations such as small scale, unnotified protests or gatherings, an officer may have difficulty identifying whether or not an offence has been committed.

This chapter also includes the offences of obstructing or assaulting a police officer in the execution of his duty. In the context of practical policing, these are often charged in addition to (or in substitution for) a more serious public order offence. Finally, the various statues addressing alcohol and disorder are explained.

Prior to the enactment of s 110 of the Serious Organised Crime and Police Act 2005, the different powers of arrest for the different offences caused numerous problems. Now, s 24 of the Police and Criminal Evidence Act (PACE) provides the power to arrest in relation to *all* the offences in the Public Order Act, provided, of course, that one of the necessity conditions applies. One of these conditions will nearly always apply in the public order context.

4.2 **Riot, Violent Disorder, and Affray**

4.2.1 **Central concepts—'Violence'**

Definition of violence

'Violence' is an ingredient of each of these offences, and is defined in s 8(3) as follows:

'violence' means any violent conduct, so that—

(a) except in the context of affray, it includes violent conduct towards property as well as violent conduct towards persons, and

(b) it is not restricted to conduct causing or intended to cause injury or damage but includes any other violent conduct (for example, throwing at or towards a person a missile of a kind capable of causing injury which does not hit or falls short).

Actual violence

In most public order situations it will be obvious to the police whether or not the actions of those present amount to 'violence'. A common sense approach should be taken by officers on the scene. Indeed, common sense is a key ingredient to the successful policing of public disorder. Throwing a punch is clearly violent, even if it does not make contact with anybody. Likewise, in a public order situation, throwing an object such as a bottle or stone into a crowd is likely to count as violence.

For riot and violent disorder, the violent conduct required can include violence towards property as well as violence towards persons. However, for the offence of affray the violence requirement can only be fulfilled by violent conduct towards *persons*.

It is a requirement of each offence that the violence used must be *unlawful*: violence used in self-defence, defence of another and prevention of crime will not count. Very often the police will need to arrest under s 1 or 2 of the POA and will be oblivious to the potential existence of a defence that the violence was not unlawful. Where violence is discussed in the remainder of this chapter, it should be assumed that it refers to unlawful violence.

Threat of violence

Each of ss 1–3 require unlawful violence or the *threat* of it.

For riot and violent disorder, a 'threat' of violence could be committed in a number of ways, for example:

- words threatening violence
- openly carrying weapons
- lunging at a person, with clenched fists.

However, for the offence of affray, words alone are not enough, because s 3(3) states that 'for the purposes of this section, a threat cannot be made by the use of words alone'.

4.2.2 Central concepts—'Person of reasonable firmness'

The offences of riot, violent disorder and affray do not require an actual victim. This is because public order offences are concerned with the offenders' conduct and the *potential effect* of that conduct (unlike offences against the person, which are concerned with harm caused to a specific person).

In riot, violent disorder and affray the violence or threat of violence simply needs to be sufficient to cause a hypothetical 'person of reasonable firmness' present at the scene to fear for his personal safety. Each of the three sections specifically confirms that 'no person of reasonable firmness need actually be, or be likely to be, present at the scene'. It is enough that a person of reasonable firmness, if they were present at the scene for any reason, would fear for their personal safety.

Even though the requirement is for the *hypothetical* person of reasonable firmness to fear for his own safety, the reaction of those who were actually present will, realistically, have important evidential value when it comes to any trial, though is less important when considering whether to arrest. It is therefore sensible for police officers to record any evidence that bystanders were in fact scared by what they witnessed. This does not have to be first-hand evidence from the bystanders: a police officer is entitled to record, and give evidence that bystanders were visibly scared, had told the officer of their fears, were shouting in fear or running away, etc.

In considering and recording such evidence police officers should be aware that not all actual bystanders will count as persons of reasonable firmness. There may be some persons present who are more easily scared than is typical— though this is relatively unlikely and it is hardly attractive for defendants to argue that such bystanders were not of reasonable firmness. There may also be some persons present who are so accustomed to such violence that they are no longer caused fear—but this does not prevent the offences being prosecuted as it is the hypothetical bystander that is the yard stick for making out the offence. Officers should exercise common sense and judgement, and should also be alert to the fact that the lack of any apparent response from a bystander does not necessarily mean they are not in fear for their personal safety: they may simply have learned not to respond with obvious alarm.

4.3 **Riot**

Section 1(1) of the Act states that:

> Where 12 or more persons who are present together use or threaten unlawful violence for a common purpose and the conduct of them (taken together) is such as would cause a person of reasonable firmness present at the scene to fear for his personal safety, each of the persons using unlawful violence for the common purpose is guilty of riot.

In practical terms, there needs to actually be a 'riot' happening before any individual can be potentially guilty of the offence of riot. For a 'riot' to occur, it is necessary for **at least 12 people** to be present and acting with a **common purpose** and **each of those 12 must use or threaten unlawful violence**.

A person commits the offence of riot when the following circumstances are fulfilled:

KEY POINTS—RIOT: ESSENTIAL FEATURES OF THE OFFENCE

1. Is there a riot?

- 12 or more people present together
- Using or threatening violence
- For a common purpose
- The conduct of the group is sufficient to cause a hypothetical person of reasonable firmness present at the scene to fear for his own safety
- The 12 or more rioters need not threaten or use violence simultaneously

2. Is the individual defendant guilty of riot?

The particular defendant:

- must have actually used, not merely threatened, violence;
- must have intended to use violence or been aware that his actions may have been violent;
- or he can be guilty of the offence as a secondary party, if aiding and abetting the person who uses violence. However, if he is not also using or threatening unlawful violence himself, he cannot make up one of the 12 (minimum) to constitute the riot.

4.3.1 **A group of at least 12, acting with a common purpose**

The common purpose is an essential element of the offence. It can exist in numerous different ways. It can be as simple and basic as celebrating a football victory, see *R v Jefferson* [1994] 1 All ER 270, where the jury were directed that a common purpose could be 'football hooliganism'. The common purpose can also be inferred from the conduct of the group. For example, if a person is present at the gate of the factory where a rowdy demonstration is being held, and there is no other reason for that person to be present, police can infer from that person's presence and position that they share in the common purpose of demonstration.

Provided that at least 12 people are acting with a common purpose, it does not matter that others are present who do *not* share that purpose. In large crowds, it may be obvious that there are at least 12 people present who have a common purpose. Police do not have to show that *every* member of the crowd shared that purpose.

The conduct of the group as a whole

The group of 12 or more do not have to use or threaten violence simultaneously (s 1(2)). It is the conduct of the group **as a whole** which matters. It needs to be such as would cause a person of reasonable firmness present at the scene to fear for his safety. It is not necessary for the acts of any of the individuals, taken alone, to have this effect.

If the group of people is dispersed over an area, or if the violence or threat of violence is sporadic, there may be doubt over whether at the time of the defendant's conduct there were 12 people acting together with a common purpose. In any situation, it will be a question of *fact*, based on the circumstances, as to whether 12 or more people were acting together. But at the point of arrest an officer can only act upon what he or she can see or hear, or is told by his or her fellow officers or those in command who may have a panoramic perspective aided by, for example, CCTV. That there may be defences to the charge, technical or otherwise, is not to the point at the time of arrest when an officer is simply trying to stop the riot.

Practical considerations

The problematic cases are likely to be the ones where the number of people involved is relatively close to 12. For example, a violent confrontation between eight people trying to gain entry to a club and five members of door staff using force to resist them is unlikely to be a riot within the meaning of s 1, even if the use of excessive force by the door staff meant that more than 12 people were acting unlawfully. In these types of circumstances, where there may be some doubt as to whether a sufficient number of people can be demonstrated to have a common purpose, a more suitable offence to consider may be violent disorder. As a matter of legal risk management, an arrest for violent disorder would be lawful and would not, if the evidence subsequently justified it, prevent a charge of riot.

In a prosecution for riot, the acquittal of a defendant can impact on the remaining defendants or suspects. If a person is acquitted, or cannot be prosecuted for evidential reasons, and their exclusion brings the total number of people acting with a common purpose to below 12, then nobody could be convicted of riot. If in any doubt, arrest for violent disorder. Following arrest, the view of the Crown Prosecution Service (CPS) will be required, particularly as the consent of the Director of Public Prosecutions (DPP) is required for a prosecution for riot; see s 7(1).

4.3.2 **The defendant's own conduct**

Provided that the context as set out above can be proved, an individual will be guilty of the offence of riot if:

1. he is part of the group which is acting with a common purpose, and
2. he **used violence** for the common purpose, and either:
    a. he *intended* to use or threaten violence, or
    b. he *was aware* that his conduct may be violent or threaten violence.

Note that in order to be guilty of riot, the defendant must actually have *used* violence—unless he is guilty as a secondary party by virtue of aiding and abetting, covered below.

Drunk or intoxicated defendants

Unusually, intoxication raises a potential specific defence to a charge of riot. Section 6(5) states that:

> For the purposes of this section a person whose awareness is impaired by intoxication shall be taken to be aware of that of which he would be aware if not intoxicated, unless he shows either that his intoxication was not self-induced or that it was caused solely by the taking or administration of a substance in the course of medical treatment.

The burden of proving this defence lies with a defendant. In practical terms, this means that a defendant will not be able to show that he did not have the sufficient intention due to intoxication, unless he can show that:

1. his intoxication was due *solely* to medical treatment (not to the interaction between alcohol / illicit drugs and medical treatment), or
2. his intoxication was caused by somebody else spiking his drink or similar, or
3. he was so intoxicated that he was incapable of forming a common purpose with the others present.

Defendants who are aiding and abetting

It is possible to be guilty of riot through aiding or abetting. In such a case, police will still need to produce evidence that that person was more than a mere bystander. For example, a person who waited around the corner from the scene of the riot, having driven his friend to the scene and having supplied him with weapons for use in the riot, would be guilty of aiding or abetting the riot. If a person is being charged as an aider and abetter, but is not also himself using or threatening unlawful violence, it will be necessary to demonstrate that in addition to that defendant (and any other defendants charged with the same) there were 12 more people acting with a common purpose engaged in violence or threatening violence.

4.3.3 **Policing of a riot**

The fact that a riot within the meaning of s 1 of the Act may be in progress does not in itself make any difference either to the powers available to the police to deal with the riot, or the way in which the powers are exercised. The requirements of s 1 as to the number of people involved, and their conduct, means that often in cases where a riot could technically be said to have occurred, the policing of the event will inevitably be more intrusive and involve greater use of force than in less serious public order offences.

Where the circumstances of a riot can be made out, police authorities are liable under the Riot (Damages) Act 1886 to pay compensation to those whose property or business is damaged by the riot. The Court of Appeal's decision in *Yarl's Wood Immigration Ltd v Bedfordshire Police Authority* [2010] 1 QB 698 concerned a claim under the Act by the private operators of the Yarl's Wood Detention Centre, following a riot at the centre in February 2002. The decision confirmed that the private company was able to claim under the Act. The sums for which the force was liable were covered by their public liability insurance.

Whilst there has been a long campaign to have the 1886 Act repealed, at the date of publication it remains in force. Following the widespread rioting in the summer of 2011, numerous claims have been submitted under the 1886 Act.

4.4 **Violent Disorder**

Definition of violent disorder

Section 2(1) of the Act states that:

> Where 3 or more persons who are present together use or threaten unlawful violence and the conduct of them (taken together) is such as would cause a person of reasonable firmness present at the scene to fear for personal safety, each of the persons using or threatening unlawful violence is guilty of violent disorder.

The obvious differences between violent disorder and the offence of riot are:

- the minimum number of people required for violent disorder is 3, and
- there is no requirement of a 'common purpose' for violent disorder.

A person commits violent disorder when the following circumstances are fulfilled:

KEY POINTS—VIOLENT DISORDER: ESSENTIAL FEATURES OF THE OFFENCE

Is there a violent disorder?

- Three or more people present together
- using or threatening violence
- the conduct of the group must be sufficient to cause a hypothetical person of reasonable firmness present at the scene to fear for his own safety.

If so, is the particular defendant guilty?

- Can have used, or merely *threatened*, violence.
- Must have intended to use violence or threaten violence, or been aware that his actions may have been violent or threatened violence.
- Can be guilty as a principal, even if only aiding and abetting: as long as he is not counted as one of the 3 people required to constitute the violent disorder.

4.4.1 **A group of at least three**

There must be at least three persons, and all three must be acting unlawfully. If three people are acting violently, but one or more of them is acting lawfully (eg it is a fight, and one of them is acting in self-defence), then the total number of people using or threatening unlawful violence is less than three. In those circumstances, none of them would be guilty of violent disorder. But this is a consideration for those responsible for charging or prosecuting: at the point of arrest, the officer can only react to what he or she can see or hear and often the lawful acts of one in the mêlée will not be apparent to the officer(s) at the point of arrest.

Similarly, if three people are charged with violent disorder, being the only three people alleged to be involved, and one of the defendants were to be acquitted at trial, it follows that the remaining defendants could not be convicted of violent disorder.

There is no upper limit on the number of people involved. There may be many cases where the numbers involved exceed 12, but where it is safer to proceed on the basis of violent disorder than for riot, for example because of difficulties in proving a common purpose.

Provided it can be established that three people were using or threatening violent disorder, it is not necessary that at least three people be charged, or convicted, or even that three particular people can be identified as being involved in the violent disorder. If only three out of five people involved in violent disorder are actually charged, and two of those are acquitted, it does not follow that the remaining two must also be acquitted. Provided it can be proved the two uncharged people were using or threatening unlawful violence, then if the last defendant also did so, he will be liable to be convicted (see *R v Warton* (1990) 154 JP 201; [1990] Crim LR 124).

4.4.2 **Present together**

Whilst the violence/threats need not be happen simultaneously, at least three people need to be present together throughout. Sporadic outbreaks will not suffice. It has been confirmed in *R v NW* (2010) 1 WLR 1426 that the expression 'present together' means no more than being in the same place at the same time. The phrase does not require any degree of co-operation between those using or threatening violence. Three or more people using or threatening violence in the same place at the same time, whether for the same purpose or different purposes, are capable of creating a intimidating prospect for others present, simply because their collective action represents a breakdown of law and order.

For example, in the following situation none of the men is guilty of violent disorder. This is because at no time are there three people present together, all threatening or using violence:

Scenario

Two men are ejected from a public house. They stand outside shouting threats at the door staff and attacking the door with a piece of wood, trying to get back in again. They then give up and go and wait for a bus at a nearby bus stop. Five minutes later one of their friends is also ejected. He also starts to shout aggressively, threatening violence towards the door staff. His friends come over to him, near to the door to the public house, but they do not join in again with threats of violence.

However, in the following version of the situation it would be appropriate to treat all three men as having committed the offence of violent disorder:

Scenario

The third man to be ejected is immediately joined by his two friends. All three men then take it in turns to try to kick the door in. Although at the time of each blow to the door, only one person is acting violently, the three men are present together throughout.

There is no upper limit on the number of people that can be involved in violent disorder. Often it will be a legally safer option to arrest a person for violent disorder rather than riot. That person can later be charged with riot. However, it would avoid the potential problem of having to prove that the arresting officer had reasonable grounds to suspect that there were 12 people present acting with a common purpose.

4.4.3 **Threats of violence**

Violent disorder can be committed using actual violence *or* threats of violence. See section 4.2.1 for what might constitute a threat of violence.

4.4.4 **Conduct of the individual**

Provided that there are at least three persons present together who are using or threatening violence, and their conduct taken together would cause the hypothetical person of reasonable firmness to fear for his personal safety, then an individual defendant will be guilty of violent disorder if:

1. He is present with the others, and
2. He **used or threatened violence**, and
    a. he *intended* to use or threaten violence, or
    b. he *was aware* that his conduct may be violent or threaten violence.

So unlike riot, the defendant need not actually have *used* violence: threat is enough.

Drunk or intoxicated defendants

Section 6(3) applies (see section 4.3.2). With violent disorder, there is no 'common purpose' element of the offence and so a defendant who raises intoxication as a defence only has two avenues open to him, which are to show either that:

1. His intoxication was due *solely* to medical treatment (not to the interaction between alcohol/illicit drugs and medical treatment); or
2. His intoxication was caused by somebody else spiking his drink or similar.

Defendants who are aiding and abetting

As with riot, it is possible to be guilty of the offence through aiding or abetting. However, a person who is only an aider or abettor cannot be counted as one of the three people required for a violent disorder to be in progress. There must be a violent disorder occurring without counting the aider or abettor.

4.4.5 **Alternative verdict**

Section 7(3) of the Act allows the jury to return a verdict of causing fear or provocation of violence as an *alternative* to a verdict of violent disorder or affray.

This only applies in the Crown Court. It enables the jury to acquit a defendant of violent disorder, but convict him of causing fear or provocation of violence contrary to s 4 of the Act. Police should note, however, that a s 4 offence cannot be committed inside a dwelling, nor can it be committed if the violence or threat of violence was solely directed towards property.

4.5 **Affray**

Definition of affray

Section 3(1) of the Act provides:

> A person is guilty of affray if he uses or threatens unlawful violence towards another and his conduct is such as would cause a person of reasonable firmness present at the scene to fear for his personal safety.

These concepts of violence and of reasonable firmness are the same as those discussed above under riot and violent disorder. The key differences between this offence and the earlier two are that:

- affray may be committed by one person, acting alone;
- the violence or threat of it must be directed at a particular person present (not at property); and
- a threat of violence in this context cannot be made by words alone.

KEY POINTS—AFFRAY: ESSENTIAL FEATURES OF THE OFFENCE

- It can be committed by one person acting alone.
- It can be committed by someone who uses or threatens violence, though the threat cannot be by words alone.
- It must be committed towards another person who is actually present.
- The conduct of the offender (or, if there is a group, of the group taken together) must be sufficient to cause a hypothetical person of reasonable firmness present at the scene to fear for his own safety.
- The offence can be committed anywhere.

Affray is not an offence against the person. Even though the violence has to be directed towards another person, it is not that person's reaction that matters. It is the reaction of the hypothetical person of reasonable firmness. This means that even though the actual person present may be terrified (perhaps because of some prior knowledge of the offender) the hypothetical bystander may not be; equally, the target of the behaviour may not feel threatened at all, but the hypothetical person may be. The charge of affray is often brought where two people are fighting. Neither may be scared, as they would be too enraged, but a bystander would be.

The person against whom the violence or threat of violence is directed must actually be present. In *I v DPP* [2002] 1 AC 285, the intended targets of petrol bombs carried by a group of youths were not present. The defendants did not attempt to use the petrol bombs, or threaten anybody with them. In quashing their convictions, Lord Hutton stated at paragraph 28 that:

> a person should not be charged with the offence [of affray] unless he uses or threatens unlawful violence toward another person actually present at the scene and his conduct is such as would cause fear to a notional bystander of reasonable firmness.

4.5.1 Threat of violence

In affray, the threat of violence cannot be committed by words alone, unlike the threat of violence element in violent disorder and riot (see 4.2.1). However, very little by way of actual conduct is required in addition to words to satisfy the requirements of the offence. For example, in *R v Dixon* [1993] Crim LR 579 CA the defendant told his dog to attack the police. The dog did indeed bite the police, though there was no evidence that it did so as a result of the defendant's command. The defendant was charged and convicted of affray. On appeal, he argued that as he had done no more than say some words, he could not be guilty of the offence. The Court of Appeal held that the words were said in order to use the dog as a way of creating fear, and upheld his conviction.

A threat of violence can be committed in many different ways and it is not possible to give an exhaustive list. In *I v DPP* (see section 4.5) the Court of Appeal confirmed that it was a question of fact whether something amounted to a threat of violence—Lord Hutton at paragraph 26 stated that the carrying of petrol bombs could, in the right circumstances, amount to a threat of violence. In *R v Thind* [1999] Crim LR 842, it was held that deliberately driving a car, at speed, towards another occupied vehicle could amount to a threat of violence in the context of an affray.

4.5.2 Affray and group behaviour

Section 3(2) of the Act provides that 'where two or more persons use or threaten the unlawful violence, it is the conduct of them taken together that must be considered for the purposes of subsection (1)'.

There will be cases where the conduct of the group taken as a whole would cause a person of reasonable firmness to fear for their own safety, but where the individual defendant's conduct taken in isolation would not. In such a case, the individual is guilty of affray provided that he personally used violence or the threat of violence.

In *R v Smith* [1997] 1 Cr App R 14 the Court of Appeal stated that affray:

> typically involves a continuous course of conduct, the criminal character of which depends on the general nature and conduct as a whole and not on particular incidents and events which take place in the course of it. Where reliance is placed on such a continuous course of conduct, it is not necessary for the Crown to identify and prove particular parts of it.

However, a series of incidents closely linked in time and location cannot necessarily be treated as a single, continuous course of conduct. Even if a number of discrete episodes of violence occur over a short period of time, care should be taken to avoid assuming that they can be treated as a continuous instance of affray. Particular attention must be paid to the alleged participants. If the participants in the different episodes vary, it would be better to regard the episodes as separate incidents rather than a continuous affray.

In *R v Flounders and Alton* [2002] EWCA Crim 1325 there were three separate incidents of alleged assaults on the victim, a few minutes apart. The first defendant was involved in the first two assaults, and the second defendant in the third assault. Although the two defendants were friends, and the background to the three confrontations was the same, neither defendant was present, or in the immediate vicinity, during the alleged assaults by the other. The two defendants were charged jointly with a single charge of affray.

On appeal it was held that the two defendants ought to have faced separate charges of affray dealing with their own conduct. This advice should be followed where there is insufficient evidence to show that two (or more) defendants were acting together in using or threatening unlawful violence.

Those who aid, abet or incite affray are liable as principals for the offence. However, just as with violent disorder, more than mere presence at the scene will be required. For example, where two people are fighting, those standing around cheering either (or both) of them on would commit the offence. Mere passive onlookers would not be liable, even if they had an interest in the outcome.

4.5.3 **Where can an affray be committed?**

Affray may be committed in private as well as in public places.

4.5.4 **Alternative verdicts**

Section 7(3) entitles a jury to acquit on a charge of affray, but convict for an offence contrary to s 4 of the Act—see section 4.4.5.

4.6 **Threatening, Insulting, or Abusive Words, Behaviour, or Writing**

Sections 4, 4A and 5 of the Act create summary only public order offences.

All three offences require the use of **threatening, insulting or abusive words, behaviour or writing**. Generally speaking, the s 4 offence is the most serious, followed by s 4A, with s 5 being the least serious. The elements of each offence are slightly different and in many cases, a suspect's behaviour may amount to an offence under more than one of the sections.

Police officers need to ensure that their account of the incident gives the CPS enough information to make an informed decision on which charge, or charges, to bring.

If the constituent elements are examined separately, the sections become easier to understand. Table 4.1 demonstrates the similarities (and differences) between the sections.

4.6.1 The meaning of 'threatening, abusive or insulting'

These words do not have a precise definition within the Act. They should be given their normal, everyday meaning.

POINT TO NOTE

Many things otherwise unobjectionable may be said or done in an insulting way. There can be no definition. But an ordinary sensible man knows an insult when he sees or hears it . . . Parliament has given no indication that the word is to be given any unusual meaning. Insulting means insulting and nothing else.

Brutus v Cozens [1973] 1AC 854, at 862

They cover conduct far wider than simply swearing and aggressive behaviour. The installation of covert surveillance cameras in changing rooms was held to amount to 'insulting behaviour' in the case of *Vigon v DPP* (*The Times*, 9 December 1997 (DC)).

While a very broad range of conduct will be covered, there are anti-social acts that might not be covered. Irritating, annoying, disgusting, even offensive, behaviour would *not* be sufficient for any of the summary public order offences. Police will need to use their judgement in deciding whether conduct is actually threatening, abusive or insulting. The surrounding circumstances and the particular characteristics of the targeted person(s) will be of significance in deciding whether the behaviour was in fact threatening, abusive or insulting. For example, words used towards certain groups (eg those who know the defendant well) may not be insulting; yet the same words might be very likely to insult, abuse, threaten—or even provoke—a different group.

Table 4.1 Comparison of Summary-Only Public Order Offences

	D's primary behaviour	D's alternative behaviour	Focus of behaviour	Intent	Location	Consequences	Specific statutory defences
s 4	Threatening, abusive or insulting words or behaviour	Distributing or displaying any writing, sign or other visible representation which is threatening, abusive or insulting	Towards another person	One of the following four scenarios applies: i) D intends to cause other person to believe that immediate unlawful violence will be used; or ii) D intends to provoke the immediate use of unlawful violence; or iii) the other person is *likely to believe* that immediate unlawful violence will be used; or iv) it is *likely* that immediate unlawful violence would be provoked. **And** D must intend his conduct to be threatening, abusive or insulting, or be aware that it may be so.	Anywhere, except where defendant and victim are both inside a dwelling (does not have to be the same dwelling)	No consequence required to be proved	No specific defence

s 4A	Threatening, abusive or insulting words or behaviour, or disorderly behaviour	Displaying (not distributing) any writing, sign or other visible representation which is threatening, abusive or insulting	A person	D must intend: i) to cause the person harassment, alarm or distress; *and* ii) D must intend his conduct to be threatening, abusive, insulting or disorderly.	As s 4 above	That person (or any other person) must actually be caused harassment, alarm or distress	i) D inside a dwelling and had no reason to believe conduct would be witnessed from outside that or any other dwelling; *and/or* ii) conduct was reasonable.
s 5	As s 4A above	As s 4A above	No focus required, but is within the hearing or sight of an actual person likely to be caused harassment, alarm or distress	D must intend conduct to be threatening, abusive or disorderly, or be aware that it may be so	As s 4 above	No consequence required to be proved	i) no reason to believe any person within hearing or sight who was likely to be caused harassment, alarm or distress; *and/or* ii) D inside a dwelling, no reason to believe the conduct could be witnessed by anyone outside; *and/or* iii) conduct was reasonable.

4.6.2 **Section 4—'Fear or provocation of violence'**

Definition of fear or provocation of violence

Section 4 provides:

(1) A person is guilty of an offence if he—

    (a) uses towards another person threatening, abusive or insulting words or behaviour, or

    (b) distributes or displays to another person any writing, sign or other visible representation which is threatening, abusive or insulting,

    with intent to cause that person to believe that immediate unlawful violence will be used against him or another by any person, or to provoke the immediate use of unlawful violence by that person or another, or whereby that person is likely to believe that such violence will be used or it is likely that such violence will be provoked.

(2) An offence under this section may be committed in a public or a private place, except that no offence is committed where the words or behaviour are used, or the writing, sign or other visible representation is distributed or displayed, by a person inside a dwelling and the other person is also inside that or another dwelling.

The following points should be noted in addition to the information set out in the table.

'Towards another person'

The target of the conduct (ie the person on the receiving end of the behaviour, or person to be provoked) must actually be present. It is not enough to be nearby, and to hear of the words or behaviour through another.

Case study

Atkin v DPP

In *Atkin v DPP* (1989) 89 Cr App R 199 customs officers and a bailiff visited the appellant's farm. The bailiff stayed outside and the customs officers went inside to talk to the appellant. The appellant said to the customs officers, in the absence of the bailiff, that the bailiff was a 'dead 'un' if he came into the house. The appellant had a gun in the room when this threat was uttered.

While the words were clearly threatening, and upon learning of the appellant's words, the bailiff did indeed feel threatened, it was held on appeal that no offence under s 4 had been committed. This was because, although the customs officers and the appellant were both inside the house, the bailiff was outside. Although the target of the threat—the bailiff—was very close by, the words 'uses towards' were held to mean uses in the presence of, and in the direction of, another person *directly*.

'Distribution/display of writing, signs etc'

This extends the range of conduct covered by s 4. It will apply to all sorts of public order policing scenarios: the display of placards at demonstrations; wearing t-shirts with slogans or pictures; wearing badges; distributing leaflets; even to putting up signs in the windows of a house.

Section 4 clearly has the potential to engage the human rights of those involved. In particular, it will frequently engage Article 9 (right to freedom of thought, conscience and religion) and Article 10 (right to freedom of expression). Both of these rights allow for restrictions to be imposed, provided the restrictions are prescribed by law, are necessary in a democratic society and are for specific reasons, such as for the protection of the rights and freedom of others. See chapter 2 for a detailed exploration of a human rights-sensitive approach to policing.

The case of *DPP v Connolly* [2008] 1 WLR 276 demonstrates the approach the courts are prepared to take to defences invoking Articles 9 and 10 of the ECHR:

Case study

DPP v Connolly [2008] 1 WLR 276

Ms Connolly was convicted on three counts of offences contrary to section 1(1)(b) Malicious Communications Act 1988. The relevant offence is committed where a person sends an item, in whole or in part, of an indecent or grossly offensive nature, intending to cause distress or anxiety to the recipient or to any other person to whom he intends it or its contents or nature to be communicated. There are clear parallels with the 'displaying and distributing' aspects of s 4.

Ms Connolly had sent pictures of aborted foetuses to various chemists. She admitted that she had sent the pictures, but maintained that such pictures were not indecent nor grossly offensive, and that the purpose of sending them was not to cause distress or anxiety, but to make a lawful protest and educate against the use of the 'morning after' pill.

On appeal, Ms Connolly argued that a prohibition on the sending of the photographs would be an unjustified interference with her rights under ECHR Articles 9 or 10.

The Court of Appeal upheld her conviction. It found that Article 10 was engaged, but that on the facts of the case, Mrs Connolly's conviction was justified under Article 10(2) as necessary in a democratic society for the protection of the rights of others. In this case the 'rights of others' were the right of employees at the pharmacies to be protected from receiving grossly offensive photographs of abortions at their place of work, where the photographs had been sent for the purpose of causing distress or anxiety.

Further examples of the scope of Article 10 as a defence to a public order offence arise in relation to s 5. See section 4.7.5.

Intention or likelihood?

As per the table below, the requirements for intent in s 4 arise in two separate places.

First, the intent to use threatening, abusive or insulting behaviour (or display threatening, abusive or insulting material). Intention may be inferred from the words, behaviour or display in a similar way to ss 1–3. Awareness may also be inferred: if it is obvious that the behaviour might be threatening, abusive or insulting then normally it can be inferred that the defendant either intended the behaviour to have this effect, or was aware that it might. Voluntary and/or self-induced intoxication does not provide a defence based on a lack of intention.

At the second stage, an essential ingredient of the offence is either the *likely* consequences of the conduct, or the defendant's *intention* as to the consequences of his own conduct. If, as a consequence of the conduct, either the target is likely to believe that immediate unlawful violence will be used against him (or another), or it is likely that such unlawful violence will be provoked, then the offence is committed and the defendant's intention as to the consequences of his conduct does not need to be considered further.

For s 4, the defendant must intend his behaviour to be threatening, abusive or insulting, and in addition either:	
(a) the defendant intends that the target should believe that immediate unlawful violence will be used against him or another (by any person);	**or (b) the defendant intends** that violence will be provoked;
or (c) it is likely that the target will believe that immediate unlawful violence will be used against him or another (by any person);	**or (d) it is likely** that violence will be provoked.

Although it will often be relevant evidentially, prosecutors do not need to prove that the target of the conduct, or target of any provoked violence, *actually* believed violence would result. The issue is whether, taking account of the particular circumstances and character of the target, the conduct was *likely* to cause that target to believe that immediate unlawful violence might result.

There may be a number of different people present, towards whom the conduct is directed. Provided at least one of those present—taking into account all the circumstances of the incident, together with their personal characteristics—was likely to believe that immediate unlawful violence might result, the offence is committed.

Immediacy of violence or anticipated violence

There is no hard and fast definition as to what may be 'immediate'. It will translate into different time periods depending on the circumstances of the case. In *DPP v Ramos* [2000] Crim LR 768, the defendant sent two letters which threatened unlawful violence to an organization which offered advice and assistance to the Asian community in West London. The letters contained threats of a bomb being detonated in the future, but did not say when this might happen.

The recipients were immediately concerned for their own safety, as well as for the safety of others. The magistrate found that the defendant intended the recipients of the letters to believe that unlawful violence would be used, but that there was no case to answer because it was not possible to infer that immediate unlawful violence would be used. In doing so, the magistrate found that an unspecified time in the future lacked the element of immediacy required in s 4. On appeal, it was held that there was nothing within the letter that could be interpreted as excluding violence occurring in the immediate future. The possibility that immediate unlawful violence would be used at any time in the future, including the immediate future, would be enough for the offence to be committed.

The concept of immediacy in s 4 is therefore capable of being applied flexibly, and in a similar way to 'imminence' for the purposes of breach of the peace: see section 3.4.

Location

An offence under s 4 can be committed either in public or in any private place, with one exception relating to homes. If both the defendant *and* the target are inside a dwelling (not necessarily the same dwelling) then no offence under s 4 is committed. A shared laundry, part of the communal area in sheltered accommodation, would not qualify as a dwelling (*Le Vine v DPP* [2010] EWHC 1128 (Admin)).

4.6.3 Section 4A—Intentional harassment, alarm or distress

Definition of intentional harassment, alarm or distress

Section 4A provides:

(1) A person is guilty of an offence if, with intent to cause a person harassment, alarm or distress, he—
  (a) uses threatening, abusive or insulting words or behaviour, or disorderly behaviour, or
  (b) displays any writing, sign or other visible representation which is threatening, abusive or insulting, thereby causing that or another person harassment, alarm or distress.

(2) An offence under this section may be committed in a public or a private place, except that no offence is committed where the words or behaviour are used, or the writing, sign or other visible representation is displayed, by a person inside a dwelling and the person who is harassed, alarmed or distressed is also inside that or another dwelling.

(3) It is a defence for the accused to prove—

    (a) that he was inside a dwelling and had no reason to believe that the words or behaviour used, or the writing, sign or other visible representation displayed, would be heard or seen by a person outside that or any other dwelling, or

    (b) that his conduct was reasonable.

The following points should be noted in addition to the information set out in the table.

Disorderly behaviour

Disorderly behaviour has exactly the same meaning as for an offence under s 5—see 4.7.2 of this chapter. For threatening, abusive or insulting behaviour, see 4.6.1.

Harassment, alarm or distress: what these words really mean

Police should bear in mind that the successful prosecution of a s 4A offence requires evidence that a person was actually caused harassment, alarm or distress. This requirement sets s 4A apart from the other offences in Part I of the Public Order Act 1986. Provided that the defendant intended any person to suffer harassment, alarm or distress, then evidence of harassment, alarm or distress on the part of anyone will be sufficient.

What do these words mean? Again, they are to be given their normal, everyday meaning—just as in 4.6.1. In *Esther Thomas v Newsgroup Newspapers Limited* [2001] EWCA Civ 1233 (a case concerning the Protection from Harassment Act 1997) Lord Phillips MR stated:

> Harassment is, however, a word which has a meaning that is generally understood. It describes conduct targeted at an individual . . . which is oppressive and unreasonable.

It is not necessary that the victim provides direct evidence that they felt harassed, alarmed or distress, although obviously if they are able to do so it will have significant evidential value. Eyewitness evidence of visible alarm or distress suffered by another person will be sufficient. For example, if as a consequence of the defendant's behaviour another person was seen to run away, this might be evidence of alarm; if a victim were to be seen bursting into tears, this would be evidence that the defendant had caused distress. For harassment, it is more difficult (though not impossible) to see how this might be proved without direct evidence from the victim.

Police officers can be victims under s 4A. However, the routine and perhaps automatic inclusion in an officer's notebook of the words 'I was harassed, alarmed and distressed' without further explanation is to be discouraged as unimaginative, contrived and unlikely to impress case hardened magistrates. If all three words are included as a matter of course, without any description of why the officer reacted in such a way, they are vulnerable to challenge. Consideration should be given to:

- Which of the three potential effects of harassment, alarm or distress did the officer *actually* feel?
- *Why* did the officer respond in this way? For example, a sole officer dealing with a number of hostile members of the public may be more likely to be alarmed by their behaviour than if he is in a large group of officers.
- What was it about the behaviour that triggered this response in the police officer?

Intent

The concept of intent is simpler for s 4A than for s 4. It must be proved that the defendant *intended* to cause a person harassment, alarm or distress. Therefore, unlike either s 4 or s 5, it is *not* sufficient to prove merely that the defendant was aware that the behaviour may be threatening, abusive, insulting or disorderly. It follows that it will be necessary to prove that the defendant intended both (i) to behave in a threatening, abusive, insulting or disorderly manner, and (ii) to cause harassment, alarm or distress to another person.

It might be difficult to obtain direct evidence of a defendant's intent as to his own behaviour. His intention can be proved by inference.

The person actually caused harassment, alarm or distress need not be the person that the defendant intended to suffer these consequences.

Defences

There are two specific defences available under s 4A(3). First, under subsection (3)(a) there is a defence that the defendant was inside a dwelling and had no reason to believe his conduct would be witnessed from outside that or any other dwelling. Second, there is a defence that the defendant's conduct was reasonable. This defence, in s 4A(3)(b), is phrased in identical terms to the defence to s 5. It is in the context of prosecutions under s 5 that the defence more commonly arises: see section 4.7.4. Once the prosecution have proved that a defendant *intended* to cause another person harassment, alarm or distress, it will be for the defendant to raise the defence of reasonableness.

4.7 **Section 5—Causing Harassment, Alarm, or Distress**

Definition of causing harassment, alarm or distress

Section 5 of the Act provides:

(1) A person is guilty of an offence if he—

    (a) uses threatening, abusive or insulting words or behaviour, or disorderly behaviour, or

    (b) displays any writing, sign or other visible representation which is threatening, abusive or insulting,

within the hearing or sight of a person likely to be caused harassment, alarm or distress thereby.

(2) An offence under this section may be committed in a public or a private place, except that no offence is committed where the words or behaviour are used, or the writing, sign or other visible representation is displayed, by a person inside a dwelling and the other person is also inside that or another dwelling.

(3) It is a defence for the accused to prove—

    (a) that he had no reason to believe that there was any person within hearing or sight who was likely to be caused harassment, alarm or distress, or

    (b) that he was inside a dwelling and had no reason to believe that the words or behaviour used, or the writing, sign or other visible representation displayed, would be heard or seen by a person outside that or any other dwelling, or

    (c) that his conduct was reasonable.

This is the least serious of the public order offences. The maximum penalty is a fine, and it is the only offence in Chapter 1 of the Act where an 'on the spot' fine can be imposed. Like sections 4 and 4A, it covers a broad range of behaviours and instances of public disorder.

The following points should also be noted.

4.7.1 **Arrest for s 5—Removal of the old requirement to warn**

It used to be the case, under the original enactment of s 5, that in order to lawfully arrest a person for a s 5 offence an officer was required to have already warned the person to desist. Section 5(4) originally provided that an officer could arrest a person without warrant if he engaged in offensive conduct which the officer warned him to stop, and he engaged in further offensive conduct immediately or shortly after that warning.

Following the amendments to s 24 PACE, s 5(4) was repealed. Now, the same principles that apply to any other offence also apply to an arrest under s 5.

This alteration in the power of arrest is more significant than for many other offences. the need for the behaviour to be repeated in the face of an official warning meant that the power to arrest did not arise for a single instance of the behaviour. Where a person did comply with an officer's warning, that person was neither arrested nor prosecuted for a s 5 offence. The fact that a person can now be arrested without such a warning has given rise to a number of concerns, particularly in relation to the exercise of a person's freedom of expression (see section 4.7.5). It remains good practice to issue a warning prior to arresting for a s 5 offence, particularly for relatively low-level conduct.

KEY POINTS—GOOD PRACTICE: WARNINGS UNDER S 5 POA PRIOR TO ARREST

In practical terms, the removal of a legal requirement that a warning be given does not remove an officer's discretion as to whether to arrest for a first infraction of s 5, or to warn prior to arrest. As a matter of good practice:

- For relatively low-level misbehaviour, particularly that aimed at a police officer rather than a member of the public, an appropriate exercise of discretion would be to warn the suspect prior to arrest. This has the additional benefit that it will be easier to prove the offence at trial if the warning has been ignored.
- Where the conduct involves a genuine exercise of the freedom of expression, if an arrest under s 5 were contemplated, it is likely that the interference with a person's Article 10 rights would be held to be disproportionate *unless* an officer first gives a warning.

This mirrors the advice provided to Crown Prosecutors:

Police officers are aware of the difficult balance to be struck in dealing with those whose behaviour may be perceived by some as exuberant high spirits but by others as disorderly. In such cases informal methods of disposal may be appropriate and effective; *but if this approach fails and the disorderly conduct continues* then criminal proceedings may be necessary.

4.7.2 Threatening, abusive, insulting or disorderly behaviour

The concepts of threatening, abusive and insulting have been dealt with in relation to s 4 (see section 4.6.1). Disorderly behaviour has, like many other concepts in Part 1 of the Act, repeatedly been said by the courts to bear its ordinary natural meaning (see *Carroll v DPP* [2009] EWHC 554 (Admin)). Whether or not a person's behaviour is disorderly is a question of fact. Police should take a common sense view. Behaviour which would be disorderly if occurring in a hospital ward or other similarly quiet environment may not be disorderly if occurring in the crowd at a football match.

Relatively peaceful behaviour can be disorderly. In *Chambers and Edwards v DPP* [2005] Crim LR 896, the defendants were anti-road protestors, attempting to obstruct a survey. They stood in front of an engineer, with one of the defendants placing his hand in front of the engineer's theodolite. After being warned by police that their conduct was disorderly (such a warning then being required) the defendants persisted and were arrested, charged and convicted under s 5 of the Act. On appeal, the Divisional Court stated, 'whether behaviour is characterised as disorderly is a question of fact for the trial court to determine'.

Within the sight or hearing of a person likely to be caused harassment, alarm or distress

It can be enough that the conduct occurs only in the presence of a police officer, or group of officers. It is important to remember that the conduct only needs to be *likely* to cause one of those officers harassment, alarm or distress. It does not need to have been the actual effect.

In *DPP v Orum* [1988] Crim LR 848 the Court confirmed that while a person likely to be caused harassment, alarm or distress *could* be a police officer, there was no reason to assume that they would react in such away, and that 'very frequently, words and behaviour which will be wearily familiar will have little emotional impact on them save that of boredom'.

In *Southard v DPP* [2007] ACD 53 DC the Court confirmed that an experienced police officer might feel harassed by an individual shouting 'fuck off' at him while he was in the process of arresting another person. Although phrases such as this are now routinely heard in public, however phlegmatic the police officer might have been, it was a sustainable decision that a likely effect was to cause him some real harassment.

It is therefore important to consider the likely reactions of any members of the public present, particularly if the police officer is not himself alarmed, harassed or distressed by the behaviour. As stated, officers must be careful not to lapse into an automatic, formulaic assumption that just because a person has behaved in a threatening, abusive, insulting or disorderly way, an offence has necessarily been committed.

4.7.3 Individual characteristics of the person witnessing the conduct

If an individual present was particularly susceptible to being caused harassment, alarm or distress, then the offence may be made out even though a person of reasonable firmness would not have reacted in the same way. The elderly, young or vulnerable are therefore afforded a degree of extra protection. Thus, for example, conduct in close proximity to a school or nursing home will be looked at differently by the courts.

First, the conduct itself might be regarded as disorderly, when it would not be so regarded elsewhere. Second, the conduct might be likely to cause harassment, alarm or distress to an elderly eyewitness, where it would not do so to those waiting outside to enter a night club.

4.7.4 **Defences**

If all the elements of the offence under s 5 are made out, there are three specific statutory defences contained in s 5(3):

- that the defendant had no reason to believe that there was any person within hearing or sight who was likely to be caused harassment, alarm or distress, or
- the defendant was inside a dwelling and had no reason to believe that the words or behaviour used, or the writing, sign or other visible representation displayed, would be heard or seen by a person outside that or any other dwelling, or
- the conduct was reasonable.

In addition to the statutory defences within s 5 itself, there is a further defence relying on a person's right to freedom of expression under Article 10, even if the conduct was not objectively reasonable.

In many situations, appropriate and proportionate policing prior to arrest (including the giving of a suitable warning) will have the dual benefit of giving the suspect the opportunity to cease the offending behaviour, and also providing good evidence negating each of these defences if the case were to proceed to trial.

Where the defendant raises a defence under s 5(3), there is an absence of appellate judicial authority as to the precise legal status of the defence for s 5. The principle distinction is whether the burden of proving the defence lies on the defendant (a 'legal burden') or whether the defendant need only raise a prima facie case, whereupon it is for the prosecution to prove its absence. The analysis of this issue in the context of s 5(3) is outside the scope of this book. However, it should be noted that different considerations may apply for the three different defences. This is of particular relevance in relation to the defence of reasonable conduct.

Defence 1—No reason to believe any person in hearing or sight

This defence arises not only where a person seeks to prove (or raises a prima facie case) that they believed there was no one present *at all* to witness the behaviour, but also the belief is that there was no one within hearing or sight who, witnessing the behaviour, would likely to be harassed, distressed or alarmed by it. The defendant must honestly believe that there was no such person present, and there must be a reasonable basis for such a belief.

The second basis is particularly important in the context of a vulnerable class of victims, who might be known to live in or frequent a certain area, but who would be unwilling or fearful to give evidence. In such a context, the use of an appropriate warning will bring home to a person that whilst their behaviour might be acceptable elsewhere, the particular location means that it is likely to cause harassment, alarm or distress to those witnessing it. For example, this might be true in the common stairwell of a block of flats, or an area outside a local shop or day centre for the elderly. If there is reliable evidence that the particular sensibilities of the local population had been drawn to a defendant's attention prior to the behaviour for which he has been prosecuted, it is likely that this particular defence would fail.

Defence 2—Defendant inside a dwelling

If the defendant is inside a dwelling, and has no reason to believe that the offensive conduct will be heard or seen by a person outside that or any other house, then he will have a defence to s 4A and s 5. Most arrests and prosecutions for s 5 offences committed by someone inside a dwelling relate to the deliberate communication to those outside, or the display of threatening, abusive or insulting writing or signs.

One situation where the defence might arise is in relation to extremely noisy behaviour disturbing others outside the house. Under normal circumstances, noisy behaviour from within a property that is causing a nuisance or distress to neighbours would be dealt with under other statutory powers. Distress caused to neighbours *inside* their homes would not even be covered by s 4A or s 5. However, where harassment, alarm or distress were being caused to those outside the dwelling, if a police officer were to inform the occupants of the dwelling of the effect of their conduct, and to warn them to stop, they would be unlikely to be able to rely on the defence under s 4(3)(a) or s 5(3)(b) in any prosecution for similar behaviour after the warning had been given.

Defence 3—Reasonable conduct

This defence arises both in relation to s 4A and s 5. There are perhaps few examples where a person could satisfy a court that their conduct was reasonable, despite acting abusively, insultingly, threatening or in a disorderly way, either with the intent of causing harassment, alarm and distress (s 4A) or where it was likely a person would be caused harassment, alarm or distress (s 5). However, such situations might include:

- emergencies, where a person might be acting under extreme pressure or stress;
- an attempt to scare off a perceived attacker (akin to self-defence or defence of another);
- extreme provocation, perhaps in relation to the 'innocent' party subject to a campaign of intimidation and harassment by others;
- a person exercising their right to freedom of expression, particularly if protesting or expressing religious or political views.

It is the last of these examples that is perhaps most controversial. There is no doubt that the exercise of Article 10 rights can, on occasion, provide a defence to what might otherwise be an offence under s 5. An early example of this was *Percy v DPP* [2001] EWHC Admin 1125. During the course of a political protest at an American air base, Percy had defaced an American flag, put it on the ground and stood on it. Following the evidence of a number of witnesses about the distress that had been caused to them, she was convicted under s 5. On appeal, the conviction was quashed. The Court held that:

> A peaceful protest will only come within the terms of section 5 and constitute an offence where the conduct goes beyond legitimate protest and moves into the realms of threatening, abusive or insulting behaviour, which is calculated to insult either intentionally or recklessly, and which is unreasonable . . . Where the right to freedom of expression under Article 10 is engaged, as in my view is undoubtedly the case here, it is clear from the European authorities put before us that the justification for any interference with that right must be convincingly established.

In *Morrow v DPP* [1994] Crim LR 58 (DC) an anti-abortion protest went beyond the use of placards and photographs when the defendants entered a clinic and acted in a disorderly way inside. At trial, they sought to rely on the defence of reasonable conduct, arguing that they were preventing crimes being committed by the abortion clinic and accordingly had the protection of s 3 of the Criminal Law Act 1967. However, the Court held that the defence under s 3 of the Criminal Law Act 1967 did not apply where an aggressive, disruptive demonstration was being held.

Morrow was decided before the Human Rights Act (HRA) came into force. However, in the context of anti-abortion protests, the case of *DPP v Connelly* (see section 4.6.2) confirmed that an interference with a person's Article 10 rights was capable of being justified under Article 10(2) in order to safeguard the rights of others.

The case of *Norwood v DPP* [2003] EWHC 1564 (Admin); (2003) Crim LR 888 confirms that there is a limit to how far the courts will allow the defence of reasonable conduct in the context of freedom of expression. It provides a very useful case study in the approach likely to be taken to the display of highly offensive material, even where the display is the bona fide expression of a person's political beliefs.

Case study

Norwood v DPP

Norwood was the regional organizer of the British National Party. He displayed a poster in his window. It contained the words (in large print) 'Islam out of Britain' and 'Protect the British People', and included a photograph of one of the twin towers of the World Trade Centre in flames on 11 September 2001, together with a crescent and star surrounded by a 'prohibition' sign.

109

On his prosecution under s 5, he argued that his conduct was reasonable. The judge found that the poster was abusive and insulting to Islam and, on its terms and in its symbols, to the followers of that religion. It was likely to cause harassment, alarm or distress and its display was not objectively reasonable within s 5(3)(c). Norwood was found guilty of the racially aggravated version of s 5 (see section 7.4.1).

On Norwood's appeal, the Divisional Court stated that the principal issue was whether his conduct went beyond legitimate protest, so that it no longer formed part of an open expression of opinion on a matter of public interest but had become *disproportionate* and unreasonable. The court decided that the Judge had been entitled to conclude that the defendant's conduct was unreasonable, having regard to the clear legitimate aim (of which s 5 is itself a necessary vehicle) to protect the rights of others and/or to prevent crime and disorder.

Norwood appealed to the ECtHR (see *Norwood v United Kingdom* (Admissibility Decision) Application No. 00023131/03). The European Court, if anything, took an even tougher line with the defendant's conduct. In unanimously holding the application to be inadmissible, the Court stated at paragraph 3:

> The general purpose of Article 17 (explained below) is to prevent individuals or groups with totalitarian aims from exploiting in their own interests the principles enunciated by the Convention . . . the words and images on the poster amounted to a public expression of attack on all Muslims in the United Kingdom. Such a general, vehement attack against a religious group, linking the group as a whole with a grave act of terrorism, is incompatible with the values proclaimed and guaranteed by the Convention, notably tolerance, social peace and non-discrimination. The applicant's display of the poster in his window constituted an act within the meaning of Article 17, which did not, therefore, enjoy the protection of Articles 10 or 14.

Article 17 provides that nothing in the Convention may be interpreted as implying for any state, group or person any right to engage in any activity or perform any act aimed at the destruction of any of the rights and freedoms set out in the Convention, or aimed at limiting those rights and freedoms to a greater extent than the Convention allows.

Neither does the exercise of religious beliefs provide an automatic immunity to prosecution. In *Hammond v DPP* [2004] EWHC 69 the defendant was an evangelical Christian preaching in public in Bournemouth town centre. During his sermon, he held a sign bearing the words 'Stop Immorality', 'Stop Homosexuality' and 'Stop Lesbianism'. A crowd of 30 to 40 people gathered, some of whom were hostile. There was a disturbance, soil was thrown at the defendant and someone was hit over the head with his placard. A police officer spoke to the defendant and asked him to take the sign down and leave the area. He refused, saying he was aware that his sign was insulting because he had had a similar reaction previously, but that he intended to return the following Saturday to preach with the sign again. H was arrested for a breach of the peace. He was subsequently charged and convicted under s 5. The Divisional Court confirmed that, while the defendant was no doubt exercising his freedom of expression, it was open to the magistrates to decide that in all the circumstances his conduct was not reasonable. In giving his judgment, LJ May stated,

> . . . the words on the sign appear to relate homosexuality and lesbianism to immorality. The justices themselves take this into consideration when they say that the words on the appellant's sign were directed specifically towards the homosexual and lesbian community, implying that they were immoral. Accordingly, not without hesitation, I have reached the conclusion that it was open to the justices to reach the conclusion that they did as to the fact that these words on the sign were, in fact, insulting.

It seems that May LJ felt he perhaps would not have convicted Hammond at first instance. Nevertheless, the defendant's conviction for an offence under s 5 was upheld, and his defence of reasonable conduct rejected.

4.7.5 Exercise of Article 10 rights, in the context of section 5 POA

It does not automatically follow that a person will be convicted of an offence under s 5 if the defence of reasonable conduct fails. Even if the conduct were unreasonable, a defendant has a potential further defence, not found in s 5, that his arrest and/or prosecution under s 5 constitutes a disproportionate interference with his right to freedom of expression. This defence arises following the decision in the case of *Dehal v DPP* [2005] EWHC 2154 (Admin). Following a long (and increasingly bitter) dispute about the interpretation of religious scripture, the defendant had put up a poster on a notice board at a Sikh temple describing the president of the temple in abusive and insulting language. There was no doubt that the ingredients of the statutory offence under s 4A were made out, and the defendant was convicted under s 4A. On appeal, the Crown Court found that the president of the temple had been harassed and distressed by the notice and that the defendant had intended to cause the president harassment, alarm or distress both by the terms of the notice and by exhibiting it as he had done. The Crown Court further held that the defendant did not have a defence of acting reasonably under s 4A(3)(b) of the Act because the test was objective and the terms of the notice were not objectively reasonable. However, on further appeal, the Divisional Court quashed the conviction. In doing so, it stated:

> In order to justify one of the essential foundations of democratic society the prosecution must demonstrate that it is being brought in pursuit of a legitimate aim, namely the protection of society against violence and that a criminal prosecution is the only method necessary to achieve that aim . . . However insulting, however unjustified what the appellant said about the President of the Temple, a criminal prosecution was unlawful as a result of

section 3 of the Human Rights Act and Article 10 unless and until it could be established that such a prosecution was necessary in order to prevent public disorder.

Dehal is of potentially wide-ranging and significant effect. It is not confined to a consideration of the proportionality of *prosecuting* someone who is exercising their Article 10 right to freedom of expression. The reasoning applies equally to the decision taken at an early stage where an officer is exercising his discretion as to whether or not to arrest an individual who, prima facie, is both exercising his Article 10 rights, but also being abusive, insulting, threatening or disorderly in breach of sections 4A or 5 of the POA.

Faced with such a situation, the officer must ask himself whether or not it is a disproportionate interference with that person's Article 10 rights to arrest them. In *Abdul v DPP* [2011] EWHC 247 (Admin) it was confirmed that where a prosecution was necessary either to prevent disorder or to protect the rights of others, the prosecution and conviction were indeed proportionate (see section 2.7.2).

Where the ingredients of a s 5 offence are established, then provided that:

- the officer has asked himself whether arrest is necessary, pursuant to one of the aims in Article 10(2),
- has given due regard to the person's Article 10 rights, and
- has (if appropriate) sought to resolve the situation without arrest,

the intervention is likely to be found subsequently to be proportionate.

4.7.6 Article 5—Detailed Case Study

A group of young males are playing a vigorous, informal game of football in a large park. They are swearing loudly at each other during the game, but the game is otherwise good-natured. A mother and her young children arrive and place themselves near where the game is taking place. The mother could have chosen to stop at any number of other places in the park, much further away from the game. The mother then complains to a passing police officer about the males' behaviour, saying that it is upsetting her children. There is no question that the behaviour is likely to cause distress in the nearby children. The police officer tells the players to quieten down, and they comply for a few minutes, before again becoming as rowdy as before.

- Are the men being threatening, insulting, abusive or disorderly? If so, is their conduct reasonable?
- Would it make a difference if the children had been playing on some swings in an area of the park fenced off as a playground, and the males had chosen to set their game of football up right next to the children's playground?

In the first scenario, there would be an argument as to whether the players were being disorderly at all if their behaviour were no worse than that in many a typical informal football game. However, depending on the language used, it might still be abusive or insulting and if it were, it need not be directed at the children in order for their distress to satisfy one of the ingredients of the offence. Nevertheless, even if the behaviour were abusive and/or disorderly, if the defence of reasonableness was raised under s 5(3), it might be difficult to establish to the criminal standard that the behaviour was unreasonable. The language used would need to be more than that which is commonly used in this kind of scenario, or it would need to be shown that the behaviour was unreasonable for some other reason: such as the players becoming aware of the distress caused to the children.

Although many of the facts are similar, different considerations apply in the second scenario. Even if it were reasonable to set up a football game right next to the children's play area (which might be open to argument), once it had been pointed out to the males that their behaviour was distressing children, and they could continue their game elsewhere in the park, the refusal to heed the warning would make it more straightforward to demonstrate that the behaviour was unreasonable.

4.7.7 Fixed penalty notices

On-the-spot fines are appropriate for specific minor offences, where the fine on conviction is likely to be little more than the value of the fixed penalty notice. The offences for which police may administer a fixed penalty notice are defined by s 1 of CJPA. These include the following, which most commonly arise in a public order scenario:

- Being drunk in a highway, other public place or licensed premises (s 12 Licensing Act 1872)
- Disorderly behaviour while drunk in a public place (s 91 Criminal Justice Act 1967)
- Consumption of alcohol in a designated public place (s 12 CJPA)
- Destroying or damaging property (s 1(1) Criminal Damage Act 1971)
- Behaviour likely to cause harassment, alarm or distress (s 5 POA)

For responses to alcohol-related public disorder, see 4.10.

Conditions for giving a fixed penalty notice

Section 2 of CJPA provides that a notice can be given if an officer has reason to believe that a person aged 10 or over has committed one of the offences listed in s 1 CJPA. The officer has to be in uniform, unless the notice is given in a police station—in which case the notice can only be *given* by an 'authorised officer'. An 'authorised officer' is one who has been authorized to issue penalty notices by the chief officer for the area in which the police station is situated; for several offences it may include police community support officers.

A person receiving a fixed penalty notice has 21 days in which to decide how to respond. He has three options:

1) Pay the penalty. This is not a formal admission or finding of guilt. It is not a conviction, and the Rehabilitation of Offenders Act 1974 does not apply.
2) Request trial for the alleged offence, in which case the normal charging decisions and procedures will follow.
3) Do nothing. The person is then subject to a fine equal to 50 per cent higher than that which he would otherwise have had to pay, and faces enforcement proceedings.

4.8 Assaulting, Resisting, or Wilfully Obstructing Police Officers

Arrests and charges for assault or obstruction of a police officer in the execution of his duty are two of the most common public order offences for which members of the public are arrested and charged. An arrest might be necessary following confrontation in the most trivial of scenarios or in a major public order event. Despite the frequency of arrests for these two offences, key aspects of these offences can throw up practical problems, even for the most alert or knowledgeable of police officers.

Section 89 of the Police Act 1996 provides for these two offences, which arise frequently in public order scenarios:

> s 89(1): Any person who **assaults** a constable in the execution of his duty, or a person assisting a constable in the execution of his duty, shall be guilty of an offence . . .
>
> s 89(2): Any person who resists or **wilfully obstructs** a constable in the execution of his duty, or a person assisting a constable in the execution of his duty, shall be guilty of an offence . . .

'Constable' includes a police officer of any rank. Similar offences exist against, *inter alia*, Police Community Support Officers by virtue of s 46 of the Police Reform Act 2002.

4.8.1 'Acting in execution of his duty'

For either offence to be committed, the officer must be acting in the execution of his duty. A police officer who is acting outside his powers or exercising his power in an unlawful way (such as disproportionately) will not be acting in the execution of his duty.

Ways in which an officer might be acting outside his powers, or exercising his powers unlawfully, include an officer who is carrying out a search unlawfully, for example a non-PACE compliant search, an officer who is trespassing on land, or an officer who restrains a person, not intending to arrest him.

For example, in *Kenlin & another v Gardiner & another* [1967] 2 QB 510 police stopped two schoolchildren who tried to run away. One of the officers caught hold of one of the boys by his arm. The police officer did not purport to arrest the boy, and his action in grabbing him was therefore an assault against the boy. As a result, the boy was able to successfully argue that he struggled in self-defence, and his conviction for assault against the officer was overturned on appeal. Similarly, in *Collins v Wilcock* (1984) 1 WLR 1172 an officer who took hold of a woman's arm to administer a caution was held to be acting unlaw-fully. Her purpose in taking hold of the woman's arm was not to attract the woman's attention but to restrain her.

However, not all physical contact short of arrest between a police officer and another person will amount to an assault. A mere tap on the shoulder, such as in *Donnelly v Jackman* [1970] 1 All ER 987, will not amount to an assault. That kind of contact is likely to be viewed by the courts as committing merely a 'trivial interference' with that person's liberty. In *Mepstead v DPP* (1996) 160 JP 475, the High Court noted that a police officer who took a man's arm, not intending to detain or arrest him but in order to draw his attention to the con-tent of what was being said to him, was acting within the execution of his duty when the man then assaulted him. In reaching this conclusion, Balcombe LJ observed:

> It is, of course, for the tribunal of fact to decide whether the physical contact goes beyond what is acceptable by the ordinary standards of everyday life and . . . if the period of contact had gone on for any length of time it may well be said to be a finding of fact, to which no reasonable court would come, to say that there was not an intention to detain.

The point at which a police officer ceases to act in the execution of his duty is the point at which he actually acts unlawfully. In *D v DPP* [2011] 1 WLR 882 a community support officer, mistaken as to the extent of her powers to detain, requested the defendant to stop and put out her hand without actually detain-ing him, and was then assaulted. The court held that at the point of the assault by the defendant, the Police Community Support Officer (PCSO) was still acting in the execution of her duty—it did not matter that her intention in putting out her hand was to effect a detention in the immediate future that, had she attempted it, would have been unlawful.

4.8.2 Officers who go to the assistance of colleagues

In *Bentley v Brudzinski* (1982) Crim LR 825, a police officer was questioning two brothers, and was seeking to keep them with him while he questioned them further. A second officer arrived and, following a nod and a point from the first officer, placed his hand on the shoulder of the man, in order to attract his atten-tion and to stop him walking away. The man punched the second officer in the face and was charged with assaulting the officer in the execution of his duty.

He was acquitted. On appeal the decision was upheld by the Divisional Court. In doing so it stated that the officer who was assaulted was acting in support of his colleague, but ought not to have been asked to stop the defendant, and was therefore acting outside the scope of his duty. The Divisional Court made it clear that the defendant *ought* to have been charged with common assault.

In *McBean v Parker* (1983) Crim LR 399, a police officer tried to search a suspect without telling him the reason for the search. There was a scuffle in which the officer's tunic was torn. A second officer then tried to restrain the suspect and was head-butted. The defendant was convicted of assaulting a police officer in the execution of his duty. On appeal the Divisional Court noted that the second officer had been present throughout and ought to have known that the search was unlawful. It was held that once the first officer began to act unlawfully and the suspect began to respond using only reasonable force, the second officer who sought to restrain him could not be acting in the execution of his duty.

In *Bentley* the assisting officer's actions amounted to unlawful interference: the physical contact was done with an intention to stop the man and so went beyond a trivial interference with the man's liberty. In *McBean*, part of the Court's reasoning was that the assisting officer ought to have known that the search was unlawful. But the more recent case of *Ali v DPP* (reported sub nom. *Cumberbatch v CPS* [2009] EWHC 3353) makes matters even more difficult for the police.

In *Ali v DPP*, officers arrived on the scene and went to assist a colleague who appeared to be attempting to arrest a man who was resisting him. The arrest was unlawful, though the officers did not know this, nor had they formed a view on whether the man had or might have committed an offence. They were simply coming to the assistance of their colleague. The man was charged with resisting each of the officers in the execution of their duty. The Divisional Court held that where the arrest of a man by a uniformed police officer is unlawful, other police officers who see what is happening and go to assist their colleague in the arrest are not acting in the execution of their duty.

In both *McBean v Parker* and *Ali v DPP* the Court rejected arguments that in circumstances where a citizen was using reasonable force to resist an unlawful arrest, the assisting officers would be acting in execution of their duty if they intervened to prevent a breach of the peace. *Cumberbatch* also followed this principle, though the Divisional Court accepted that if there were an 'independent, free-standing breach of the peace, the position would be different'. In that case, the violent behaviour of the woman arrested was found to be inextricably linked to the unlawful arrest and detention of her father, and the arresting officer, whilst not directly involved in the arrest of the father, was part of the team who were there to transport him post-arrest.

Taken together, these cases suggest that where officers simply assist colleagues who are acting unlawfully, **the assisting officers will not be acting in execution** of their duty *even if* they are unaware—and have no reason to suspect—that their colleagues are acting unlawfully.

In contrast, in *Sutton & Ors v Commissioner of Police for the Metropolis* [1998] EWCA Civ 1333, Lord Justice Kennedy accepted that an officer who assisted in forming part of a cordon could be acting in the execution of his duty even if the arrest which the cordon sought to protect was itself unlawful: 'otherwise any police officer instructed to form part of a cordon, in order to be sure that he is acting in the execution of his duty, must first investigate the legality of the incident he is being asked to cordon off'.

In *DPP v Meaden* (2004) 1 WLR 945, police had a warrant to search a property and persons found within it. The procedure adopted was to search one room, and then use that as a 'sterile' room in which to keep the respondent until the rest of the property had been searched. Whilst the first room was being searched the respondent was detained in the bathroom. He threw a cigarette lighter at an officer and was charged with assaulting and wilfully obstructing an officer in the execution of his duty. He argued that the officer was not acting in the execution of his duty, as the police had no power to detain him and restrict his movement within the property whilst the search was continuing.

The Divisional Court held that the statutory powers under which the warrant was issued enabled the police to detain the respondent for the purpose of searching him, and enabled the police to use reasonable force for the purpose of executing the warrant. Lord Justice Rose said at paragraph 32:

> Here the warrant authorised a search of premises and persons for controlled drugs and documents connected with drugs offences. That authority, to be meaningful, had, as it seems to me, to enable the search to be effective. It could not be effective, particularly in premises on two floors, presently occupied by a number of people, if the occupiers were permitted to move about freely within the premises while the searches were going on. Although I accept it is for the police to show, and the burden upon them is a heavy one, that the use of force was necessary and reasonable, it seems to me to be entirely reasonable that officers should seek, by no more force than is necessary, to restrict the movement of those in occupation of premises while those premises are being searched.

Accordingly, the officers were acting in execution of their duty. The appeal was allowed and the case remitted to the magistrates to continue the hearing.

4.8.3 'Assaults' and 'resists or wilfully obstructs'

Assault

The section 89(1) offence is an offence that involves an assault, in the ordinary sense of the term with which the police are familiar. This means that a member of the public who makes physical contact with a police officer in lawful self-defence, or accidentally, or in lawful defence of another, is not 'assaulting' that officer. The section 89(1) offence would therefore not be made out.

Resist or wilfully obstruct

This means more than simply refusing to answer questions put by police. A suspect has the right to remain silent and is under no legal duty to assist the police (even though it might be thought that his civic duty is to assist the police): therefore, in order to amount to behaviour which resists or wilfully obstructs the suspect's behaviour must go further than this—such as a suspect who actually runs away from police when the police show him their warrant cards and attempt to question him (*Sekfali and others v DPP* [2006] EWHC 894 (Admin)). The obstruction does not need to be physical—abusive and uncooperative behaviour can amount to obstruction.

Where a person is under a legal duty to assist the police, failing to assist may amount to a section 89(2) offence. This may arise in public order situations where an officer is attempting to prevent a breach of the peace and calls for assistance or makes a request of those involved. An alternative offence to one under s 89(2) would be the common law offence of refusing to aid and assist a constable in the execution of his duty.

'Wilfully' simply requires the suspect to be acting deliberately.

Following the amendment to s 24 PACE, the general power to arrest without a warrant applies to both s 89(1) and s 89(2) offences.

4.9 Obstruction of Emergency Workers

Sections 1 and 2 of the Emergency Workers (Obstruction) Act 2006 create the offences relating to the obstruction of emergency workers:

s 1: Obstructing or hindering certain emergency workers who are responding to emergency circumstances;

s 2: Obstructing or hindering those who are assisting emergency workers responding to emergency circumstances. This includes members of the public lending assistance to emergency workers, whether or not the emergency worker actually arrives after the member of the public.

Section 1(2) defines emergency workers. The broad categories are:

- Fire fighters, whether they employed by a fire and rescue authority or their official duties including fire fighting;
- Ambulance workers, whether employed by the NHS or acting on its behalf;
- Those transporting blood, organs, equipment or personnel on behalf of the NHS; and
- Coastguards and lifeboat crews.

Emergency circumstances are those where there are circumstances, present or imminent, which are causing or are likely to cause death, serious injury or illness (or the worsening of it) and serious harm to the environment, buildings or property. They include the situation where a person responding has reasonable grounds for believing they responding to what is, or may be, an emergency. This would include responding to both hoax and mistaken emergency calls.

The CPS guidance states that 'there is strong public interest in prosecuting such cases once the evidential test is met'. In each case, the maximum punishment is a fine (not exceeding level 5). While the offence is therefore suitable for 'mere' obstruction, such as blocking access, giving misleading information or interfering with equipment, the CPS advise that where conduct obstructing an emergency worker would also constitute a more serious offence (eg s 4A of the POA 1986) it would normally be appropriate to charge the more serious offence. However, provided the arresting officer records the full extent of the conduct, it would be lawful to arrest for obstruction, and defer the charging decision to a later time, when the full evidential picture has been obtained.

There is a defence of reasonable excuse. Whether or not such a defence would apply would depend on all the circumstances of the case.

4.10 **Alcohol**

The close link between alcohol and disorder, violence and anti-social behaviour is reflected in a number of specific offences, as well as powers available to the police and local authorities. These provisions aim both to deal with drunken behaviour, and to seek to prevent it occurring in public. The measures set out here are a mixed bag, which itself reflects the piecemeal approach to legislation.

See chapter 10 for alcohol-related offences in the context of football matches. Both traffic offences and the licensing of the sale of alcohol and are beyond the scope of this book.

4.10.1 **Specific alcohol-related offences**

Being drunk in a public place

Section 12 of the Licensing Act 1872 creates the offence of being drunk in a highway, other public place or licensed premises. A 'public place' includes any place to which the public have access: this could include premises which charge an entrance fee, such as an art gallery.

There is no statutory definition of 'drunk'. Whether or not a person is drunk is a question of fact (affected in part by that individual's tolerance of alcohol) and is a matter for which police officers need to use their experience and common sense—the use of an intoxiliser is to be confined to traffic stops. Drug intoxication does not qualify. If a person is under the influence of both drink and drugs, a court may ultimately have to decide whether, excluding the drug-related element of intoxication, the person had consumed sufficient alcohol to significantly affect their steady self-control (see *Neale v R MJ E (a minor)* (1985) 80 Cr App R 20).

This is an offence of strict liability, and the reason for the person coming to be in a public place (or on the highway) is irrelevant. The section implies that the person, in being 'found', will be insensible. This is indeed how the section is typically applied. However, there is no requirement that the person actually be unconscious.

There also is a more serious offence under s 12, of being drunk in charge of a carriage, horse, cattle, or steam engine, or of being drunk when in possession of a loaded firearm.

Drunk and disorderly behaviour

Section 91(1) of the Criminal Justice Act 1967 provides that any person who, while drunk, is of disorderly behaviour in any public place is guilty of an offence. The definition of a public place is as set out above. 'Disorderly behaviour' is not defined, but is to bear its ordinary, natural meaning, as for section 5 of the POA 1986. (See section 4.7.2)

Definition of refusal to leave licensed premises: s 143 of the Licensing Act 2003

Section 143(1) provides that:

A person who is drunk or disorderly commits an offence if, without reasonable excuse—

(a) he fails to leave relevant premises when requested to do so by a constable or by a person to whom subsection (2) applies, or

(b) he enters or attempts to enter relevant premises after a constable or a person to whom subsection (2) applies has requested him not to enter.

'Relevant premises' are defined in s 159 of the Act as:

• licensed premises, or
• premises in respect of which there is in force a club premises certificate, or
• premises which may be used for a permitted temporary activity by virtue of Part 5 of the Act.

'Person to whom subsection (2) applies' includes:

• anybody who works at the premises, whether paid or unpaid;
• the holder of the premises licence in the case of a licensed premises;
• the designated premises supervisor under such a licence;
• any member or officer of the club, in the case of premises holding a club premises certificate; and
• the premises user, in the case of premises at which there is a permitted temporary activity under Part 5 of the Licensing Act 2003.

If one of the above listed persons makes a request that a drunk or disorderly person leave the premises, s 143(4) of the Act provides that a constable *must* help to expel that person from the premises, and help to prevent them from entering the premises. He may use reasonable force to do so—see *R v Semple* [2010] 2 All ER 353.

4.10.2 Section 1 of the Confiscation of Alcohol (Young Persons) Act 1997

Section 1(1) of the Confiscation of Alcohol (Young Persons) Act 1997 gives a police officer power to require surrender of alcohol, or anything that appears to be alcohol, if he reasonably suspects that a person in a 'relevant place' is in possession of alcohol and reasonably suspects that either:

- he is under the age of 18, or
- he intends any of the alcohol to be consumed by a person under 18, or
- a person under 18 has recently been with him, or is currently with him, and has recently consumed alcohol.

'Relevant place' means simply any public place other than licensed premises. 'Public place' has the meaning given under 'Drunk in a public place', under section 4.10.1.

When making a request for surrender of alcohol under s 1(1), the officer must also:

- require the person to state his name and address, and
- inform the person of his suspicion, and
- inform the person that failing to comply with the request, without reasonable excuse, is an offence.

In a manner similar to CJPA below, ss 1AB(2) and 1AB(3) provide, respectively, disposal powers and an offence of failing to comply without reasonable excuse.

4.10.3 Section 27—Violent Crime Reduction Act 2006

This section provides the police with power to give a direction ('a s 27 direction') to an individual to leave an area, and prohibiting him from returning for a period not greater than 48 hours from the giving of the direction, if satisfied that the test in s 27(2) is met.

The test in s 27(2) is that the individual's presence in that area is:

- likely, in all the circumstances, to cause or contribute to the occurrence of alcohol-related crime or disorder in that area, or
- likely, in all the circumstances, to cause or to contribute to a repetition or continuance there of such crime or disorder, and

121

- that giving a s 27 direction is necessary, to remove or reduce the likelihood of such crime or disorder occurring (or a repetition or continuance of such crime or disorder) in that area in the period for which the direction will have effect.

The s 27 power should be used proportionately, reasonably and with discretion, in circumstances where it is considered *necessary* to prevent the likelihood of alcohol-related crime or disorder. Failing to comply with a s 27 direction is an offence.

KEY POINT—DIRECTIONS UNDER S 27 VIOLENT CRIME REDUCTION ACT 2006

A s 27 direction *must*:

- be given in writing
- clearly identify the area to which it relates
- specify the period for which the individual is prohibited from returning to the area.

A s 27 direction *can*:

- require the individual to whom it is given to leave the area immediately, or at a time specified by the constable giving the direction
- impose requirements on how that individual is to leave the area
- impose requirements about the route that individual takes to leave the area
- be withdrawn or varied by a constable.

A s 27 direction *cannot*:

- be varied to extend for a period beyond 48 hours
- prevent the individual from accessing the place where he resides, or from attending any place he is required to attend for work, training, medical treatment, or under any enactment, or under any order of a court or tribunal.

If giving a s 27 direction, the constable must make a record of the terms of the direction and the locality it relates to, the individual to whom it is given, the time it is given, and the period during which the individual is prohibited from returning to the locality. If the constable reasonably suspects the individual to be under 16, he may remove that individual to a place where he resides or a place of safety.

4.10.4 Designated Public Places Orders (DPPOs)

Section 13 of the CJPA allows local authorities to designate areas for this purpose only where they are satisfied that: **nuisance or annoyance to the public**, or **disorder**, have been associated with drinking in that place.

It is for the local authority, rather than the police, to be satisfied that public nuisance, annoyance or disorder has been associated with drinking in the area concerned and that a designation order under s 13 is appropriate. The procedures for consultation for, and timing and publicity of, DPPOs is contained in the Local Authorities (Alcohol Consumption in Designated Public Places) Regulations 2007.

Once a DPPO is in place, if a constable reasonably believes that a person is or has been consuming, or intends to consume, alcohol in a designated public place he has the power to require that person not to drink alcohol in that place and to surrender any alcohol or alcohol containers (including sealed containers) in his possession. Prior to such a request by a police officer, it is not an offence to drink alcohol in a DPP (designated public place).

Consumption of alcohol in a designated public place

Definition of consumption of alcohol in a designated public place

Section 12 of CJPA provides:

(1) Subsection (2) applies if a constable reasonably believes that a person is, or has been, consuming alcohol in a designated public place or intends to consume alcohol in such a place.

(2) The constable may require the person concerned—

    (a) not to consume in that place anything which is, or which the constable reasonably believes to be, alcohol;

    (b) to surrender anything in his possession which is, or which the constable reasonably believes to be, alcohol or a container for alcohol.

(3) A constable may dispose of anything surrendered to him under subsection (2) in such manner as he considers appropriate.

(4) A person who fails without reasonable excuse to comply with a requirement imposed on him under subsection (2) commits an offence and is liable on summary conviction to a fine not exceeding level 2 on the standard scale.

(5) A constable who imposes a requirement on a person under subsection (2) shall inform the person concerned that failing without reasonable excuse to comply with the requirement is an offence.

Where a DPPO is in place, s 12(2) gives police the power to require members of the public to refrain from drinking alcohol, and to confiscate containers of alcohol from members of the public **if the officer reasonably believes that the person is consuming alcohol, or that they have been, or are about to.** The officer does not have to prove that a container has alcohol in it, but does need to have reasonable grounds to believe that it contains alcohol. When making a requirement under s 12(2) the officer *must* warn the person that if they fail to comply without a reasonable excuse, they commit an arrestable offence. The confiscated alcohol may be disposed of in such a manner as he considers appropriate. A refusal to comply with the direction to stop drinking and/or to surrender the container will constitute an offence.

While the local authority may only create a DPP if there has been public nuisance, annoyance or disorder associated with drinking, once the order is in place, there is no requirement that the officer have a reasonable belief or suspicion that the person will, if they consume the alcohol, contribute to public nuisance, annoyance or disorder. To impose such a requirement might have made enforcement of the DPPO significantly more difficult in practice. However, the lack of this threshold does mean that there is the potential to apply the directions under s 12 in an overzealous manner. An officer should exercise considerable discretion in enforcement.

4.10.5 Drinking Banning Orders

General features

Drinking Banning Orders (DBOs) can be applied for by police or local authorities (similar to anti-social behaviour orders) against persons over the age of 16 whose use of alcohol has led to alcohol-related crime or disorder. They can therefore be useful against those who cause persistent public-order related nuisances. The minimum period for such an order is two months, and the maximum is two years.

Under s 1(2) of the Violent Crime Reduction Act (VCRA), a DBO can impose 'any prohibition on the subject which is necessary for the purpose of protecting other persons from criminal or disorderly conduct by the subject while he is under the influence of alcohol'.

Section 1(3) of that Act requires all DBOs to contain 'such prohibition as the court making it considers necessary' relating to the subject's ability to enter premises holding a premises licence or club license which authorizes the sale or supply of alcohol. Common (and useful) kinds of prohibitions which the police might wish to seek include ones that:

- Prohibit the person from entering certain named licensed premises
- Prohibit the person from entering any licensed premises in a specific geographic area
- Prohibit the person from consuming alcohol in a specific geographic area.

Like anti-social behaviour orders, the VCRA provides for an interim order which can be imposed if the court considers it just to do so, pending hearing of the final application. In some circumstances, the court can order the offender to attend an 'approved course' to address their alcohol misuse. A full exposition of when an application is appropriate, how to gather evidence for and apply for a DBO, and the appropriate prohibitions to seek is beyond the scope of this book: the appropriate link to the CPS and Home Office guidance is provided at the end of the chapter.

DBOs on conviction

Section 6 of the VCRA enables a DBO to be made on conviction where the convicted offender is over 16, and committed the offence whilst under the influence of alcohol. This is a matter for discussion between the police and CPS. In order to obtain a DBO on conviction, the prosecution will need to present evidence to satisfy the court that the DBO, and each of the prohibitions sought, are necessary and proportionate. This is an important power for police to bear in mind when gathering evidence about the index offence. Even if a DBO is unlikely to follow the arrest (or conviction) under consideration, it may well be important evidence capable of being relied upon in a future application.

4.11 **Public Nuisance**

Public nuisance is a common law offence, also known as common nuisance, committed if a person:

> **does something not warranted by law, or fails to do something which he is under a legal duty to do**

and as a result, either:

- there is a danger to the life, health, property or comfort **of the public**, or
- **the public's** ability to exercise their ordinary rights is obstructed.

The essence of the offence is that injury is caused to a section of the general public. Historically, it covered a large number of activities now covered by specific statutory legislation, particularly environmental, social or public health, such as keeping pigs near a public street and feeding them with offal. In *R v Rimmington* (2006) 1 AC 459 the House of Lords held that although public nuisance remained an offence at common law, most offences formerly chargeable as public nuisance were now covered by statute and should be prosecuted under the relevant statute unless there was good reason for doing otherwise.

Examples of behaviour which the courts have recently found to amount to public nuisance include conspiring to extinguish the floodlights at a Premier Division football match which would have plunged thousands of attendees into darkness, holding an 'acid house' party where there was loud music, disruption to traffic, woodlands being littered with excrement, and obstructing the highway.

It therefore will not apply where the behaviour affects only one person, or where the behaviour is a series of acts against a number of specific individuals, such as sending threatening packages to a number of specific individuals, or making obscene phone calls to a number of individual women—even if those individuals all live in the same community.

A bomb hoax could also amount to the offence (although this too is now the subject of a specific offence under s 51 of the Criminal Law Act 1977):

> In the ordinary course a hoax message which . . . inconvenienced only the recipient would lack the necessary public element. Very different would be a hoax message of the existence of a *public* danger, such as a hoax telephone call that an explosive device has been placed in a railway station. A hoax message of this character is capable of constituting the offence even though made to one person alone. This is because the message . . . was expected and intended to be passed via the police to users and potential users of the railway station. *In other words, the message was the means whereby the caller intended to cause public alarm and disruption.*
>
> R v Rimmington, paragraph 42 [emphasis added]

The principle that emerges, as confirmed in *R (Hope and Glory Public House Ltd) v City of Westminster Magistrates' Court* [2009] EWHC 1996 can be summarized in two key points:

- what is a public nuisance is a question of fact; and
- the public nuisance need not be very indiscriminate or very widespread, provided there is an effect on a sufficiently large number of members of the public to amount to something more than private nuisance.

In practice, although it remains an offence, considerable caution should be exercised before arresting a person for public nuisance. There will be only rare occasions where public nuisance is the only identifiable crime that has been committed. If the conduct does not clearly fall within the definition of a different offence, the officer should ask himself whether the conduct is criminal in character at all.

Further reading

- CPS Guidance to Prosecutors on Public Order Offences Incorporating The Charging Standard:
  <http://www.cps.gov.uk/legal/p_to_r/public_order_offences/>
- Home Office and CPS information on Drinking Banning Orders:
  <http://www.cps.gov.uk/legal/d_to_g/drinking_banning_orders/>,
  <http://www.homeoffice.gov.uk/drugs/alcohol/drinking-banning-orders/>

NOTES

NOTES

Processions, Assemblies, and Demonstrations

5.1 **Introduction**

One of the guiding principles of our common law is that a citizen is free to do anything not forbidden by the law. The incorporation of articles of the European Convention on Human Rights (ECHR) into our domestic law adds to the protections already present in our common law by placing restrictions on the interference with Convention rights. Specific protection is given in the ECHR to freedom of expression (Article 10) and freedom of peaceful assembly and freedom of association (Article 11).

Citizens of the UK are entitled to expect that peaceful assemblies, processions and demonstrations will not just be *permitted*, but will be positively *facilitated* by the police. This principle is emphasized by the European Court of Human Rights (ECtHR) in *Plattform Arzte fur Leben v Austria* (1988) 13 ER 204:

> A demonstration may annoy or give offence to persons opposed to the ideas or claims that it is seeking to promote. The participants must, however, be able to hold the demonstration without having to fear that they will be subjected to physical violence by their opponents; such a fear would be liable to deter associations or other groups supporting common ideas or interests from openly expressing their opinions on highly controversial issues affecting the community. In a democracy, the right to counter-demonstrate cannot extend to inhibiting the exercise of the right to demonstrate.
>
> Genuine, effective freedom of peaceful assembly cannot, therefore, be reduced to a mere duty on the part of the State not to interfere: a purely negative conception would not be compatible with the object and purpose of Article 11 . . . Article 11 sometimes requires *positive measures to be taken*, even in the sphere of relations between individuals, if need be.

So the obligation on the state—and thus the police—goes beyond non-interference and extends to the *facilitation* of lawful, peaceful protest.

However, the right to assemble, process or demonstrate is not an unqualified or unfettered right. The starting point is the duty of the protesting citizen in many cases to notify the police if they are planning a procession. While, in most cases, there is no legal duty to give notice of an assembly, the responsible citizen would also understand that intrusive policing of a peaceful demonstration is less likely if plenty of warning is given to the police. Given adequate notification and cooperative protestors (eg with regard to the setting of conditions), the police will be able to accommodate and facilitate lawful protest in the vast majority of cases.

The principle powers relating to the notification and policing of processions and assemblies are found in Part II of the Public Order Act 1986 (in this chapter, 'the Act' or the POA). This chapter focuses on those sections and the way they apply to the planning and policing of processions and assemblies.

It is also necessary to consider the other powers that apply to assemblies on the highway in public places, and obstruction of the highway.

5.2 **Definitions**

5.2.1 **'Procession'**

'Procession' itself is not defined in the Act. Normally it will not be in issue. In *Commissioner of Police for the Metropolis v Kay* [2007] 1 WLR 2915 the Court of Appeal considered whether the regular, monthly Critical Mass cycle ride in Central London amounted to a procession. It referred to the following definition of 'procession' from the Concise Oxford Dictionary:

1. A number of persons or vehicles moving forward in an orderly fashion
2. The action of moving in such a way
3. A relentless succession of people or things.

However, this dictionary definition is not exhaustive. For example, s 11 POA would include people moving forward together who are *individually* behaving in a disorderly way.

In *Flockhart v Robinson* [1950] 2 KB 498 it was held that the essence of a procession was that it proceeded along a route. However, it need not be a fixed or pre-determined route: see the judgment of Lord Rogers at 37–44 and the judgment of Lord Carswell at 61 in *Kay*. Nor does a procession have to have a pre-arranged starting point or a pre-arranged destination. Participants might be on foot, on bicycles like in *Kay*, in motor vehicles, such as a demonstration by London taxi drivers in their cabs, or a mixture of different forms of transport, such as a motorized float with an accompanying marching band in a street carnival.

A procession that comes to a temporary halt does not become an assembly, then a procession once more if it moves off again. However, once a procession reaches its final destination, it may turn into an assembly, depending on what the participants then do (this will be discussed later in this chapter). In most cases it will not be necessary for the senior officer at the scene to distinguish between the two because in practical terms the officer's legal powers will be the same. Provided he has in mind his powers under Part II of the Act, he does not have to have in mind whether he or she is acting under section 12 or section 14.

5.2.2 **'Public place'**

Definition of public place

Section 16 defines 'public place' as:

(a) any highway, or in Scotland any road within the meaning of the Roads (Scotland) Act 1984, and

(b) any place to which at the material time the public or any section of the public has access, on payment or otherwise, as of right or by virtue of express or implied permission.

This is a wider definition than for the purposes of some other legislation. It will include private roads, leisure centres, public gardens or parks, shopping centres, amusement parks, and other places that the public can access. Private land is included if the public have an implied right to be there, such as the grounds of a stately home which has opened to the public. (For a discussion of implied permission, see the explanation of trespass in section 9.2.1.)

5.2.3 'Assembly'

Definition of assembly

An assembly is defined in section 16 as 'an assembly of 2 or more persons in a public place which is wholly or partly open to the air'. 'Assembly' is to be given its everyday meaning: a group of people gathered together in one place for a common purpose.

Prior to 20 January 2004 the section required '20 or more persons' to be present in order for the section to apply. It is no exaggeration to say that this amendment to two persons now gives the police the power to regulate *any* gathering of any size in any public place which is open to the air. Even a married couple present together in a local park in order to exercise their dog would theoretically fall within the definition of an assembly.

The presence of the two or more people in one place must be more than incidental. They must intend to assemble: a crowd of people present in a market square to do their shopping will not fall within the section. However, if some members of that crowd stop to listen to a radical preacher in the square, the section probably will apply: they could be regarded as an assembly as in listening to the preacher they have a common purpose.

The 'open to the air' requirement means that indoor theatres, lecture halls, even some sports stadiums, are *not* covered by the Act. However, venues open to the air offering similar facilities are covered. For the new generation of sports stadiums with retractable roofs (such as the Millennium Stadium in Cardiff) it seems the Act will apply when the roof is retracted but will not apply if it is completely closed.

A single person cannot form an assembly, but they can be treated as remaining part of an assembly if they have temporarily separated from the main group. In the case of *Broadwith v Chief Constable of Thames Valley Police* [2000] Crim LR 924 Mr Broadwith had distanced himself from an assembly and then sought to enter a part of the highway that was, pursuant to conditions imposed under the Act, closed to the assembly. He appealed against, *inter alia*, his subsequent conviction for knowingly failing to comply with a condition contrary to s 14(5) of the Act. On appeal, it was confirmed by the Divisional Court that:

> groups . . . can only consist of individuals. It may be necessary according to the particular circumstances, in order to ensure that an assembly proceeds on

permitted lines, to take steps in relation to controlling the movements of particular individuals.

Mr Broadwith was found to have remained part of the assembly despite his geographical distance from it at the time of arrest, which was suggested (though not found as a fact) to be 100 yards.

5.2.4 'Demonstrations and protests'

Traditionally in domestic law, no formal distinction has been drawn between a procession or assembly that is a demonstration (political or otherwise) as opposed to one that has no such purpose. This position has been altered by the Serious Organised Crime and Police Act 2005 (SOCPA), but only in relation to a small area around the Houses of Parliament, where demonstrations are subject to specific notification and authorization procedures (see section 5.4.5).

Nowhere in public order legislation is the concept of a 'protest' defined. A protest may take many forms. Some may involve serious, even deliberate, criminality, which could itself even be the primary purpose of the event. Where a person attempts to mask criminality behind the claim of 'protest', they can have no expectation of special treatment. By contrast, the courts will take particular care when scrutinizing decisions taken during the policing of genuine 'political' protests or demonstrations. This is because of both the importance the courts have traditionally attached to the expression of political ideas, and also because s 12 of the Human Rights Act obliges all courts to take specific account of the Freedom of Expression enshrined in Article 10.

5.3 Processions

5.3.1 The requirement for advance notice of a procession

Section 11 of the Act requires that in most cases the organizers of a procession are obliged to give advance notice of the intended procession to the police.

Definition of advance notice of a procession

Section 11 of the Act states:

(1) Written notice shall be given in accordance with this section of any proposal to hold a public procession intended—

(a) to demonstrate support for or opposition to the views or actions of any person or body of persons,

(b) to publicise a cause or campaign, or

(c) to mark or commemorate an event,

unless it is not reasonably practicable to give any advance notice of the procession.

> (2) Subsection (1) does not apply where the procession is one commonly or customarily held in the police area (or areas) in which it is proposed to be held or is a funeral procession organized by a funeral director acting in the normal course of his business.

There is no separate legal concept of an 'unlawful procession'. A failure by the organizers to comply with section 11 is an offence but it does not render the procession itself unlawful. Nor does it necessarily follow that those taking part in the procession are committing an offence.

5.3.2 **Which processions require notification?**

The following process needs to be applied to consider whether an obligation arises (or arose) under section 11 of the Act:

1) Is it a procession? If so,
2) Is the intention of the procession covered by subsection 11(1)? If so,
3) Does the procession fall within either of the two exceptions in section 11(2)?

The first question is addressed at section 5.2.1 of this chapter. Subsection 11(1) is very wide, including all protests, campaigns, celebrations or commemorations. While almost all processions are likely to be covered, a 'fun run' organized merely to allow the participating joggers to enjoy going for a run would not fall within the section. However, if the organizers decided that the run was to be a sponsored run in aid of a local charity, the event would probably be covered by 11(1)(b) because while the primary aim might be to raise money, it would almost certainly also be intended to raise the profile of the cause for which the money was being raised.

Section 11(2) contains just two exemptions from the requirement to give advance notification of processions falling within s 11(1). Firstly, funeral processions organized by a professional funeral director are exempt. Public outpourings of grief that are not organized by a funeral director as part of the funeral will not be.

The second exemption is for a procession 'commonly or customarily held in the police area'. For traditional cultural events, such as a Good Friday procession, such an exemption clearly applies. But for how long does an event have to have been taking place to qualify as commonly or customarily held?

The case of *Kay*, first heard in March 2007, concerned the monthly Critical Mass cycle ride around the streets of central London that has taken place on the last Friday of each month since April 1994. Mr Kay, a participating cyclist, argued that there was no requirement to notify the Metropolitan Police, either because the event did not fall within s 11(1) or, if it did fall within s 11(1), it was exempt as being an event commonly or customarily held.

Did the event fall within s 11(1)?

The event is said to have no identifiable organizers, and although it begins from the same point each month, its route and destination vary. Pauses are sometimes made at points where a cyclist has been killed in an accident. Mr Kay argued that there was no formal motive for the event and it was suggested that different cyclists might attend with widely differing intentions. To the extent that a cyclist attended simply to enjoy the experience of cycling along the highway in a large group of cyclists, this intention would not fall within subsections (a)–(c) of s 11(1). However, it was found at first instance (*R (Kay) v Commissioner of Police for the Metropolis* [2006] 1 Pol LR 111) that a group of people in a procession could have a 'collective intent' and, if the dominant purpose was to highlight a cause, this collective intention would fall within section 11(1). This finding was not appealed, so the subsequent appeals to the Court of Appeal and the House of Lords proceeded on the basis that it *was* a procession that fell within the meaning of s 11(1).

Was the event commonly or customarily held? Mr Kay claimed that the Critical Mass cycle ride was customarily held as it had started from the same place on the last Friday of every month since April 1994. Against this, the Commissioner of Police argued that:

- A radical change of route to any customary procession altered the character and customary nature of the procession. However, the Divisional Court did not agree that a radical change of route altered the nature of a procession, or gave rise to any other justification requiring notice of what was commonly or customarily held in the police area.
- There had not been the constancy of intention for the purposes of s 11(1) of the Act, as the aims of the demonstration had altered over the 13 years since it began. The Divisional Court concluded on the evidence that the dominant collective intention had not significantly changed over time.

As a result of its findings on these two issues, it was decided by the Divisional Court that there was no requirement for notification.

However, the Court of Appeal (by a majority) disagreed: *R (Kay) v Commissioner of Police for the Metropolis* [2007] 1 WLR 2915. In overturning the decision, it found that the Critical Mass cycle ride, having no consistent route or end point, was not a procession commonly or customarily held. The majority in the Court of Appeal emphasized that the case was determined on its own facts. Its reasoning included the following observations:

- Neither route, destination nor timing were determinative of whether or not a procession was customary. There was no single feature that was determinative of whether or not a procession was commonly or customarily held.

- However, the direction in which any procession moves and its destination is certainly material, if not integral, to the issue of repetition which is at the heart of what is commonplace or customary.

This decision was itself overturned by the House of Lords in *R (Kay) v Commissioner of Police for the Metropolis* [2008] 1 WLR 2723. The House of Lords held that a procession *could* be commonly or customarily held, despite it following no pre-determined route. Lord Phillips of Worth Matravers stated at paragraph 16,

> I am in no doubt that the Critical Mass cycle rides that take place month after month have so many common features *that any person would consider that each month the same procession takes place* . . . I would identify the common features as follows: the procession is made up of cyclists; the procession starts at the same place; the procession takes place in the Metropolitan Police area; the procession starts at 6pm on the last Friday of every month; those who join the procession do so with a common intention; the procession is recognised and publicised with a single name . . . the procession chooses its route on a follow-my-leader basis'.

> [emphasis added]

Lord Matravers went on to observe at paragraph 22,

> . . . because of its spontaneous nature and because those who take part in it know where and when it is to start, it seems unlikely that Critical Mass now involves any advance planning or organization. If that is the true position I do not see how section 11 can have any application to Critical Mass.

The follow key practical points arise out of the case of *Kay*:

- Section 11(2) does not require a procession to be unfailingly held at a regular appointed time. A May Day procession would not lose its 'customary' status simply because it was cancelled due to bad weather the year before.
- It is the procession that must be customarily held, not the underlying cultural custom it reflects. A new procession to celebrate an ancient custom would not be exempt from the notification requirement.
- Minor alterations from year to year in the nature or route customarily held would not cause a procession to lose its exempt status. A Remembrance Day parade remains the same procession even if, for some reason, the organizers choose a different route from church to war memorial, or, indeed, a slightly different starting or end point in any particular year provided that, having regard to all the circumstances, the procession remains the same.

5.3.3 **Who is an organizer?**

The Act does not contain a definition of the word 'organizer'. In most cases it will be clear by a person's conduct whether or not they are an organizer of a procession, though the use of the internet and smart phones has the potential to obscure who is working behind the scenes to make a procession occur.

Difficulties in identifying whether or not an individual is an organizer tend to arise in relation to the 'problem' processions where the risk of disorder or disruption is greatest.

Whilst 'organizer' is to be given its everyday meaning, this does not always mean it will be obvious who counts as an organizer. For example, is a steward of a march an organizer? Is the publisher who sets out the format for the flyers for a demonstration an organizer?

The case of *DPP v Baillie* [1995] Crim LR 426 is the only modern case that deals directly with the type of conduct that will make a person an organizer. The case concerned the organization of an assembly rather than a procession, but the same principles of construction would apply to either aspect of public event planning. The police believed that a 'festival' was going to take place, although they had not received formal notification of the date or venue. Mr Baillie was identified as distributing flyers with information about the festival. He also provided information via a telephone answering machine and answering phone calls. At first instance, Mr Baillie was found to be an organizer of the event.

Although the appeal was allowed on different grounds, the Divisional Court found that there was sufficient evidence available to regard Mr Bailie as an organizer of the event. Whilst Mr Baillie's involvement could be categorized as merely disseminating information, in circumstances where there was no official or public announcement about the details of the festival an individual disseminating the details of the event would in normal terms be sufficient to count as an organizer.

The majority in *Flockhart v Robinson* [1950] 2 KB expressed the view that 'the person who organises the route is the person who organises the procession'. However, this definition is likely to be at once both too narrow and too wide. It is too narrow in that it would not catch the publicizers (such as Mr Baillie), but too wide in that it might include a steward who is merely directing a procession, or the cyclists at the head of the column of a Critical Mass procession, rather than participating in the arrangements necessary for the event to occur in the first place. In contrast to this, in his minority judgment in *Flockhart*, Finnemore J stated:

> The mere fact that a person takes part in a procession would not of itself be enough. I do not think that the fact that the defendant was the leading person in the procession would by itself be enough, although it might be some evidence to be considered . . . I think organising a procession means something in the nature of arranging or planning a procession.

The issues raised in *Baillie* have obvious parallels with the difficulties sometimes encountered in identifying the organizers of actions by animal rights or environmental activists. The problems of identification of an organizer in the case also foreshadowed the problems that now arise in relation to the publicizing of events via the internet and messaging services. Taking into account the limited case law and the rapid developments in information technology over the last 20 years, it is suggested that, as a general rule, a participant is not to be regarded as an organizer unless:

- prior to the event, he takes an active part to some degree in the planning, preparation or facilitation of, or publicity for a procession, or
- during the event, he can be identified as deliberately directing or influencing the route, progress or activities of the procession and its participants.

As ever, every case will turn on its facts.

5.3.4 **Notice requirements imposed on the organizer**

Unless the procession falls within one of the exceptions set out above, the organizer of a procession is obliged by s 11 to give advance notice to the police. The organizer is only relieved of the requirement to give advance notice if it is not reasonably practicable to do so. This does not apply to uncertainties such as the exact start point or time etc, but only to the lack of opportunity to provide notice in advance. Section 11(1) only provides an exemption for spontaneous processions, or those organized at very short notice. There is no formal minimum time between organization and a procession below which the organizer is exempt from providing notice. However, the exemption is likely to apply only to those processions organized in a matter of hours, rather than days, since days would easily enable the organizer to give the police notice. Even those processions organized in a matter of hours would not prevent an organizer giving the police late notice.

Contents of notice

The notice must be in writing, see s 11(1). Section 11(3) provides that the notice must specify:

(1) the date when it is intended to hold the procession,
(2) the time when it is intended to start it,
(3) its proposed route, and
(4) the name and address of the person (or of one of the persons) proposing to organize it.

A notice must supply all of this information, and a notice that does not do so will not satisfy the requirements of s 11. However, there is no legal requirement that the notice be in any particular form. The standard forms provided by police forces for members of the public will inevitably request significantly more information than that set out above. The organizer commits no offence if he refuses to supply this information, however important the police may feel the information is to allow them to plan for the procession properly.

However, an inability or unwillingness to provide other information, such as the reason for the procession and the numbers expected to attend, is very likely to impact upon the police decision whether or not to impose conditions and the nature of those conditions (see section 5.3.5).

Timing and delivery of notice

Section 11(4) states that the notice must be delivered to a police station in the police area in which it is proposed the procession will start. It does not have to be delivered to the closest police station, but may be delivered to *any* police station, provided it is to the correct constabulary.

The written notice may be delivered by hand or, in certain circumstances, by recorded delivery. Section 11(5) and 11(6) set precise times for the service of notice on the police.

Section 11(5) provides that if the amount of notice given is more than six clear days then service may be provided by way of *recorded* delivery (not first class post) or hand delivery. However, the notice *must be delivered*. The organizer is not entitled to rely on any presumption that because the notice has been sent, it has been delivered. It would obviously be sensible for any organizer to check that a notice has actually been delivered, rather than assume that it has arrived.

If notice is not provided more than six clear days before the procession, it must be delivered to the appropriate police station by hand. If it is not reasonably practicable to deliver the notice more than six clear days before the procession is intended to be held, then the obligation remains on the organizers to deliver (by hand) the notice as soon as is reasonably practicable.

Interpreted strictly, there is no minimum time prior to the intended start of a procession beyond which the obligation to give written notice stops. Even hours before an intended procession is due to begin, an organizer remains obliged to hand deliver written notice.

Offences relating to notification

Offences arising out of a failure to provide notification (or correct notification) do not arise until the procession is actually held. Section 11(7) creates two offences relating to notice:

- s 11(7)(a)—the organizer is guilty of an offence if he fails to satisfy the notice requirements set out in 11(1) and 11(3)–(6);
- s 11(7)(b)—the organizer is guilty of an offence where the date of the procession, start time or route is different from the date, time or route specified in the notice.

There are two defences available to an organizer who is prosecuted:

- In relation to either offence, under section 11(8) the organizer has a defence if he is able to prove that he did not know of, and neither suspected nor had reason to suspect, the failure to satisfy the notice requirements or the difference of date, time or route.

- In relation to an offence under s 11(7)(b) arising from a difference from the notified date, time or route, under section 11(9) the organizer has a defence if he is able to prove that the difference arose either from circumstances beyond his control, or as a result of something done with the agreement of a police officer or by his direction.

5.3.5 **Powers to impose conditions on processions under section 12**

All processions are subject to the potential imposition of conditions under s 12.

Section 12 does not replace or override any other statutory or common law powers available to the police, nor does the option of imposing conditions under section 12 oblige the police to use powers under it rather than alternatives. The police retain their full common law powers to prevent a breach of the peace, whether or not conditions have been imposed under s 12. There may be circumstances where the police take action on a different legal basis which has a similar (even identical) effect on a procession to the imposition of conditions.

The House of Lords stated in *R (Laporte) v Chief Constable of Gloucestershire* [2007] 2AC 105 that:

> The rights to freedom of expression, and assembly and association, which are protected by Articles 10 and 11 of the ECHR respectively, are of the greatest importance to the proper functioning of any democracy. Any intrusion upon the rights, either by the developing common law or by the intervention of statute law, has to be jealously scrutinised.

It must be anticipated that, if asked to do so, the courts will closely examine the basis for the imposition under Part II of the Public Order Act 1986 of any conditions on processions or assemblies.

When can conditions be imposed on a procession?

Section 12(2) draws a distinction between two stages in relation to a procession. The later stage is the procession and the immediate build up to it, defined as the point from which 'persons are assembling with a view to taking part'. The first stage is any time prior to this point.

Conditions can be imposed at any time, either prior to, during the build up (as defined in section 12(2)) or during the procession itself. Conditions can be imposed whether or not notification of the procession has been given by the organizers.

Who can impose the conditions on processions?

Conditions can only be imposed by the 'senior police officer'.

Prior to a procession being held (the 'first stage' described above), this is the chief police officer for the area in which the procession is to be held. This power may be delegated under s 15 of the Act to an assistant chief officer (ie assistant chief constable or assistant commissioner).

During a procession, 'senior police officer' simply means the most senior officer present at the scene. It is important that when planning the policing of a procession, those in overall command consider carefully *who* at the scene will be the officer responsible for undertaking this role.

How are conditions to be communicated?

If conditions are imposed prior to the later, build up, stage they *must* be in writing. Furthermore, they must be *'given* in writing' to the organizers. The word 'given' is not defined, and would probably include the conditions being posted to the organizers. However, given that criminal proceedings may result if an organizer does not comply with the conditions, steps should always be taken to ensure that (i) the organizers have received, and understood, the conditions, and (ii) the police can *prove* proper service of the conditions. Ideally this should be achieved during a face-to-face meeting on a day *prior* to the procession, though the realities of policing and lack of cooperation from the organizers may demand sub-optimal service of conditions.

Plainly if the organizers do not wish to identify themselves, service of written conditions becomes difficult, though the maxim must be for the police to do their best to serve those who appear to be organizers. As a matter of risk management, police commanders could do worse than advertising intended conditions on social network media and so forth so as to demonstrate to any reviewing court their good faith in attempting to communicate the conditions sought to be imposed.

The case of *Brehony v Chief Constable of Greater Manchester* [2005] EWHC 640 concerned the imposition of conditions on an assembly under s 14, rather than a procession under s 12, but the same principles must apply. The Divisional Court stated that in advance of the event, the notice imposing conditions should include:

- each of the bases the chief officer was relying upon in seeking to impose conditions; and
- the reasons for forming that belief.

The reasons do not have to be given in detail but must be sufficient to enable the organizers to understand *why* conditions are being imposed, and to enable a court (if the matter goes to court) to assess, once the judge is presented with evidence as to the facts, whether the belief was reasonable or not. The conditions must be clear, in order to avoid genuine confusion on the part of the organizers of the procession.

During the second stage, ie in the immediate build-up to or during the procession, conditions do not have to be in writing. Section 12(1) refers to conditions being 'imposed' on organizers and/or participants, but does not specify the way in which the conditions being imposed are to be communicated during a procession. Some thought should always be given in advance to what steps will be required to ensure effective communication with the participants. If it is anticipated prior to a procession that the imposition of conditions during the procession might become necessary, it is vital that careful thought is given in advance to the method of communication with the crowd. Methods of communication are likely to include police amplified audio systems (loudhailers), personal communications by police officers and, potentially, social network and messaging sites. It was accepted (without argument) in *Brehony* that there was no obligation to give reasons for conditions imposed at the time of the procession.

What is the basis for imposing conditions?

Conditions may only be imposed under section 12(1) if, having regard to the intended (or actual) time or place of the procession, the circumstances in which it will be held and its route, the senior police officer reasonably believes either that:

- the procession may result in **serious** public disorder, **serious** damage to property or **serious** disruption to the life of the community; or that
- the purpose of organizers is the intimidation of others with a view to compelling them not to do an act they have a right to do or to do an act they have a right not to do.

The requirement of reasonable belief means that it is good practice that the senior officer records *at the time* the basis for his or her belief. The test is the same in relation to stage 1 or stage 2, although the basis for the belief is likely to be different at each stage. The most important aspects to consider are the 'circumstances' of the procession. This word is wide enough to cover such matters as the conduct of participants at previous processions organized by the same people, or the actions or plain intentions of the organizers, eg to foment violence or serious disorder.

However, the time and route must not be ignored—it can easily be envisaged how a procession might have the potential to cause confrontation if it occurred at a particular time or location (eg outside a mosque at Friday prayers) where the same participants and focus would not pose such a risk to public order in a different place or at another time. Another obvious example is the routes taken by processions of the Orange Orders in Northern Ireland.

The concept of 'disruption to the life of the community' in section 12(1)(a) is not a legal term commonly found elsewhere in English law. In *Re Murphy* (Northern Ireland Court of Appeal, unreported, 11 July 1991) on the corresponding words in the Public Order (NI) Order 1987 Hutton LCJ observed that:

> . . . in applying those words it is appropriate for the senior officer to take account, not only of physical matters such as the disruption of traffic and the

blocking of streets, but also of the annoyance and upset which may be caused to a community by a procession passing through it, if it is shown that as a consequence there is disruption to life in that community.

'Community' extends beyond those who are resident in the area, and would include workers, local businesses and their customers.

The senior officer must believe that the procession may result in *serious* public disorder; damage to property; disruption to the life of the community. The requirement that the negative impact be serious is a threshold requirement: a degree of disruption which is less than serious would not justify even very minor conditions being imposed. The word 'serious' is not, and could not sensibly be, defined. However, it must mean more than minimal and will be dependent upon all the factual circumstances, which the senior officer would do well to record.

For example, the mere fact that traffic would be slowed, even halted, over several hours to allow a procession to take place might still amount to serious disruption, such that the threshold would be met for the imposition of proportionate conditions to limit such disruption to traffic.

'Disruption' should be treated separately from the motivation or conduct of the organizers. Entirely well-meaning organizers may still attempt to organize a procession which may cause serious disruption to the life of the local community. The procession (or, under s 14, assembly), or the participants in it, do not have to be the source or initiator of the anticipated disorder. For example, the senior officer is entitled to take into account the interaction with a counter-demonstration, if there is the prospect of a counter-demonstration occurring. In paragraph 96 of the first instance decision in *Austin v Commissioner of Police for the Metropolis*, Tugendhat J stated:

> I do not accept the submission that the power to impose conditions can only be exercised under either section where the disorder results from the assembly or procession itself, and not from other groups, even if they have broken away from the assembly or procession. The provisions of s 12(1)(a) and 14(1)(a) include no reference to the source of the risk (as contrasted with subsection (1) (b), where the risk must emanate from the organisers).

There are at least three potential circumstances where a legal challenge to the imposition of conditions can be anticipated:

- Firstly, prior to the event by judicial review, perhaps challenging the nature of the conditions imposed or the assessment of the senior officer of the prospect of serious consequences or intimidation.
- Secondly, as a defence to a prosecution of an organizer or participant for breaching the conditions.
- Thirdly, in a civil action after the event, perhaps claiming infringement of the right to assemble and/or freedom of speech.

It may well be that in the event of such a challenge, the court would be reluctant to interfere with the reasonable assessment of an experienced police officer. The court is likely to give such an officer a margin of operational latitude. However, any challenge brought would require the court to satisfy itself that the senior officer *honestly* believed that the basis for imposing conditions was present, and that he had sufficient (ie objectively reasonable) grounds on which to properly reach this conclusion. Such grounds can be based upon intelligence, including intelligence to which public interest immunity (from disclosure) might apply.

The senior officer does not need to be satisfied that, in the absence of conditions, damage, disorder or disruption would *definitely*, or would *probably*, occur. He or she needs to be satisfied only that they *may* occur (see *Brehony*, paragraph 20). However, the prospect of serious consequences needs to be real rather than theoretical or fanciful.

Intention to intimidate

Intimidation is not defined in the Act. A case that dealt with the meaning of intimidation under the predecessor Act to the POA was *R v Jones* (1974) 59 Cr App R 120, where it was suggested that intimidation included 'putting persons in fear by the exhibition of force or violence or the threat of violence or the threat of force or violence; and there is no limitation restricting the meaning to cases of violence or threats of violence to the person'. If this observation were followed, then intimidation would include putting someone in fear of having property damaged, which need not be that person's property. The observations in *R v Jones* are extremely helpful in that they should focus the senior officer's mind on the threat of force or violence.

However, the definition from *Jones* set out above is not comprehensive: in *Thomas v National Union of Mineworkers (South Wales Area) and others* [1986] 1 Ch 20, Scott J expressed the view that the presence of large numbers of silent, glowering striking miners outside a colliery could itself be intimidating.

Picketing (now covered by the Trade Union and Labour Relations (Consolidation) Act 1992 (TULRCA)) is dealt with at section 6.6. It is a good example of the problem in identifying the line between intimidation and (for example) persuading a person by other means, such as shaming them into changing their behaviour. A worker might decline to cross an entirely peaceful picket line because of a fear of embarrassment or shame if identified as a strike-breaker.

In the context of anti-abortion campaigners protesting outside a clinic, the Divisional Court said the following in *DPP v Fidler* [1992] 1 WLR 91:

> The evident purpose of the demonstrators' behaviour was to embarrass and shock and shame those concerned into abstaining from abortion. In my judgment, the justices were right to find that this purpose, thus implemented, was a purpose of dissuasion rather than one of compulsion.

Behaviour by participants in a procession that was likely to embarrass or shame members of the public is unlikely, by itself, to be sufficient to amount to intimidating conduct. The extent to which a deliberate attempt to shock members of the public might cross the line from dissuasion into compulsion or intimidation will be fact-sensitive.

The very purpose of many processions is to seek to alter the views, opinions or actions of other people. However, there will be occasions where the purported legitimate purpose is little more than a pretext for intimidatory behaviour by the participants. Nevertheless, even in these cases there will often be practical difficulties in establishing that there are reasonable grounds to believe the *purpose* of the organizers is to intimidate others, rather than such intimidation arising from the number of participants, subject matter of the protest or style of the protest. Obviously, the behaviour of the participants on previous occasions will be of some relevance, as will the publicity materials which the organizers are either planning to use at the procession or have prepared for other occasions. The senior police officer is entitled to infer from the behaviour of the organizers that their intent is to cause intimidation, provided that the basis for this inference is evidentially sound (which, again, may include intelligence materials).

KEY POINTS—THRESHOLD FOR IMPOSING CONDITIONS ON A PROCESSION

Conditions may only be imposed under s 12 if, having regard to

- the time or place; and
- the route or proposed route; and
- the circumstances of the procession;

the senior officer believes on objectively reasonable grounds that the procession *may* result in *serious*

- public disorder;
- damage to property;
- disruption to the life of the community; or

if it is reasonably believed that the *intention* of the organizers is

- the intimidation of others with a view to compelling them not to do an act they have a right to do, or to do an act they have a right not to do.

5.3.6 What conditions can be imposed?

Section 12(1) states that, provided the threshold conditions discussed above are met, the senior officer:

> . . . may give directions imposing on the persons organising or taking part in the procession such conditions as appear to him *necessary to prevent* such disorder, damage, disruption or intimidation, including conditions as to the

145

route of the procession or prohibiting it from entering any public place specified in the directions.

The key is that the conditions must be 'necessary to prevent' the particular problems identified. Given that s 12 must also be interpreted in accordance with Articles 10 (freedom of expression) and 11 (freedom of assembly) of the ECHR, the conditions will also have to be proportionate to the problems the senior officer is trying to prevent.

The express proviso in ECHR Article 11(2) states, 'No restrictions shall be placed on the exercise of these rights other than such as are prescribed by law and are necessary in a democratic society in the interests of national security or public safety, for the prevention of disorder or crime'.

Therefore the fundamental test for any condition under consideration is that it must be:

(1) **relevant** to the particular problem;
(2) **necessary** to prevent the particular problem; and
(3) **proportionate** to the anticipated scale and/or seriousness of the problem.

There is no formal difference between the conditions that can be imposed in advance and those that can be imposed during the immediate build up or procession. However, there are obvious practical differences between what is feasible to impose by way of condition during the procession itself, compared to that which can be the subject of negotiation and agreement around a table some time in advance.

It will normally be straightforward to identify conditions that relate directly to the risks identified and are capable of reducing the prospect of these events unfolding. However, any 'standard' conditions are vulnerable to criticism, particularly on the grounds of lack of relevance to the individual risk factors presented by the procession. Instead, it is better that each time notification of a procession is given thought should be given by the police commanders to each particular proposed condition afresh.

Section 12(1) singles out for particular consideration alterations to the route of the procession and/or prohibition from entering any specified public place. It is easy to see how these particular features of a procession could be altered via a condition which would have the effect of reducing the risk of the consequences set out above, for example, by altering the route of the procession to avoid a particular flash point. However, section 12(1) should not be read as suggesting that conditions concerning the route should be considered in preference to others. The obvious categories of conditions that should be considered by police commanders include those dealing with:

- date, time and duration of procession
- route
- exclusion from a particular place

- number of participants
- the gathering point or points
- stewarding
- items to be carried by participants, eg placards and banners
- use of items such as loudhailers, whistles and air horns
- the extent to which vehicles or animals will be permitted on the procession
- the use of masks, scarves, hats, balaclavas or face paint.

This last feature is subject also to section 60 and 60AA of the Criminal Justice and Public Order Act 1994 (CJPOA) and is dealt with in more detail in section 5.5.4. However, the presence of those s 60/60AA powers does not prevent conditions with similar effect being imposed under section 12. It will be of mutual benefit to the police, organizers and participants if such a condition can be discussed and publicized in advance of a procession.

Conditions must also be proportionate. If a senior officer were able to satisfy the court that a condition were necessary to prevent the adverse consequences, it would normally also be proportionate. However, this will not necessarily be the case. It was confirmed in *Austin* at first instance (at paragraph 92) that conditions which are so demanding, that they amount *in effect* to a ban, are an improper use of the power and so are unlawful on ordinary public law principles. So it is important that any such conditions do not in effect prevent the procession from occurring.

It is important for police commanders to bear in mind that, while it will normally be the disorder or damage by the participants in the procession that is to be the subject of hopefully 'preventive' conditions, there are cases where it may be necessary to impose conditions on a procession in order to prevent misconduct by other people who are not directly involved in it. The most frequent example of this is the procession that prompts either a counter-demonstration, or risks provoking a hostile response by onlookers. Race-related processions are particularly prone to this type of response.

In these circumstances, the police should try to protect, rather than restrict, the rights of those participating lawfully, as far as they are able to do so with the resources available. In *Brehony*, the following statement from the decision of the ECtHR in *Ärzte für das Leben v Austria* (1988) 13 EHRR 204 was specifically approved. It is a very helpful guide on the approach to be taken to policing processions or demonstrations where there is the prospect of a counter-demonstration:

> A demonstration may annoy or give offence to persons opposed to the ideas of claims that it is seeking to promote. The participants must, however, be able to hold the demonstration without having to fear that they will be subjected to physical violence by their opponents; such a fear would be liable to deter associations or other groups supporting common ideas or interests from openly expressing their opinions on highly controversial issues affecting the community. In a democracy the right to counter-demonstrate cannot extend to inhibiting the exercise of the right to demonstrate.

However, in many cases minor curtailment of an innocent participant's freedom of expression will be entirely proportionate. For example, participants who hold extreme political views on immigration may wish to hold a peaceful procession through an area which has a very large population of migrants. Even though the tone of the procession was to be measured, the very presence of these marchers in the area may make violence very likely. To police such a procession through the sensitive area would be possible, but may require an immense use of police resources that could be saved if the route of the march were altered by just a few streets. Such a condition could probably be successfully defended as relevant, necessary and proportionate. That said, to alter protestors' desired route or time, etc, should always still be regarded as a measure of last resort.

As stated, for an intended procession, conditions which are so demanding that they amount in effect to a ban, are an improper use of the power under section 12, and as such are unlawful on ordinary public law principles. However once a procession is under way, conditions can be imposed which would have the practical effect of bringing the procession to a (premature) end.

Offences

Both organizers and participants may be guilty of knowingly failing to comply with conditions imposed under s 12(4).

Organizer: In order to prove that an offence has been committed by an organizer it will be necessary to show the following matters:

(1) He was an organizer—see above;
(2) The condition in question was imposed under section 12. It will not normally be sufficient for the senior office to rely on any direction given by him and it should be assumed that he will need to show that at the time he gave the direction, he was intending to impose a condition under section 12 of the Act;
(3) The condition was lawful;
(4) The organizer knew of the condition. Provided the guidance set out above as to meeting with the organizers is followed, for written conditions this should not pose a problem. However, a particular organizer may not have attended a planning meeting and some organizers of protests (such as of the more radical anti-globalization or green protestors) are unlikely to wish to reveal themselves as organizers, as to do so makes the police's job easier and reduces the element of 'surprise' which such organizers often seek;
(5) The organizer knowingly failed to comply with the condition. 'Knowingly' in this context includes deliberately not making enquiries or closing one's mind.

If the above elements are established, the organizer may still have a defence if he can show that the failure to comply arose from circumstances beyond his control. Provided an organizer has take reasonable efforts to bring the conditions to the attention of the participants, and has complied with other conditions relating to the stewarding of the procession, it is likely that he would not be held criminally liable for sudden behaviour by participants that he was unable to control. However, the burden of establishing such a defence is on the defendant.

Participant: A participant is also guilty of an offence under section 12(5) if he knowingly fails to comply with a condition. Similar elements must be proved to those set out above. However, in relation to an individual participant, it may be more difficult to prove that the participant knew about the condition. Where it is practicable to do so, it would be wise for police officers first to inform participants of a particular condition and then to warn them to comply with the same before finally seeking to effect an arrest. Arrests are, of course, labour intensive and remove officers from the scene, thereby reducing the overall resilience of the police presence. The giving of a warning may assist in avoiding the need to arrest, but also if an arrest is necessary, will demonstrate both a proportionate response and assist in proving the participant knew of the condition.

The reality is that the use of conditions on processions is fraught with difficulty when the organizers do not wish to cooperate with the police. But the judicious use of conditions is worthwhile even in such circumstances, not least as it provides a useful contextual backdrop for the police if the procession in question generates litigation against the police.

5.3.7 **Powers to ban processions**

Section 13 of the Act sets out the circumstances in which processions may be banned.

Section 13 makes a distinction between the banning of processions in London and those outside London. The two regimes are different.

In either case, in order to seek to impose a prohibition, the chief officer must believe, on reasonable grounds, that whatever powers are exercised under section 12, they will not be sufficient to prevent the public procession (or processions) from resulting in serious public disorder. Such a belief must be based on reasonable grounds. It is likely that on most occasions the principle basis for a ban would be recent serious or escalating violence at similar or related processions.

The only consequence that justifies prohibition is the potential for **serious public disorder**: disruption to the community, damage to property (if it does not amount to public disorder) or intimidation are not a sufficient basis, however serious or high the likelihood.

If challenged, any ban on processions is likely to be subject to close judicial scrutiny under the Human Rights Act. It is likely that the requirement of proportionality will be carefully considered and it is suggested that it will only be found satisfied in cases where the chief officer is able to demonstrate that, given the resources available to him, there were no reasonable policing options available that would have reduced the risk of violence to an acceptable level, such that the option of seeking to ban a procession (or processions) really was the last resort.

Banning processions outside London

Section 13(1) and (2) provide:

(1) If at any time the chief officer of police reasonably believes that, because of particular circumstances existing in any district or part of a district, the powers under section 12 will not be sufficient to prevent the holding of public processions in that district or part from resulting in serious public disorder, he shall apply to the council of the district for an order prohibiting for such period not exceeding 3 months as may be specified in the application the holding of all public processions (or of any class of public procession so specified) in the district or part concerned.

(2) On receiving such an application, a council may with the consent of the Secretary of State make an order either in the terms of the application or with such modifications as may be approved by the Secretary of State.

Outside London, a chief officer seeking to impose a ban must first apply to the council for the district within which the procession or processions are due to take place for an order prohibiting all public processions in the district or specified classes of public processions, either in the whole district or in part of it. Unlike within London, the Secretary of State has no direct involvement.

Further, the wording of s 13(1) suggests that, unlike s 13(4), the chief of police has no discretion as to whether or not he makes the application. If he is of the view that conditions will be insufficient to prevent serious public disorder, he 'shall' apply to the council for a banning order. It is then for the district council to decide whether to agree to the prohibition sought.

Banning processions within London

Within London, the power to ban processions is contained in s 13(4):

(4) If at any time the Commissioner of Police for the City of London or the Commissioner of Police for the Metropolis reasonably believes that, because of particular circumstances existing in his police area or part of it, the powers under section 12 will not be sufficient to prevent the holding of public processions in that area or part from resulting in serious public disorder, he may with the consent of the Secretary of State make an order prohibiting for such period not exceeding 3 months as may be specified in the order the holding of all public processions (or of any class of public procession so specified) in the area or part concerned.

Commissioners of Police for the City of London or for the Metropolis may make an order prohibiting all processions, or a specified class of processions in the whole or part of the area. However, in order to do so, the Commissioner must first seek the consent of the Secretary of State. The Secretary of State has no power to initiate the process.

Local authorities within the London area have no direct input into whether or not a ban is imposed. Subject to the consent of the Secretary of State, it is the two Commissioners who decide whether it is necessary to seek to ban public processions. They are not obliged to seek a ban, but have a discretion as to whether or not to seek to do so.

Scope and duration of ban

Section 13 provides that the duration of the ban may be any period up to, but not exceeding, three months. Proportionality is again a vital consideration. The chief officer remains under an obligation:

(i) to seek only the duration which is the minimum reasonably necessary to prevent serious public disorder
(ii) to apply to have the prohibition revoked or varied as soon as the basis for seeking the prohibition no longer applies, or as soon as the risk of disorder needs can be managed without a total prohibition.

Prior to the Human Rights Act it may have been felt fairer, clearer and simpler to ban all processions rather than to specify a particular group or particular type of procession that was likely to cause serious public disorder. Now, a total ban would be at significant risk of legal challenge on the basis that it was a disproportionate, unnecessary and/or arbitrary curtailment of a person's rights under Articles 10 or 11 of the Convention. There is no definition or guidance on how a prohibited class of procession is to be specified. Provided it is realistic to do so, the chief officer should attempt expressly to limit any prohibition sought, such as by limiting the prohibition to specific organizers, groups of organizers, types of procession and/or geographical areas.

Section 13(5) provides that any prohibition may be revoked or varied by the same process applying to the original application. Having approved a prohibition, a district council (or, in London, the Secretary of State) does not have power to vary or revoke a prohibition unless it is approached by the chief officer. This would not prevent an informal approach being made to the chief officer.

Offences

If processions (or a particular class of procession) have been banned in the area, a person, knowing the public procession is banned, is guilty of an offence if he:

• organizes a banned procession, contrary to s 13(7);
• participates in a banned procession, contrary to s 13(8); or
• incites others to do so, contrary to s 13(9).

A person may be guilty of the offence of organizing a banned procession whether or not the procession actually takes place.

5.4 **Assemblies**

The principle statutory provision governing the powers to control public assemblies is s 14 of the POA. However, over the last 20 years, the relatively limited power to impose conditions on assemblies under s 14 of the POA has been supplemented by a number of further statutory powers to control specific types of assembly, including:

- The creation of the 'trespassory assembly' under the POA sections 14A–14C and the powers to deal with it, including the power to turn people away who might be on their way to a trespassory assembly;
- The offence of trespass on designated sites: s 128 SOCPA;
- Demonstrations near the Houses of Parliament, regulated by sections 132–138 of SOCPA.

The powers under s 14 are addressed first, followed by these later powers. The definition of an assembly set out at 5.2.3 relates only to gatherings that are subject to the powers under the POA. Other Acts have their own definitions of the type of assembly the powers are to cover.

In addition to the recent legislation, there a number of Acts of local effect, in particular the Metropolitan Police Act 1839, that contain specific public order powers. These local powers are beyond the scope of this book.

5.4.1 **Powers to impose conditions on assemblies**

There is no notification requirement in the POA in relation to assemblies. It requires little thought to see how such a requirement would be unworkable—friends meeting together in the park for a picnic would be required to notify the police of their intention.

However, the circumstances in which conditions can be imposed on assemblies under section 14 of the Act follow closely those under s 12 relating to processions. The range of conditions that can be imposed is more limited, reflecting the somewhat more predictable impact of a static gathering.

Organizers of an assembly

Conditions can only be imposed on the organizers of an assembly and not the participants. See section 5.3.3 for the question of who may or may not be an organizer.

Who can give directions?

Prior to an assembly taking place, s 14(2) states that it is the chief officer who must give the directions imposing conditions on the assembly. As with processions, this power may be delegated. Once an assembly is in progress, directions may be given by the most senior in rank of the police officers present at the scene.

When can conditions be imposed on an assembly?

As for a procession, conditions may be imposed only if, having regard to the time and place of the assembly, the senior officer present reasonably believes that:

(a) the assembly may result in **serious**:

   public disorder;

   damage to property; or

   disruption to the life of the community; or

(b) the purpose of the persons organizing the assembly is the intimidation of others with a view to compelling them not to do an act they have a right to do, or to do an act they have a right not to do.

These matters are dealt with in detail at section 5.3.5 in relation to processions.

What format should the conditions take?

Conditions imposed by (or through the delegated authority of) the chief officer in advance of the assembly must be recorded as directions in writing. There are no specific provisions as to the service of these directions on the organizers. If the directions are sent in the post, it is important that the police do their best to verify that the organizers have received and understood the conditions prior to the assembly taking place. This may best be achieved by face to face meetings or visits by the police to the apparent organizers.

Directions given while an assembly is in progress may be given verbally. However, it is highly desirable that the officer imposing the conditions records in writing at the time or immediately afterwards:

- the name or names of the organizers that the conditions were communicated to;
- the conditions imposed;
- the reasons for each of the conditions imposed;
- the basis for the officer's belief that it was necessary to impose such conditions.

> **KEY POINTS—GOOD PRACTICE: GIVING DIRECTIONS IMPOSING CONDITIONS UNDER S 12 OR S 14**
>
> Prior to the procession/assembly or build up:
>
> - Must be in writing
> - Must be communicated in writing to the organizers
> - May be delivered by post, but this will provide little evidence of knowledge by the organizers
> - Best practice is to arrange one or more meetings with the organizers, prior to the day of the procession
> - For awkward or evasive organizers, consider video evidence of personal service
> - Consider use of social network media.
>
> During the assembly/procession or build up:
>
> - Need not be in writing: no mandatory method of communication
> - Loudhailers/loudspeakers to be available
> - Consider use of social network media
> - Once imposed, change the conditions as little as practically possible.

What are the conditions that can be imposed on an assembly?

The nature of the conditions that can be imposed upon an assembly are limited. However, these powers can be used alongside other statutory or common law powers, such as those to prevent a breach of the peace. Under section 14(1) the senior officer can only impose conditions relating to:

- the place at which the assembly may be (or continue to be) held;
- its maximum duration;
- or the maximum number of persons who may constitute it.

Such conditions can only be imposed to the extent that they appear to be necessary to the officer in order to prevent the anticipated disorder, damage, disruption or intimidation. In order for any condition to be valid, it must be:

- relevant to the particular problem;
- necessary to prevent the particular problem; and
- proportionate to the anticipated scale and/or seriousness of the problem.

Case study

Imposition of conditions on an assembly

The police learn that a group of friends are planning a party, open to the public, in a public park. The party is to celebrate a high-profile cricket match. Previous similar events have been attended by large numbers of people, with a sound system playing patriotic songs, to which the crowd sing along. Previous events have peaceful to start with, but degenerated into drunken disorder late in the evening. There has been no history of confrontation between rival supporters.

A condition could be imposed for a finish time well before disorder is likely. However, conditions prohibiting the presence of alcohol or the playing of music, although relevant, are not conditions that can be formally imposed under s 14. There may be other powers available, such as local authority powers, to deal with alcohol (see section 4.10.4) and noise.

Although there are particular assemblies which may be prohibited (see further in this chapter), there is no general power to ban an assembly. A condition that amounts to a ban on an assembly would not be lawful. However, once an assembly is in progress, a direction could be imposed that would bring the assembly to an immediate end.

In *Moos v Commissioner of Police for the Metropolis* [2011] EWHC 957 (Admin) the High Court specifically endorsed this exercise of powers under s 14 of the Act. In that case, the static Climate Camp demonstration had occupied, and completely blocked, Bishopsgate in the City of London during the working day. There had been disorder during the day, albeit primarily at a different location. In the evening the senior police present imposed a condition that the assembly must stop. Officers dispersed the assembly by using an advancing line of police officers, and force was used against those who refused to leave. The Court concluded at paragraph 63:

> As to the decision to terminate the demonstration and clear the Climate Camp, by force if necessary with the aid of section 14 of the 1986 Act, *in our judgment this was fully justified*. The demonstration had lasted the best part of 12 hours—quite long enough to take full advantage of rights under Articles 10 and 11 of the Convention—and those wishing to remain were intent on continuing to block the highway, which was a main thoroughfare into and out of the City. The prolongation of the demonstration, thus blocking the highway until the morning, had no justification and would continue to cause serious disturbance and disruption to traffic and pedestrians wishing to use the highway. The police had a duty to clear the highway, which could not be done without removing the protestors by force if necessary.

In *Moos*, significant factors that led to the finding that the direction was lawful was that the demonstration had been allowed to continue for 12 hours and that there was a complete obstruction of the highway. In circumstances where either the highway is not obstructed or a protest has only just commenced, the senior officer must consider whether it would be a proportionate interference with the Article 10 and 11 rights of the protestors to bring the protest to an immediate end: it might be in certain circumstances. At the time of publication, *Moos* is understood to be the subject of appeal.

Similar reasoning underpinned the decision in *Hall & Ors v Mayor of London (On Behalf of the Greater London Authority)* [2011] 1 WLR 504, [2010] EWCA Civ 817. The Mayor of London had been granted an order for possession of Parliament Square Gardens (PSG) against the demonstrators in the 'Democracy Village' which had set up camp in Parliament Square. An injunction was also

155

granted, requiring the removal of any structures they had erected and to leave PSG. The Court of Appeal noted at paragraph 48:

> They have been allowed to express their views and assemble together at the location of their choice, PSG, for over two months on an effectively exclusive basis. It is not even as if they will necessarily be excluded from mounting an orthodox demonstration at PSG in the future. Plainly, these points are not necessarily determinative of their case, but, when it comes to balancing their rights against the rights of others, they are obviously significant factors.

In extreme circumstances, it might be lawful for the police to temporarily detain those assembled in order to manage a safe, controlled dispersal: see further section 3.5 on the relevant exercise of the common law power to prevent a breach of the peace.

Care must be taken in how the conditions are drafted. Times, numbers and locations should be as specific as possible. A vague condition is open to misinterpretation or confusion (genuine or otherwise). For example, a direction that 'the maximum number of people shall be no greater than that permitted by the fire regulations' may appear on the face of it to leave no room for confusion. Which fire regulations apply? Even if they are identified, the fire regulations may not impose a specific maximum, or the limit may differ for different parts of a building or for different functions.

KEY POINTS—IMPOSITION OF CONDITIONS WHICH MAY BRING AN ASSEMBLY TO AN END

There is no power to ban an assembly under the powers in s 14 of the POA:

- A condition may be imposed which brings an assembly to a premature end
- Consider the proportionality of the proposed conditions
- In considering proportionality and the Article 10 or 11 rights of those assembled:
  - Consider whether they have been given sufficient opportunity to exercise those important rights
  - You may balance their rights with those of others, such as local residents, businesses and users of the highway
  - Consider whether, in all the circumstances, the limitation of these rights is proportionate to the interference involved in order to upholding other people's rights.

5.4.2 Offences

A person who organizes a public assembly and knowingly fails to comply with a condition imposed under section 14(1) is guilty of an offence under section 14(4). A person who takes part in a public assembly and knowingly fails to comply with a condition imposed under this section is guilty of an offence under section 14(5). In either case, if the prosecution is able to establish a breach of the condition, just as with processions, it is a defence for a person to prove that the failure arose from circumstances beyond his control.

5.4.3 Additional statutory powers to control assemblies

These different powers are designed to deal with specific and different circumstances; there is no common principle running through them. Definitions, concepts and court decisions do not necessarily apply outside the specific situation and statutory power under consideration.

Trespassory assemblies

The power to ban and control access to trespassory assemblies arises under section 14A–14C POA. These powers appeared for the first time when the section was inserted by the CJPOA. This new legislation was passed against a perceived background of rising public concern about the impact of large gatherings that trespassed on private ground or historical sites, such as the Castlemorton Common Festival near Malvern, Worcestershire in 1992. There is significant overlap with the type of activity covered in chapter 9, which deals the unlawful use of land in more detail.

In a similar way to s 13 of the Act, s 14A provides different regimes for seeking a prohibition inside and outside London.

The central aspects of Section 14A state:

14A Prohibiting trespassory assemblies

(1) If at any time the chief officer of police reasonably believes that an assembly is intended to be held in any district at a place on land to which the public has no right of access or only a limited right of access and that the assembly—

    (a) is likely to be held without the permission of the occupier of the land or to conduct itself in such a way as to exceed the limits of any permission of his or the limits of the public's right of access, and

    (b) may result—

      (i) in serious disruption to the life of the community, or

      (ii) where the land, or a building or monument on it, is of historical, architectural, archaeological or scientific importance, in significant damage to the land, building or monument,

he may apply to the council of the district for an order prohibiting for a specified period the holding of all trespassory assemblies in the district or a part of it, as specified.

(2) On receiving such an application, a council may—

    (a) in England and Wales, with the consent of the Secretary of State, make an order either in the terms of the application or with such modifications as may be approved by the Secretary of State; or

    (b) . . .

(3) Subsection (1) does not apply in the City of London or the metropolitan police district.

157

(4) If at any time the Commissioner of Police for the City of London or the Commissioner of Police for the Metropolis reasonably believes that an assembly is intended to be held at a place on land to which the public has no right of access or only a limited right of access in his police area and that the assembly—

(a) is likely to be held without the permission of the occupier of the land or to conduct itself in such a way as to exceed the limits of any permission of his or the limits of the public's right of access, and

(b) may result—

    (i) in serious disruption to the life of the community, or

    (ii) where the land, or a building or monument on it, is of historical, architectural, archaeological or scientific importance, in significant damage to the land, building or monument,

he may with the consent of the Secretary of State make an order prohibiting for a specified period the holding of all trespassory assemblies in the area or a part of it, as specified.

What is a trespassory assembly?

There are four necessary ingredients to a trespassory assembly:

(1) There must be (or it must be anticipated there will be) an assembly of **twenty or more** persons: see s 14A(9). The reduction in the number of people required to constitute an assembly for the purposes of s 14 of the Act from twenty down to two does *not* apply to s 14A–14C.

(2) The assembly must be held on land which is in the open air: s 14A(9). Section 14A does *not* apply to assemblies inside buildings.

(3) The assembly must take place on land to which the public has no right of access or only a limited right of access: s 14A(1) and 14A(4).

(4) The assembly is likely either:

- to be held without the permission of the occupier of the land, or to conduct itself in such a way as to exceed the limits of the occupier's permission, or
- to conduct itself in such a way as to exceed the limits of the public's right of access: s 14A(1)(a) / 14A(4)(a).

It is not necessary that the trespassory assembly be open to the public. A ticket-only event, or one from which the public were excluded for more informal or unofficial reasons, is included.

Grounds for seeking the prohibition of a trespassory assembly

The grounds for seeking the prohibition of a trespassory assembly are that the chief officer (either the Chief Constable or the Commissioner) believes, on reasonable grounds that:

- a trespassory assembly is intended to be held within the policing area;
- the assembly may result in either (i) serious disruption to the life of the community, or (ii) where the land, or a building or monument on it, is of

historical, architectural, archaeological or scientific importance, significant damage to the land, building or monument.

'Reasonably believes' involves the state of knowledge discussed at section 5.3.5. The chief officer must believe it is *likely* that the assembly will be trespassory, but need only believe that serious disruption, etc, *may* result. It follows that the evidence that there will be a trespassory assembly may need to be stronger than the evidence of the risk of disruption or damage.

Given that the power only arises if the assembly is anticipated to take place on land where the occupier has not given consent (or consent as to the full extent or character of the assembly), in many cases there will be no formal publicity for the event, or notification of it. The information on which the chief officer will be acting is likely to include the history of behaviour at previous assemblies held at the location, or assemblies elsewhere organized or attended by similar people. Intelligence may be relied upon, even if the source of nature of it is potentially subject to public interest immunity from disclosure.

The test for serious disruption to the life of the community is addressed above in relation to sections 12 and 14 of the Act. However, the community in which a trespassory assembly takes place may be very different from most processions or assemblies. The majority of processions take place in, or near, urban areas. By contrast, trespassory assemblies can occur anywhere, and will frequently happen in rural areas. While the assembly may occur some distance away from where the local community lives, it is also likely that the local infrastructure will be less able to accommodate a large influx of people or vehicles because of fewer, smaller roads, less frequent rubbish collections, lack of toileting facilities and so forth. Further, the level of noise that would amount to serious disruption may be lower in a rural rather than an urban setting.

The Act sets out no formal test or list establishing whether a particular site is of historical, architectural, archaeological or scientific importance. Many sites, particularly those that include listed buildings or sites of special scientific interest, very likely be included. However, there may be areas that do not obviously fit into this category. For example, the fact that an assembly may take place in an Area of Outstanding Natural Beauty is not itself sufficient, but may be a significant factor in the police seeking to invoke the provisions.

'Significant damage' is also not defined. It will include a lesser degree of damage than serious damage required in s 12 of the Act. In the context of the sensitive sites that s 14A aims to protect, anything more than insignificant damage is likely to be sufficient.

The power to seek a prohibition only arises in respect of an anticipated assembly. However, once the assembly is taking place, the police retain the power to impose conditions under s 14, including a direction bringing the assembly to a premature end.

The power to prohibit a trespassory assembly is *in addition to* common law powers to prevent a breach of the peace. However, prior to a trespassory assembly taking place, provided attendance by 20 or more people is anticipated, the powers under s 14A are of significantly wider application, for two reasons.

- Firstly, there is no requirement of imminence: a trespassory assembly can be prohibited as soon as the test set out below is made out, provided the exercise of the section 14A power is proportionate.
- Secondly, the test of 'serious disruption to the life of the community' and 'significant damage' to the site, includes conduct that would not amount to a breach of the peace.

A gathering which is permitted by the occupier of the whole of the land on which it takes place cannot be prohibited under section 14A, however disruptive or damaging it is likely to be to the local community. Permission granted by the occupier will rarely be completely unconditional. An obvious example, and relevant to the sorts of problems the section was intended to tackle, is that in most circumstances an occupier giving a person permission to be on his land will not also give that person permission to deliberately or recklessly damage the occupier's property. A person who enters onto land with such an intention will be trespassing. So too will somebody who entered the land without that intention, but who later in the day decides to commit such damage.

This distinction is an important one because there are circumstances where the initial gathering might well be (or appear to be) non-trespassory, but later change in nature if those present exceed the occupier's conditions of permission to be there. It may be that the chief officer has reasonable grounds to suspect that it will be the behaviour of those attending *after* they have gained entry to the land which will render the assembly a trespass.

The House of Lords confirmed in *DPP v Jones* [1991] 2 AC 240 that a group of people who sought to demonstrate on the highway were not trespassers, provided that the demonstration was peaceful and did not obstruct the highway (see section 5.6.3 for the facts of this case). It was confirmed that there is a right to peaceful assembly on the highway provided (i) there is no obstruction and (ii) such an assembly would be neither a public nor a private nuisance. That case also confirmed that section 14A–C are not capable of capable of turning people into trespassers who would not otherwise be trespassing:

- there is no power to prohibit a non-trespassory assembly, and
- if no power to prohibit the assembly exists, then a person who attends a gathering cannot be rendered a trespasser merely by their failure to comply with a prohibition.

Procedure outside London for obtaining a prohibition

Outside London, the procedure is governed by section 14(A)(1) and (2):

- The chief officer applies under section 14A(1) of the Act to the council of the district where it is anticipated the assembly will occur. The application does not have to be made in any particular format. There is no statutory requirement that it be in writing. Unless there is great urgency, it would not be appropriate for there to be no contemporaneous written record made of the application. It can safely be assumed that the local authority and the Secretary of State will require at least a summary of the grounds for asserting that the power arises. If the statutory criteria are met, it will normally be clear why it is necessary to exercise the power, but for completeness this should be considered separately.

- The application is for an order prohibiting the holding of all trespassory assemblies, either throughout the district or a specified part of it, for a specified period.
- Upon receiving such an application, a council may, with the consent of the Secretary of State, make an order either in the terms of the application or with such modifications as may be approved by the Secretary of State: s 14(A)(2).

If made, the order does not need to be in writing, but if it is not in writing, must be recorded in writing as soon as practicable after being made.

Procedure within London

Under section 14A(4) of the Act, if the Commissioner of Police for the City of London or the Commissioner of Police for the Metropolis believes that the conditions for imposing a prohibition on trespassory assemblies is satisfied, he may with the consent of the Secretary of State make an order prohibiting the holding of all trespassory assemblies in the area or a specified part of it, for a specified period.

There is no statutory procedure set out for obtaining the consent of the Secretary of State. Again, unless there is great urgency, it would not be appropriate for there to be no contemporaneous written record made of or accompanying the request for consent. If consent is given, the order must be recorded in writing as soon as practicable after being made: s 14A(8).

Section 14(A)4 does not provide the Borough Councils with any role in the prohibition of trespassory assemblies. There is no specific procedure for the Secretary of State to make or approve modifications, although it can be assumed that such proposals may be made prior to consent being given and/or a renewed application by the Commissioner.

Terms and duration of ban

Under section 14A(6), the maximum duration of the prohibition is four days. The area covered cannot exceed an area represented by a circle with a radius of five miles from a specified centre. Within this area (or such smaller area as may have been specified), *all* trespassory assemblies are prohibited. There is no power to distinguish a particular assembly or type of assembly. An order made can be varied or revoked by following the same procedure set out in s 14A(1)–(2) or s 14A(4). It follows that while the maximum duration of a single ban is four days, subsequent bans could take effect as a rolling prohibition, provided a renewed application were made on each occasion.

Although a single prohibition is limited in length and geographical effect, and addresses only those assemblies that are unlawful, the chief officer is nevertheless obliged to consider whether the prohibition is both necessary and proportionate. It might be assumed that, as the prohibition can only be sought if there is a risk of serious disruption to the life of the community, or significant damage to a sensitive site, it would follow that it would be proportionate to impose the prohibition. However, the chief officer must specifically consider the impact of the prohibition on the participants' Article 11 rights.

In *R v Tunbridge Wells Borough Council and Another ex p The Gypsy Council for Education, Culture, Welfare and Civil Rights and Another* (QBD 7 September 2000, unreported) a parish council cancelled a local horse fair, which had in previous years been attended by large numbers, including many travellers and Romanies, and had become associated with serious disruption. Despite the cancellation, the chief constable anticipated the attendance of large numbers of travellers and Romanies, and believed that this would lead to a trespassory assembly, likely to cause serious disruption to the life of the community. Accordingly, he applied for a prohibition order. The borough council passed the application to the Secretary of State, who approved the application. Shortly before the gathering was anticipated to take place, an application for judicial review was made of the decision to grant the application. The grounds included that:

- there had been no, or insufficient, investigation of the risk of serious disruption;
- no consideration had been taken of the fact that the right to hold the horse fair arose through prescription;
- the prohibition had disproportionate impact on the Article 8 and 11 rights of the Romanies.

The High Court found that the Romanies' Article 8 and 11 rights were indeed engaged by the prohibition, but that the Secretary of State had expressly considered their rights in reaching the decision to approve the prohibition. The court was also satisfied that there were reasonable grounds to anticipate serious disruption, and that the prohibition was a proportionate measure to protect the rights of the local community.

POINT TO NOTE

Section 14A in context: Area of Prohibition?

While a chief officer considering a prohibition order under section 14A will be keen to keep the area as small as practicable, it must be borne in mind that a uniformed officer's powers to stop and turn back vehicles under section 14C can only be exercised within the area subject to the prohibition. It may therefore still be necessary, in order to give effect to the powers under section 14C, to designate an area of prohibition wider than the specific location where the assembly is anticipated to take place.

Offences

A person who organizes an assembly the holding of which he knows is prohibited by an order under s 14A is guilty of an offence under s 14B(1). A person who incites another to participate in a prohibited assembly is also guilty of an offence under s 14B(3).

A person who takes part in an assembly which he knows is prohibited by an order under s 14A is guilty of an offence under s 14B(2).

Power to stop those attending a trespassory assembly

Section 14C provides the police with a power to stop people from attending at a trespassory assembly before they reach the immediate vicinity of the assembly. If successful, this should prevent large-scale confrontation at the site that the police are trying to protect. The power is exercisable against a person travelling on foot or by any other means.

Section 14C provides that if:

- a police constable,
- in uniform,
- reasonably believes that a person is on his way to an assembly within the area to which an order under section 14A applies, and
- reasonably believes that assembly is likely to be an assembly prohibited by that order,

he may (a) stop that person, and (b) direct him not to proceed in the direction of the assembly. If a person fails to comply with these directions, he is guilty of an offence.

This power may itself only be exercised within the area to which the order applies. It follows that under no circumstances may a person be stopped and turned back if they are either outside the specific area in the order, or are further than five miles from the location specified in the order.

> **KEY POINTS—STOPPING PEOPLE ON THEIR WAY TO A PROHIBITED ASSEMBLY**
>
> - The police officer must be in uniform.
> - The power is exercisable against people on foot and in vehicles.
> - The police officer can only take action within the area covered by the particular s 14A prohibition.

- The police officer must have reasonable grounds for believing both that:
  - the person is on their way to an assembly within the area; and
  - the assembly is likely to be a trespassory assembly.
- The person can be stopped and directed not to proceed in the direction of the assembly.
- A person who fails to comply with a direction is guilty of an offence.

5.4.4 Trespass on designated sites

Section 128 of SOCPA (as amended by s 12(1) of the Terrorism Act 2006) creates the offence of trespass on designated sites. Under s 128(1) a person (who may be alone or with others) commits an offence if he enters, or is on, any protected site in England and Wales or Northern Ireland as a trespasser.

Land is a protected site if it is either:

- land subject to a nuclear site licence (within the meaning of the Nuclear Installations Act 1965); or
- a site which has been designated by order.

A site may be designated by order if it forms part of Crown Land, belongs to the Queen or the Prince of Wales in a private capacity, or it appears to the Secretary of State that it is appropriate to designate the site in the interests of national security. Orders made by the Secretary of State under s 128 now include a large number of premises, including military sites such as RAF Fairford, GCHQ, royal residences such as Sandringham, Highgrove House and parts of Windsor Castle, Chequers and a large number vulnerable political buildings in Whitehall, including Downing Street. Areas to which the public have access are not designated. It is anticipated that the police force in whose area such a site exists will have been formally notified.

It is a defence for a person charged with an offence under this section to prove that he did not know, and had no reasonable cause to suspect, that the site in relation to which the offence is alleged to have been committed was a protected site. However, s 131(2) of the Act authorizes the Secretary of State to may take such steps as he considers appropriate to inform the public of the effect of any designation order, including, in particular, displaying notices on or near the site to which the order relates.

In practice, it is likely that protected sites will have high barriers at the perimeter, which will be clearly marked, warning that the site is a protected site. However, if such a site exists within a particular force area, the police force concerned should satisfy itself that the degree of signage is sufficient to prevent a trespasser from arguing that they did not know, and had no reasonable cause to suspect, that they were entering a protected site.

Section 128 provides for a power to arrest any person trespassing at these sites, or who is attempting to gain entrance to these sites. The individual does not need to be participating in an assembly or demonstration, although they may well be. They do not need to be committing any other criminal offence. There is clearly the potential for it to be widely used in the policing of demonstrations at many sensitive locations.

5.4.5 **Demonstrations in Whitehall, Westminster**

Sections 132–138 of SOCPA created an entirely new, and separate, regime for the regulation of demonstrations in the vicinity of the Houses of Parliament, within a one kilometre radius of Parliament Square. A detailed consideration of the ramifications of this statutory scheme for the policing of demonstrations in (or passing through) Whitehall is beyond the scope of this book. The area represents a tiny proportion of the country, but as it includes the focus for many of the large-scale protests held in the United Kingdom, it is necessary to briefly summarize the framework set out by SOCPA.

The scheme differentiates between demonstrations and gatherings of any other nature. Despite this unique departure from the traditional approach to public order law, 'demonstration' is not defined in the Act. One dictionary definition, that of the online Oxford Dictionary, is 'a public meeting or march protesting against something or expressing views on a political issue'. The modern, sophisticated protestor may attempt to avoid the operation of Part IV of SOCPA, by arranging what is said not to be a demonstration. For example, it is likely that the organizers of the 'Guerilla Gardening' event in Parliament Square on 1 May 2000 would have argued that the event they were arranging was a celebration, not a demonstration. It is suggested that, for the purposes of SOCPA, for an event to constitute a demonstration it would normally be necessary for a major element of the event to be the intention either to show approval or disapproval of, or even simply to highlight, a particular cause.

A demonstration can be a procession or an assembly, or both. However processions and assemblies are treated differently:

Assemblies: By operation of SOCPA s 132(6), s 14 POA does *not* apply to a public assembly if it is a demonstration in a public place in the s 132 designated area. The SOCPA scheme applies—notification must be given and the regime for imposition of conditions is different.

Processions: By operation of SOCPA s 132(3), public processions that are governed by sections 11–13 POA (including those exempt from notification under Section 11(2)) are *not* subject to the SOCPA statutory scheme, but remain to be notified and policed in accordance with the POA, as set out in detail above.

In practice the SOCPA statutory scheme, rather than the POA, applies to all static demonstrations that take place within a one kilometre radius of the Houses of Parliament (except industrial pickets outside a place of work, under s 220 of TULRCA, for which see section 6.6). The area to which this scheme applies covers most of Whitehall and the area surrounding the

165

Houses of Parliament. The precise description of the designated area is found in paragraph 2 of the SOCPA (Designated Area) Order 2005 (SI 2005/1537). A static demonstration within this zone will not avoid the SOCPA scheme because it takes place prior to or following a procession outside the zone.

The procedure can be broken down into notification/seeking of authorization, imposition conditions/authorization by the Commissioner, and compliance with conditions in a similar way to that for processions or assemblies under the Public Order Act.

Requirement to obtain authorization

Under s 132(1) any person who:

(a) organizes a demonstration in a public place in the designated area, or
(b) takes part in a demonstration in a public place in the designated area, or
(c) carries on a demonstration by himself in a public place in the designated area,

is guilty of an offence if, when the demonstration starts, authorization for the demonstration has not been given by the Commissioner of Police for the Metropolis. It is a defence for a person accused of an offence under this section to show that he reasonably believed that authorization had been given.

A person seeking authorization for a demonstration must give written notice to the Commissioner—s 133(1). If reasonably practicable, the notice must be given not less than six clear days before the day on which the demonstration is to start. If six clear day's notice is not reasonably practicable, then notice must be given as soon as reasonably practicable. In any event, notice must be given not less than 24 hours before the time the demonstration is to start. It follows that 'spontaneous' demonstrations are no longer permissible within the designated area.

Although this may be a substantial inroad into the British citizen's traditional liberties, the European Court of Human Rights has previously noted in the case of *Ziliberberg v Moldova* (App. No. 61821/00, 4 May 2004) that 'the requirement to obtain authorization for a demonstration is not incompatible with Article 11 of the Convention'. The ECtHR has confirmed both that the SOCPA regime is, in principle, similarly compliant with Article 11, and that a criminal sanction for failure to comply with the requirements for notification is not of itself disproportionate: *Rai and Evans v United Kingdom* (App. Nos. 26258/07 and 26255/07).

If the demonstration is to be carried on by more than one person, any one (or more) of the persons organizing the demonstration can give notice to the Commissioner. Under s 133(4), the notice, which must be delivered to a police station in the metropolitan police district by hand or by recorded delivery, must include the following:

(a) the date and time when the demonstration is to start,
(b) the place where it is to be carried on,

(c) how long it is to last,
(d) whether it is to be carried on by the person giving notice or by (or including) another,
(e) the name and address of the person giving the notice.

It follows that an organizer could post the notice to an outlying police station within the Metropolitan police area and time it to arrive on a Saturday. In such circumstances it might be a close run thing as to whether all such police stations would be able to process their mail sufficiently quickly to enable the public order branch to be alerted to the notice.

Authorization must be given

If a notice complying with section 133 has been validly served, s 134 states that the Commissioner *must* give authorization for the demonstration to which the notice relates. However, when giving authorization, s 134(3) provides that he may impose such conditions as are, in his reasonable opinion, necessary for the purpose of preventing:

(a) hindrance to any person wishing to enter or leave the Palace of Westminster,
(b) hindrance to the proper operation of Parliament,
(c) serious public disorder,
(d) serious damage to property,
(e) disruption to the life of the community,
(f) a security risk in any part of the designated area, or
(g) risk to the safety of members of the public (including those taking part in the demonstration).

In legal terms there is unlikely to be a substantial difference between reasonable opinion and reasonable belief. However, the basis for imposing conditions is very much wider than that under s 14 of the Public Order Act. The specific references to ensuring that the proper functioning of (including access to) parliament, together with the absence of the adjective 'serious' when considering disruption to the life of the community, make it clear that the threshold for imposing conditions under s 134 SOCPA is significantly lower than under the Public Order Act.

The imposition of conditions

Conditions may be imposed prior to the demonstration. They may also be varied or added to by the senior officer at the scene during the demonstration.

The power to impose conditions is wide and unfettered other than by considerations of proportionality and necessity. Section 134(4) specifically notes that the conditions might include requirements as to:

(a) the place where the demonstration may, or may not, be carried on,
(b) the times at which it may be carried on,
(c) the period during which it may be carried on,

(d) the number of persons who may take part in it,

(e) the number and size of banners or placards used,

(f) maximum permissible noise levels.

Details of the authorization and conditions to be imposed in advance of the demonstration must be communicated in writing to all people who have provided notification.

During the demonstration, s 135 provides that the senior police officer at the scene (ie any of the officers present who are equal in rank to the most senior rank present) may impose additional conditions, or vary any conditions previously imposed. These conditions are to be imposed by giving directions to those present taking part or organizing the demonstration. The senior police officer may vary or impose additional conditions to the extent that he reasonably believes that it is necessary to do so to safeguard the same matters as those set out in s 134(3).

Each person who takes part in or organizes a demonstration in the designated area is guilty of an offence contrary to s 134(7) if he knowingly fails to comply with a condition imposed which is applicable to him, or he knows or should have known that the demonstration is carried on otherwise than in accordance with the particulars set out in the authorization by virtue of subsection. A person taking part in or organizing the demonstration who knowingly fails to comply with a condition which is applicable to him and which is imposed or varied by a direction under this section is guilty of an offence (s 135(3) of SOCPA). It is a defence for him to show that the failure to comply arose from circumstances beyond his control.

Prohibition on loudspeakers

With certain specific, limited exceptions that do not relate to protesting per se, s 137 prohibits the use of loudspeakers at demonstrations within the designated area. Even the use of loudspeakers inside motor vehicles is prohibited, unless it is in use solely for the entertainment of the driver and/or any passengers inside the vehicle, *and* is operated so as not to give reasonable cause for annoyance to persons in the vicinity.

A person who operates or permits the operation of a loudspeaker in contravention of s 137 is guilty of an offence and is liable on summary conviction to a fine not exceeding level 5 on the standard scale, together with a further fine not exceeding £50 for each day on which the offence continues after the conviction.

5.5 Sections 60 and 60AA of the Criminal Justice and Public Order Act 1994

Under normal circumstances, the power to stop and search a member of the public must be based on s 1 of the Police and Criminal Evidence Act (PACE), and requires reasonable grounds to suspect that the subject of the search is in possession of stolen or prohibited articles. However, provided the necessary prior authorization has been given, ss 60 and 60AA of the CJPOA provide the police with two further powers that can be routinely deployed in the context of the policing of processions and assemblies.

Section 60 of the CJPOA allows an officer in uniform to search any person or vehicle for offensive weapons or dangerous instruments.

Section 60AA allows an officer in uniform to require a person to remove (and the officer to seize) any item which the constable reasonably believes that person is wearing wholly or mainly for the purpose of concealing his identity.

These powers have been the cause of anxiety for organizers and participants of demonstrations, and have been the subject of legal challenges.

It is important that officers making authorizations and carrying out searches or requiring removals under ss 60 and 60AA understand the requirements which make such actions lawful. Although the basis for authorization may be similar, the powers under ss 60 and 60AA are considered separately to avoid confusion.

In outline, the relevant stages are:

- under s 60:
  - authorization
  - steps to be taken prior to search
  - conduct of the search
  - seizure/disposal of items.
- under s 60AA:
  - authorization
  - suspicion on the part of the officer
  - permitted action
  - seizure/disposal of items.

5.5.1 Authorization under section 60

No searches can be carried out under s 60 unless prior authorization has been given. Under s 60(1), authorization must be given by an officer of at least the rank of inspector. If an inspector or chief inspector gives an authorization, he must inform an officer of the rank of superintendent or above as soon as is reasonably practicable.

Under s 60(1), the officer may give authorization if he reasonably believes:

(a) that incidents involving serious violence may take place in any locality in his police area, **and** that it is expedient to give an authorization under this section to prevent their occurrence, or

(b) that persons are carrying dangerous instruments or offensive weapons in any locality in his police area without good reason.

'Offensive weapon' has the meaning given by s 1(9) of PACE. 'Dangerous instruments' means any instruments which have a blade or are sharply pointed.

The two limbs are entirely independent of each other. If the officer reasonably believes that people in the locality are carrying dangerous instruments or offensive weapons, he can give an authorization without considering it expedient to do so. There is a difference between the states of mind between the two limbs. Both require the officer's belief to be based on reasonable grounds. However, the first limb requires the officer to believe that incidents involving serious violence *may* be committed. It is not necessary for him to believe that such incidents are inevitable. Under the second limb it is necessary for the officer to believe that persons within the locality are *in fact* carrying dangerous instruments or offensive weapons.

The meaning of 'expedient' in the context of similar stop and search powers previously contained within s 44 of the Terrorism Act 2001 is considered in detail at section 8.2.3. 'Expedient' means something less than necessary. In practical terms, the person giving the authorization must consider it likely that the stop and search powers would be of significant practical value and utility in seeking to prevent acts of serious violence. The Home Office's *Stop and Search Manual* confirms that 'section 60 powers should not be used to avoid using the normal powers or dealing with routine crime problems. Authorizations must be made on the basis that exercising the power is a proportionate and necessary response to achieve the purpose for which parliament provided the power'.

The manual goes on to suggest that an authorization under s 60 must be based on intelligence or relevant information. The examples given are:

- violence between particular groups;
- previous incidents of violence at or connected with particular events or locations;
- a major increase in robberies at knife point in a small area; or
- reports that individuals are regularly carrying weapons in a particular area.

However, there are no formal limits on the circumstances in which a s 60 authorization would be appropriate. Its use is of potentially significant value in policing protests where there has been serious violence at similar events in the past, or there is good intelligence to suggest that there will be violence.

Any authorization shall be in writing, signed by the officer giving it and shall specify the grounds on which it is given, the locality in which and the period during which the authorization is to last. Where it is not practicable to record the authorization in writing at the time, it must be recorded as soon as it is practicable to do so.

The area covered by the authorization must be precisely identified. The whole of the area must be contained within the police area of the authorizing officer's force. For the British Transport Police, 'area' means 'any locality in or in the vicinity of any policed premises'. As a s 60 authorization has the potential to engage several articles of the ECHR, it follows that the authorizing officer must consider whether the authorization is a proportionate response to the potential for violence, and if so, to satisfy himself that the geographical extent and duration of the authorization are also proportionate.

The maximum duration of the authorization is 24 hours. However, an officer of or above the rank of superintendent may direct that the authorization shall continue in existence for a further period of up 24 hours. This may only be done if that officer has had regard to offences which have been committed, or are reasonably suspected to have been committed in connection with any activity falling within the scope of the original authorization, and considers that it is expedient to continue the authorization.

The continuation of an authorization must also be recorded in writing at the time of the continuation. Where it is not practicable to do so at the time, it must be recorded as soon as is practicable thereafter.

In practical terms, unless there are exceptional circumstances, it is important that s 60 authorizations are only made in the context of carefully planned operations, due to the need to have the opportunity fully to brief officers before the operation commences.

5.5.2 **What does the authorization cover?**

The authorization under section 60 confers on any constable in uniform power:

(a) to stop any pedestrian and search him or anything carried by him for offensive weapons or dangerous instruments;

(b) to stop any vehicle and search the vehicle, its driver and any passenger for offensive weapons or dangerous instruments.

The most significant feature of this power is found in s 60(5). This section confirms that, for the duration of the authorization, within the specified area the officer may stop and search any person or vehicle he thinks fit, **whether or not he has grounds for suspecting that that person or vehicle is carrying weapons or articles of that kind**.

The power to search anyone an officer may see fit is confined to searching for weapons or dangerous instruments. A search conducted under s 60 for any other purpose would be unlawful, although if in the process of a legitimate s 60 search, evidence of a different offence (or a prohibited item) were to be found, the officer may act on what he has found. Moreover, the individual officer must act lawfully. It would be an unlawful act of discrimination to stop a person simply because they were a particular ethnicity, or male, for example. However, as for searches under the Terrorism Act 2005, it is acceptable to take into account the person's ethnic appearance as one factor among others leading to the stop, provided it is relevant to the nature of violence / carrying of weapons in the area (such as, for example, at a time of heightened gang violence between gangs in a specific area, recognized to be of a particular ethnicity). Other possible relevant factors might include: gender, age, dress, whether the person is alone or in a group, the location or their behaviour.

5.5.3 Steps to be taken prior to the search

The case of *Osman v Southwark Crown Court* (1999) COD 446 confirmed that searches undertaken under s 60 still fall to be conducted in accordance with s 2 of PACE. Both the legal requirements of s 2 of PACE and Part 3 of Code of Practice A should be followed.

It follows that, prior to searching a person under s 60, the officer should firstly tell the person that he is being detained for the purposes of a search, then:

- the officer's name and the name of the police station to which he is attached
- the object of the proposed search
- the grounds for the officer proposing to make the search—here, that there is an authorization under s 60 of the CJPOA in place in that location.

The officer must then inform the person of his or her entitlement to a copy of the record of the search, and lastly, attempt to obtain the consent of the person to be searched, and/or the owner of the vehicle to be searched (see PACE Code of Practice A 3.2).

If an officer fails to provide the necessary information, the search will be unlawful. Any force then used during the search would constitute an assault, and reasonable force used by the person resisting the search would not be unlawful.

Similar consequences would follow if the person were not given the opportunity to consent, as the force used by the officer would be likely to be found to be disproportionate.

A person who fails to stop, or fails to stop their vehicle, when requested, is guilty of an offence.

Conduct of search

The search must be conducted in accordance with s 3 of Code A to PACE. In particular, it should be remembered:

- Reasonable force should only be used as a last resort, and if it is necessary in order to conduct a search or to detain the person or vehicle for the purposes of the search.

- There is normally no power to require a person to remove any clothing in public other than an outer coat, jacket or gloves.

Seizure and/or disposal of items

Section 60(6) provides that if in the course of the search the officer discovers a dangerous instrument or an article which he has reasonable grounds for suspecting to be an offensive weapon, he may seize it. Section 60 entitles the officer to retain the item. The owner may later apply for its return under the Police (Retention and Disposal of Items Seized) Regulations 2002.

5.5.4 **Authorization under section 60AA**

Section 60AA is intended to assist in the policing of two different types of problem that have arisen with increasing frequency in recent years. The notes of guidance to authorizing police officers that accompany PACE Code of Practice A describe these as, 'to prevent those involved in intimidatory or violent protests using face coverings to disguise identity', or in response to reports of 'previous incidents of crimes being committed while wearing face coverings to conceal identity'.

These two scenarios are likely to cover almost every instance where authorization under section 60AA is appropriate. It is principally the use of section 60AA in relation to assemblies and processions that is covered in this chapter.

If authorization has been given under section 60, this automatically operates as an authorization under section 60AA. However, there is a further power to make an authorization only under section 60AA. The authorization may only be made by an officer of at least the rank of inspector. Identical requirements apply to those under section 60 in relation to duration, location, the notification of an officer at least of the rank of superintendent, the requirement that the authorization be in writing and the provisions for extending the duration of the authorization.

The officer may give an authorization under section 60AA if he reasonably believes:

(a) that activities *may* take place in any locality in his police area that are likely (if they take place) to involve the commission of offences; and
(b) that it is expedient, in order to prevent or control the activities, to give an authorization under this subsection.

While the nature of the offences are not specified, the requirement that the making of an authorization be 'expedient' requires a link between the offences under consideration and the wearing of items likely to conceal a person's identity. The period authorized should be no longer than appears reasonably necessary to prevent, or seek to prevent, the commission of offences.

Suspicion on the part of the officer

Once an authorization under either section 60 or section 60AA has been given, section 60AA(2) authorizes any constable in uniform:

(a) to require any person to remove any item which the constable reasonably believes that person is wearing wholly or mainly for the purpose of concealing his identity; and

(b) to seize any item which the constable reasonably believes any person intends to wear wholly or mainly for that purpose.

Unlike the stop and search powers under section 60, this power does require the officer to have a reasonable belief that the item under consideration is being worn either wholly, or mainly, to conceal that person's identity. The demonstrator may suggest that the mask is being worn as part of the demonstration, to highlight or emphasize a particular issue. However, the use of masks by protestors to conceal their identity, particularly if they are intent on unlawful conduct, is a tactic now widely used. Therefore, if the officer has reasonable grounds to believe that the protestors (or some of them) intend to act unlawfully, and masks or similar items are being worn by some or all of the protestors, the officer is very likely to be able to satisfy a court that he had an honest and reasonably held belief that the item was being used wholly or mainly to conceal that person's identity. It is not necessary to prove that the individual in fact had any such intention.

In many cases the grounds for requiring a person to remove the item will be obvious. However, it will not always be straightforward: the wearing of hats and scarves in summertime may give rise a reasonable belief that the items were being used to conceal a person's identity, but this would be a more difficult connection to make on a very cold day.

Cyclists participating in demonstrations might wear a helmet, sunglasses and an anti-pollution mask, all of which are normal, even desirable, items for cycling. However, if the cyclist is stationary, or in very slow moving procession, and after an informal conversation refuses to remove the items, this might be sufficient to amount to reasonable grounds to believe that they are not being worn for cycling purposes, but *at that time* are being worn mainly to conceal the person's identity. This sort of situation is a good example of the importance of officers attempting to achieve an outcome through communication and persuasion rather than immediately relying on their statutory powers.

Permitted action under section 60AA

Under section 60AA, an officer is only allowed to require the removal of, and then to retain, items that are either being worn to conceal identity or which the officer believes the person intends to wear wholly or mainly to conceal their identity. There is no power to search for any items.

If the person refuses to remove the article, they are guilty of an offence under section 60AA(7). There is no specific power to remove the item from the person. Once the person has been arrested, the item could be removed at the custody suite, in order for the arrested person's photograph to be taken, pursuant to PACE s 64A(2). The power to seize and retain items under section 60AA is identical to that set out in section 60.

5.6 Obstruction of the Highway

Many public assemblies and almost all processions will impact on the use of the highway. Section 137(1) of the Highways Act 1980 provides:

> If a person, without lawful authority or excuse, in any way wilfully obstructs the free passage along a highway he is guilty of an offence and liable to a fine not exceeding [level 3 on the standard scale].

A person obstructing the highway may also be guilty of a public nuisance, see section 4.11.

5.6.1 Meaning of 'highway'

When considering whether the offence is being committed, police need to be certain that the protesters are in fact obstructing something that counts as a highway. The road and the pavement are both highways. The definition of a highway in the Highways Act 1980, section 328(1) and (2), relies on the understanding of 'highway' that has been built up by case law. The Act's definition is this:

> highway means the whole or part of a highway other than a ferry or waterway [and] where a highway passes over a bridge or through a tunnel, that bridge or tunnel is to be taken for the purposes of this Act to be part of the highway.

The meaning of highway as understood by the courts is essentially a way over which a public right of passage exists. Roads, pavements, bridleways and other routes over which the whole public has the right to pass will be highways. Note that the route has to be truly public in nature to count as a highway. If it is only open to a section of the public, such as members of a church parish, it is not a highway.

5.6.2 'Obstruction'

In order to for there to be an obstruction, the highway does not have to be completely blocked. A partial obstruction (provided it is not trivial) is sufficient. However, in order for an obstruction to amount to an offence it must also be an *unreasonable* use of the highway. Recent cases confirm that the use of the highway to conduct an assembly or public protest will, in many circumstances, constitute a reasonable use.

5.6.3 **Reasonable use**

In *DPP v Jones* [1999] 2 AC 240 the question arose whether or not a person protesting on the highway was trespassing on it. A group of (at least) 21 protestors gathered on the verge of a main road near to Stonehenge to protest, although there was no evidence that the group intended to trespass at the site itself. The inspector present decided this was a trespassory assembly and gave directions under s 14A of the POA to the assembly to move off. The defendants refused, were arrested and subsequently convicted of an offence under s 14B of the Act. The Divisional Court upheld their convictions, holding that the public's right of access to the public highway is limited to the right to pass and repass, and to do anything incidental or ancillary to that right. As the peaceful assembly was not incidental to the right to pass and repass, it exceeded the limits of the public's right of access, and so the protestors were trespassing on the highway.

On appeal, the House of Lords was divided 3–2. The majority recognized that there *was* a right to use the highway for purposes other than simply to pass and re-pass. Giving the lead majority judgment, Lord Irvine found there was no trespass, stating (p 257D–E):

> I conclude therefore the law to be that the public highway is a public place which the public may enjoy for any reasonable purpose, provided the activity in question does not amount to a public or private nuisance and does not obstruct the highway by unreasonably impeding the primary right of the public to pass and repass: within these qualifications there is a public right of peaceful assembly on the highway.

This represented a significant development in the use of the highway for peaceful assembly, regardless of its purpose. It affects both trespass on and obstruction of the highway, as well as public nuisance. In the context of picketing, see also *Hirst and Agu v Chief Constable of West Yorkshire* (1987) 85 Cr App R 143, discussed further in section 6.6.

The right to use the highway to exercise freedom of speech was taken further in *Westminster City Council v Haw* [2002] EWHC 2073 (QB). The claimant council sought an injunction preventing Mr Haw from continuing his long-term, static demonstration against the war in Iraq on the pavement by Parliament Square. It relied on the argument that his demonstration constituted an obstruction of the highway and contravened s 137. The pavement was 11 feet wide and Mr Haw and his protest occupied approximately two feet of the width of the pavement. Because of the layout of Parliament Square, the pavement where the protest is held is not very busy. The High Court held that Mr Haw was causing a wilful obstruction, which was not *de minimis*. However, he was exercising his right to freedom of speech, which ought to be protected if possible. The Court found that, taken in the round, Mr Haw's use of the highway was not unreasonable and an injunction was refused.

There was no evidence in either case that the obstruction being considered by the courts was preventing pedestrians or vehicles from freely passing on the highway. In *DPP v Jones*, both the majority and minority of the House of Lords agreed that that if the highway were substantially impeded then the use would be unlikely to be reasonable. Whether or not a particular gathering or activity would constitute an obstruction of the highway is a question of fact for the magistrates (see *DPP v Jones* at p 257 F–H).

It follows that, although the use of the highway to hold an assembly is not automatically unlawful, it is likely to become so if the assembly is preventing free passage along the highway. If this occurs, the police are entitled to enforce s 137 of the Highways Act 1980 whether or not the threshold of serious disruption to the life of the community (as is required to take action under sections 12 or 14 of the Public Order Act) has been reached: see for example, in the context of picketing, *Broome v DPP* [1974] AC 587, discussed at section 6.6.

A sit-down protest will not usually constitute a reasonable use of the highway. In *Birch v DPP* [2000] Crim LR 301 the defendant, together with about seven to eleven others, sat or lay down in the road, deliberately causing a complete obstruction. The defendant maintained his actions were a reasonable use of the highway as he was attempting to prevent crimes being committed at the adjacent chemical plant, which was the focus of the protest. At first instance he was convicted of obstructing the highway.

In dismissing the appeal, the Divisional Court accepted that it was *possible* for the prevention of crime to be a lawful excuse for obstructing the highway. However, if the defence is to be raised, it will be necessary for evidence to be called to establish the facts necessary to show that (1) a breach of the peace or serious crime was about to be committed and (2) that the defendant's actions were no more than was reasonably necessary to prevent that crime. Such an argument in the defendant's case was described as 'hopeless'.

If, despite advice from the police, a 'freedom of expression' assembly continues to block a pavement or carriageway, then reference to the powers under s 137 of the Highways Act 1980 should be considered. However, given the rights to assembly and freedom of speech, there may be circumstances in which it would be disproportionate to direct the assembly to disperse immediately, particularly if the participants can be persuaded to adapt their behaviour to avoid or minimize the extent or duration of the obstruction. See section 5.4.1 on imposing directions on an assembly in order to bring it to an end.

5.7 Specific Types of Assembly or Meeting

There are a number of specific situations where particular powers exist to intervene to protect, or to disperse, an assembly or meeting. Meetings held indoors, whatever their nature, are not 'assemblies' for the purposes of the Public Order Act 1986. In the absence of an invitation, the police have no general right to attend at an indoor *private* meeting. However, the fact that a meeting is taking place cannot be a reason to prevent the police attending, where they would otherwise have power to do so, such as to prevent a breach of the peace (see for example *McLeod v Commissioner of Police for the Metropolis* [1994] 4 All ER 553).

The situation is different for a *public* meeting. If a meeting is truly open to the public, then a police officer would be entitled to attend like any other member of the public. (If attending purely as a member of the public, the officer would not necessarily be acting in the execution of his duty.)

It has been confirmed in *Thomas v Sawkins* [1935] 2 KB 249, that where a breach of the peace is reasonably apprehended at a public meeting, held on private premises, the police may attend uninvited. In that case, attendance was said not to be limited to where a breach of the peace is imminent, provided it is likely: see p 255, per Lord Hewart CJ. However, the decision of the House of Lords in *Laporte* has confirmed that imminence is the threshold requirement for a breach of the peace, which must be present in order to justify any intrusive policing action, however minor (see further section 3.4).

Thus, if the organizers of a public meeting expressly withdraw their consent for police officers to be present, it is likely that they will only have the power to remain on the premises if there is an imminent risk of a breach of the peace. It would clearly be lawful for police officers to remain outside, and to re-enter prior to a breach of the peace occurring. Moreover, because, as confirmed in *Laporte*, the concept of imminence is flexible, and it would be too late for the officers to remain outside until (perhaps due to the sound of a disturbance) they were to learn that a breach of the peace was already occurring, there may well be circumstances in which their continued presence at the meeting would be lawful. As in all cases of preventative action to prevent a breach of the peace, the power to intervene is entirely fact-dependent.

5.7.1 Public meetings

Section 1(3) of the Public Meeting Act 1908 provides a power which is still in force and of which police may make use at public meetings, where a person or persons present are attempting to disrupt the business of that meeting.

Section 1 provides that:

(1) Any person who at a lawful public meeting acts in a **disorderly** manner for the purpose of preventing the transaction of the business for which the meeting was called together shall be guilty of an offence . . .

(2) Any person who incites others to commit an offence under this section shall be guilty of a like offence.

(3) If any constable reasonably suspects any person of committing an offence under the foregoing provisions of this section, he may if requested to do

so by the chairman of the meeting require that person to declare to him immediately his name and address and, if that person refuses or fails so to declare his name and address or gives a false name and address he shall be guilty of an offence . . .

The conduct need only be disorderly. It does not need to be either threatening or abusive but it has to be done with the intention of preventing business of the meeting. Voicing disapproval or vigorous agreement, putting questions to, even challenging the speaker would not be sufficient (*Wooding v Oxley* 9 Car. & P. 1).

What powers do the police have to intervene when their assistance is requested to control a controversial meeting convened by a public body? Prior to 1960, there was no general right to attend meetings of local authorities. Such a right now exists under s 1 of the Public Bodies (Admissions to Meetings) Act 1960 and s 100A of the Local Government Act 1972. Both of these sections include the assertion that the right is without prejudice to any power of exclusion to suppress or prevent disorderly conduct or other misbehaviour at a meeting.

The case of *R v Brent Health Authority exp Francis* [1985] QB 869 confirmed that a public authority has a common law power to exclude the public from what would normally be a public meeting, if it is the only practical way of carrying on the business of the authority. In coming to the conclusion that there must be such a power, Forbes J stated at p 878:

> The purpose of giving the public the right to attend meetings is so that they can inform themselves of what is going on. They are not given the right to disrupt meetings and, of course, the right is not a right to participate in anything that is going on, but merely to observe and hear what is going on. It is since 1960 that the all too prevalent habit has grown up of political opponents of one kind or another getting their supporters to descend on public meetings to disrupt them by rowdy and noisy behaviour, and shouting down all the arguments which the opponents do not wish to hear.

This power to exclude disruptive attendees is a separate common law power from that which applies to a breach of the peace. It is exercised by the public authority, not the police. There is no threshold requirement of imminence. However, quite apart from their powers to prevent a breach of the peace, police officers would be acting in the execution of their duty if they assisted in enforcing such an exclusion—not least because to do so would be to prevent offences being committed under s 1 of the Public Meetings Act 1908.

5.7.2 **Election meetings**

Special protection is given to public political meetings during the formal election campaign prior to both parliamentary and local government elections. During these periods, a person who acts in a disorderly manner (or incites others to do so) is guilty of an offence contrary to s 97(1) of the Representation of the People Act 1983 (RPA), provided the purpose of the disorder is to prevent the transaction of the business for which the meeting was called.

Under a very similar power to that in the Public Meetings Act 1908, a constable may, if requested by the chairman of the meeting and if he reasonably suspects any person of committing an offence under this section, require the disorderly or inciting person to provide his name and address immediately. Failure to provide a correct name and address would constitute a further offence under s 97(3) of the RPA 1983, as well as satisfying one of the general arrest conditions under s 24 PACE.

5.7.3 Church services

Section 2 of the Ecclesiastical Courts Jurisdiction Act 1860 created two different types of offences:

- **Riotous, violent, or indecent behaviour**, provided it takes place in any cathedral, church, chapel, churchyard, burial ground or other certified place of religious worship—which may, under Places of Worship Registration Act 1855, include Jewish worship. This offence may be committed at any time.
- **Molesting, disturbing, vexing**, or **troubling**, or (by any other unlawful means) **disquieting** or **misusing** any preacher or clergyman in the process of conducting a religious service at one of these places.

The Act prohibits behaviour that would not constitute an offence under the Public Order Act 1986. It potentially covers almost any deliberately disruptive behaviour during a church service, including entirely peaceful but disruptive protest. While the statute is now over 150 years old, the particular protection it provides to religious worship is consistent with upholding a person's right to practise their religion, now specifically preserved in Article 9 of the ECHR. However, under the Places of Worship Registration Act 1855, the offences relate only to Christian or Jewish worship.

5.8 Dispersal Orders

Sections 30–36 of the Anti-social Behaviour Act 2003 (ASBA) create a free-standing regime giving the police extra powers where specific areas have been identified as having a problem with anti-social behaviour, and have been authorized as such.

The outline of the scheme is:

- The authorization, made in relation to a specific area
- Powers of direction and dispersal exercised within an authorized area
- Removal of children to their home between 9pm and 6am

In February 2011, the Home Office issued a consultation document entitled *More Effective Responses to Anti-social Behaviour* and it may be that the Dispersal Order is shortly to be amalgamated into a new statutory regime.

5.8.1 **The authorization process**

The police officer formally giving authorization must be of the rank of at least superintendent, described in ASBA 2003 as the 'relevant officer' (s 36). He may consider giving an authorization under s 30(1) where he considers that, in any locality in his police area, 'any members of the public have been intimidated, harassed, alarmed or distressed as a result of the presence or behaviour of groups of two or more persons in public places'. The power to grant an authorization therefore only arises in relation to intimidation, harassment, alarm or distress that has already been suffered. 'Public place' is defined in s 36 in almost identical terms to that in s 16 of the POA—see section 5.2.2 of this chapter.

The statutory threshold is low: no specific conduct needs to have caused the reaction in the public, indeed mere presence is sufficient. However, there must be a causal link between this reaction and the presence or behaviour of at least two people. The authorization is designed to deal with trouble spots, rather than isolated incidents of anti-social behaviour. The decision to make an authorization will need to be proportionate and, under s 31(2), cannot be given without the consent of the local authority, or each local authority, whose area includes the whole or part of the relevant locality.

The authorization, granted with the consent of the local authority, must:

- be in writing,
- be signed by the relevant officer giving it, *and*
- specify the relevant locality,
- specify the grounds on which the authorization is given, and
- specify the period during which the powers conferred are exercisable.

The ground on which the authorization is given must do more than simply recite the ingredients of s 30(1): unless specific grounds are set out, the authorization is invalid. See *Sierny v DPP* [2006] EWHC 716 (Admin), where Nelson J said at paragraphs 28–29:

> The section is designed to ensure that there is a proper thought-out basis for making the authorizisation and expressing that basis in written form, which can later be examined and challenged, and which explains to the police, who may later be required to give dispersal directions, information as to the nature of the problem which gave rise to the authorisation and hence in what circumstances the need for directions may arise . . . What is necessary is that there should be a *brief, relevant and concise summary of the nature of the material which gives the authorising officer the grounds for his belief.*
>
> [emphasis added]

Although specific conduct must be considered in the authorization, once it is granted, the powers exercisable by officers are not limited to any particular type of behaviour or scenario, see *R (Parminder Singh) v Chief Constable of the West Midlands Police* [2006] 1 WLR 3374, discussed below.

Once given, the authorization must be published in an authorization notice—a different document from the written authorization itself. Section 31(3) provides that publication may be:

- publishing an authorization notice in a newspaper circulating in the relevant locality; and/or
- posting an authorization notice in some conspicuous place or places within the relevant locality.

The authorization notice must state that the authorization has been given, and specify the relevant locality, and the period during which the powers under the authorization are exercisable.

An authorization may be withdrawn by the officer who gave it, or any other officer whose police area includes the relevant locality, whose rank is the same as, or higher than, that of the original authorizing officer. Before withdrawing an authorization, consultation must take place with the local authority.

Section 31(9) specifically allows the existence of multiple authorizations, potentially covering overlapping areas, based on different behaviours or durations. A withdrawal of one authorization will not affect the validity of other authorizations covering the same locality.

5.8.2 **Direction and dispersal**

Once an authorization has been given, any officer in uniform may exercise the powers under s 30(4), provided he has reasonable grounds for believing that the presence or behaviour of a group of two or more persons in any public place in the relevant locality, has resulted, or is likely to result, in any members of the public being intimidated, harassed, alarmed or distressed. Neither the group, their behaviour, nor the 'victims' need have any similarity or connection with those specified in the original authorization: see *Parminder Singh* at paragraphs 101–102.

The directions under s 30(4) that the officer may give are:

- that the persons in the group disperse—either immediately, or within a time specified by the officer;
- that anybody who is not a resident within the relevant locality is to leave the locality—again, either immediately or within a specified time;
- a direction prohibiting anyone who is not a resident within the locality from returning to it within a specified period (not exceeding 24 hours).

A person who knowingly contravenes one of these directions commits an offence under s 32(2).

The case of *Parminder Singh* concerned a heated protest taking place inside a theatre complex in Birmingham City Centre. The protest was by members of the Sikh community, angered by a play that they felt was blasphemous. Protests took place over several days, and on the day in question had included an invasion of the auditorium in which the play was being shown and a protest in the foyer. At the time of the protests, two authorizations had already been given covering the area, intended to address completely different forms of behaviour. A direction to disperse was given by the police, and when the appellant refused he was arrested, and subsequently accepted a caution for an offence under s 32(2).

The use of the dispersal powers to control a protest, as opposed to anti-social behaviour, was challenged. The Court of Appeal observed that there no easy definition of what is or is not a protest, and that there may be a blurred line between protest and anti-social behaviour. It noted that, while the threshold for conduct justifying a direction to disperse is *lower* than that, required to imposed conditions on an assembly under POA s 14 or 14A, the authorization requires anti-social behaviour to have already occurred (albeit on a previous occasion), rather than showing a likelihood it will occur.

While the exercise of powers under s 30(4) could have a serious impact on the exercise of Article 9, 10 and 11 rights, these rights carry with them the duty to exercise them responsibly. The Court of Appeal confirmed that, provided the powers were used proportionately, the rights of a protestor were still protected. At paragraph 89–90 Hallet LJ stated:

> 89. . . . 'alarm or distress' in some circumstances may not be sufficient to justify a dispersal direction. One or two particularly sensitive members of the public may be alarmed or distressed by conduct that would not or should not offend others. All of us who have the privilege of living in a free and democratic society must on occasions suffer some inconvenience caused by protests and protesters. Whether or not a group's behaviour on any particular occasion warrants a dispersal direction will depend on the circumstances. Police officers must act proportionately and sensibly, as the officers claim they did here.

> 90. They cannot act on a whim. *Both authorizations and dispersal directions must be properly justified on an objective basis.* If used improperly or disproportionately they may be challenged. Articles 10 and 11 are there to protect the peaceful and lawful protest. The rights of the protester are not overridden.
>
> [emphasis added]

There is no need to demonstrate that an individual given a direction had acted (or even was likely to act) in an anti-social way, see paragraph 94:

> The exercise of the powers under section 30 depends on the effect of conduct on members of the public by a group acting as a group. It does not depend on proving that any individual has behaved reprehensibly.

183

The powers under s 30(4) cannot be used in relation to peaceful industrial pickets under TULRCA s 220, or processions under s 11 of the POA, provided notice has either been given or is not required: where a person is lawfully exercising a specific right granted under these two acts, the authorization and dispersal order do not apply.

5.8.3 Removal of children to their home

Between 9pm and 6am s 30(6) gives a uniformed officer a power to take a person under the age of 16 back to their place of residence if:

- they are found in any public place in the relevant locality;
- he has reasonable grounds for believing the person is under the age of 16 and not under the effective control of a parent or a responsible person aged 18 or over.

The power does not require a specific authorization to have been given—it arises automatically on an authorization being granted. The power cannot be exercised if the officer has reasonable grounds for believing that, if taken back to their home, the person would be likely to suffer significant harm. If this power is exercised, the local authority must be informed.

In *R (W) v Commissioner of Police for the Metropolis* [2007] QB 399 the exercise of the power routinely to take children home was challenged. The Court of Appeal stated that the power under s 30(6) was not to be exercised arbitrarily. The purpose of s 30(6) was to both protect children from the physical and social risks of anti-social behaviour by others and to prevent children from themselves participating in anti-social behaviour.

At paragraph 35 of its judgment, the Court of Appeal gave specific guidance as to the scope and operation of s 30(6):

- Section 30(6) does not confer a power to remove children simply because they are in a designated dispersal area at night.
- The discretionary power can only be used if, in the light of its purpose, it is reasonable to do so.
- All constables must have regard to circumstances such as
  - the age of the child;
  - how late at night it is;
  - whether the child is vulnerable or in distress;
  - the child's explanation for his or her conduct and presence in the area; and
  - the nature of the actual or imminently anticipated anti-social behaviour.

The exercise of the power under s 30(6) includes a power to use reasonable force—see paragraph 19 of the judgment in *W*.

Further reading

- *DPP v Jones* [1999] 2 AC 240
- The Home Office *Stop and Search Manual*—this provides a straightforward and readable guide to the implementation of section 60 searches. [The flow chart on page 20 of this manual appears to be incorrect in its use of the word 'necessary']
- The Cabinet Office paper of June 2009, *Understanding Crowd Behaviours: Guidance and Lessons identified* contains detailed consideration of crowd behaviour and crowd management, and contains guidelines for good crowd management. It is available online at <http://www.cabinetoffice.gov.uk/sites/default/files/resources/guidancelessons1_0.pdf>

NOTES

NOTES

Professional Protest and
Direct Action

6.1 **Introduction**

The last twenty years have seen a growth in the number of protestors prepared to act unlawfully to further their cause. The phrase used to describe many of the more publicized actions of such groups is 'direct action'. This is often a euphemism for acts such as trespass, criminal damage or deliberate economic disruption which may amount to crime and well as civil wrongs.

That said, there is a well established and arguably *noble* distinction between non-violent civil disobedience of the kind advocated and exemplified by Henry Thoreau, Mahatma Ghandi or Martin Luther King, and direct action which is less respectful of persons or property. When planning the public order response to radical groups—be they environmental, animal rights or anti-globalization—the police would do well to note and understand the distinction.

There is a world of difference between those who would stage fundamentally peaceful (if deeply inconvenient) 'sit down' protests or 'occupations' at the headquarters of multi-national companies and those who would storm those same headquarters, using violence or intimidation to gain entry and retain possession.

So 'direct action' can mean many different things, ranging from the studiously peaceful through to the decidedly non-peaceful. Understanding which group is at large on any particular police operation is very important in terms of getting the tone, resources and tactics of the police operation right.

The most recent high-profile cause associated with groups who use 'direct action' is climate change and the environmental 'green' movement. Other causes in the last 20 years have included animal rights (especially animals subjected to scientific experiments or intensive farming), anti-capitalism, anti-globalization and various anti-war movements. A number of 'common ingredients' may feature at events organized by such groups:

- A sincerely held belief that it is morally, even *legally*, acceptable to break the law in furtherance of the greater good of the cause.
- Well educated, intelligent, imaginative organizers who are committed to putting significant effort into planning new, publicity-seeking methods of protest.
- A disillusionment or cynicism about using traditional democratic institutions as an effective way to bring about change. This can translate into suspicion or downright hostility towards genuine efforts by the police to facilitate lawful protest.
- Deliberate decisions *not* to engage with police in advance of an event.
- The spreading of disinformation in order to wrong-foot the policing operation.
- A very broad spectrum of attendees. Some will be veteran protestors from the studiously peaceful wing of protesting. Some will be casual supporters, who wish to lend support by their presence and who may get caught up in

'crowd mentality'. Others may be best described as 'rent-a-mob'—attendees who are attracted to the opportunity to cause trouble rather than attending out of any true support for the cause.

Casual supporters may form the majority of those attending at larger events. There is however a well-recognized tendency for these casual supporters to tolerate unlawful conduct by fellow protestors, and even to imitate them, if they become angered by a perception that the police are being heavy handed or overreacting, or simply because they get caught up in the excitement of the event and the crowd's activity.

The policing of protests or 'events' by radical direct action groups needs to be proactive and intelligence-led, with exquisitely careful briefing of the frontline officers prior to the event. The police have the legal duty to strike a balance between facilitating lawful protest on the one hand, and on the other hand intervening to prevent an escalation of disorder before restoring order becomes impossible. The timing of such interventions is therefore legally and practically sensitive.

This chapter focuses on the legal powers available to deal with protest that has become, or imminently threatens to become, unlawful. It offers solutions to a few of the problems recognized as commonly arising. Some of the statutory powers, and their potential use, are demonstrated in the case studies 'Toad Hall' and 'Hedgerow Airport'.

6.1.1 **Specific legislation**

During the 1980s and early 1990s the protest groups posing the greatest and most persistent challenges to public order policing were animal rights organizations and the anti-hunt lobby. While the ban on fox hunting has led to a decrease in protests against hunting, animal rights organizations have remained both active and creative in adapting their activities. As a result, more efforts have been made to introduce legislation to control the activities of animal rights protestors than for any other protest group since the peak of industrial unrest.

The Protection from Harassment Act 1997 (in this chapter, 'the Act' or PHA) was originally intended to address neighbourhood disputes, personal vendettas, and stalkers. Nevertheless, the tactic of some animal rights activists (for example, those opposing Huntingdon Life Sciences and its associates) of intimidating commercial partners, employees and their families led to significant numbers of injunctions being granted under the Act to restrict the activists' conduct.

While the potential for the Act to assist in protecting those working within this sector was apparent, a number of difficulties resulted from using it in a way which was not originally anticipated.

As a result, a number of further statutory offences and associated powers have been created:

- Section 1A and 3A of the PHA. These expanded the ability to use the Act against protestors. See sections 6.2.2 and 6.2.3.
- Section 42 of the Criminal Justice and Police Act 2001 (CJPA). This gives the police power to give directions stopping the harassment of a person in his home. See section 6.3.
- Section 42A of the CJPA. This created the offence of harassment of a person in his home. See section 6.3.

In addition, sections 145 and 146 of the Serious Organised Crime and Police Act 2005 (SOCPA) created specific offences of (i) interference with contractual relationships so as to harm animal research organizations, and (ii) the intimidation of persons connected with animal research organizations. Unlike the harassment offences, this legislation is confined to the sphere of scientific animal research, See section 6.4.

6.2 The Protection from Harassment Act 1997

The broad framework of the 1997 Act is as follows:

- Section 1 prohibits harassment, which can be committed in a number of ways.
- Section 2 creates the criminal offence of harassment.
- Section 3(1) creates a civil cause of action for harassment.
- Section 3(3) empowers the High Court and County Court to grant injunctions to prevent further harassment where it has already occurred.
- Section 3(6) creates the offence of breach of such an injunction.
- Section 4 creates a more serious criminal offence than s 2, of putting people in fear of violence.
- Section 5 provides for a similar power as s 3(3), known as a restraining order. This can be imposed on conviction for an offence under s 2 or s 4.

The *only* difference between 'criminal' harassment' in s 2 and the tort ('civil wrong') in s 3 of the 1997 Act is the standard of proof required at court. There is also a specific crime of racially aggravated harassment—see section 7.4.1 of chapter 7.

6.2.1 What constitutes harassment?

Definition of course of conduct

Section 1(1) of the 1997 Act states:

(1) A person must not pursue a course of conduct—
(a) which amounts to harassment of another, and
(b) which he knows or ought to know amounts to harassment of the other.

Section 2 of the 1997 Act creates the criminal offence of harassment, and section 3 makes harassment a civil tort, which can give rise to damages and which can be prevented with an injunction. Section 7(2) states that references to 'harassing' a person include alarming the person or causing them distress, but no further definition is offered.

Three civil decisions demonstrate the looseness of the definition of harassment.

In *Majrowski v Guy's & St Thomas' NHS Trust* [2006] UKHL 34, Baroness Hale stated at paragraph 66:

> All sorts of conduct may amount to harassment. It includes alarming a person or causing her distress: section 7(2). But conduct might be harassment even if no alarm or distress were in fact caused. A great deal is left to the wisdom of the courts to draw sensible lines between the ordinary banter and badinage of life and genuinely offensive and unacceptable behaviour.

In *Ferguson v British Gas Trading Limited* [2009] EWCA Civ 46 the Court of Appeal held that persistent, erroneous letters from a utility company threatening a former client with having her supply cut off, or being referred to credit agencies in relation to a non-existent debt, were capable of amounting to harassment. The Court confirmed that 'a real person is likely to suffer real anxiety and distress if threatened in the way which Ms Ferguson was'.

In *Thomas v News Group Newspapers Ltd* [2001] EWCA Civ 1233 the Court of Appeal stated at paragraph 30 that harassment 'describes conduct targeted at an individual which is calculated to produce the consequences described in section 7 and which is oppressive and unreasonable'.

Similarly:

- Persistent telephone calls about what may have (initially) been a legitimate complaint were potentially capable of amounting to harassment—*DPP v Hardy* [2008] EWHC 2874 (Admin).
- Legitimate commercial pressure to repay a business debt could become harassment if the conduct ceased to be merely unattractive and unreasonable and became oppressive and unacceptable: *S&D Property Investments Ltd v Nisbet* [2009] EWHC 1726 (Ch).

In cases involving public protest, the courts have been noticeably more cautious in finding that acts of protest constitute harassment.

Case study
Animal rights protests at the University of Oxford

In *University of Oxford v Broughton* [2008] EWHC 75 (QB), the Court distinguished between daily contact between animal rights protestors and workers attending a laboratory for their work (which might be harassment) and occasional protests outside the university's graduation ceremonies. Having reminded itself that 'Free speech includes not only the inoffensive but the irritating, the contentious, the heretical, the unwelcome and the provocative' (see *Redmond-Bate* at section 3.6.2), the Court went on to note that, in relation to the graduation ceremonies, 'Nowhere in the University's evidence does any witness speak of feeling harassed, alarmed or threatened. The language is all in terms of irritation and the loss of enjoyment'.

Key points

- The courts will be slow to find that a genuine exercise of the right to freedom of expression is harassment.
- Conduct which is repeatedly targeted at the same individual, day after day, might constitute harassment, even though less frequent repetition of similar conduct would not.

However, this does not mean that irritation and loss of enjoyment could not amount to harassment, particularly if it is endured over a period of time. In *Broughton* the Court did not rule out the possibility that similar protests in the future might constitute harassment, particularly if loudhailers were persistently used.

The mental element of harassment

Where a single individual is the victim of harassment, it is necessary to show that the harasser knew *or ought to have known* that the course of conduct amounts to harassment (s 1(1)(b)).

This is a purely objective test, based on the facts of which the harasser was aware or ought to have been aware. Except for cases where the acts complained of only just amount to harassment, this should be an easy test to satisfy. However, where harassment is based on a number of different victims, the test as to intent is stricter.

6.2.2 **What amounts to a course of conduct?**

One victim, at least two occasions

For harassment to become actionable under the Act, there must be a 'course of conduct'. This requires either:

- under s 1(1), conduct on at least *two* occasions towards *one* person, or
- under s 1(1A), in the case of conduct towards two or more people, conduct on at least *one* occasion towards *each* of them.

Two occasions of conduct towards one person does not *automatically* mean that a course of conduct is established. The course of conduct must also amount to harassment.

Thus two isolated, unconnected instances of conduct causing distress to another person might not amount to harassment if it was nothing more than coincidence that linked the two occasions (see for example, in the domestic context *R v Curtis* [2010] EWCA Crim 123). Nevertheless, the suggestion by the harasser that the two instances were a mere coincidence would have to be carefully examined.

There must be at least two occasions of harassing conduct for the offence under s 1 to be made out. The closer together that the occasions are in time, the greater the chance that they will be interpreted as a single instance of conduct.

Conversely, the longer the period of time between each occasion, and the smaller the number of incidents, the less likely it is that they would amount to a course of conduct. A jury direction along these lines is now standard in criminal cases.

Where there is a time lag of several months it may be difficult to demonstrate a sufficient connection between the events to establish a course of conduct. While this will apply more clearly for domestic or neighbourhood disputes, the considerations are different for political activists who are running a campaign. In such cases, even a long time lag may be no bar to finding a course of conduct, as the connection can be established due to the *basis* of the contact between the activist and the victim which arises only due to the activists' campaign, rather than (for example) the proximity of people's homes.

Conduct in relation to two or more people

The introduction of s 1(1A) made a substantial difference to the way in which harassment can be committed.

Definition of conduct in relation to two or more people

Section 1(1A) provides:

A person must not pursue a course of conduct—

(a) which involves harassment of two or more persons, and

(b) which he knows or ought to know involves harassment of those persons, and

(c) by which he intends to persuade any person (whether or not one of those mentioned above)—

　(i) not to do something that he is entitled or required to do, or

　(ii) to do something that he is not under any obligation to do.

Section 7(3)(b) provides that the course of conduct must relate to at least one occasion in respect of each person.

While a corporate body (such as a company or partnership) cannot be the direct victim of harassment, it is often the activities of the organization that are the focus of the activists' conduct rather than any one individual. So while subsection 1A could potentially be used where a family is being harassed, it is actually designed to deal with situations where activists are focused on an organization, and are targeting the employees or contractors of that organization.

As can be seen from subsections (b) and (c) of s 1(1A), to establish a course of conduct against multiple victims the test for intent is very different from the test for harassment of a single victim.

Firstly, it must be shown that the harasser knew, or ought to have known, that the course of conduct would involve harassment—as for harassment under s 1(1).

Secondly, it must also be shown that the motive for the harassment is to persuade *any person* (which in this context *includes* an organization) either to stop doing something they are entitled to do, or to do something they are not obliged to do. An obvious situation is where the employees of a company are harassed in order to put pressure on the employer to change its business activities, for example by stopping animal experiments.

Where the harasser is a campaigner, the nature of the campaign itself is likely to be the best evidence of the activist's underlying intent. For example, if a delivery driver for suppliers of building materials is targeted by activists whose campaign goal is to stop the construction of a particular building, it should be simple to show that the activists' intention is to persuade the suppliers to stop delivering materials to the site, ie to stop them doing something that they are entitled by law to do.

6.2.3 **Aiding and abetting**

In a carefully orchestrated campaign many individual protestors may play small roles, which looked at individually might not amount to harassment but which together contribute to a harassment campaign. Section 7(3A) of the Act is designed to cover such a situation:

> (3A) A person's conduct on any occasion shall be taken, if aided, abetted, counselled or procured by another—
>
> (a) to be conduct on that occasion of the other (as well as conduct of the person whose conduct it is); and
>
> (b) to be conduct in relation to which the other's knowledge and purpose, and what he ought to have known, are the same as they were in relation to what was contemplated or reasonably foreseeable at the time of the aiding, abetting, counselling or procuring.

This is a complicated way of saying that where someone has assisted (ie aided abetted, counselled or procured) someone else to act in a certain way, *both the act and the intention* are attributable to the assister. For example, if person A assists both B and C each to do a single act and, if both single acts had been committed by a single person they would have constituted a course of conduct, then—provided the assistance can be proved—A is to be treated as having pursued that course of conduct himself.

Case study

Action against multiple people

A, B and C are campaigners against the seal fur trade, and have identified X Ltd as a company involved in the trade. A prints copies of graphic photographs of the corpses of seal pups killed in the trade, and gives the copies to B and C. B attends outside the primary school attended by one of the children of an employee of X Ltd and hands the pictures of the dead seal pups to the child. C does a similar thing to another child of the employee, who attends a different primary school.

- The conduct, in showing gruesome pictures to young children, would clearly be capable of forming part of a course of conduct amounting to harassment.
- The intention of the campaigners can be established by reference to the campaign itself: the intention is clearly to put pressure on the children's father (and through him, X Ltd) to stop their involvement in the fur trade.
- Although only one act has been committed in relation to each child, taken together they amount to a course of conduct.
- A has aided both B and C in their actions. Under s 7(3A)(a) of the Act, both acts are attributable to A, and would amount to a course of conduct by him.
- A has therefore committed the offence of harassment under s 1(1A) of the PHA.

6.2.4 Defences to allegations of harassment

Definition of defences to allegations of harassment

Section 1(3) states:

(3) Subsection (1) or (1A) does not apply to a course of conduct if the person who pursued it shows—
   (a) that it was pursued for the purpose of preventing or detecting crime,
   (b) that it was pursued under any enactment or rule of law or to comply with any condition or requirement imposed by any person under any enactment, or
   (c) that in the particular circumstances the pursuit of the course of conduct was reasonable.

Exemptions (a) and (b) are more likely to arise where the person accused of harassment is a police officer, or where they act on behalf of a public or statutory body (including county court bailiffs, traffic wardens, etc).

The fact that harassment might arise in the context of preventing or detecting crime does not *in itself* amount to a defence. The course of conduct at the heart of the alleged harassment must be specifically for the purposes of the prevention or detection of crime, and in most cases this means that the defendant will have to show that the course of conduct was *necessary* to prevent crime: *Dowson v Chief Constable of Northumbria (No. 1)* [2009] EWHC 907 (QB).

195

It is exemption (c)—'in the particular circumstances the pursuit of the course of conduct was reasonable'—that is most likely to arise in the context of the policing of protests or direct action where activists will often seek to argue that their conduct is reasonable.

The exercise of the right to protest can mean that certain conduct is considered reasonable that might in a non-protest context be harassment. See, for example, the approach of the court to demonstrations outside the graduation ceremonies of Oxford University at 6.2.1 of this chapter. Freedom of expression and freedom of association have to be protected by the courts (see section 2.7.2) and in *Oxford University v Broughton* the court referred to the need for 'the most careful scrutiny' when considering possible restraints upon freedom of expression. However, where there is evidence that the conduct has crossed the line from public protest into the harassment of individuals, the defence of reasonable conduct will be more difficult to establish. As ever, each case will turn on its particular facts and context.

There are close parallels between the harassment defences and the statutory defence to an offence under s 5 of the Public Order Act 1986 (POA)—see section 4.7.4. However, there is a conflict between a victim's right to be protected from harassment within the meaning of s 1(1A) and the protestor's right to freedom of expression protected by s 1(3)(c). This is because the very purpose of much legitimate protest is to seek to persuade people not to do something that they are otherwise entitled or required to do (such as a company who have contracted to supply an animal research organization, who are therefore legally required to supply the organization with goods) or to make them do something they do not want to do.

Underlying the potential defence in s 1(3)(c) is the need to balance the rights of the protestor with the rights of the person who feels (or is likely to feel) harassed.

The s 1(3)(c) defence is therefore likely to avail a protestor who conducts his protest in a proportionate and reasonable manner, even if the consequence of the protest is to cause another person to feel harassed. In the earlier example, the anti-fur trade campaigner who deliberately caused distress to young children by showing them photographs of seal pup corpses would be unlikely to be able to convince a court that such conduct was reasonable. However, if the campaigner had sent a letter to two directors of X Ltd, explaining their concerns about the treatment of seal pups, accompanied by a similar photograph, it might be arguable that it was reasonable to demonstrate to the directors the reality of the fur trade.

Protest which takes place in breach of the terms of an injunction in force at the time of the protest cannot be reasonable behaviour: in *DPP v Moseley* (*The Times*, 23 June 1999) protestors continued to protest at a mink farm even after an injunction had been obtained against them which prevented them from doing so. The magistrates' decision that the conduct was reasonable under s 1(3)(c) was overturned by the High Court. It held that, where protests were continued in breach of an injunction, the magistrates were bound to accept that the respondents could not prove reasonableness under s 1(3)(c).

Exercise of freedom of expression, even freedom of the press, can nevertheless constitute harassment. This was confirmed in *Thomas v News Group Newspapers Ltd* [2001] EWCA Civ 1233. This case concerned the repeated (and allegedly unnecessary) reference to the claimant's race in a series of newspaper articles criticising her for making a complaint about a private joke between police officers about an asylum seeker. The Court of Appeal confirmed that:

- the publication of press articles calculated to incite racial hatred of an individual is an example of conduct capable of amounting to harassment under the 1997 Act (paragraph 37);
- the test (for whether a series of articles amounts to harassment) requires the publisher to consider whether a proposed series of articles, which are likely to cause distress to an individual, will constitute an abuse of the freedom of press.

6.2.5 **The offence of harassment**

Section 2 of the Act confirms that a person who pursues a course of conduct amounting to harassment is guilty of a summary only offence.

Police should note that the offence is complete once the second incident of conduct has taken place. This means that behaviour towards another that would not constitute an offence under s 5 of the POA can nevertheless constitute criminal behaviour if, by its repetition (either towards a single person or a number of people), it forms part of a course of conduct under the Act.

6.2.6 **The offence of putting people in fear of violence**

Definition of the offence of putting people in fear of violence

Section 4 of the Protection from Harassment Act 1997 provides:

A person whose course of conduct causes another to fear, on at least two occasions, that violence will be used against him is guilty of an offence if he knows or ought to know that his course of conduct will cause the other so to fear on each of those occasions.

This offence, which is triable either way and can lead to a prison sentence of up to five years, is intended to cover the most serious cases of harassment, involving the deliberate threat of *violence*. Just as for 'straightforward' harassment, the mental element requires that the defendant knew or ought to have known that the conduct would cause a fear of violence in another. The test is whether a reasonable person, in possession of the same information as the defendant, would know.

6.2.7 **Injunctions and restraining orders**

Where evidence of campaigns of harassment have been demonstrated, the courts have been pragmatic in the scope of the injunctions ordered, the terms of the prohibitions, the identities of the defendants and the measures to be taken to 'serve' the injunction. Whilst it is not part of the function of the police to seek injunctions on behalf of potential victims (an injunction being a private, civil remedy for which the potential victim must be the applicant), an understanding of their scope and existence is important to the police for several reasons:

- It would be appropriate for the police to advise the victim of harassment that they may be able to seek an injunction, and should therefore obtain their own legal advice.
- Injunctions have become a useful tool against the more determined direct action groups. The existence (or absence) of such an injunction is a significant factor in the planning of protests by organizers as well as in the proactive policing response.
- Officers may be asked to assist in providing witness statements—normally in support of such injunctions. There is no reason in principle why, if asked, an officer ought not provide such evidence, provided that the police do not become embroiled in the substantive merits of the issue under protest (ie do not enter the political fray) and certainly any officer giving such a statement would be well advised to confirm with a senior officer that it is appropriate to do so in any particular case.
- Breach of the terms of such an injunction constitutes a criminal offence under s 3(6). Therefore, once an injunction is in place, the police may be called upon to enforce its terms by arresting those who have breached it.
- The existence and terms of an injunction have the potential to have a major impact on the policing of protests.

An injunction (or, following conviction, a restraining order) may be granted to protect a company, not simply an individual or individuals: *R v Buxton* [2010] EWCA Crim 2923, where environmental protestors had obstructed a section of railway used by trains carrying coal and caused a loss of about £8,000 to the company that owned the coal.

Injunctions in the civil courts

An injunction may be sought by the victims in the civil courts to prevent harassment, or anticipated harassment. The injunction can be sought proactively or after harassment has already occurred to seek to prevent it recurring. The requirements to be satisfied differ as between the injunctions sought by a single victim (under s 3(1)) and those sought on behalf of multiple victims.

At the pre-trial stage where an interim injunction is sought, an applicant will have to show evidence of a prima facie case that at least one incident has occurred (or been threatened) that would, if repeated, amount to harassment. There would have to be evidence to demonstrate that, in the absence of an injunction, there was a substantial risk that the behaviour was likely to recur. At the hearing for a final injunction, the alleged facts on which the claim is based must, as in other civil claims, be proved on the balance of probabilities.

The civil courts adopt a three stage process in determining applications for injunctions under the 1997 Act:

1. Whether there is a real prospect that the acts on which the application is brought will be proved (or, for a final injunction, whether the matters *are* proved);
2. Whether, on the basis of the facts proved (or likely to be proved) there is a reasonable anticipation that further acts will be committed;
3. Whether an order against an individual defendant is reasonably to be regarded as necessary for the protection of the claimants' legitimate interests. An alternative formulation of this, see section 37(1) of the Senior Courts Act 1981, is whether it is *just and convenient* to make an order in the terms sought. See, for example, *UPS Ltd & Ors v Stop Huntingdon Animal Cruelty & Ors* (LTL 17/2/2011, unreported) where the court held that it would normally be just and convenient to grant an injunction where the court reasonably supposed there to be a continuing threat, requiring the coercive power of a court order to mitigate it.

The precise matters that must be proved in order to persuade a court to grant an injunction will vary depending on factors such as what prohibitions are sought and what the alleged behaviour of the harasser is. In *Hall v Save Newchurch Guinea Pigs (Campaign)* [2005] EWHC 372 (QB) (the highly publicized Darley Oaks Farm campaign) the Court noted that:

> Since the decision of the House of Lords in *Cream Holdings Limited and others v Banerjee and others* [2004] UKHL 44, [2003] 3 WLR 918, a more stringent test must be applied where the injunction sought will encroach upon an individual defendant's rights to freedom of expression.

In relation to the s 1(1A) version of harassment (multiple victims), a civil injunction may be applied for by either an individual who is subjected to harassment or the target of the campaign, ie the person who the harasser is seeking to persuade not to do something that he is entitled or required to do, or to do something that he is not under any obligation to do. Where commercial interests or institutions are involved, it will increasingly be the corporation, or its business clients/suppliers, who are the claimants in such injunctions—rather than their employees or individual contractors.

The identity of defendants in civil injunctions

Often, it will be difficult to confirm the identity of all the individuals involved in the harassment. This can be for a number of reasons. Activist organizations often have a complicated, or simply disorganized, structure, or may be too large or shifting in their composition to be capable of tidy identification. Furthermore, often no one individual is prepared to accept that they are an organizer. The activists may also take deliberate steps to conceal their identity.

If evidence can be produced which details the efforts made to identify the activists, and showing links between the activist organization and unlawful conduct or harassment in the past, the courts try to take a pragmatic approach to these types of problems. Under Part 19.6 of the Civil Procedure Rules it is possible for one identified defendant to act as a 'representative' of other, unnamed protestors.

See, for example, in *Smithkline Beecham Plc v Avery* [2009] EWHC 1488 (QB) where the activist groups, the Animal Liberation Front (ALF) and Stop Huntingdon Animal Cruelty (SHAC), could not be named defendants because as unincorporated associations they were not recognized as legal persons. Using Part 19, the Court made a 'representation order', the effect of which was that named defendants who could be proved to be members of those organizations were ordered to act as representatives of any other persons who held that same interest. One of the named defendants, the press officer for the ALF, was held to be a suitable representative defendant for 'all persons acting as members, participants or supporters or in the name of the unincorporated association known as the Animal Liberation Front'. However, under Part 19 the Court's permission is required to actually *enforce* such an injunction against the unnamed persons. The Court in the *Smithkline* litigation had declined to do this (see [2007] EWHC 948 (QB)) on the grounds that it would be unjust to make an order against unidentified persons without giving them an opportunity to be heard and without giving some consideration to their individual circumstances. The Court of Appeal has confirmed, in the subsequent case of *Astellas Pharma Ltd and others v Stop Huntingdon Animal Cruelty and others* [2011] EWCA Civ 752, that the Court's approach was appropriate. In *Astellas*, the Court of Appeal also declined to express a view on whether an unnamed person, bound by an injunction made in proceedings where a representation order was made, was a 'defendant' for the purposes of s 3(6) PHA (which would mean they could be arrested for breach of the injunction's terms).

6.2.8 Restraining orders in the criminal courts

Where a defendant is convicted of an offence under either s 2 or s 4 of the PHA, the sentencing court may make a restraining order. The order can be made for the purpose of protecting the victim(s) of the offence(s) or any other person mentioned in the order from further conduct which amounts to either harassment or which will cause a fear of violence.

Where a restraining order is sought, both the prosecution and the defence may lead further evidence that would be admissible in a civil application for an injunction under section 3. Any person mentioned in the order is entitled to be heard on the hearing of an application for a restraining order.

Under s 5A of the Act, the Criminal Court may also make a restraining order following the *acquittal* of a defendant. It may only do so if it considers it *necessary* to do so to protect a person from harassment by the defendant. The test for the court as to whether an order is necessary is one of evaluation, rather than application of a normal burden or standard of proof. However, the facts on which the court is to base its evaluation must be proved to the civil standard.

Once it is in place, the restraining order has a very similar effect to a civil injunction: those named in the order are prohibited from the behaviour specified in the order.

6.2.9 Breach of an injunction or restraining order

Breach of an injunction or restraining order issued under the PHA is a criminal offence. Whether a prohibition has been imposed via a civil injunction or criminal court restraining order, the penalty for breach is the same: on conviction on indictment, up to five years' imprisonment (or a fine, or both) or on summary conviction, up to six months' imprisonment or a fine not exceeding the statutory maximum, or both. There is a potential defence of 'reasonable excuse'.

Under sections 3(3)–3(5) of the Act, a claimant who has the benefit of a civil injunction can apply for a warrant for the arrest of someone who without reasonable excuse breaches the terms of the injunction. Whether or not an individual has applied for a warrant, a constable may, under the usual arrest provisions of s 24 of the Police and Criminal Evidence Act (PACE), arrest a person where there are reasonable grounds to suspect he has, without reasonable excuse, done anything which he is prohibited from doing by the injunction.

6.3 Harassment of a Person in his Home

Section 42 and 42A of the Criminal Justice and Police Act 2001 (CJPA) set out specific police powers and specific offences arising where a protest (or other form of protestor action) takes place at, or in the vicinity of, a person's home. The sections are only relevant where the action takes place outside a person's own home. However, the police will need to consider these sections whenever action takes place (or is anticipated to take place) that targets the home (or vicinity of the home) of an individual.

6.3.1 **The offence of harassment of a person in his home**

In summary, section 42A of the CJPA provides as follows:

42A Offence of harassment etc of a person in his home

(1) A person commits an offence if—
    (a) that person is present outside or in the vicinity of any premises that are used by any individual ('the resident') as his dwelling;
    (b) that person is present there for the purpose (by his presence or otherwise) of representing to the resident or another individual (whether or not one who uses the premises as his dwelling), or of persuading the resident or such another individual—
        (i) that he should not do something that he is entitled or required to do; or
        (ii) that he should do something that he is not under any obligation to do;
    (c) that person—
        (i) intends his presence to amount to the harassment of, or to cause alarm or distress to, the resident; or
        (ii) knows or ought to know that his presence is likely to result in the harassment of, or to cause alarm or distress to, the resident; and
    (d) the presence of that person—
        (i) amounts to the harassment of, or causes alarm or distress to, any person falling within subsection (2); or
        (ii) is likely to result in the harassment of, or to cause alarm or distress to, any such person.
(2) A person falls within this subsection if he is—
    (a) the resident,
    (b) a person in the resident's dwelling, or
    (c) a person in another dwelling in the vicinity of the resident's dwelling.

POINT TO NOTE

'Dwelling' takes the definition contained in s 8(1) of the Public Order Act 1986—'any structure or part of a structure occupied as a person's home or as other living accommodation (whether the occupation is separate or shared with others)'—and includes a tent, caravan, vehicle, vessel or other temporary or movable structure.

The offence of harassment of a person in his own home by a defendant therefore has four ingredients.

1. **Presence**: outside or in the vicinity of a person's home. 'Vicinity' potentially covers a significantly wider area in a rural area than in a city centre. Entrances to the common areas of a block of flats, or the entrance to a private gated road would both be covered.

2. **Purpose**: to convince the resident not to do something that he is entitled or required to do, or to do something that he is not under any obligation to do. Section 42A(1)(b) allows the target of the conduct to either be the resident, or some other visitor. The third person might be a family member (eg the children of a director of a company building coal-fired power stations), but might equally be a visitor to the dwelling. In such a case, the purpose is either to convince the third person to change his future conduct, or to put pressure on the third person to persuade the resident to change his conduct.
3. **Intent or knowledge**: the offence requires either an intention to cause the resident harassment alarm or distress, or the knowledge of a likelihood that the resident will be caused this. Or, the offence can be committed where the defendant ought reasonably to have known this was the likely result. Subsection (4) provides that 'a person (A) ought to know that his presence is likely to result in the harassment of, or to cause alarm or distress to, a resident if a reasonable person in possession of the same information would think that A's presence was likely to have that effect'.
4. **Consequence**: the presence of the defendant needs to either result in harassment, alarm or distress, or be likely so to do.

Unlike s 1(1) of the PHA, this offence does not require a course of conduct. It can therefore be used for one off acts of home-targeted harassment.

Section 42A(1)(b) of the CJPA specifies that while the action needs to focus on putting pressure (harassment, alarm or distress) on a particular resident or visitor, the person whose behaviour the action is ultimately directed towards *influencing* need not be that resident or visitor. It could be another individual altogether, such as the resident or visitor's employer. The harassment, alarm or distress that is intended or anticipated can be that of the specific resident, a person in his dwelling, or even a person in a *different* dwelling, provided it is in the vicinity of the person's dwelling. Harassment, alarm or distress caused (or likely or intended to be caused) to the neighbours would be sufficient to complete the offence.

The offence under s 42A does not require the defendant to have previously been given a direction by a constable under s 42. The maximum sentence is 51 weeks (s 42A(5)).

Case study

Harassment of a person in his home

Dr Scalpel works at a clinic where abortions are carried out. He lives in a detached house in a small cul-de-sac with his wife and child. One morning when Mrs Scalpel and her child are walking to the shops, they see an anti-abortion campaigner at the end of their road. As they walk past, the campaigner shouts and Mrs Scalpel, 'What a pretty little child. But your husband kills other people's children, how can you live with a child murderer? You must be as bad as him'. Mrs Scalpel is extremely upset by this comment.

- This is a one-off incident, but under s 42A there is no need for there to be a course of conduct.
- The protestor is present in the vicinity of Mrs Scalpel's home.
- The protestor's intent is clearly to persuade Dr Scalpel (either directly, or through his wife) to stop undertaking abortions at the clinic.
- The protestor either knew, or ought to have known, that the comment would cause Mrs Scalpel distress.
- The conduct has in fact caused Mrs Scalpel distress.
- An offence under s 42A is complete.
- Similar behaviour towards a next door neighbour, aimed at causing distress either to the neighbour or Dr Scalpel, would also amount to an offence.

6.3.2 Power to give directions to stop the harassment of a person in his home

Section 42 of CJPA gives a constable power to give directions to a person (or persons) at a scene in order to try to prevent the harassment of a person in his home. Unlike the application for an injunction under the PHA, this section grants specific powers to the police to prevent future harassment of a person in their home.

When does the power to give directions arise?

Section 42(1) of CJPA 2001 provides:

(1) Subject to the following provisions of this section, a constable who is at the scene may give a direction under this section to any person if—

  (a) that person is present outside or in the vicinity of any premises that are used by any individual ('the resident') as his dwelling;

  (b) that constable believes, on reasonable grounds, that person is present there for the purpose (by his presence or otherwise) of representing to the resident or another individual (whether or not one who uses the premises as his dwelling), or of persuading the resident or such another individual—

    (i) that he should not do something that he is entitled or required to do; or

    (ii) that he should do something that he is not under any obligation to do; and

  (c) that constable also believes, on reasonable grounds, that the presence of that person (either alone or together with that of any other persons who are also present)—

    (i) amounts to, or is likely to result in, the harassment of the resident; or

    (ii) is likely to cause alarm or distress to the resident.

The conditions that are necessary in order for the power to arise have parallels with, but are not identical to, s 42A. The conditions are:

1. **Presence**: the person is present outside or in the vicinity of any premises that are used by any individual as his dwelling.
2. **Purpose**: the constable must believe on reasonable grounds, that the person is present for the purpose of putting pressure on the resident (or another individual) to change their future legitimate conduct.
3. **Consequence**: the constable believes on reasonable grounds that the conduct amounts to harassment, or is likely to cause harassment, alarm or distress to the resident. If there is no potential for the resident to be harassed, then no direction can be given.

However, even if these conditions are satisfied, an officer cannot give directions if there is a more senior-ranking officer also at the scene (s 42(6)(a)). So it is the most senior officer present who must give the directions.

There is no specific defence (or exclusion) of reasonable conduct, similar to that in s 1(3)(c) of the PHA. However, it is almost inevitable that if the same behaviour would constitute reasonable conduct under the 1997 Act, it would not be harassment for the purposes of s 42(1)(c)(i) above.

What directions may be given?

Section 42(2) of CJPA provides:

> A direction under this section is a direction requiring the person to whom it is given to do all such things as the constable giving it may specify as the things he considers necessary to prevent one or both of the following—
> (a) the harassment of the resident; or
> (b) the causing of any alarm or distress to the resident.

Therefore, provided that the constable believes the directions are necessary to prevent harassment, alarm or distress, the potential scope of the directions is very broad. However, it remains the case that, as when considering the power to give directions at all, the officer must have reasonable grounds to believe that the specific directions are *necessary*.

There is one specific set of directions that *cannot* be given under this section, which is the right to refrain from peacefully picketing a place of work, ie acts that can be potentially lawful under s 220 of the Trade Union and Labour Relations (Consolidation) Act 1992 (TULRCA), see section 6.6 of this chapter.

Section 42(4) confirms that the requirements can include a requirement (a) to leave the vicinity of the premises in question, or (b) to leave that vicinity *and* not to return to it within such period as the constable may specify, up to three months. Again, the officer must have reasonable grounds to believe that the duration period is necessary.

Where there are a number of people present, the constable may notify them individually or as a group. In either case, the requirement to leave the vicinity may be to do so immediately or after a specified period of time. A direction under this section may be given orally.

However, it is vital for practical risk management purposes that a record is kept of the wording of the direction, as well as to whom it was given, where and when. The legality of any future arrest and viability of associated prosecution will depend on proving precisely what direction was given and to whom. It would therefore be strongly advisable to carefully draft and prepare the directions in writing *prior* to giving them, and also to provide all those people notified of the direction a copy of the directions in writing. It would also be good practice digitally to record the process of service of the notices.

Under subsection (5), the constable may make exceptions to the direction, as he sees fit. Such exceptions may themselves be subject to conditions. For example, a constable could direct that protestors leave and do not return, subject to the exception that they may return to protest at a certain time each week, with the exception subject to the condition that there be no more than a specified number of protestors present, or that particular protestors are not to return. Clearly, if there are to be any exceptions, this increases the need for absolute precision, and a written record of the full terms of the direction and proof of service or delivery of the same.

There is a power under s 42(6) CJPA to vary or withdraw a direction previously given. While there is no formal avenue for appealing a direction given under s 42, the decision to give such a direction would be susceptible to judicial review. The process of judicial review requires the claimant to exhaust other avenues of appeal before bringing a claim. In practical terms, it will be necessary for a dissatisfied protestor to request from the police a review of the direction before seeking judicial review. If such a request is received, it would be incumbent on the police to give it due consideration, not least because a refusal to do so could itself be susceptible to challenge.

If a direction were made which were not necessary, or did not satisfy the requirements of s 42 for any other reason, this would provide a defence to a potential charge arising either from an alleged breach or from an alleged obstruction/assault of an officer in the execution of his duty. It might potentially render an arrest unlawful.

Breach of s 42

There are two summary offences arising from breaches of s 42, which are entirely separate from the s 42A offence.

The first is failing to comply with a constable's direction (s 42(7)).

The second is where a person returns to the vicinity of the premises in question before the expiry of the period specified in the direction, for the purposes of s 42(1)(b).

Both are summary only offences. In order to prove the offence, there is no requirement to demonstrate that a resident has suffered harassment as the essence of the offence is the breach of the direction.

206

6.4 **Specific Animal Research Offences**

The legislation discussed above is not confined to animal rights protests, though it is often deployed against such activists. However, there are two specific offences enshrined in sections 145 and 146 of SOCPA that do apply specifically to action taken against animal research organizations. 'Animal research organizations' has a very specific meaning. It refers to persons or organizations designated under various sections within the Animals (Scientific Procedures) Act 1986. Other activities that raise animal rights issues, such as hunting, fishing, the fur trade, live animal exports, etc, are *not* covered.

For both s 145 and s 146, on conviction in the magistrates' courts a defendant faces imprisonment of up to 12 months or a fine not exceeding the statutory maximum, or both. On conviction on indictment the maximum sentence is five years' imprisonment, a fine, or both.

6.4.1 **Interference with contractual relationships**

Section 145 provides:

145 Interference with contractual relationships so as to harm animal research organisation

(1) A person (A) commits an offence if, with the intention of harming an animal research organisation, he—
   (a) does a relevant act, or
   (b) threatens that he or somebody else will do a relevant act,
   in circumstances in which that act or threat is intended or likely to cause a second person (B) to take any of the steps in subsection (2).

(2) The steps are—
   (a) not to perform any contractual obligation owed by B to a third person (C) (whether or not such non-performance amounts to a breach of contract);
   (b) to terminate any contract B has with C;
   (c) not to enter into a contract with C

(3) For the purposes of this section, a 'relevant act' is—
   (a) an act amounting to a criminal offence, or
   (b) a tortious act causing B to suffer loss or damage of any description;
   but paragraph (b) does not include an act which is actionable on the ground only that it induces another person to break a contract with B.

(4) For the purposes of this section, 'contract' includes any other arrangement (and 'contractual' is to be read accordingly).

(5) For the purposes of this section, to 'harm' an animal research organisation means—
   (a) to cause the organisation to suffer loss or damage of any description, or
   (b) to prevent or hinder the carrying out by the organisation of any of its activities.

The aim of this provision is to criminalize the unlawful pressure put on the clients, financial backers, and contractors, etc, of animal research organizations, rather than necessarily on the specific individuals employed by such organizations.

The above section is fairly precise. The essential ingredients are:

- the doing of a criminal or tortious act, or the threat of it;
- with the intention (or where it is likely) that as a consequence the target company will either terminate contracts, not enter into contracts or decline to perform contract obligations with an animal research organization.

Excluded from this offence is conduct which is 'simply' the unlawful inducement to breach a contract. There is also a further important exemption to s 145 concerning trade disputes. If the action is being taken pursuant to a bona fide trade dispute (rather than a sham dispute), and the dispute falls within Part IV of TULRCA, then no acts done wholly or mainly in contemplation or furtherance of such a dispute are covered by s 145.

6.4.2 Intimidation of persons connected with animal research organizations

Section 146 SOCPA states:

(1) A person (A) commits an offence if, with the intention of causing a second person (B) to abstain from doing something which B is entitled to do (or to do something which B is entitled to abstain from doing)—

    (a) A threatens B that A or somebody else will do a relevant act, and

    (b) A does so wholly or mainly because B is a person falling within subsection (2).

'Relevant act' is an act amounting to a criminal offence, or a tortious act causing B or another person to suffer loss or damage. The people falling within subsection (2) of the Act include a very wide group of people associated with either commercial or academic animal research, and specifically includes the 'spouse, civil partner, friend or relative of, or a person who is known personally to' such people.

There are three ingredients to this criminal offence:

1. **Act or threat**: of a crime, or tort causing loss/damage
2. **With the intention**: of causing a person to stop doing something they are entitled to do, or to do something they are not obliged to do
3. **To a person**: who works, or is connected with animal research in any one of a wide variety of ways, or to their family, friends or personal acquaintances.

6.5 Contamination or Interference with Goods

The contamination or interference with goods—particularly consumer items—has long been a method of either attracting attention to a certain company's conduct, or a direct effort to cause that company harm. Section 38(1) of the POA creates a number of different offences connected with the contamination of goods, if it is done with the intention of causing injury, loss, public alarm or anxiety:

(1) It is an offence for a person, with the intention—
    (a) of causing public alarm or anxiety, or
    (b) of causing injury to members of the public consuming or using the goods, or
    (c) of causing economic loss to any person by reason of the goods being shunned by members of the public, or
    (d) of causing economic loss to any person by reason of steps taken to avoid any such alarm or anxiety, injury or loss,

to contaminate or interfere with goods, or make it appear that goods have been contaminated or interfered with, or to place goods which have been contaminated or interfered with, or which appear to have been contaminated or interfered with, in a place where goods of that description are consumed, used, sold or otherwise supplied.

The section covers conduct going far beyond the tampering with jars of food on supermarket shelves.

6.5.1 Intention

Section 38 only relates to conduct which is done with the intention of causing:

- public alarm or anxiety;
- injury to members of the public, through consuming or using the goods;
- economic loss to any person—including a company—due to either the goods being shunned by members of the public, or the cost of steps taken to avoid alarm, anxiety, injury or loss.

While this type of activity is often associated with a 'cause', any further purpose beyond the immediate consequence is irrelevant to the offence. Provided one or more of the above consequences is intended, the perpetrator may have no further goal in mind.

6.5.2 What conduct does section 38(1) cover?

Section 38(1) relates to interference with 'goods'. These are described in s 38(5) as 'substances whether natural or manufactured and whether or not incorporated in or mixed with other goods'. This will cover food, ingredients, components or assembled items. There is no limit on size: the section applies as equally to aircraft engines as it would to jars of baby food.

The conduct includes:

- contamination with anything—the contaminant itself need not be harmful;
- interfering with goods—which would cover tampering with in any way, such as removing batteries, or removing safety features;

- making it look as if a product has been contaminated or interfered with—for example, by placing a (fake) warning label on the item;
- placing goods which have been contaminated or interfered with (or made to look as if they have been) on the shelf of a shop, or in the display cabinet of a café, vending machine, etc, anywhere where they are sold, consumed, used, or supplied. This does not have to be a public place, so would apply to assembly lines, warehouses, distribution centres, etc.

6.5.3 Threats or claims of tampering under section 38(2)

Section 38(2) states:

> It is also an offence for a person, with any such intention as is mentioned in paragraph (a), (c) or (d) of subsection (1), to threaten that he or another will do, or to claim that he or another has done, any of the acts mentioned in that subsection.

This subsection covers both the threat of tampering by any person, and also the claim that goods have been contaminated/interfered with by any person. The claim does not have to be true, so hoaxes are treated in a similar way to actual tampering. A hoax could itself be made with the intention of causing injury, such as if it related to safety devices or medicines.

There is a defence to s 38(2) of good faith contained in s 38(6):

> The reference in subsection (2) to a person claiming that certain acts have been committed does not include a person who in good faith reports or warns that such acts have been, or appear to have been, committed.

This defence would potentially assist people who learn of the contamination, and media who report it. However, the circumstances will be very limited in which such claims are made where one of the harmful intentions set out in s 38(1) is made out, but the person making the claim is nevertheless acting in good faith. A hypothetical example might be where an employee learns of contamination of goods, but his employer decides for commercial reasons not to publicize the fact of the contamination.

6.5.4 Possession of articles with a view to the commission of an offence

Section 38(3) states:

> (3) It is an offence for a person to be in possession of any of the following articles with a view to the commission of an offence under subsection (1)—
>
> (a) materials to be used for contaminating or interfering with goods or making it appear that goods have been contaminated or interfered with, or
>
> (b) goods which have been contaminated or interfered with, or which appear to have been contaminated or interfered with.

Like s 38(1), an offence under this section could be committed in a huge variety of ways, from the possession of even a small number of fake labels, or contaminated items, to the possession of tools for sabotaging complex pieces of machinery.

6.6 **Picketing**

The change over recent years in the court's attitude to peaceful picketing is highlighted by the dissenting judgment of Lord Denning MR in *Hubbard v Pitt* [1976] QB 142 at 177:

> Picketing is lawful so long as it is done merely to obtain or communicate information, or peacefully to persuade; and is not such as to submit any other person to any kind of constraint or restriction of his personal freedom . . .

Although it was the minority view in 1976, Lord Denning's words have subsequently been endorsed by the Divisional Court in *Hirst and Agu v Chief Constable of West Yorkshire* (1987) 85 Cr App R 143.

A picket will often involve a degree of obstruction of the highway. However, provided the degree of obstruction does not amount to an unreasonable use of the highway, the obstruction will not make the picket unlawful. In *Hirst and Agu* there was a protest outside a furrier's shop. Animal rights supporters handed out leaflets, held banners and attracted groups of passers-by who blocked the street. Organizers were prosecuted under s 137 of the Highways Act 1980. The Divisional Court confirmed that whether the activity was or was not reasonable was a question of fact. Glidewell LJ stated at p 150:

> It may be decided that if the activity grows to an extent that it is unreasonable by reason of the space occupied or the duration of time for which it goes on that an offence would be committed, but it is a matter on the facts for the magistrates.

This approach was specifically approved by the Court of Appeal in *Jones v DPP* [1999] 2 AC 240—see chapter 5.6.3. These cases demonstrate a consistency between the law on assemblies, picketing, breach of the peace, obstruction of the highway and public nuisance (see also the box below).

KEY POINTS—ASSEMBLIES, PICKETS AND PROTESTS ON THE HIGHWAY

In each case, an activity is likely to be lawful if:

- It is peaceful (and a breach of the peace is not imminent)
- It is a reasonable use of the highway by reference to the location, size and duration of the event
- Other people are not unduly restricted in their use of the highway

> Particular regard must be paid to freedom of expression. If it arises, proportionality must be considered. It will often be proportionate to allow a peaceful, albeit obstructive, event on the highway to continue temporarily, in order to allow a degree of exercise of the freedom of expression.

The situation is different if the picketers' purpose is to *prevent* free passage along the highway. In *Broome v DPP* [1974] AC 587, Lord Reid stated at 597H–598A:

> . . . it would not be difficult to infer as a matter of fact that pickets who assemble in unreasonably large numbers do have the purpose of preventing free passage. If that were the proper inference then their presence on the highway would become unlawful.

In *Broome v DPP* the defendant had, while picketing, gone beyond attempting to communicate with a lorry driver and had stood in the road to obstruct the vehicle so that he could speak to the driver. His conviction for obstruction of the highway was upheld: see further section 5.6.3.

Section 241 of TULRCA criminalizes specific behaviour which may arise in the context of picketing. Although found in an Act dealing with industrial relations, the section itself is *not* directed solely at industrial disputes. It is of general application to picketing, whether in relation to trade disputes or any other cause. However, when pickets are used in the context of a trade dispute, there is specific statutory protection for peaceful, primary pickets: see section 6.6.2.

'Secondary picketing' is the practice of picketing in a location other than the principle site of the protest. Outside the employment context, the distinction between a primary and a secondary picket has little legal significance. As an exercise of the rights to freedom of expression or assembly, such a protest still has the protection of Articles 10 and 11 of the ECHR. Equally, TULRCA s 241, the POA, PHA powers and the full breach of the peace powers all apply to secondary or non-employment pickets.

Neither the statutory offences under TULRCA s241, nor the right to picket peacefully outside one's place of work (s 220), affect the scope of the power to take action to prevent an imminent breach of the peace.

6.6.1 Unlawful pickets: intimidation or annoyance by violence

Section 241 TULRCA states:

241 Intimidation or annoyance by violence or otherwise

(1) A person commits an offence who, with a view to compelling another person to abstain from doing or to do any act which that person has a legal right to do or abstain from doing, wrongfully and without legal authority—

    (a) uses violence to or intimidates that person or his spouse or civil partner or children, or injures his property,

(b) persistently follows that person about from place to place,
(c) hides any tools, clothes or other property owned or used by that person, or deprives him of or hinders him in the use thereof,
(d) watches or besets the house or other place where that person resides, works, carries on business or happens to be, or the approach to any such house or place, or
(e) follows that person with two or more other persons in a disorderly manner in or through any street or road.

The section is not confined to trade and industrial disputes. It has been used in numerous other contexts, including animal rights protests, environmental protests, and demonstrations outside abortion clinics. In the non-industrial context, there are overlaps with the PHA and section 42 and 42A of CJPA in the types of behaviour prohibited.

However, for arrests or prosecutions under s 241, the conduct must be for the specific purpose of compelling another person to (i) abstain from doing something he has the right to do or (ii) do any act which he has a legal right to abstain from doing. The use of the phrase 'with a view to' confirms that the defendant does not have to succeed in compelling a person to change his behaviour.

'Compulsion' means more than persuasion or dissuasion, even if persuasion is to be achieved by causing embarrassment or shame. In *DPP v Fidler* [1992] 1 WLR 91, a number of protestors outside an abortion clinic had been charged and acquitted of a similar charge to that under s 241. Nourse LJ stated (p 97):

> It seems plain enough that the purpose of the anti-abortion group in watching and besetting the clinic was to stop abortions from being carried out there, but it is equally plain that the means employed to implement this purpose were confined to verbal abuse and reproach and shocking reminders of the physical implications of abortion. *Physical force was neither used nor threatened. The evident purpose of the demonstrators' behaviour was to embarrass and shock and shame* those concerned into abstaining from abortion. In my judgment, the justices were right to find that this purpose, thus implemented, was a purpose of dissuasion rather than one of compulsion.
>
> [emphasis added]

There are likely to be situations where the prospect of humiliation is just as powerful a disincentive as intimidation or the fear of violence (see further in this chapter). Nevertheless, Nourse LJ's comments reflect the approach to be taken following the introduction of the Human Rights Act 1998 (HRA) and the importance now attached to the freedom of expression.

If a controversial protest is mounted, which is likely to cause offence or feelings of harassment, then the differences between the offences under TULRCA s 241 and harassment must be considered. Section 241 criminalizes specific conduct that might not constitute a course of conduct amounting to harassment, but only if the *purpose is to compel* a person to do (or abstain from doing) something they are not obliged to do. Section 241 addresses:

- **Use of violence**, s 241(1)(a): this will almost inevitably cover conduct that will also constitute other criminal offences, such as offences against the person, or POA offences.
- **Intimidation**, s 241(a): the word 'intimidate' has its usual everyday meaning. The person (or spouse, civil partner or child) must actually be intimidated, although it is not necessary to show the intended outcome of the intimidation is achieved. It includes, but is not limited to violence or the threats of violence (*R v Jones* (1974) 59 Cr App 120). In *Thomas v National Union of Mineworkers* [1986] Ch 20, Scott J stated at p 55C–E:

  > Some 50 to 70 striking miners attend at the colliery gates daily. Six of them are selected to stand close to the gates. The rest are placed back from the road so as to allow the vehicle conveying the working miners to pass. Abuse is hurled at the vehicle and at the men inside . . . It is taking place not on isolated instances but on a daily regular basis. . . . I really do not think it can be sensibly suggested that picketing or demonstrating of this sort . . . would be otherwise than highly intimidating to any ordinary person.
  >
  > . . . a large number of sullen men lining the entrance to a colliery, offering no violence, saying nothing, but simply standing and glowering . . . would, in my opinion, be highly intimidating.

- **Damage to property**, s 241(1)(a): it is difficult to see how this would cover conduct that would not also be criminal damage.
- **Persistent following**, s 241(1)(b): this can be on foot or by car. A single person may commit the offence. Provided that persistent following is shown (together with intent), there is no requirement that the conduct itself would amount to harassment, or even irritating conduct.
- **Follows in a disorderly manner**, s 241(e): provided two or more people are involved in disorder, this following does *not* have to be persistent—a single occasion will be sufficient.
- **Hiding or obstructing use of tools, clothes or property**, s 241(1)(c): under most circumstances, it will be obvious if this conduct occurs. However, the conduct must still include within it at least an element of unlawfulness: if the defendant does no more than he is legally entitled (or empowered) to there will be no offence. For example, in *Fowler v Kibble* [1922] 1 Ch 487 the defendant prevented miners who were not members of a particular union from using safety lamps. However, the defendant's union had previously agreed with the employer that safety lamps were only to be provided to certain workers, which did not include the miners. Had it not been for this agreement, the defendant may well have been guilty of an offence. However, as the agreement with the employer entitled the defendant to deprive the miners of access to safety lamps, his conduct was not unlawful, and therefore not a breach of (the precursor to) s 241(1)(c).

- **Watching and besetting**, s 241(d): it will be a question of fact whether the conduct of picketers constitutes 'watching and besetting'. These words have their usual, everyday meaning. In the case of 'besetting' this means to surround and harass. The phrase, 'the house or other place where that person resides, works, carries on business or happens to be' in s 241(1)(d) means that the offence can be committed anywhere, provided the target is either at the location of the watching/besetting, or it is anticipated that he will attempt to approach it.

It is likely that a greater latitude would be permitted for picketing at a place of work or commercial premises, compared to someone's home, where even a minimal presence might constituted watching or besetting. However, there are limits to what is permitted, even at industrial premises. At p 76 of the judgment in *Thomas v NUM*, Scott J confirmed that mass picketing (meaning picketing where, by sheer weight of numbers the entrance to premises is blocked, or entry is prevented) would constitute both a nuisance (see section 4.11 for the meaning of 'nuisance') and an offence under the precursor to s 241.

6.6.2 **Lawful picketing**

When s 241 is considered in the specific context of industrial relations, it is important that it is considered alongside s 220 of the same Act, which provides:

220 Peaceful picketing

(1) It is lawful for a person in contemplation or furtherance of a trade dispute to attend—
   (a) at or near his own place of work, or
   (b) if he is an official of a trade union, at or near the place of work of a member of the union whom he is accompanying and whom he represents,

   for the purpose only of peacefully obtaining or communicating information, or peacefully persuading any person to work or abstain from working.

In light of the additional protection afforded to any peaceful picketer following the introduction of the HRA into domestic law and the decisions in *Jones v DPP* and *Hirst and Agu*, s 220 confers little *additional* protection to the worker/trade union official:

- Unless the picketer is a trade union official, it only applies to a picketer at or near his *own* place of work, so would not include, for example, picketing outside his employer's headquarters (unless that was also where he worked);
- The defence is limited to obtaining or communicating information, or peaceful persuasion of people to work/abstain from work. As is seen from the decision in *Broome v DPP*, even stopping a vehicle on the highway to speak to the driver takes the picketer outside the protection of s 220.

It is unclear whether a mass picket consisting solely of 'silent, glowering' workers would fall within the protection of s 220: the decision in *Thomas v NUM* confirms the common sense analysis that such behaviour might well be intimidating. However, if the picket was calm (ie no imminent threat to the peace) and consisted only of trade union officials and workers outside their own place of work, there is a strong chance that the picketers would benefit from the s 220 defence. Similarly, despite the words of warning in *Broome v DPP* that a mass picket risked the inference being drawn that the purpose of the picket was to obstruct the highway, a degree of obstruction in what would otherwise be a peaceful picket falling within s 220 would probably be tolerated by the courts.

6.7 **Further Specific Powers**

In addition to the standard offences and powers, such as those under the POA, there are a number of specific statutory provisions covered in other chapters that are particularly likely to arise when dealing with direct action:

- Aggravated trespass: see section 9.3;
- Section 14(1)(b) of the POA, giving the power to impose directions on an assembly where an officer reasonably believes that the purpose of the persons organizing it is the intimidation of others with a view to compelling them not to do an act they have a right to do, or to do an act they have a right not to do: see 5.4.1;
- In relation to environmental or anti-war protests, the offence of trespass on designated sites, contrary to section 128 of SOCPA may be of particular relevance, depending on the location of the protest: see section 5.4.4;
- Trespass on the site of a diplomatic mission, consular premises or the private residence of a diplomatic agent, contrary to s 9 of the Criminal Law Act 1977. This is likely to be of particular significance in anti-war protests, or protests against the actions of foreign governments: see 9.10.2.

6.8 **Detailed Case Study: Animal Rights Protests**

Background

At Toad Hall Farm, toads are bred for use in animal research by various laboratories around the country. The farm is in a very rural location. The toads are bred in a large barn about 200 metres from the farmhouse, where the breeder and farmer Mr Mole and his family live. The barn is close to the border with another farm, the occupier of which, Mr Green, dislikes Mr Mole.

On 1 December 2010, ten masked people dressed as frogs or toads broke into the barn and released hundreds of toads. Entry to the barn was probably gained via Mr Green's land. The event received much publicity, and the responsibility for the incident was claimed by a group called the Amphibian Freedom Army (AFA). The AFA website is registered to a person called Edward, who states he does not go on protests with the AFA, but supports their goals.

Since that time, there has been a very small demonstration outside the entrance to the farm on most Saturday mornings, when the unmarked delivery vans arrive to take the toads away. The demonstrations are noisy but peaceful, except for when the vans arrive or leave, when a few protestors sometimes throw themselves in front of the vans' wheels. Other protestors have been seen writing down the number plates of the vans that attend. The delivery company is called Superfast Deliveries, a family-owned business and not a registered company.

Stage 1

1 December 2011 is approaching. On the AFA website a protest is publicized for the anniversary of the 'liberation'. This is anticipated to be a large protest. Although the website says it will be a peaceful protest on the grass verge outside Mr Mole's farm, the website shows photographs taken by activists during the previous year's liberation. Mr Mole has received letters saying 'we will leave you alone if you stop breeding toads'.

Mr Mole wants to know from the police if the Saturday morning protests can be stopped. He does not want the anniversary protest to go ahead.

Discussion

The police have a duty to *facilitate* lawful, peaceful protest. They also have a duty to protect persons and property from violence, damage or intimidation.

Provided that the Saturday morning protests remain peaceful, as protests on the grass verge of the highway, that did not obstruct traffic, they would be likely to be a reasonable use of the verge of the highway, and—following *Duncan v Jones*—would not be a trespassory assembly. Accordingly, s 14A POA would not apply, and there is no power to ban the regular protests under s 14 POA.

Are the Saturday morning demonstrators committing the offence of harassment of a person in his home, under s 42A of CJPA? In a rural area, the entrance to the farm, even if it is several hundred yards away, is probably close enough to be regarded as being in the 'vicinity'. Were the protests to be remain confined to each Saturday, and were not so large as to be intimidating in themselves, a regular protest would probably not amount to harassment under s 42A.

Therefore, provided the regular meetings remain peaceful, there would be no power to prevent them taking place.

In the absence of specific evidence that the anniversary event was planned to involve trespass on Mr Mole's farm (or to operate as a diversion to allow others to trespass) then it too should be facilitated. Nevertheless, at the planning stage, specific consideration should be given to the potential for imposition of conditions on the assembly, either under s 14 or breach of the peace powers. This will require careful briefing to sergeants and inspectors, and the planning to have available loudhailers, etc, to ensure effective communication with the protestors.

Mr Mole should be asked to show the letters, and allow them to be copied. This is for a number of reasons. For example:

- If the person who sent the letters can be identified, there remains the potential to investigate links to the 2010 crime, or to help identify the planners of the 2011 event.
- The sending of the letters *may*, depending on their content, constitute offences under the Protection from Harassment Act 1997, or s 146 of SOCPA. The author of the letters clearly has written them with the intention of persuading Mr Mole to stop breeding toads for animal research. If the letters contain threats, then an offence under s 146 SOCPA has been committed.
- The letters might be relevant to the giving of a direction under s 42 CJPA.

Unless a course of conduct amounting to harassment had occurred, Mr Mole would not be able to seek an injunction under the Protection from Harassment Act 1997. However, he should be told to seek his own legal advice to consider or pursue this.

Stage 2

Matters escalate slightly in the weeks prior to the anniversary. One of the van drivers notices a sign saying 'Superfast are Superevil'. He tells Mr Mole he is reluctant to visit the farm again as he does not know how the protestors learned of the name of his company and he fears reprisals against his company. A person called Andrew has come forward who describes himself as a spokesman for the Toads, but says he is not a member of AFA. He formally notifies the police that there will be a demonstration outside the farm on the anniversary and that he expects 60 people to attend. Numerous comments on the AFA website indicate that some people intend to attempt to break in to the barn again on 1 December 2011.

Mr Green has refused permission for police to go onto his land to police the protest.

Discussion

As stated above, the notified assembly does not become a trespassory assembly merely because attempts at trespass are anticipated. However, it is clear that a more substantial policing operation will be required and the risk of trespass and criminal damage will clearly be a factor in the conditions it is appropriate to impose. The identification of an organizer has the potential to make the communication of any likely conditions more straightforward, but make no direct difference to the power to impose conditions.

The reference by the protestors to Superfast being 'Superevil' raises the issue of how this business came to be identified. As the vans are unmarked, have they been traced via the registration numbers? If so, it is possible that a crime has been committed; perhaps in relation to the Data Protection Act in relation to the DVLA records, or the interception of records/correspondence of Mr Mole, Superfast or the laboratories.

Is showing the sign 'Superfast are Superevil' an offence? In the context of a single demonstration, it would probably be just about be defensible on the basis of the exercise of Article 10 rights, therefore reasonable conduct. However, it is clear that Superfast has now been identified by the AFA as a potential avenue to disrupt the trade in toads. Any intimidation or threats made towards the company or its drivers would be likely to infringe s 145 or s 146 of SOCPA.

The police do not have the power to go onto Mr Green's land under s 17 PACE, as the land does not constitute 'premises'. However, they do not need a specific statutory power, Mr Green's refusal of permission cannot operate so as prevent the police from entering his land if such entry was be necessary in order to prevent crime and/or a serious breach of the peace, or to prevent serious injury. However, entry onto his land ought to be avoided unless it is *strictly necessary*, and limited to such incursions as are necessary, including the number of officers going onto the land, and how long they remain. Officers policing the event should be specifically briefed in relation to this possibility, so that they are clear of the very limited circumstances in which such entry would be defensible. Particular care must be taken to ensure that Mr Green's crops are not damaged by the police unnecessarily.

6.9 **Detailed Case Study: Hedgerow Airport**

Stage 1

The 'Happy Camper' protest movement announces that they intend to demonstrate against the construction of a second terminal at Hedgerow Airport. A week of 'fun, festivities, awareness and action' is planned for the first week of August. The Happy Camper movement is a loose affiliation of a number of different organizations, encompassing people with different agendas, from anti-capitalists and veteran road building protestors to mainstream green politicians and local residents who object to the development. The organizers, who have not identified themselves publicly, state that they will occupy a site near to the current airport and the site of the proposed second terminal, where they will erect a 'Happy Camp' and organize workshops, raise awareness and plan the week's activities. Hedgerow Airport itself is private land.

Intelligence suggests that the majority of the demonstrations are likely to be peaceful, although it is understood that within the campers there will be a number of people who have previously been associated with unlawful activity at protests. Intelligence suggests that least one building occupation is planned, and a major demonstration on the penultimate day of the week at the airport itself.

Discussion

The focus in the weeks prior to a major event of this nature will clearly be on the gathering of accurate intelligence, making attempts to establish meaningful contact with the organizers, arranging for adequate numbers/types of police resources and liaising with other organizations or individuals likely to be affected by the protest.

The refusal of people to identify themselves as organizers must not prevent the police from seeking to identify the organizers, and initiating contact with them.

The availability of specialist teams (such as climbing or lock-on teams) is becoming almost inevitable in light of the frequency with which this type of direct action is now used.

Serious consideration should be given to seeking prohibition of this potentially trespassory assembly, under s 14A of the Public Order Act 1986 (see chapter 5). However, this is not a guaranteed solution:

- A particular legal hurdle might arise in relation to s 14A: if the majority of local residents are themselves *against* the new terminal, a temporary camp of protestors might be welcomed, rather than deprecated, by the 'community'. However, the test of 'serious disruption to the community' is not determined by reference to the majority. If a significant minority in the local community faced serious (unwelcome) disruption, this would be satisfied.
- Is the prohibition is a necessary or proportionate measure, given the potentially significant impact it would have on the freedom of assembly/expression in the context of public protest? In order to demonstrate proportionality, reliable evidence would have to be available as to the risk of serious disruption. The combination of knowledge of the extent of action/disruption on previous occasions, together with specific intelligence (rather than general perceptions) about the upcoming event is clearly **crucial** to this assessment.
- Even if an order were granted under s 14A, it would be entirely ineffectual if a local landowner gave permission to the Happy Campers to use his land. However, the police do not have the option of waiting to see if (or where) the assembly takes place: s 14A only applies to anticipated assemblies. Therefore, if the decision is that an application under s 14A should be made, the possibility that a local landowner might give consent is not in itself a reason to delay making an application.

Wherever possible, efforts should be taken to contact the organizers and attempts made to convince them that the best prospect for lawful, peaceful protests to go ahead is for the organizers to liaise and cooperate with the police. If such steps cannot be demonstrated, it may make it more difficult to justify subsequent measures taken. The necessity defence will only assist the police during the demonstration if they can demonstrate that the necessity to act has not arise through prior fault on their own part (see *Rigby v Chief Constable of Northamptonshire* [1985] 1 WLR 1242).

Stage 2

A day earlier than announced, the Happy Campers unexpectedly occupy a field very close to Hedgerow Airport. The landowner (i) has not given permission, (ii) regards the campers as trespassers, and (iii) says that if the police do not remove the campers, he will.

The protesters erect a string boundary around the campsite, and put up signs headed 'squatter's notice', stating that the tents are the protestors' homes and any force used to evict them would be unlawful under section 6 of the Criminal Law Act 1977.

Numbers at the site start rising to several hundred, and although the atmosphere is friendly towards the police, several protestors have been spotted who are well known to be associated with illegal direct action. Some are wearing scarves round their faces when outside the tented areas.

Discussion

The 'squatter's notice' is likely to be of no legal effect, as the tented site would not constitute 'premises' within the definition provided in the Criminal Law Act 1977. Note that, while the definition of dwelling in Part 1 of the POA includes a 'tent', the definition in the Criminal Law Act 1997 does not.

The lawful occupier is entitled to use reasonable force to eject the trespassers from his land. The police can neither require the occupier to permit the protestors to remain, nor can they require him to eject them. If, as a result of the landowner seeking to eject the trespassers, there was an imminent risk of a breach of the peace, the police would be under a *duty* to intervene.

Now that the location of the site for the Happy Camp is known, further consideration would have to be given to whether or not the grounds to impose conditions prohibit the assembly under s 14 of the POA are satisfied. As the assembly is already taking place, s 14A of the POA cannot be used. The occupier may use reasonable force to eject the protestors, should he be determined to do so. This situation therefore requires consideration of the rights of the occupier, of the wider community, the protestors and the businesses likely to be affected by the protest.

Occupier

The occupier has right to the peaceful occupation of his own land under Article 1 of Protocol 1 to the ECHR. This has not been incorporated into domestic law. However, in assessing proportionality, the landowner's rights are to be considered: the Happy Campers have no right to remain, even if they are doing so pursuant to an attempt to exercise their own right to freedom of assembly. The landowner should not be put under undue pressure to allow the Happy Campers to remain.

If an agreement can be brokered for the occupier to suspend measures to evict the trespassers until the end of the protest, this does not mean that the Happy Campers cease to be trespassers. With the permission of the occupier, the police will have the power to enter the camp, and the protestors would have no legal authority to exclude them.

Securing the forbearance of the landowner for the duration of the week may be the most straightforward way of facilitating the Happy Campers' rights to freedom of assembly and expression.

Local community

While many members of the local community will be sympathetic to the campers, and even if the landowner were to agree, the occupancy of the field may give rise to problems not directly associated with protest, such as traffic, site safety, sanitation, etc. If an order under s 14A is not made, but the site reaches capacity, restrictions on access by further protestors would be inevitable.

Local business

The proximity of the camp to the airport raises particular considerations as to the prospect for unlawful direct action. Despite the very vulnerable nature of air travel, the unnecessary use of anti-terrorism powers against protestors is now strongly discouraged.

Previous similar demonstrations have involved masked protestors causing criminal damage and violent confrontation with both police and security staff at businesses. It is likely that a s 60AA CJPOA authorization for the duration of the protest will be necessary to enable the police to remove scarves and masks. If the intelligence and/or experience, it might be necessary to give a 'full' s 60 authorization, allowing the Happy Campers to be searched for offensive weapons or dangerous instruments. However, the threshold test of 'serious violence' is a high one.

The Happy Campers have no right to protest on the site of the airport, or to process on the roads leading to the terminal buildings: *Appleby v UK* [2003] 37 EHRR 38 (see section 2.7.3). Efforts must be made to facilitate a lawful procession/demonstration outside the airport, despite the Happy Campers' reference to 'action' being a clear warning that there will be some protestors who will not be satisfied with a purely lawful, peaceful protest. There are two quite separate justifications for proportionate interference in the Happy Camper's planned protests outside the airport itself:

- *Ezelin v France* 1991 14 EHRR 362 confirms that the unlawful intentions of some protestors does not deprive their fellow, law-abiding protestors of their rights. However, this does not mean that the police should agree to an event taking place in a way which would—however unwittingly—facilitate unlawful activity by a minority within the group.

• There will inevitably be other business premises outside the airport that are commercially associated with air travel or air freight, which will also be targets. Deliberate disruption of the business of the airport and nearby companies associated with it will certainly amount to 'disruption to the life of the community'.

Further conditions can therefore be imposed on both the Happy Camp and any protesting assemblies that spring up during the week. It would be sensible to identify and maintain dialogue with the organizers of the Happy Camp itself so that any conditions imposed—whether at the Happy Camp or in relation to specific daily protests—can be efficiently communicated to the campers. This is not a substitute for also communicating these conditions at the protests.

Further reading

- *Thomas v National Union of Mineworkers* [1986] Ch 20
- *Hall v Save Newchurch Guinea Pigs (Campaign)* [2005] EWHC 372
- *Smithkline Beecham Plc v Avery* [2009] EWHC 1488
- *Oxford University v Broughton* [2008] EWHC 75

NOTES

NOTES

7

Race, Religion, and Sexual Orientation: Hate Crime and Public Order

7.1 **Introduction**

The practical difficulties of striking a balance between the rights of different groups, or between such groups and individuals who hold strong beliefs about them (often expressed in strong terms) can be significant. One of the most high profile 'events' of recent years has been the so-called 'war against terror'. This has been the focus for many demonstrations and counter-demonstrations. These in turn have attracted the interest of groups associated with public disorder and offences.

In a public order scenario such as a demonstration, where there is a strong focus on a particular county or religious issue, there is obvious potential for racial or religious tensions to be stirred up. There is the potential at such events for behaviour to go beyond legitimate expression and fall into the category of hate crime.

In addition to facilitating legitimate protest and protecting the right of different groups and individuals to freedom of expression (human rights policing is covered in chapter 2), police must be aware of the specific criminal offences which might be committed. This chapter explains the various offences which exist in relation to race, religious belief, sexual orientation and disability hate crime.

KEY POINTS—RACE, RELIGION AND SEXUAL ORIENTATION

The relevant legislation is:

Race:

- Part III of the Public Order Act 1986 (in this chapter, 'the Act' or the POA). This covers actions, publications and performances intended or likely to stir up racial hatred;
- Racially aggravated offences, under s 28 and s 31 of the Crime and Disorder Act 1998.
- For football offences relating to racist chanting, see chapter 10.

Religion:

- Part IIIA of the POA, Hatred against Persons on Religious Grounds;
- Religiously aggravated offences, under s 28 and s 31 of the Crime and Disorder Act 1998.

Sexual orientation:

- Part IIIA of the POA (inserted by s 74 of the Criminal Justice and Immigration Act 2008).

The POA treats race-related offences differently to the way it treats offences related to religion. A degree of criticism or hostility towards a person's religious (or philosophical) beliefs remains generally acceptable in today's society, and is protected by freedom of expression under Article 10. The POA at s 29J protects this freedom to be critical:

> Nothing in this Part shall be read or given effect in a way which prohibits or restricts discussion, criticism or expressions of antipathy, dislike, ridicule, insult or abuse of particular religions or the beliefs or practices of their adherents, or of any other belief system or the beliefs or practices of its adherents, or proselytising or urging adherents of a different religion or belief system to cease practising their religion or belief system.

Similarly, in relation to sexual orientation and practices the POA contains the following provision at s 29JA:

> In this Part, for the avoidance of doubt, the discussion or criticism of sexual conduct or practices or the urging of persons to refrain from or modify such conduct or practices shall not be taken of itself to be threatening or intended to stir up hatred.

These sections make explicit the distinction between criticism, even vehement criticism, of a particular religion or sexual orientation, and *actual hatred or hatred-driven acts towards people* who are of that religion or sexual orientation. This is covered further at 7.3.3 in this chapter. No such distinction is drawn in relation to race.

It should be noted that, under s 24A(5) of PACE, a person other than a constable has no powers of arrest in relation to the crimes created by Parts III (relating to racial hatred) and IIIA (relating to sexual orientation and religious hatred) of the POA.

7.2 **Race**

7.2.1 **What is 'race'?**

Definition of racial hatred

Section 17 of the POA defines 'racial hatred' as:

> hatred against a group of persons . . . defined by reference to colour, race, nationality (including citizenship) or ethnic or national origins.

'Racial' hatred is defined here *by reference to* colour, race, nationality or ethnic or national origins. It is a very broad definition and is applied in a non-technical way by the courts. The purpose of the section is to combat racism and xenophobia (see *R v Rogers* [2007] 21 AC 62). It does not require the victim to be from a particular identifiable race, or even a specific group of races. 'Ethnic origin' is not limited to strict racial or biological origins. 'Race' is a word that is imprecise.

Some uncertainty has arisen in relation to cultural or religious subsets of a particular nation or broader ethnic group. In *Mandla v Lee* [1983] 2 AC 548, it was held that to constitute an ethnic group, there would need to be a number of common characteristics such as a shared history, language, culture, literature, religion or geographical origin.

The courts have held that:

- Jews are protected under the definition, although a Jew can be of any ethnic origin.
- Sikhs constitute a racial group, although Hindus do not.
- Rastafarians do not constitute a distinct racial group, although they would, like followers of Hinduism, be protected under the laws against religious hatred.
- Romany Gypsies constitute a group that would fall under the section, but the wider travelling community would not—see *Commission for Racial Equality v Dutton* [1989] QB 783.

Groups against whom someone could be guilty of inciting hatred would include 'foreigners', 'immigrants' (see *R v Rogers*) or 'Asians'. This is so, even though each of these terms, if used by an offender, could cover a person of almost any ethnic background.

7.2.2 Stirring up racial hatred

Sections 17–23 of the POA create offences covering a wide range of potential behaviour, provided that in each case the act was done either:

(1) With the *intention* to stir up racial hatred, or
(2) Where, having regard to all the circumstances, it is *likely* that as a result racial hatred will be stirred up.

The offender's intent can be proved by looking at all the circumstances. See section 4.6.2 for the problems surrounding intent in relation to s 4 of the POA.

It will often be easier to establish that it was *likely* that racial hatred would be stirred up, than to establish that somebody actually *intended* to stir it up. However, where only likelihood can be proved, each of the statutory offences contains a specific defence of 'innocent' conduct, possession, performance, etc. These specific defences vary slightly from section to section and are considered below.

The conduct covered by this part of the POA includes:

- Words, behaviour or display of written material: s 18
- Publishing or distributing written material: s 19
- Public performance of play: s 20
- Distributing, showing or playing a recording: s 21
- Broadcasting or including programme in cable programme service: s 22
- Possession of racially inflammatory material: s 23

Corporations as well as individuals may be guilty of these offences. Under s 28 of the POA, if it can be shown that the offence was committed with the 'consent or connivance' of a director, manager, secretary or similar officer (or a person purporting to act in any such capacity), that individual is also guilty of the offence. For corporate bodies run by their members, individual members may be guilty of an offence.

KEY POINTS—RACIAL HATRED: SUMMARY OF OFFENCES IN PART III POA

A. The acts covered by the offences:

- Words, behaviour or display of written material: s 18
- Publishing or distributing written material: s 19
- Public performance of play: s 20
- Distributing, showing or playing a recording: s 21
- Broadcasting or including programme in cable programme service: s 22
- Possession of racially inflammatory material: s 23

B. Intent or likelihood: in each case the act must be done either:

- with the intention to stir up racial hatred, or
- where, having regard to all the circumstances, it is likely that as a result racial hatred will be stirred up.

Words, behaviour and written material

Section 18 of the POA provides that:

> A person who uses threatening, abusive or insulting words or behaviour, or displays any written material which is threatening, abusive or insulting, is guilty of an offence if—
>
> (a) he intends thereby to stir up racial hatred, or
> (b) having regard to all the circumstances racial hatred is likely to be stirred up thereby.

Section 18 covers similar behaviour to sections 4 and 4A of Part I of the POA. See section 4.6.1 for a discussion of the meaning of 'threatening, abusive or insulting words or behaviour', and 'displays any written material which is threatening, abusive or insulting'.

Material or behaviour that is racially inflammatory but not threatening, abusive or insulting is not covered by either this section or any other within Part III of the POA. For example, if a group of young black men were messing about and one used the word 'nigger' towards one of his friends, his conduct in using that word in that context would probably not amount to threatening, abusive or insulting behaviour (see 4.6.1). It would not therefore be caught by s 18, even if the word 'nigger' is itself capable of being racially inflammatory.

However, a lot of racially inflammatory material or behaviour *is* likely to be threatening, abusive, or insulting. For example, derogatory and offensive descriptions of or claims about a particular racial group—such as 'all Asian men are perverts who secretly want to groom white underage girls'—is racially inflammatory and would clearly be considered insulting by the majority of the population.

The offence can be committed in public or in private. It is a defence for the accused to prove that he was inside a dwelling and had no reason to believe that the words or behaviour used, or the written material displayed, would be heard or seen by a person outside that or any other dwelling.

Whether the words, behaviour or written material is either intended or likely to stir up racial hatred is a matter of fact. 'Likely to' has the same meaning as that in s 4 of the POA: see 4.6.2 under the heading 'Intention or likelihood'.

This is the racial hatred offence that will most commonly be committed. It will potentially arise in the context of anti-social/threatening behaviour, and also at protests and demonstrations where members of (for example) far-right groups like the English Defence League are likely to be present, such as protests that relate to Islam, or the 'war on terror'.

The statutory defence

There is no specific statutory defence of 'reasonable conduct' to a s 18 stirring racial hatred offence, nor to any of the offences of stirring up racial hatred. Once the courts find that an expression was intended to, or was likely to, stir up racial hatred, that expression would not by definition be reasonable.

In circumstances where there was no intent to stir up racial hatred, but racial hatred was nonetheless likely to be stirred up, s 18(5) of the POA provides a potential defence. This defence will apply if the defendant is able to demonstrate that he was *not aware* that his words or behaviour (or the written material) might be threatening, abusive or insulting.

POINT TO NOTE

Where

i) it can be shown that racial hatred was likely to be stirred up, and

ii) it can be shown that the defendant was aware his behaviour, words (or material) was threatening, abusive or insulting,

it will not matter that the defendant was *unaware* that those threatening, abusive or insulting words, behaviour or material were likely to stir up racial hatred.

Expressions which are intended or likely to incite racial hatred would fall within the restriction imposed by Article 17 of the ECHR, which says that:

Nothing in this Convention may be interpreted as implying for any State, group or person any right to engage in any activity or perform any act aimed at the destruction on any of the rights and freedoms set forth herein or at their limitation to a greater extent than is provided for in the Convention.

They would therefore *not* attract the potential protection of freedom of expression under Article 10 (see section 2.7.2). The position is potentially different for offences under ss 4A, 5, and the religious/sexual orientation offences under s 29B (see 7.3.3).

Publishing or distributing written material

Section 19 of the POA provides that:

(1) A person who publishes or distributes written material which is threatening, abusive or insulting is guilty of an offence if—
   (a) he intends thereby to stir up racial hatred, or
   (b) having regard to all the circumstances racial hatred is likely to be stirred up thereby.

The publishing and distribution of material must be to the public or a section of the public. The circulation of material by a political party to its own members would not therefore fall within s 19. However, the distribution at a political rally of pamphlets likely to stir up racial hatred, where attendance at the rally was not confined to members of that party, could constitute an offence.

Where *intent* to stir up racial hatred is not provable (ie it is only the likelihood of doing so in issue), there is a potential defence under s 19(2) if the accused can prove

i) that he was not aware of the content of the material, *and*
ii) did not suspect and had no reason to suspect that it was threatening, abusive or insulting.

An innocent person distributing racially inflammatory material inside sealed envelopes who had no reason to suspect he was distributing such material would therefore have a defence.

Mere possession of material is *not* an offence under s 19, although it may well be under s 23, dealt with below.

Possession of racially inflammatory material

Section 23 of the POA provides that:

(1) A person who has in his possession written material which is threatening, abusive or insulting, or a recording of visual images or sounds which are threatening, abusive or insulting, with a view to—
   (a) in the case of written material, its being displayed, published, distributed, or included in a programme service, whether by himself or another, or
   (b) in the case of a recording, its being distributed, shown, played, or included in a programme service, whether by himself or another,

is guilty of an offence if he intends racial hatred to be stirred up thereby or, having regard to all the circumstances, racial hatred is likely to be stirred up thereby.

(2) For this purpose regard shall be had to such display, publication, distribution, showing, playing, or inclusion in a programme service as he has, or it may reasonably be inferred that he has, in view.

Effectively, this section covers the possession of any material likely to stir up racial hatred, provided that:

- the person has it in his possession; *and*
- it is threatening, abusive or insulting; *and*
- it is in his possession with a view to it being displayed, published, distributed, shown, played or included in a programme; *and*
- he intends racial hatred to be stirred up, or it is likely racial hatred will be stirred up.

'Recording' means any record from which visual images or sounds may be reproduced. It would include material stored on a computer hard drive or smartphone, as long as that hard drive or phone was in the possession of the suspect or the accused. The person in possession of the material need not be the person intending to disseminate it: it is sufficient that the material is being held with a view to its dissemination by someone else.

Provided that no intent is shown (ie only a likelihood of racial hatred being stirred up is shown), there is a potential defence under s 23(3) if the person in possession of the racially inflammatory material can prove:

- that he was not aware of the content of the written material or recording; *and*
- did not suspect that it was threatening, abusive or insulting; *and*
- had no reason to suspect that it was threatening, abusive or insulting.

This defence might at first glance seem difficult to prove. In some cases it will be difficult, such as where a large number of placards are present in somebody's office or home. However, there are other circumstances, such as the presence of racially inflammatory material on the hard drive of a computer shared by several flatmates, or accessed by someone other than the owner, where it may be easier for a defendant to rely on the defence.

Public performance of play

Section 20 of the POA provides that:

(1) If a public performance of a play is given which involves the use of threatening, abusive or insulting words or behaviour, any person who presents or directs the performance is guilty of an offence if—

   (a) he intends thereby to stir up racial hatred, or

(b) having regard to all the circumstances (and, in particular, taking the performance as a whole) racial hatred is likely to be stirred up thereby.

This section broadly covers those who direct or produce stage plays or live shows. An actor is not liable (even as a secondary party) solely by reason of their taking part, unless, without reasonable excuse, they perform otherwise than in accordance with their directions.

A person who has presented or directed a play like this may be liable even if he is not present at the performance. However, provided there was no *intent* to stir up racial hatred, he will have a defence under s 20(2) he is able to prove any of the following:

- that he did not know, and had no reason to suspect, that the performance would involve the use of the offending words or behaviour; or
- that he did not know and had no reason to suspect that the offending words or behaviour were threatening, abusive or insulting; or
- that he did not know and had no reason to suspect that the circumstances in which the performance would be given would be such that racial hatred would be likely to be stirred up.

Section 20(3) states that performances given solely or primarily for the purposes of rehearsing, or making a recording of the performing, or enabling the performance to be included in a programme service are not covered by the s 20 offence.

There are a number of technical details regarding who is liable under this section, and in what circumstances. Detailed consideration of this section is beyond the scope of this book.

Distributing, showing or playing a recording

Section 21 of the POA states:

(1) A person who distributes, or shows or plays, a recording of visual images or sounds which are threatening, abusive or insulting is guilty of an offence if—
   (a) he intends thereby to stir up racial hatred, or
   (b) having regard to all the circumstances racial hatred is likely to be stirred up thereby.

A recording means any record from which visual images or sounds may, by any means, be reproduced.

Provided no intent is proved, there is a defence if an accused is able to show that he was not aware of the content of the recording and did not suspect, and had no reason to suspect, that it was threatening, abusive or insulting.

Broadcasting a programme

Section 22 of the POA states:

(1) If a programme involving threatening, abusive or insulting visual images or sounds is included in a programme service, each of the persons mentioned in subsection (2) is guilty of an offence if—
 (a) he intends thereby to stir up racial hatred, or
 (b) having regard to all the circumstances racial hatred is likely to be stirred up thereby.

The people identified in s 22(2) are as follows:

- The person using the offending words or behaviour;
- Any person by whom the programme is produced or directed (not simply the lead producer or director);
- The person providing the programme service, ie the 'broadcaster'.

In the absence of evidence of specific *intent* to stir up racial hatred, there is a general defence if a person did not know (and had no reason to know) that the offending material was threatening, abusive or insulting. There are also individual defences available to each of the three groups of people if they are able to show they did not know (and had no reason to suspect) either that a programme would be broadcast including the material, or that the circumstances in which the material would be broadcast were such that racial hatred would be likely to be stirred up.

7.3 **Religion and Sexual Orientation**

Part IIIA of the POA creates a group of offences committed when a person does a specific act with the intention of stirring up religious hatred or hatred on the grounds of sexual orientation. The elements of the offences are similar, but not identical, to those relating to the incitement of racial hatred in Part III of the POA.

For each of the Part IIIA offences, the elements of the offence are the same regardless of whether the hatred is in relation to religious belief or sexual orientation. There are slightly different statutory defences: see section 7.3.4.

7.3.1 **Definition of religious hatred**

Definition of religious hatred

Section 29A of the POA defines religious hatred as 'hatred against a group of persons defined by reference to religious belief or lack of religious belief'.

The section refers to hatred 'against a group of persons'. However, hatred towards a particular individual, if based on their personal religious conviction (or lack of belief) rather than anything they had done, would normally be caught by s 29A as it would be hatred against the group of persons having that belief, albeit targeted at an individual.

For example, hatred against a person in response to actions that person had taken which offended a particular religious group (such as Salman Rushdie's penning of the *Satanic Verses*, or a vicar who burned the Koran) would not necessarily fall within the Act, because the reason for the hatred would not be the religious belief of Salman Rushdie or the vicar's, but their actions in writing the *Satanic Verses* and burning the Koran. However, hatred against the same individual, if based on that individual's religious beliefs or practices, would constitute an attack on the group sharing that belief.

The reference to 'lack of religious belief' is not confined to atheism. It applies to those who lack a particular religious belief. For example, it could cover a particular sub-division of a religion—or anyone who does not have the same set of religious beliefs as the offender. It has the potential to cover *any* difference in religious belief. However, it would not extend to persons defined by a purely philosophical belief. In this respect it is narrower than the scope of protection against discrimination in the employment field.

There is a significant practical difference between the legal concepts of racial hatred and hatred on the grounds of religious belief. While it would be very unusual for a person to stir up racial hatred against their own race, it is very well recognized that people frequently stir up hatred against followers of the same religion, but who may not have quite the same beliefs. There are many examples of this today, just as there are stretching back for many hundreds of years.

7.3.2 Definition of hatred on the grounds of sexual orientation

Definition of hatred on the grounds of sexual orientation

Section 29AB states that hatred on the grounds of sexual orientation means, 'hatred against a group of persons defined by reference to sexual orientation (whether towards persons of the same sex, the opposite sex or both)'.

The section therefore covers hatred on the grounds of homosexuality, heterosexuality and bisexuality. It does not extend to hatred based on a preference for particular sexual acts or lifestyles, or to transgender individuals or groups of transgender individuals.

7.3.3 **Stirring up hatred on grounds of religious belief or sexual orientation**

The specific offences under Part IIIA of the POA of stirring up hatred on the grounds of religious belief or sexual orientation follow very closely the family of offences relating to the incitement of racial hatred. The sections contain language that is often identical, and are even set out in the same order. In light of the similarities, while section 29B (threatening words and behaviour with intent to incite hatred) is addressed in detail, the contents of section 7.2.2 are not repeated in relation to Part IIIA of the Act. Table 7.1 at the end of this section summarizes the locations of each offence, and demonstrates both the differences and similarities between the two groups of offences.

The three major differences between the offences of incitement to racial hatred, and hatred on the grounds of religious belief or sexual orientation are:

- For each of the offences in Part IIIA, the defendant must have *intended* to stir up hatred on the grounds of religious belief or sexual orientation. The offence is not made out if there was only a likelihood that hatred would be stirred up.
- An essential element of each offence is that the relevant conduct is threatening. Unlike in Part III, it is not sufficient if the behaviour is abusive or insulting. It must also be threatening.
- Unlike for Part III, for charges of incitement to hatred on the grounds of religious belief or sexual orientation, there are specific defences aimed at protecting freedom of expression: see section 7.3.4.

The combination of these three factors mean that the scope of these offences are significantly narrower than for the offences of inciting racial hatred.

Section 29B: Words, behaviour and written material

Section 29B provides that:

(1) A person who uses threatening words or behaviour, or displays any written material which is threatening, is guilty of an offence if he intends thereby to stir up religious hatred or hatred on the grounds of sexual orientation.

(2) An offence under this section may be committed in a public or a private place, except that no offence is committed where the words or behaviour are used, or the written material is displayed, by a person inside a dwelling and are not heard or seen except by other persons in that or another dwelling.

(3) ...

(4) In proceedings for an offence under this section it is a defence for the accused to prove that he was inside a dwelling and had no reason to believe that the words or behaviour used, or the written material displayed, would be heard or seen by a person outside that or any other dwelling.

...

This section closely follows s 18. However, the words, behaviour or written material must be threatening, not merely abusive or insulting. Language or conduct that ridicules or insults religion, religious beliefs, or adherents of a particular religion but is not threatening will not be sufficient. This is so, even if it could be shown that the intent behind the insulting behaviour is to stir up hatred on grounds of religious belief.

For the issues surrounding the concept of 'intent', and what may constitute 'threatening' see sections 4.6.2 and 4.6.1 in relation to s 4 of the Act.

The key points table below sets out the remaining offences in Part IIIA of the POA. With the modifications described above, each offence is effectively identical to the equivalent offence relating to racial hatred. Table 7.1 at the end of this chapter summarizes the similarities and differences between the offences in Parts III and IIIA of the Act.

KEY POINTS—HATRED ON GROUNDS OF RELIGIOUS BELIEF/SEXUAL ORIENTATION: SUMMARY OF OFFENCES IN PART IIIA POA

A. The acts covered by the offences

- Threatening words, behaviour or display of written material: s 29B
- Publishing or distributing written material which is threatening: s 29C
- Public performance of play involving the use of threatening words or behaviour: s 29D
- Distributing, showing or playing a recording of visual images or sounds which are threatening: s 29E
- Broadcasting threatening visual images or sounds, or including same programme in cable programme service: s 29F
- Possession of material which is threatening: s 29G

B. Intention

- In each case the act must be done with the intention to stir up hatred on the grounds of religious belief or sexual orientation.

7.3.4 Defences under Part IIIA of the POA

There are two specific defences under Part IIIA of the Act. They are contained in s 29J and s 29JA, set out at the start of this chapter. They are designed to protect freedom of expression and in particular, two types of activity:

- discussion or criticism of religious beliefs, and religious or sexual practices;
- attempts to persuade others to change either their religious beliefs or sexual practice.

Section 29J of the Act protects freedom of expression in relation to religious belief. In addition to the discussion, criticism or expression of dislike, and the protection for people urging others to change their belief, there is specific protection for language or conduct which ridicules, insults or abuses either a religion or religious practices.

Section 29JA of the Act protects freedom of expression in relation to sexual orientation. Again, there is specific protection for discussion or criticism of sexual conduct. There is no specific protection for expression that amounts to ridicule, insults or abuse. However, because the offences themselves require the behaviour to be threatening before an offence is committed, there is no real need for such protection.

Case study

Distinguishing between words or behaviour aimed at a religious or sexual practice, and words or behaviour aimed at the *people* who endorse that practice

While this difference is important, it is not always easy to identify. One way of thinking about it is that there is a difference between attacking the belief, and attacking the person who holds the belief. This is shown in the following two examples.

Islam versus right-wingers

A right-wing group holding banners stating 'Islam is a crazy religion' would probably be protected by s 29J, as this banner slogan refers to the religion itself. In contrast, a banner with the words 'Islam out of Britain' has been interpreted as an attack on the followers of Islam, in that it suggests that they should leave Britain. In *Norwood v DPP* [2003] EWHC 1564 (Admin) Lord Justice Auld stated that it could not be dismissed as a protest against the tenets of the Muslin religion, as distinct from 'an unpleasant and insulting attack on its followers generally'.

Sexual orientation versus 'moral majority' Christians

Similarly, an evangelical Christian protesting with leaflets and a banner stating that 'Homosexuality is a sin' would probably be protected by s 29JA, whereas if he or she were handing out leaflets or holding a banner stating 'Go to Hell, All Homosexuals!' he or she would not.

The defences are confined to Part IIIA of the Act. They do not cover threatening, abusive or insulting words or behaviour charged under s 4, s 4A or s 5 of the Act. This leads to an anomalous situation:

- If defendant A has used abusive and insulting, but not threatening, behaviour with the intention of inciting religious hatred, he could be charged with an offence under s 5 of the POA (perhaps the religiously aggravated version of those offences) and would only have the benefit of the 'reasonableness' defence under that section.

- By contrast, if defendant B has also used *threatening* behaviour with the intention of inciting religious hatred, he could be charged with an offence under s 29B of the Act, and would therefore have the potential benefit of the freedom of expression defence under s 29J.

This is not necessarily a sterile, legalistic analysis. In the case of *DPP v Hammond* [2004] EWHC 69, the defendant had held up a sign bearing the words 'Stop Immorality', 'Stop Homosexuality' and 'Stop Lesbianism' (see 4.7.4 for a more detailed account of this case). He was charged with an offence under s 5 of the Act. The defence of reasonable conduct failed, and the defendant was convicted of the offence. His conduct was clearly not threatening—but was held by the magistrates to be insulting to towards the gay and lesbian community, by implying that they were immoral. With reservation, the Divisional Court felt unable to interfere with this assessment.

Even if the charge been brought after the change in the law, as the defendant was not charged with an offence under s 29B, he would not have been entitled to rely on the s 29JA defence that he was doing no more than criticising 'sexual conduct or practices or the urging of persons to refrain from or modify such conduct or practices', a defence which might well have succeeded. If the statutory defence cannot apply in these sorts of circumstances, it seems odd that it would apply to more serious incidents where there has been threatening, rather than merely insulting, conduct.

Table 7.1 Comparison of Offences under Parts III and IIIA of The Public Order Act 1986

	Part III Racial Hatred: **Intent or likelihood** of racial hatred being stirred up Conduct/words may be **threatening, abusive or insulting**	Part IIIA Hatred on Grounds of Religious Belief / Sexual Orientation: **Intent must be shown** (not merely likelihood) and **conduct/words must be threatening**
Definition	s 17	s 29A (Religious Belief) s 29AB (Sexual Orientation)
Offences		
Words, behaviour or display of written material	s 18	s 29B
Publishing or distributing written material	s 19	s 29C
Public performance of play	s 20	s 29D
Distributing, showing or playing a recording	s 21	s 29E

(Continued)

Table 7.1 (*Cont'd*)

	Part III Racial Hatred: **Intent or likelihood** of racial hatred being stirred up Conduct/words may be **threatening, abusive or insulting**	Part IIIA Hatred on Grounds of Religious Belief / Sexual Orientation: **Intent must be shown** (not merely likelihood) and **conduct/words must be threatening**
Broadcasting or including programme in cable programme service	s 22	s 29F
Possession of material with a view to it being displayed, published, distributed or broadcast, etc	s 23	s 29G
Freedom of expression defence?	None	s 29J (Religious Belief) s 29JA (Sexual Orientation)

7.4 **Hate Crime, Aggravated Offences, and Sentences**

Where there is evidence that an offence has been motivated by, or accompanied by, hostility towards a person based on their race, religious belief, sexual orientation or disability, the offence may be treated as an **aggravated offence**.

There are three separate ways this can be achieved:

- by statute law creating specific aggravated forms of *particular* offences;
- via a statutory direction to consider crimes as aggravated if there are elements of 'hate crime' present;
- by the court taking all of the circumstances of the offence into account in deciding its seriousness.

7.4.1 **Specific racially or religiously aggravated offences**

Under sections 29–32 of the Crime and Disorder Act 1998 (CDA), separate offences are created, constituting racially or religiously aggravated versions of the principal offences of assault, criminal damage, harassment, and offences under sections 4, 4A and 5 of the POA. It is only for these specific offences that a separate, racially/religiously aggravated version of the offence has been created.

In each case, under section 28 the racially or religiously aggravated version of the relevant offence is committed if either:

- at the time of committing the offence, or immediately before or after, the offender demonstrates towards the victim hostility based on the victim's membership (or, on the part of the offender, the presumed membership) of a racial or religious group (s 28(1)(a)); or

- the offence is motivated (wholly or partly) by hostility towards members of a racial or religious group, based on their membership of, or association with, that group (s 28(1)(b)).

In *Jones v DPP* [2011] 1 WLR 833 the court confirmed that there is no requirement to demonstrate any specific intent on the part of the offender under s 28(1)(a)—the prosecution need only show a *demonstration* of racial or religious hostility. In other words, it is an objective test: looking at how matters appear to be, rather than what was actually in the defendant's mind. However, under s 28(1)(b) it is different. There, the test is subjective, looking at what was in the defendant's mind—the prosecution must be able to show that the offence was motivated, at least in part, by hostility towards members of the relevant racial or religious group.

'Racial group' means a group of persons defined by reference to race, colour, nationality (including citizenship) or ethnic or national origins. 'Religious group' means a group of persons defined by reference to religious belief or lack of religious belief. These are exactly the same definition as for the specific race/ religious hate crimes within Part III of the POA.

The offences for which the CDA (ss 29–32) provides a corresponding racially or religiously aggravated offence are:

- Assaults: s 29 CDA
- Criminal damage: s 30 CDA
- Public Order Offences (s 4, 4A and 5 POA): s 31 CDA
- Harassment: s 32 CDA.

Case study

Barry and Charlie

Barry and Charlie, two doormen, throw three drunk men out of a night club. The last man falls to the ground, at which point Barry kicks him. As Barry walks back into the night club, Charlie says, *'That was a good dig you gave him!'* At this point Barry says, *'Yeah, well I hate darkies'.*

In kicking the man on the ground, Barry appears to have committed the offence of assault. The words used immediately after the attack demonstrate a hostility based on the victim's membership—or, on Barry's part, the presumed membership—of a racial group: see *R v Rogers* [2007] 21 AC 62. The victim's *actual* racial/ethnic background is irrelevant. Barry is therefore likely to be guilty of the racially aggravated version of the offence of assault under s 29 CDA.

However, on the basis of the above facts, Barry would probably *not* be guilty of the offence of using threatening words or behaviour intended or likely to stir up racial hatred, contrary to s 18 of the POA because his motive in kicking the man was to satisfy his own dislike, rather than to stir up racial hatred in other people; and because it is unlikely that racial hatred would be stirred up simply by Barry's kick or his comment afterwards, given by way of explanation.

The situation would have been different if, while kicking one of the men, Barry had shouted at the ejected group words along the lines of, '*If you darkies come back again, you'll all get some of this*'. Barry has clearly demonstrated threatening behaviour. Having regard to all the circumstances, it seems likely that racial hatred would be stirred up. It would not be necessary to show that this was Barry's intent: the elements of an offence contrary to s 18 of the POA would be made out.

If the aggravating ingredients can be demonstrated, it is the policy of the Crown Prosecution Service (CPS) to prosecute for these more serious offences. **It is therefore vital that such evidence be gathered and recorded as close to the time of the offence as possible, even if the individual has not been arrested for an aggravated offence.**

7.4.2 Increased sentences for aggravation related to race, religious belief, disability or sexual orientation

The specific statutory provisions dealing with this are s 145 and s 146 of the Criminal Justice Act 2003 (CJA). Race and religious belief are covered by s 145, disability and sexual orientation by s 146.

Section 145 only applies to those race/religion offences *not* covered by ss 29–32 of the CDA (see 7.3.1). However, it applies precisely the very formulation set out in s 28 of the CDA as to the circumstances in which the offence is to be regarded as racially or religiously aggravated: see section 7.3.1.

Under s 146(2), the circumstances where an offence is to be regarded as aggravated for a reason related to disability or sexual orientation are:

(a) that at the time of committing the offence, or immediately before or after doing so, the offender demonstrated towards the victim of the offence hostility based on—
  (i) the sexual orientation (or presumed sexual orientation) of the victim, or
  (ii) a disability (or presumed disability) of the victim, or

(b) that the offence is motivated (wholly or partly)—
  (i) by hostility towards persons who are of a particular sexual orientation, or
  (ii) by hostility towards persons who have a disability or a particular disability.

This is effectively identical to the test at s 28 of the CDA. 'Disability' means *any* physical or mental impairment, a very much wider definition that that found in the equality legislation.

If the circumstances are proved, the court *must* treat that fact as an aggravating factor, and *must* state in open court that the offence was so aggravated. **It is therefore important to obtain and record contemporaneous evidence of any features of the offence, or surrounding circumstances, that suggest that hatred or hostility may have played a part in the offence.** Even if a suspect is not arrested for an aggravated offence, it is nevertheless necessary to record or evidentially capture any such features. This enables an informed decision to be taken either at the charging stage as to which charge to prefer, or at the sentencing stage as to whether to refer the court to s 145/s 146 of the CJA.

Case study

Flag waving and goading by members of the Pakistani and Indian communities

Scenario 1—after sporting events between the countries

In the local urban community there are two fairly distinct areas, one populated predominantly by the Pakistani (Muslim) community, the other by an Indian (Hindu) community. It has become common after sporting events between the two countries for young men from the community of the victorious nation to drive down the streets of the other community, sounding their car horns, cheering, and draping the national flag of their country out of the window. This often leads to angry, sometime violent confrontations between groups of youths in the street.

Is an offence being committed?

Patriotic behaviour, or expressions of affection or devotion towards a particular country or religion would not normally amount to the stirring up of hatred against another racial or religious group. Such behaviour would be accepted by most members of society, in the context of celebrating a sporting match or similar. In this scenario, it might be thought to make a difference that the drivers are deliberately targeting the streets where the residents originate from the other nation. The inference is that they are deliberately goading them. However, what is the conduct that could be said to be criminal? It is not threatening, it may not even be abusive or insulting, so Part III of the POA does not apply. A better way to deal with this behaviour, which, if deliberately goading, is unreasonable, is via the exercise of powers to prevent a breach of the peace, if imminent violence is threatened by such conduct.

Scenario 2—after the Mumbai bombing attacks

In the immediate aftermath of the Mumbai attacks of 26 November 2008 (where the attackers approached Mumbai from Pakistani territorial waters), young men from the Pakistani community drive down streets in predominantly Indian areas in urban England, sounding their horns, cheering and waving the Pakistani flag out of the window.

Is an offence being committed?

The behaviour is the same as scenario 1, but the context is completely different. There is little doubt that the behaviour would, in the circumstances, be at the very least insulting, perhaps disorderly. Given recent events, the conduct is within the hearing or sight of a person likely to be caused harassment, alarm or distress by it. It could not be said to be reasonable behaviour.

At the very least, an offence contrary to s 5 POA has been committed. The behaviour is not threatening, because the young men are simply driving through the streets cheering, and so no offence under Part IIIA of the POA arises. However, the offence appears to be motivated (wholly or partly) by hostility towards members of a racial group—the Indian community—based on their membership of that group. There would therefore appear to be prima facie evidence of an offence under s 31 of the CDA—a racially or religiously aggravated public order offence, probably the racially or religiously aggravated version of s 4A or s 5 of the POA.

7.4.3 **Other hate crime**

For other hate crimes (eg motivated by a person's gender, philosophy, age— even support of a particular football team, etc), a court would still be entitled to treat such a motive as an aggravating factor when sentencing. This would be part of the court's general power to consider all the surrounding circumstances when reaching a decision as to the seriousness of the offence. For example, in the CPS sentencing manual for assault, one aggravating factor is identified as 'Offence motivated by hostility towards a minority group, or a member or members of it'. **It is therefore important to record any evidence that might suggest that such a motivation existed, even if there is no specific statutory mechanism applicable to the protection of that minority.**

7.5 **Powers of Entry, Search, and Forfeiture**

7.5.1 **Powers of entry and search**

There are specific powers granted to the police to enter premises to search for material or recordings which are suspected to be in a person's possession in contravention of either s 23 (race) or s 29G (religious belief/sexual orientation) of the POA. The powers of entry and search are contained in s 24 (race) and s 29H (religious belief/sexual orientation). The power is only exercisable on a warrant:

- If a magistrate is satisfied that there are reasonable grounds for suspecting that a person has possession of written material or a recording in contravention of s 23 or s 29G of the POA, the magistrate may issue a warrant authorizing any constable to enter and search the premises where it is suspected the material or recording is situated.

- A constable entering or searching premises under such a warrant may use reasonable force if necessary.

7.5.2 **Forfeiture**

The power of forfeiture is exercised by the court following conviction for offences under s 18/s 29B (if it relates to the display of written material), s 19/s 29C (publishing or distributing written material), s 21/s 29E (distributing, showing or playing a recording), or s 23/s 29F (possession of material with a view to it being displayed, published, distributed or broadcast).

If a person is convicted of one of these offences, the court shall order the forfeiture of any written material or recording which is:

- produced to the court; and
- shown to the court's satisfaction to be written material or a recording to which the offence relates.

Because of this power of forfeiture, it is important that all relevant material is seized and retained until the outcome of any criminal proceedings.

7.6 **Prosecution of Offences**

The consent of the Attorney General is required prior to the commencement of proceedings under Parts III and IIIA of the POA. This requirement arises only at the stage of charge—no permission is required for arrest or investigation.

If convicted of an offence under Part III or IIIA, the maximum sentence on conviction is seven years' imprisonment and/or a fine (on indictment) or six months and/or a fine not exceeding the statutory maximum (summary conviction).

The maximum sentences that can be imposed for the specific racially or religiously aggravated offences under the CDA are generally higher than for the non-aggravated offences. For example, for the aggravated form of the s 4/4A POA offences, the maximum sentences are two years' imprisonment and/or a fine (on indictment) or six months and/or a fine not exceeding the statutory maximum (summary conviction). At a Crown Court trial for the aggravated form of the s 4/4A POA offence, the jury may find the defendant guilty of the non-aggravated form of the offence.

Further reading

- *Mandla v Lee* [1983] 2 AC 548
- *R v Rogers* [2007] 2 AC 62 on the broad approach taken to the concept of race
- Addison, N., *Religious Discrimination and Hatred Law* (Oxford: Routledge Cavendish, 2007)

NOTES

Terrorism

8.1 **Introduction**

Terrorist threats pose risks to the lives of the community in countless ways and generate specific public order challenges. Dealing with scenarios where acts of terrorism are threatened or anticipated, or the aftermath of such an attack or attempt may require public order powers to be exercised on a large scale, in rapid time and in a decisive and sometimes intrusive manner. The powers to deal with attacks that are imminent or underway have been supplemented by specific terrorism-related statutory powers.

In addition to these specific terrorism-related statutory powers, the police are able to use other statutory powers (such as those under the Public Order Act 1986) and general common law powers as appropriate. These powers are discussed in detail in other chapters and are included here only in relation to specific applications in relation to the threat of terrorism.

The main powers available to the police are contained in the Terrorism Act 2000 (referred to in the remainder of this chapter as 'the Act'). The powers relate to:

- cordons,
- parking, and
- stop and search.

The powers to stop and search have been the subject of substantial revision under the Terrorism Act 2000 (Remedial) Order 2011, which came into force on 18 March 2011. This followed the decision in *Gillan and Quinton v The United Kingdom* (2010) 50 EHRR 45 in which the European Court of Human Rights (ECtHR) declared that the regime under ss 44–46 of the Act was unlawful. Those sections are now deemed replaced by the provisional ss 47A–47C. However, the remainder of the statutory powers granted by the Act remain in effect.

There are specific powers relating to terrorism (such as intelligence and aviation security) that are beyond the scope of typical public order scenarios and thus this book.

8.1.1 **In what kinds of circumstance are terrorism powers needed?**

The police need powers to keep order in many different circumstances arising from actual, anticipated or suspected terrorism. For example:

- Someone suspected to have been involved in plotting a terrorist attack discards a bag and the contents have been strewn across a busy shopping street. The public are in no immediate danger, but the police need to keep busy shoppers and inquisitive passers-by away from the potentially important evidence. What might the police do?
- There is a suspicious package in the same street. The police need the power to keep everyone a safe distance away, including keen office workers who want to get back to work after their lunch break. What might the police do?

- There is a bomb threat in an enclosed space such as an underground railway tunnel. Whether or not the threat is real, if everyone panics and tries to leave at once people will be pushed and crushed. What powers might the police use to control where and how the public reach safety?

In relation to scenarios of this kind, see the section on cordons at section 8.2 of this chapter.

- In the wake of a terrorist attack it is feared that there will be further atrocities by members of the same group. The police need the power to search people for items which might be used in terrorism, even if they cannot justify particular grounds for suspicion against each individual stopped. What might the police do?
- In relation to this kind of scenario, see the section on s 47A Terrorism Act 2000 authorizations for stop and search, and other stop and search powers, at sections 8.4–8.5 of this chapter.
- Intelligence suggests there is a terrorist with a gun on a packed commuter train. The police need to keep people on the train for as long as reasonably necessary to find him and deal with the threat, without either causing a panic or alerting the terrorist. What powers might the police use?
- A bomb has detonated. The police need the power to do everything at once, ie to get people to safety in a controlled way, to keep people away from the scene, and to take steps to avert another attack. What powers might be available to the police?

This chapter will cover the various cordons, parking-related powers and stop and search powers that will be of use to the police in this kind of pressured situation, in that order. At the end of this chapter some miscellaneous terrorism-related powers for public order officers will be identified. But first, what does 'terrorism' mean?

8.1.2 The meaning of 'terrorism' in the Terrorism Act 2000

'Terrorism' is defined in section 1(1) and 1(2) of the Act. It means the use or threat of action where the:

- action involves serious violence against a person or serious damage to property; endangers a person's life, other than that of the person committing the action; creates a serious risk to the health or safety of the public or a section of the public; or is designed seriously to interfere with or seriously to disrupt an electronic system; and
- the use or threat of such action is **designed to influence** the government or an international governmental organization **or to intimidate** the public or a section of the public (except for the use or threat of action which involves the use of firearms or explosives which does not have to satisfy this criterion); and

249

- the use or threat is **made for the purpose of advancing a political, religious or ideological cause.**

This definition covers terrorism both domestically and abroad and the planning for any such action:

- 'Action' includes action outside the United Kingdom;
- 'Person' and 'property' means any person, or property, wherever situated;
- 'The public' includes the public of a country other than the United Kingdom;
- 'The government' means not only any United Kingdom government but also the government of any other country.

8.1.3 **Meaning of 'terrorist'**

For the purposes of the exercise of counter-terrorism powers, a terrorist is defined under s 41 of the Act as either a person who has committed one of a number of particular offences specified in the Act, or who is or has been concerned in the **commission, preparation or instigation** of acts of terrorism, as defined in the Act.

8.2 **Cordons**

The Act gives the police a specific statutory power to establish a cordon in relation to terrorism—in addition to the common law powers dealt with at section 3.6.4.

In summary, the Act grants the police powers, to be used where it is considered expedient for the purposes of terrorist investigation, to:

- designate areas to be cordoned off with police tape or otherwise;
- do this urgently, if necessary;
- whilst the cordon is in place, control who and what is present in the area of the cordon; arrange for the removal or movement of vehicles within the area; and restrict access to the area;
- extend the duration of the cordon past 14 days, up to 28 days if required.

These powers are set out in detail below.

8.2.1 **Statutory cordons: ss 33–36 Terrorism Act 2000**

Sections ss 33–36A of the Act provide for the designation of areas, and the implementations of cordons around those areas, for the purposes of the terrorist investigation. A cordoned area is simply an area which has been 'designated' under s 33.

How is a cordoned area identified?

Under normal circumstances it is anticipated that police tape will be used, but other methods such as barriers, vehicles or officers could be used if considered appropriate by a constable (s 33(4)). For example, in certain circumstances it might be appropriate simply to restrict access to an area by marking entrance doors, gates or fences to inform the public that the area is cordoned off.

The duty in s 33 of the Act is to arrange for the cordoned area to be demarcated so far as is 'reasonably practicable'.

8.2.2 Who can designate an area to be cordoned?

Table 8.1 Who can designate an area to be cordoned?

Area		Force	Rank
Outside Northern Ireland	Wholly or partly within police area	An officer for police area X	At least superintendent
Transport network	Except in Northern Ireland: • on track (including bridges, tunnels, level crossings, etc) • on network (ie the system of track and other installations) • in a station (including station approaches, forecourts and car parks, etc) • in a light maintenance depot • on other land used for purposes of or in relation to a railway • on other land in which a person who provides railway services has a freehold or leasehold interest. (See s 44(4A), s 34(1A) and the Railways and Transport Safety Act 2003, s 31(1)(a)–(f). For detailed definitions see s 75, Railways and Transport Safety Act 2003, and the further provisions it refers to.)	British Transport Police Officer	At least superintendent
In Northern Ireland		A member of the Police Service of Northern Ireland	At least superintendent
Ministry of Defence (outside or in Northern Ireland)	Land, vehicles, vessels, aircraft and hovercraft for naval, military or air purposes. Includes most Ministry of Defence land (see s 34(1B) Terrorism Act and the Ministry of Defence Police Act 1987, s 2). An area relating to a particular incident or operation where the assistance of the Ministry of Defence Police has been requested by another police force under Ministry of Defence Police Act 1987 s 2(3A).	Ministry of Defence Police	At least superintendent

Any less senior officer has the power to make a designation if he considers it necessary by reason of urgency: s 34(2). However, if an urgent designation is made under s 34(2), the officer making the designation shall, as soon as is reasonably practicable:

- make a written record of the time at which the designation was made; and
- ensure that a police officer of at least the rank of superintendent is informed— see s 34(3).

The officer who is informed of an urgent designation made by a less senior officer must then either confirm the designation, or cancel it. If cancelled, the cancellation takes effect from such time as he may direct—see s 34(4)(a). If he cancels the designation he must make a written record of the cancellation and the reason for it: s 34(4)(b).

8.2.3 In what circumstances can a designation be made?

A designation may be made *only* if the person making it considers it expedient for the purpose of a terrorist investigation: s 33(2).

Under s 32, a terrorist investigation means an investigation of:

- the commission, preparation or instigation of acts of terrorism;
- an act which appears to have been done for the purposes of terrorism;
- the resources of a proscribed organization;
- the possibility of making an order under s 3(3) (proscribing an organization); or
- the commission, preparation or instigation of an offence under the Terrorism Act 2000, or under Part 1 of the Terrorism Act 2006 other than ss 1 or 2.

It follows from this definition that there *must* be an element of investigation, or intended investigation, in order for an area to be subject to a cordon. The investigation does not need to have started by the time the cordon is in place.

There will be circumstances where the police will wish to impose cordons for reasons connected with terrorism that will not include investigation. For example, the police, together with other organizations, may wish to conduct a training rehearsal of an evacuation, or some other contingency exercise, which might involve the imposition of cordons. Whilst the 'investigation of . . . the preparation of acts of terrorism' would probably cover measures taken to prevent a particular terrorist attack, it probably does not cover purely precautionary preventative action where no specific threat has been identified. In such a case it is likely that the police will need to continue to rely on their more general powers, either from common law and/or or relying on permission from the landowners.

'Expedient' is not defined in the statute. It is likely that the courts would apply the same meaning as was previously applied to expedient' under s 44. 'Expedient' is not as high a test as 'necessity'. The person making the designation must consider it likely that cordoning the area would be of *significant practical value and utility* for the purpose of a terrorist investigation.

8.2.4 **Duration of a designation**

A designation has effect during the period beginning when it was made and ending with a date or time specified in the designation: s 35(1). The maximum period that can be initially specified is 14 days: s 35(2).

A designation may be extended by the person who made it, or a person who could have made it of at least the rank of inspector: s 35(3). The extension must specify the additional period during which the designation is to have effect: s 35(4). There is no provision for granting an extension urgently.

A designation shall not have effect after the end of the period of 28 days beginning on the day on which it is made: s 35(5). In other words, a designation cannot be extended beyond a total period of 28 days.

KEY POINTS

Designated cordoned areas under the Terrorism Act 2000

- It must be expedient for the purpose of a terrorist investigation for the area to be cordoned off
- Expediency is a lower threshold than necessity
- Officer designating an area must be at least a superintendent, unless it is urgent in which case a lower ranking officer can designate
- If a lower ranking officer designates, a superintendent must be informed as soon as reasonably practicable and must confirm or cancel the designation
- A written record must be kept
- The designation must specify the duration
- The maximum duration is 14 days, extendable to a maximum 28 days.

8.2.5 **What special police powers are there in relation to a designated area?**

Under s 36(1) a constable in uniform has the following significant powers in relation to a designated area, *whether or not it has yet been demarcated* with tape or by other means:

- to order a person in a cordoned area to leave it immediately;
- to order a person immediately to leave premises which are wholly or partly in or adjacent to the cordoned area;
- to order the driver or person in charge of a vehicle in a cordoned area to move it from the area immediately;
- to arrange for the removal of a vehicle from a cordoned area;
- to arrange for the movement of a vehicle within a cordoned area;
- to prohibit or restrict access to a cordoned area by pedestrians or vehicles.

These powers can be exercised in relation to any person. There are no pre-conditions to be fulfilled in relation to any individual (such as reasonable suspicion).

8.2.6 **Offences**

It is an offence to fail to comply with an order, prohibition or restriction imposed by virtue of s 36(1) and s 36(2).

It is a defence to prove a reasonable excuse: s 36(3). As necessity is a general defence in criminal law, a 'reasonable excuse' will include circumstances that would not reach the standard required for a necessity defence such as where, due to physical infirmity, a person might not be able to comply immediately with a direction to leave an area.

KEY POINTS

Maintaining cordoned areas under the Terrorism Act 2000

- Cordoned area can be demarcated by any appropriate method
- The method must be sufficient to clearly inform the public the area has been cordoned off
- A constable in uniform may
  - order a person in a cordoned area to leave it immediately
  - order a person immediately to leave premises which are wholly or partly in or adjacent to the cordoned area
  - order the driver or person in charge of a vehicle in a cordoned area to move it from the area immediately
  - arrange for the removal from (or movement within) a cordoned area of a vehicle
  - prohibit or restrict access to a cordoned area by pedestrians or vehicles
- An officer can start to give the above orders *before* the cordoned area has been demarcated.

8.2.7 **Cordons at common law**

The broad powers available to the police under the common law can, in principle, provide legal justification for establishing a cordon. The relevant common law powers are those relating to:

- breach of the peace, and
- necessity.

Where the cordon is restricting a person's direction of movement, rather than detaining them, it is now accepted that, provided it is **necessary** to do so, the police have both a common law power and (for private land) the implied consent of a landowner to impose a cordon, see *DPP v Morrison* [2003] EWHC 683 (Admin) at paragraphs 4 and 25. Chapter 3 provides a more detailed discussion of these powers. Common law cordons are more flexible than the statutory powers and may therefore be of particular assistance to deal with short-term crises.

Case study

The police receive reliable intelligence that a terrorist is inside a busy railway station at rush hour, attempting to plant a bomb. They need to achieve evacuation of the station, while also trying to detect the bomber in case he attempts to leave—perhaps to detonate the bomb elsewhere. The police also need to prevent unsuspecting members of the public from entering the railway station. This may be best achieved by the use of two cordons: an inner one to allow people to leave safely and/or catch the terrorist, and an outer one to prevent members of the public from entering the station.

The inner cordon, designed in part to apprehend the terrorist, will come within the definition of an 'investigation' for the purposes of sections 32 and 33 of the Act.

The outer cordon could also be justified under the Act, in that part of its purpose will be to prevent the investigation becoming hindered or contaminated by incoming members of the public. However, even if its imposition did not fall within the scope of the statute such that it would otherwise be unlawful (see chapter 3), it would clearly fall within the scope of the necessity defence and/or s 3 of the Criminal Law Act 1967. It could also potentially be justified to prevent a breach of the peace: see chapter 3.

Continuing the above example, in a public order situation like this it may be necessary to impose the cordons in such a way that members of the public are not free to leave, in any direction. Here are three possible ways the situation could develop:

Example 1

While the threat of an attack remains, there might still be individual members of the crowd who wish to leave as they think that the police action is unnecessary, or an overreaction.

Example 2

Alternatively, the threat to public safety having passed, there may be the risk of a rush by angry, late commuters to catch the next train home.

Example 3

A less likely (but not unrealistic) scenario might be if a false rumour were to spread among the crowd that the bomber had been caught and the crowd becomes hostile, believing that they should now be released. There becomes a risk of the whole crowd, or a section of it, rushing to break through the cordon.

In a situation where the police have decided not to let anybody leave, the police will need to justify this 'false imprisonment' at common law. The legal justification could be provided by common law powers relating to:

- necessity (in the first, second or third example), and/or
- breach of the peace (in the second or third example).

If there were no alternative, and the detention were relatively brief, then (on the basis of the House of Lords decision in *Austin v Commissioner of Police for the Metropolis* [2009] 1 AC 564) the public's right to liberty under Article 5 would not be engaged.

A common law cordon can be maintained for as long as is reasonably required and in contrast to the set-up procedures of a cordon under the Act, one can be made on the spur of the moment by **any** constable, using his or her judgement. However, if the cordon is part of an absolute containment, the case of *Moos v Commissioner of Police for the Metropolis* [2011] EWHC 957 means that in order for it to be lawful, other possibilities will need to have been considered and discounted (see sections 3.6.4 and 3.6.5 for a discussion of *Moos* and *Austin*).

It is important to stress that in situations of actual or threatened terrorist attack, police officers should, above all else, do what they honestly and reasonably believe to be necessary to prevent loss of life. Doing 'the right thing' will generally coincide with acting lawfully. The courts are not eager to criticise police officers who, in the heat of the moment, do their best to save life.

8.3 Parking Restrictions Expedient for the Prevention of Terrorism

Sections 48–51 of the Act provide a separate, independent and relatively uncontroversial power to authorize the imposition of parking restrictions and prohibitions for specified areas.

As with cordons, the restrictions can be imposed where considered expedient for the prevention of acts of terrorism.

8.3.1 Authorizations for parking restrictions

There is no requirement for confirmation by the Home Secretary, unlike the now defunct s 44 authorizations. In other respects the initial authorization process, set out in s 48, has similarities with s 44:

- The required level of seniority is as set out in Table 8.2. Unlike cordons, there is no provision for urgent authorizations by a less senior officer.

- An authorization may be given only if the person giving it considers it expedient for the prevention of acts of terrorism. In most circumstances, this test is likely to be examined with less scrutiny than a section 44 authorization.
- The authorization must be in writing. If an authorization is given orally, the person giving it shall confirm it in writing as soon as is reasonably practicable.
- All roads affected must be specified in the authorization (although for an area encompassing several roads, it is probably permissible to specify the area and all the roads therein).
- The duration of the authorization must be specified. The maximum duration is 28 days.

An authorization can be renewed by following the same procedure.

Table 8.2

Where is the specified area or place?	What force must the police officer making the s 48 authorization be from?	What rank must the police officer making the s 48 authorization be?
Whole or part of the metropolitan police district	Metropolitan Police	At least Commander
Whole or part of City of London	City of London	At least Commander
Whole of part of Northern Ireland	Northern Ireland	Assistant Chief Constable
Any other area	The force for the area	Assistant Chief Constable

8.3.2 Prohibitions, restrictions and directions as to parking

Once an authorization has been given, a constable in uniform may prohibit or restrict the parking of vehicles on a road specified in the authorization. This includes suspending parking places. This is to be carried out by placing a traffic sign on the road concerned.

A constable in uniform may also order a driver or someone with control of a vehicle to move it if it is parked in contravention of a restriction or prohibition imposed under the Act.

8.3.3 Offences

It is an offence for a driver—or someone with control of a vehicle—to park, or fail to move a vehicle in contravention of a prohibition or restriction. The penalties are significantly more serious than fixed penalties for normal parking offences. Parking in contravention of a restriction can result in a fine not exceeding level 4 on the standard scale (s 51(5)), and defying the direction of a constable to move a vehicle can result in a fine, a sentence of imprisonment of up to 51 weeks, or both.

It is a defence for the person to prove that he had a reasonable excuse for the act or omission in question. However, as for the cordon offences, it is likely to be difficult establish such a defence. For example, possession of a disabled person's badge is not of itself a defence to a contravention offence (s 51(3)(4)). It might be reasonable to refuse to move a vehicle if the driver knew that they were over the limit for alcohol consumption, or were unable to drive due to being injured or unwell.

8.4 **Stop and Search Powers under the Act**

The operation of stop and search powers under the Act was drastically altered by the Home Secretary in July 2010 and March 2011, following the judgment of the European Court of Human Rights in the case of *Gillan and Quinton*. The background to this judgment is explained in the case study in 8.5 of this chapter.

In the context of the exercise of terrorism powers, racial or cultural profiling is to be discouraged. When exercising their powers, the Equality Act 2010 makes it unlawful for police officers to discriminate against, harass or victimize any person on the grounds of the 'protected characteristics' of age, disability, gender reassignment, race, religion or belief, sex and sexual orientation, marriage and civil partnership, pregnancy and maternity. This has important implications for the exercise of the powers of stop and search under either section.

8.4.1 **Stop and search on reasonable suspicion that the person is a terrorist**

Under section 43(1) of the Act a constable may stop and search a person whom he reasonably suspects to be a terrorist to discover whether he has in his possession anything which may constitute evidence that he is a terrorist. Importantly:

• The suspicion must be based on reasonable grounds;
• The constable does not have to be in uniform;
• Any officer with the powers of a constable can exercise this power anywhere in the United Kingdom;
• There is no requirement for an authorization under s 47A to have been given.

This power to stop and search without arresting is in addition to the power to arrest and detain set out in s 41. The investigation, arrest and detention of terrorism suspects are beyond the scope of this book.

Under s 43(4) a constable may seize and retain anything which he discovers in the course of a search of a person under subsection (1) or (2) and which he reasonably suspects may constitute evidence that the person is a terrorist. The power to stop and search does not arise unless the officer suspects *beforehand* (on reasonable grounds) that the person he is considering stopping may be a terrorist.

The conduct of a s 43 search is governed by the Police and Criminal Evidence Act 1984 (PACE) Code of Practice A. The search must be carried out by an officer of the same sex as the person being searched. Code of Practice A states that reasonable suspicion:

- can never be supported on the basis of personal factors;
- cannot be based on generalizations or stereotypical images of certain groups or categories of people as more likely to be involved in terrorism;
- must rely on intelligence or information about, or some specific behaviour by, the person concerned.

Unless the police have a description of a particular suspect, or group of suspects, a person's physical appearance or the fact that the person is known to have a previous conviction cannot be used alone or in combination with each other (or any other personal factor) as the reason for searching that person. However, the person's conduct can of course give rise to a reasonable suspicion, such as their behaviour at or near a location which has been identified as a potential target for terrorists.

8.4.2 **Power to enter and search premises**

There is also a power under section 42 to search premises following the issue of a warrant if there are reasonable grounds for suspecting that a person whom the constable reasonably suspects to be a terrorist is to be found there. This remains unaffected by the *Gillan and Quinton* judgment.

8.5 **The Power to Stop and Search following Authorization**

The case of *Gillan and Quinton,* the criticisms of the previous regime made by the European Court of Human Rights, and the government's response to the decision are summarized below. These events set the context for the exercise of the 'new' stop and search powers under s 47A of the Act.

Case study

The Facts in *Gillan and Quinton v United Kingdom*

Two pedestrians were stopped and searched under s 44(2), under authorizations covering the Metropolitan Police area which had been confirmed by the Home Secretary.

Mr Gillan was a PhD student who came to London to protest peacefully against an arms fair being held at the ExCel Centre, Docklands, in east London. He was riding his bicycle near the centre when he was stopped by two police officers. They searched him and his rucksack and found nothing incriminating. They gave him a copy of the Stop/Search Form 5090 which recorded that he was stopped and searched under s 44 of the Terrorism Act. The search was said to be for 'articles concerned with terrorism'. The whole incident lasted about 20 minutes.

Ms Quinton was a freelance journalist. She went to the ExCel Centre to film the protests taking place against the arms fair. She was stopped by a female police officer near the Centre and was asked to explain why she had appeared out of some bushes. She was wearing a photographer's jacket and carrying a small bag and a video camera. She explained she was a journalist and produced her press pass. The officer searched her, found nothing incriminating, and gave her a copy of Form 5090. This recorded that the object and grounds of the search were 'POTA' (which the court thought was a reference to the Terrorism Act 2000 rather than the previous Prevention of Terrorism Acts). The form showed the length of the search as five minutes, but Ms Quinton estimated it lasted for 30.

8.5.1 The legal challenge in *Gillan*

The legal challenge to these two incidents was taken all the way through the English courts to the European Court of Human Rights. The ECtHR held that the use of coercive powers to require an individual to submit to a detailed search of his person, clothing and belongings amounted to a clear interference with his right to respect for private life, ie his Article 8 rights.

Because of the following factors, the ECtHR held that the interference was *not* justified, and was therefore unlawful:

- The police's discretion to authorize stop and search powers, and to use them once authorized, was very wide and there was no real curb on that power.
- The test of 'expedience' in s 44 was much lower than that of 'necessity' and therefore during the authorization process there was no requirement upon the police or the state to assess the *proportionality* of the authorization.
- There was no real check on the issuing of authorizations: demonstrated by the fact that the Metropolitan Police authorization had been continually renewed in a 'rolling programme' ever since the very first authorization had been granted.
- There was a huge discretion bestowed upon individual officers deciding to use the s 44 powers, as they were not required to have reasonable suspicion. Rather, the decision to search could be based upon a 'hunch' or 'professional intuition'.

The ECtHR referred to the many thousands of searches that had taken place under s 44, and the fact that not a single one of these searches had ever led to an arrest for a terrorism related crime. The Court considered that there was a real risk of arbitrariness in the way the power could be used. The s 44 powers as enacted by Parliament therefore could not be said to be in accordance with the law.

8.5.2 Government's reaction

Following the final judgment by the ECtHR being delivered on 28 June 2010, the UK government suspended the application of ss 44–47 on 8 July 2010 and then conducted a review of counter-terrorism and security powers. The review's report, published on 26 January 2011 (Cm 8003), concluded that a power to stop and search individuals and vehicles without reasonable suspicion in tightly circumscribed circumstances was operationally necessary.

On 17 March 2011, acting under s 10(2) of the Human Rights Act, the Home Secretary laid before Parliament the Terrorism Act 2000 (Remedial) Order 2011, referred to in this chapter as 'the Terrorism Order'. The Terrorism Order came into effect on 18 March 2011.

8.5.3 Terrorism Act 2000 (Remedial) Order 2011

The Terrorism Order provides that the Terrorism Act 2000 is to have effect as if:

- ss 44–47 of the Act have been repealed and replaced by three entirely new sections, ss 47A–47C, and
- a new schedule 6B added, dealing with authorizations under the new s 47 regime.

An entirely new Code of Practice has been issued, covering the both the operation of the new sections and the conduct of searches authorized by the amended Act. Paragraphs 2.18–2.26(c) of PACE Code of Practice A (which governed searches under the repealed ss 44–47) are also to be treated as revoked.

The Terrorism Order provides for a system of authorization. When an authorization is granted, then within the area of authorization police officers have limited powers to search people and vehicles for the purpose of discovering whether there is anything which may constitute evidence either that (i) the vehicle is being used for the purposes of terrorism, or (ii) that the person being searched is a terrorist within the meaning of the Act. Provided the power is exercised for this purpose, there is no requirement for a reasonable suspicion.

8.5.4 The authorization process

An authorization under s 47A may only be made by an officer of the rank of assistant chief constable or above (in the case of the Metropolitan or City of London Police, a commander). Authorizing officers must be either substantive or on temporary promotion to the qualifying rank: officers 'acting up' may not give authorizations.

The authorization must apply to a specified area or place (which may include the internal waters, but not territorial waters, of England and Wales). The key requirements for an authorization under s 47A(1) are that the authorizing officer:

- reasonably suspects that an act of terrorism will take place; and
- considers that—
  - the authorization is necessary to prevent such an act; and
  - the specified area or place is no greater than is necessary to prevent such an act; and
  - the duration of the authorization is no longer than is necessary to prevent such an act.

The requirement of **necessity** applies to the authorization itself, as well as its area and duration of effect. This marks an important change from the old statutory scheme, which merely required that the authorization be 'expedient'. The expediency test continues to apply to the less intrusive measures of cordons or parking restrictions.

Section 3.1 of the Code of Practice provides clear guidance on the factors to include when considering making an authorization. An authorization may only be given where there is intelligence or circumstances which lead the authorizing officer to reasonably suspect that an act of terrorism will take place. In deciding whether an authorization is necessary, the following factors may be taken into account, but are insufficient by themselves to justify an authorization:

- There is a general high threat from terrorism.
- A particular site or event is deemed to be high risk or vulnerable.

In order to satisfy him or herself that the authorization is indeed necessary, the authorizing officer must have considered, and excluded, other powers as being insufficient to deal with the threat (ie that the use of the power is proportionate). The Code of Practice specifically excludes as a valid basis for making the authorization that the use of the powers might provide public reassurance, or be a useful deterrent or intelligence-gathering tool.

The period of authorization starts when a senior officer gives authorization. At this time he must state when the authorization is due to finish—at a time and date no later than the end of a 14-day period, including the day on which the authorization was given.

Authorizations should, where practicable, be given in writing. Where an authorization is given orally, it should be confirmed in writing as soon as possible after it is given. The Code of Practice sets the aim of supplying the written authorization to the Secretary of State. Annex C to the Code of Practice is a detailed, 11-page authorization document that requires the senior officer to address matters such as the intelligence on which the authorization is based, information demonstrating that all officers involved in exercising section 47A powers will receive appropriate briefing in the use of the powers, and about how the powers will be used, and why. See paragraph 3.2.7 of the Code of Practice:

> 3.2.7. Tactical Deployment: The authorising officer should provide information about how the powers will be used and why. This may include the use of vehicle checkpoints, stops and searches of individuals entering or leaving particular sites such as rail stations, sports stadiums etc (depending on the nature of the threat and the place(s) and area(s) specified). The authorising officer should indicate whether officers will be instructed to conduct stops and searches on the basis of particular indicators (eg behavioural indicators, types of items carried or clothes worn, types of vehicles etc), or whether the powers will be exercised on a random basis, or exercised using a combination of these tactics. If the powers are to be exercised on a random basis, the authorising officer should indicate why this is necessary, including why searches based on particular indicators are not appropriate, and should set out the parameters of the stop and search operation.

8.5.5 Confirmation by the Secretary of State

Where practicable, an authorizing officer should inform the Home Office that he or she intends to give an authorization, and provide a draft of that authorization, before it is given.

Once an authorization has been made, the Secretary of State must be notified of any authorization. If the authorization is specified to exceed 48 hours, the Secretary of State must confirm the authorization within 48 hours, or the authorization will cease to have effect at that point.

The Secretary of State may cancel the authorization or, if confirming the authorization, substitute an earlier time/date for the authorization to end, or confirm a narrower geographical area than in the original authorization. The authorizing officer may subsequently reduce the duration or area of the authorization, and this decision does not require the confirmation of the Secretary of State.

For authorizations that last less than 48 hours, there is no requirement for confirmation by the Secretary of State, although the authorization may still be cancelled by the Secretary of State within this period.

8.5.6 Rolling authorizations

One of the matters that led to the previous s 44 regime being categorized as disproportionate by the ECtHR was that there had been very long periods of time when the old 48-hour authorization periods had rolled into each other. Rolling authorizations (whether under 48 hours or longer) are not permitted under the new regime. A successive or replacement authorization must be sought, demonstrating that there has been a fresh assessment of both the intelligence *and* the necessity to seek an authorization.

8.5.7 **The briefing**

The Code of Practice stresses the central importance of the briefing to all officers who may use their s 47A powers. The written authorization/confirmation process requires the authorizing officer to set out the details of the planned tactical deployment of the s 47A stops. In order to ensure that this scope of deployment, as confirmed by the Secretary of State, is indeed reflected during operations, the officers involved in conducting the stops must receive clear instructions as to the intended deployment. For risk management reasons, officers involved in such instructions or briefings should record clearly the content of the same—see the auditable requirement, in paragraph 4.2.10 of the Code of Practice, which states:

> In order to demonstrate that the powers are used appropriately and proportionately, the briefing process must be robust and **auditable**. All officers involved in the process should be reminded that they are fully accountable in law for their own actions.
>
> [emphasis added]

If the exercise of s 47A powers is challenged, it may prove crucial to any justification that the police are able to show that the officer conducting the search:

• was briefed as to the appropriate and proportionate exercise of the power in the circumstances of the particular authorization; and
• did not exceed the scope of the briefing, and exercised the s 47A powers proportionately and appropriately.

The briefing may direct that officers are to stop and search pedestrians or vehicles in a certain location at random, provided this formed part of the plan within the original written authorization, and the necessity to take such a step can be demonstrated.

8.5.8 **Powers to stop and search under the authorization**

The authorization must state whether it applies to the search of vehicles—together with their drivers and passengers—(s 47A(2)) or pedestrians (s 47A(3)), or both. The stop and search can only take place within the area/place, or areas, included within the authorization.

Under s 47A(2), for vehicles, a constable in uniform may stop a vehicle and search:

(a) the vehicle;
(b) the driver of the vehicle;
(c) a passenger in the vehicle;
(d) anything in or on the vehicle or carried by the driver or a passenger.

The stop and search is permitted only for the purpose of discovering whether there is anything which may constitute evidence that the vehicle concerned is being used for the purposes of terrorism, or the person is involved in terrorism.

For pedestrians, under s 47A(3), a constable in uniform may stop a pedestrian and search:

(a) the pedestrian;
(b) anything carried by the pedestrian.

Again, the stop and search is permitted only for the purpose of discovering whether there is anything that may be evidence the person stopped is a terrorist.

The Code of Practice for the exercising of the stop and search powers under s 47A (which also covers the authorizations) is separate from PACE Code of Practice A. The Code of Practice (at 4.1.1) recommends that, when exercising s 47A powers, officers should have a basis for selecting individuals or vehicles to be stopped and searched. This basis will be either objective factors (based on intelligence, and in accordance with the briefing) or the selection of individuals or vehicles at random, according to the plan set out in the authorization.

POINT TO NOTE

The Code of Practice directs all officers to consider the following matters:

s 47A Terrorism Act 2000 Searches: Code of Practice, Paragraph 4.1.3

When selecting individuals to be stopped and searched, officers should consider the following:

Selecting an individual or vehicle using indicators

a. Geographical Extent—What are the geographical limits of the authorization and what are the parameters within which the briefing allows stops and searches to be conducted?
b. Behaviour—is the person to be stopped and searched acting in a manner that gives cause for concern, or is a vehicle being used in such a manner?
c. Clothing—could the clothing conceal an article of concern, which may constitute evidence that a person is a terrorist?
d. Carried items—could an item being carried conceal an article that could constitute evidence that a person is a terrorist or a vehicle is being used for the purposes of terrorism?

Selecting individuals 'at random'

What are the geographical and other parameters of the operation as set out in the authorization?

> **Explanation**
>
> Officers should be reminded of the need to explain to people why they or their vehicles are being searched.

A s 47A search is confined to the removal of headgear, footwear, an outer coat, a jacket or gloves.

If stops and searches are being conducted on the basis of objective factors, officers should be alert to the need to consider whether using their s 43 powers would be more appropriate. The Code of Practice is clear that officers should only use the s 47A powers if they are satisfied that they cannot meet the threshold of reasonable suspicion which would have entitled them to use other police powers. If an officer has a reasonable suspicion that a person is a terrorist, then regardless of the fact that a s 47A authorization is in place, the search which that officer conducts will properly fall within the scope of s 43 and that is the power that the officer should exercise.

Officers should take care to avoid any form of racial or religious profiling when selecting people to search under s 47A—ie the decision to search someone should not be made just because they are believed to belong to a particular racial or religious group. Great care should be taken to ensure that the selection of people is not based *solely* on ethnic background, perceived religion or other protected characteristic (see section 8.4.1). A potential suspect's appearance or ethnic background will sometimes form part of specific intelligence, provided as part of the briefing under an authorization. A decision to search a particular person under s 47A on the basis of their appearance could then be made if that person fits the description given in the briefing.

The Code of Practice is at pains to emphasize that, in recent years, terrorism-related acts have been carried out or attempted in the UK by White, Black and Asian British citizens.

Section 5 of the Code of Practice sets out the general requirements relating to the stops and searches, such as the need to show courtesy and respect to the person stopped, and the need to detain the person being searched for the minimum time required to complete the search.

While there is no statutory requirement for specific information to be given prior to the search, the Code of Practice stresses the importance of providing information to the person stopped such as the fact that they have detained for the purposes of search, the reasons for the stop, and the object of the search. Although the search might still be technically lawful if this information were not given, such a failure might provide the person stopped which the opportunity to argue that the stop was not in accordance with s 47A, as the officer did not in fact have the purpose required in s 47A(2)/(3).

The officer must make a record of the search at the time or as soon as is practicable after the search is completed. The record must include:

(a) a note of the self-defined ethnicity of the person searched, and, if different, the ethnicity as perceived by the officer making the search;
(b) the date, time and place the person or vehicle was searched;
(c) the object of the search;
(d) the nature of the powers under section 47A, the fact an authorization has been given and the reason the person or vehicle was selected for the search;
(e) the officer's warrant number or other identification number and duty station (the officer is not required to provide his name if he reasonably believes that recording names might endanger the officers).

A record should be offered to the person at the time. Provided the person applies for a written statement confirming the fact of the s 47A(2)/(3) search within 12 months, the written statement must be provided.

After searching an unattended vehicle, or anything in or on it, an officer must leave a notice in it (or on it, if things on it have been searched without opening it) recording the fact that it has been searched, and provided similar information to that set out above.

8.5.9 Police Community Support Officers

Provided they have been designated under the Police Reform Act 2002, and they are in the company of a constable who is supervising them, under s 47A, Police Community Support Officers (PCSOs) can stop:

- any pedestrian;
- any vehicle.

They may then search:

- anything carried by a pedestrian;
- anything carried by a driver or passenger;
- any vehicle;
- anything on or in a vehicle.

However, a PCSO is not allowed to search a person or their clothing.

8.5.10 Power to seize items

Under s 47A(6), the police officer may seize and retain anything which is discovered during the course of the search and which it is reasonably suspected may constitute evidence that the vehicle is being used for the purposes of terrorism or that the person being searched is a terrorist.

Nevertheless, provided the search is lawful, if other matters come to light (such as prohibited articles or controlled drugs), the officer can seize these other items if entitled to do so under other statutory powers. The person may, depending on the nature of any suspected offence that comes to light (and the general arrest powers under s 24(6) of PACE) face arrest for any offence, not simply those under the Act.

8.5.11 **Monitoring, supervision and community engagement**

In order to maintain the community's confidence in the police, supervising officers must monitor the use of stop and search powers. They should consider in particular whether there is any evidence or trend suggesting the powers are being exercised on the basis of stereotyped images or inappropriate generalizations. The statistical data on these searches must be retained, made available to community representatives. (There is a separate obligation to provide similar figures to the Home Office.)

The Code of Practice also mandates the police to engage with the local community where s 47A authorizations have been made: see section 6. When planning a counter-terrorism search operation, police authorities and the local CONTEST strategic partnership should be involved at the earliest opportunity to provide advice and assistance in identifying mechanisms for engaging with communities.

8.5.12 **The future of the authorization and stop and search regime**

Amendments very similar to those contained in the Terrorism Order are contained in the Protection of Freedoms Bill and it is anticipated that the bill will be passed during 2011. There is a 'sunset' clause in the Terrorism Order which provides that upon the provisions of the bill coming into force, the Terrorism Order will automatically cease to have effect.

The Terrorism Order does not create any specific new offence of failing to stop or obstructing a police officer acting under s 47A, although it may be that any formal amendment to the Terrorism Act 2000 will reintroduce offences of this nature. Nonetheless, failing to cooperate with an officer deploying s 47A would be capable of constituting the offence of wilful obstruction of a constable in execution of his duty, under s 89(2) Police Act 1996.

8.6 **Other Powers Exercisable**

The anti-terrorism powers have proved to be controversial and it is recognized that their use (particularly their overuse) may contribute to a mistrust of the police and damage to community relations.

The Code of Practice encourages the use of other stop and search powers which are available to the police, such as:

- s 60 Criminal Justice and Public Order Act 1994: offensive weapons and dangerous instruments (dealt with in chapter 5);
- s 1 PACE: stolen articles, offensive weapons, articles made or adapted for use in the course of or in connection with relevant offences, articles with blade or point in public place, fireworks;
- s 139B Criminal Justice Act 1988: offensive weapons on school premises;
- s 47 Firearms Act 1968: not dealt with in this book but which in essence says that an officer may search a person he suspects may be in possession of a firearm or ammunition in a public place (or in a vehicle in a public place);
- s 27 Sporting Events (Control of Alcohol etc) Act 1985: alcohol at sporting events (dealt with in chapter 10).

All these stop and search powers require *either* authorization *or* reasonable suspicion as set out in Table 8.3.

Table 8.3 Principle Powers of Stop and Search Available to Constables

Statute and section	Searching for . . .	Reasonable grounds to suspect, or statutory authorization?
PACE s 1	Stolen articles, offensive weapons, articles with blade or point, fireworks	Reasonable grounds to suspect
Misuse of Drugs Act 1971	A controlled drug	Reasonable grounds to suspect
Criminal Justice Act 1988, s 139B	Offensive weapons on school premises	Reasonable grounds to suspect
Firearms Act 1968, s 47	Firearm or ammunition in a public place (or in a vehicle in a public place)	Reasonable grounds to suspect
Sporting Events (Control of Alcohol etc) Act 1985, s 27	Alcohol at sporting events	Reasonable grounds to suspect
Criminal Justice and Public Order Act 1994, s 60	Offensive weapons and dangerous instruments	Prior statutory authorization required
Terrorism Act 2000, s 47A (de facto amendment)	Anything that may be evidence the person stopped is a terrorist/vehicle used in terrorism	Prior statutory authorization required
Terrorism Act 2000, s 43	for evidence that the person searched is a terrorist	Reasonable grounds to suspect

If the legal test for the use of any of these powers is met, then these powers can also be used in a terrorist context if necessary.

8.6.1 **When should the police rely on their legal powers?**

It remains an important goal of modern practical policing that it should, where possible, be by consent (see Appendix A of Charles Reith, *A New Study of Police History* (London: Oliver and Boyd, 1956)); this is often repeated by chief officers, including after the August 2011 riots.

The PACE Code of Practice A 1.5, although it relates to the exercise of stop and search powers other than s 47A, makes it clear that a member of the public should *not* be searched unless the officer is satisfied that there is a legal power to search:

> An officer must not search a person, even with his or her consent, where no power to search is applicable. Even where a person is prepared to submit to a search voluntarily, the person must not be searched unless the necessary legal power exists, and the search must be in accordance with the relevant power and the provisions of [Code A]. The only exception, where an officer does not require a specific power, applies to searches of persons entering sports grounds or other premises carried out with their consent given as a condition of entry.

To use force to search someone where the use of such force is not necessary (because the person might be willing to consent to the search) would constitute an assault on that person. It is vital that the person to be searched be given the opportunity to cooperate, where practicable.

Although the existence of the legal power is a necessary pre-requisite, the Code A 3.2 also stresses the need to obtain the person's consent if possible:

> The co-operation of the person to be searched must be sought in every case, even if the person initially objects to the search. A forcible search may be made only if it has been established that the person is unwilling to co-operate or resists. Reasonable force may be used as a last resort if necessary to conduct a search or to detain a person or vehicle for the purposes of a search.

While Code A does not apply to s 47A searches, these general observations would still govern the conduct of these searches.

8.7 **Taking Photographs/Collecting Information**

Section 58 of the Act, 'Collection of information', provides that a person commits an offence if he either collects or makes a record of information of a kind likely to be useful to a person committing or preparing an act of terrorism, or he possesses a document or record containing information of that kind.

'Record' includes a photographic or electronic record. The section therefore potentially criminalises the taking of photographs, if those photographs are likely to be useful to somebody committing or preparing an act of terrorism.

Any sightseer might take a picture of a royal residence, or political building, even a police officer. Protestors involved in direct action might also take pictures as souvenirs of the day. In both of these situations, it is conceivable that the photograph might potentially be useful to a person planning an act of terrorism. However, there is a statutory defence at s 58(3), 'It is a defence for a person charged with an offence under this section to prove that he had a reasonable excuse for his action or possession'. Tourism, journalism, making a souvenir, or even photographing a police officer whom the photographer believes to be acting unlawfully would probably all amount to 'reasonable excuse'. There is no such thing as an offence of photographing a police officer and the right to take innocent photographs of public buildings and even police officers is not suspended by a s 47A authorization.

Similarly, the possession of a camera could, in some circumstances, be an item of evidence suggesting the person stopped is a terrorist. However, in most cases the possession of a camera will be entirely innocent.

If there is objective evidence leading to the reasonable suspicion that a person is taking photographs in order to assist a person committing or preparing an act of terrorism, then that person can be searched under s 43 of the Act. However, if there is not such a reasonable suspicion, the photographer is in no different position for the purposes of s 47A than any other member of the public.

Section 58A provides that a person who elicits or attempts to elicit information about an individual who is or has been a member of Her Majesty's forces, a member of any of the intelligence services, or a constable, which is likely to be useful to a person committing or preparing an act of terrorism, or who publishes or communicates such information, commits an offence.

Like s 58, this section will not ordinarily be available to arrest a person taking a photograph of a police officer. Whilst it is *conceivable* that the information in that photograph might be of use to somebody committing or preparing an act of terrorism, the same defence of reasonable excuse as s 58 applies. While there have been numerous successful convictions under s 58A, there have been no convictions directly relating to the simple taking of pictures in a public order scenario.

8.8 **Terrorist Clothing**

Under s 13 of the 2000 Act a person in a public place commits an offence if he (a) wears an item of clothing, or (b) wears, carries or displays an article, in such a way or in such circumstances as to arouse reasonable suspicion that he is a member or supporter of a proscribed organization.

The list of proscribed organizations is found in Schedule 2 of the Act.

8.9 **Glorifying or Encouraging Terrorism**

Another terrorism-related power of potential use to the police in public order scenarios, particularly protests, is contained in section 1 of the Terrorism Act 2006 (passed in the wake of the July 2005 London bombings). This section creates the offence of the encouragement of terrorism:

(1) This section applies to a statement that is likely to be understood by some or all of the members of the public to whom it is published as a direct or indirect encouragement or other inducement to them to the commission, preparation or instigation of acts of terrorism or Convention offences.

(2) A person commits an offence if—
    (a) he publishes a statement to which this section applies or causes another to publish such a statement; and
    (b) at the time he publishes it or causes it to be published, he—
        (i) intends members of the public to be directly or indirectly encouraged or otherwise induced by the statement to commit, prepare or instigate acts of terrorism or Convention offences; or
        (ii) is reckless as to whether members of the public will be directly or indirectly encouraged or otherwise induced by the statement to commit, prepare or instigate such acts or offences.

This covers not just written statements but communications of any description (s 20(6)). Banners, posters, and so on will be included.

Under s 1(3), a statement which:

- glorifies the commission of past or future acts of terrorism,
- and from which members of the public reading, or hearing, or seeing it could *reasonably* be expected to infer that the glorified conduct is conduct that they should emulate,

will count as a statement that is likely to be understood by members of the public as indirectly encouraging the commission or preparation of acts of terrorism. 'Glorification' is defined by section 20(2) as including any form of praise or celebration. Indirect encouragement is not defined, and, at a minimum, might cover conduct that gave only relatively minor encouragement to others to commit acts of terrorism. Moreover, the offences can be committed recklessly, without any need to establish proof on the part of the defendant. The person making the statement need not even sympathize with the cause giving rise to terrorism: extreme ridicule or abuse of a person's religion could provide indirect encouragement to that person to respond with an act of terrorism. If someone were to be convicted of, or even arrested for, making a statement that gave minor encouragement to others to commit or prepare for an act of terrorism, but had made the statement so only recklessly, the potential for curtailment of the freedom of speech would arise. Discretion and proportionality remain crucial aspects of the officer's decision making.

No prosecutions under s 1 of the Terrorism Act 2006 have challenged that section's compatibility with a person's Article 10 right to freedom of expression. It is very likely that if a statement clearly, unambiguously, encourages or glorifies terrorism, the courts would have little hesitation in finding that it fell within the Article 10(2) qualification.

Further reading

- *Gillan and Quinton v The United Kingdom* (2010) 50 EHRR 45, [2010] Crim LR 415, 28 BHRC 420, [2010] ECHR 28, 50 EHRR 45
- The Code of Practice relating to s 47A and Schedule 6B to the Terrorism Act 2000 (contains a copy of s 47A and Schedule 6N): <http://www.homeoffice.gov.uk/publications/counter-terrorism/terrorism-act-remedial-order/code-of-practice?view=Binary>
- Lord Carlile of Berriew's annual reports into the operation of the Terrorism Act 2000, found at: <http://security.homeoffice.gov.uk/legislation/independent-review-legislation/>
- Lord Carlile's review of the definition of terrorism: <http://security.homeoffice.gov.uk/news-publications/publication-search/terrorism-act-2000/carlile-terrorism-definition.pdf>
- The Government's response: <http://security.homeoffice.gov.uk/news-publications/publication-search/terrorism-act-2000/hs-response-report-terrorism-def>
- The Stop and Search Action Team's 'Stop and Search Manual', published by the Home Office and available at: <http://police.homeoffice.gov.uk/news-and-publications/publication/operational-policing/stopandsearch-intermanual1.pdf>

NOTES

NOTES

9

Unlawful Use of Land

9.1 **Introduction**

> . . . at a very early stage in the development of the common law it was recognised that even apparently harmless intrusions onto land, without permission, can for no apparent reason escalate into troublesome disturbance, commotion and violence . . .
>
> (Lord Justice Judge, *Porter v Metropolitan Police Commissioner*, 1999)

This chapter deals with the trespass-related powers available to police in situations where a person's or group's presence in a particular place is unwelcome, or is the cause of disorder or crime. Whilst trespass to land is a civil concept, there are a number of trespass-related criminal offences, such as aggravated trespass, created by the Criminal Justice and Public Order Act 1994 (CJPOA). These various offences are explained, in addition to the powers and offences that exist in relation to unauthorized encampments.

9.2 **Civil Trespass**

9.2.1 **The legal concept of 'trespass'**

Many of the powers in this chapter are based on the legal concept of trespass. In essence, a person trespasses if he intentionally enters someone else's land and does not have permission or a legal right to be there. It is also possible for a person to commit trespass not through his own physical presence on land but by causing some substance such as water, or rubbish, to be present on the land, but it is trespass through the presence of individuals which will commonly arise in the public order context.

A person who has the owner or occupier's permission to be on their land will not usually be trespassing, unless he goes beyond the scope of the permission which he has been given. This is illustrated in case study A below.

Case study

Case study A: Environmental protestors occupying premises of a major oil company

A major oil company in London Docklands is hosting an annual conference about the future of sustainable energy. It has been widely publicized and tickets have been sold to a variety of people including industry stakeholders, politicians, university groups and members of the public. The conference is taking place in the ground-floor auditorium of the company's Docklands headquarters, and the toilet facilities and lunch facilities are all in the public areas of the ground floor.

Unknown to the organizers, a number of the attendees are members of a climate change protest group. During the lunch break, several of them decide to hold a protest. Before the afternoon session begins, they peacefully enter the lift and manage to get into the company boardroom on the 17th floor, which is currently unused. They lock themselves in and commence negotiations with the company by telephone. In the entire process, they avoid causing any damage to property. The company wants them out as soon as possible, and calls the police.

Recognizing trespass

- Each ticket holder has the company's permission to be in the areas of the Docklands premises in which the conference is taking place.
- However, the attendees who enter the lift and subsequently make their way into the boardroom do not have permission, explicit or implicit, to be present in those areas. They are trespassing.

....

9.2.2 Trespass, 'self-help' and the role of the police

The police have no powers of arrest for trespass per se, as it is not in itself a criminal offence. However, in relation to civil trespass, the police may become involved where the rightful owner or occupier of the land wishes to evict the trespassers without recourse to the courts.

Police may also become involved where the landowner has obtained a possession order and an eviction is taking place using court-appointed or private bailiffs. The purpose of a police presence in that circumstance would be to keep the peace. (The Civil Procedure Rules Part 55 procedure for taking possession of land is beyond the scope of this book and is not covered further.)

The common law right to evict those trespassing on one's land is a right recognized by our law and known as 'self-redress' or 'self-help'. It can be used lawfully if trespassers have been asked to leave and have refused. The rightful owner or occupier may then remove the trespasser(s) from the land using no more force than is reasonably necessary. He may ask others to assist him. The involvement of the police is in *facilitating the lawful removal*.

In case study A, if the company asks the trespassers to leave and they refuse and the company requests the assistance of the police to remove them, the police can lawfully assist. The force used by the police must be reasonable and proportionate, as must the force used by anyone from the company, or used by any private security firm being used for the same purpose. Disproportionate force would be likely to amount to an assault. For example, picking up a protestor and carrying them whilst struggling into the lift and outside of the Docklands company headquarters is likely to be reasonable; using a second officer to assist in restraining the struggling protestor would also probably be reasonable; the use of batons or CS gas, however, is unlikely to be reasonable—depending upon for how long the occupation has gone on. There may come a point when an increase in the level of force to be used can be justified. When briefing the frontline officers on the use of force in a situation like this, it is important to emphasize that the trespassers are not committing any criminal offence by simply trespassing on the company's property.

277

In *Porter v Metropolitan Police Commissioner* (20 October 1999, unreported) the Court of Appeal confirmed that it is appropriate for the police to assist in situations such as this. In *Porter*, the appellant refused to leave the showroom of the London Electricity Board, following a dispute with staff. The police at Kentish Town received a message 'female refusing to leave' and attended to try to mediate a peaceful resolution, which was unsuccessful. The appellant was carried out of the showroom by four police officers, whilst struggling, and in the course of the struggle the group crashed into a wall, resulting in some of the officers and the appellant ending up on the floor. Importantly, the court noted that the CCTV evidence showed the police officers' approach to be calm, measured and using the minimum of force. The Court of Appeal said, *inter alia*, that:

- Whilst the matter was 'only civil' (as opposed to any criminal offence being committed) this was an area of life affecting community peace.
- The police were the obvious organization to contact.
- Private security guards or firms, who might also be used to enforce the owner's rights, would lack the responsibility and accountability to the public owed by the police.
- If the police did not attend in such a situation, those who could not afford private security firms would call on friends and colleagues for immediate help, with the serious risk that the police would be called to the scene later rather than sooner to bring to an end a breach of the peace which their earlier presence might well have prevented.
- It would have been irresponsible if the police had informed the London Electricity Board that they would not attend.

In *Porter* the issue was raised—although not finally resolved—whether, in physically intervening to remove the claimant, the police were acting in the execution of their duty. The judgments of Lord Justice Judge and Lord Justice May suggest that, in a self-help scenario, the police act in the execution of their duty because of the general duty to keep the peace. Lord Justice Sedley in his judgment thought that the police acted as volunteers, ie not in the execution of their duty. The question was left open by the Court of Appeal.

Given that the Court of Appeal has so far declined to provide a definitive answer to the status of a police officer attending at the scene of an ongoing civil trespass, what practical steps can an officer take to ensure that any intervention is lawful? A simple answer—and the approach impliedly endorsed by the Court of Appeal in *Porter*—is that the aim ought to be to approach the problem in a similar way, regardless of whether the officer is acting as a volunteer or as a police officer.

The following advice may assist, although each situation will turn on its own facts:

- Assess each situation carefully and consider whether immediate steps to prevent an imminent breach of the peace are required.
- Attempt to mediate a negotiated outcome.

- Assess whether it is appropriate to assist the occupier to remove the trespasser, taking into account all the circumstances including what other attempts there have been to ask the trespassers to leave, the level of disruption being caused, whether it is a clear cut case of trespass or whether there is any doubt as to who is the rightful occupier, and so on. If assisting, no more than reasonable force should be used. Bear in mind that an officer assisting in this way could subsequently be found to be acting as a volunteer rather than a police officer, which would affect the powers available to the police and provide a defence to a charge for an offence of assault/wilful obstruction of an officer in the execution of his duty. Whilst the powers to arrest for assault/wilful obstruction of an officer in the execution of this duty (covered at section 4.8) would not be available where a police officer is acting as a volunteer, an evictee who assaults an officer could be arrested for the alternative offence of common assault. If possible this should be covered by a comprehensive briefing before the event.
- Continuously assess the risk of a breach of the peace. If, at any point during the eviction, it is considered that a breach of the peace is imminent, or the person (or persons) resisting commits an offence, then in responding to that change of events the police are likely to be acting in execution of their duty.

See chapter 3 for police powers available in the context of breach of the peace.

9.2.3 **Self-help and using violence to secure entry to a property**

Section 6(1) of the Criminal Law Act 1977 makes it a criminal offence for any person to use or threaten violence, without lawful authority, to secure entry into premises if there is somebody present on those premises at the time who is opposed to the entry and the person using or threatening violence knows that there is such a person on the premises.

There are certain important exemptions to the section for persons with a *residential* interest in the premises, in particular residential occupiers who have been ejected from their own home by trespassers ('displaced residential occupiers') or 'protected intending occupiers' within the meaning of s 12A of the Criminal Law Act 1977, which would include a person temporarily out of their home while it was being refurbished. In these cases, if the trespasser is required to leave by the displaced resident (or protected intended resident) and refuses to do so, the trespasser commits an offence under s 7 of the Criminal Law Act 1977.

It will be important for any police officers attending such situations to satisfy themselves about the legal status of the person inside the premises, the person seeking entry and their interest in the property. It may be that police intervention is required either to protect the resident (if an offence under s 6 is being committed), or assist the person outside the property, even arrest the occupier, if there are reasonable grounds to suspect an offence under s 7. If a s 7 offence is suspected, s 17 of the Police and Criminal Evidence Act 1984 provides a power of entry and search to a constable in uniform who reasonably suspects that the offender is on the premises.

This situation is an exception to the usual legal position that the eviction of a residential occupier requires a court order for immediate possession, as at 9.2.2 of this chapter. Public order situations such as 'occupations', like the one in case study A, are unlikely to be affected by this section unless protesters have managed to take over and secure the premises.

9.3 **Aggravated Trespass**

Definition of aggravated trespass

Section 68 of the Criminal Justice and Public Order Act 1994 (CJPOA) provides:

(1) A person commits the offence of aggravated trespass if he trespasses on land and, in relation to any lawful activity which persons are engaging in or are about to engage in on that or adjoining land, does there anything which is intended by him to have the effect:
   (a) Of intimidating those persons or any of them so as to deter them or any of them from engaging in that activity;
   (b) Of obstructing that activity; or
   (c) Of disrupting that activity.

Trespass is not defined in CJPOA. It will carry its ordinary definition from the civil law of trespass. As per 9.2.1 of this chapter, the person need not be a trespasser from the moment he first enters the land. He may become a trespasser at some later point when he begins to exceed the scope of his permission to be there, despite the fact that initially he might have had a ticket to be present in a conference centre, or might have had a right of way over a field.

9.3.1 **'On land'**

Section 68 CJPOA does not define land, and it has been left to case law to clarify what is included. Although originally enacted to limit the activities of trespassing hunt saboteurs and animal rights activists, it is now clear that 'land' includes buildings, ie it is no longer the case that aggravated trespass can be committed only in the open air: see *DPP v Chivers & ors* (2011) 1 All ER 367.

Further, s 68(5) provides:

(5) In this section 'land' does not include—
   (a) the highways and roads excluded from the application of section 61 by paragraph (b) of the definition of 'land' in subsection (9) of that section; . . .

The effect of this (with reference to s 61(9)(b)) is that it is not possible to commit a s 68 offence on a highway, *except if it is a highway which falls into one of the following three categories*:

1. A 'footpath, bridleway or byway open to all traffic' within the meaning of Part III of the Wildlife and Countryside Act 1981. With reference to the 1981 Act,
   - 'footpath' means a highway over which the public have a right of way on foot only, other than such a highway at the side of a public road;
   - 'bridleway' means a highway over which the public have the following, but no other, rights of way, that is to say, a right of way on foot and a right of way on horseback or leading a horse, with or without a right to drive animals of any description along the highway;
   - 'byway open to all traffic' means a highway over which the public have a right of way for vehicular and all other kinds of traffic, but which is used by the public mainly for the purpose for which footpaths and bridleways are so used.
2. A 'restricted byway' within the meaning of Part II of the Countryside and Rights of Way Act 2000. With reference to the 2000 Act,
   - a 'restricted byway' means a highway over which the public have restricted byway rights, with or without a right to drive animals of any description along the highway, but no other rights of way. Restricted byway rights mean:
     - a right of way on foot
     - a right of way on horseback or leading a horse, and
     - a right of way for vehicles other than mechanically propelled vehicles.
3. A cycle track under the Highways Act 1980 or the Cycle Tracks Act 1984. With reference to those acts, 'cycle track' means a way constituting or comprised in a highway, being a way over which the public have the following, but no other, rights of way, that is to say, a right of way on pedal cycles (other than pedal cycles which are motor vehicles within the meaning of the Road Traffic Act 1988) with or without a right of way on foot.

For a definition of 'highway' generally, see section 5.6 in chapter 5.

9.3.2 Lawful activity which persons are engaging in or about to engage in

'Persons'

In order for the s 68 offence to be committed there must be *at least two people* (aside from the trespassers) who are:

- present or about to be present on the land or adjoining land, and
- engaging in or about to engage in lawful activity.

In *DPP v Tilly* [2002] Crim LR 128, no s 68 offence was committed where trespassers damaged genetically modified crops with the intention of interrupting the activity of growing those crops, because there were no people physically present at the time the trespassers caused the damage. Mrs Justice Rafferty in her judgment gave the following explanation of s 68:

> it contemplates and is designed penally to mark a situation in which people are meant to be intimidated, or cannot get on with what they are entitled to do . . . to suffer inconvenience or anxiety they must be present.

In *Tilly* there was no suggestion that the crop owners were about to approach the fields. Had that been the case, the case would likely have been decided differently.

'Lawful activity'

Definition of 'lawful activity'

This is defined in s 68(2) of CJPOA:

> Activity on any occasion on the part of a person or persons on land is 'lawful' for the purposes of this section if he or they may engage in the activity on the land on that occasion without committing an offence or trespassing on the land.

In cases involving organized 'direct action' from experienced protest groups, such as the environmental/green lobby, police may encounter protestors who try to persuade them that the activity taking place is not lawful and that therefore they—the protestors—are not committing an offence under s 68 CJPOA. In most situations, officers will be justified in making arrests if their own assessment of the situation (which of course must be informed and based on reasonable grounds) is that the activity is *apparently* lawful. Technical arguments about lawfulness can be fought out in court as part of the campaigners' defence to any subsequent criminal proceedings, rather than allowing them to interrupt the normal policing of difficult public order situations.

The approach of the courts has been to look at the lawfulness of the activity overall, and not to be concerned if some small part of the activity was potentially unlawful. Where *part* of the activity taking place *might* be unlawful, the approach of the court has been to look at what it was that, in a general sense, the trespassers were trying to interrupt. In *Nelder v DPP* (*The Times*, 11 June 1998) trespassers disrupting a hunt argued that two of the hunt participants were on land which they had no permission to be on. The magistrate approached the matter on the basis that the intention had been to interrupt the hunt's lawful activity and on areas where the hunt was acting lawfully. On appeal, the court indicated that if the hunt's *central objective* had been to hunt on land over which they had no permission to go, or if the protestors had confined their protest to a period when a significant proportion of the hunters were trespassing, then no s 68 offence would be made out. Similarly, in *Hibberd v Director of Public Prosecutions* [1996] EWHC Admin 280, the court held that a potential breach of health and safety regulations on the part of persons carrying out tree felling did not make the activity of land clearance, taken 'as a whole', unlawful.

Police should note that an element of common sense and public protection comes to bear. The court in *Hibberd* indicated that a s 68 offence may not be made out if a trespasser disrupted tree-felling activity which was taking place in such a way as to cause imminent danger to members of the public, such as by landing on the motorway.

In *R v Jones (Margaret) and others* (2007) 1 AC 136 campaigners had sought to argue that activity at military bases—such as loading equipment onto ships to be transported for use in Iraq—was unlawful, as it was carried out in pursuit of the Iraq war. Their argument rested on the assertion that these activities were carried out in pursuit of an unlawful war of aggression: a crime in international law. The House of Lords held that the reference to 'offence' in s 68(2) was to be understood as referring to something which was an offence in domestic criminal law, which the crime of 'war of aggression' was not.

Another argument run by the campaigners in that litigation as a defence to charges of criminal damage was that their actions had been taken in accordance with s 3(1) of the Criminal Law Act 1967, which provides that:

> A person may use such force as is reasonable in the circumstances in the prevention of crime, or in effecting or assisting in the lawful arrest of offenders or suspected offenders or of persons unlawfully at large.

They argued that the damage caused to a fence and military tanks was necessary to prevent the commission of war crimes (see *Ayliffe v DPP* (2006) QB 227). The approach taken by the Divisional Court in that case is worth noting. Mr Justice Jack said, simply, that there was no connection between the campaigners' acts and the prevention of alleged crimes: 'The reality is that these were protests and . . . not attempts to prevent crimes' (paragraph 82).

Case study

Case study B: Anti-abortion campaigners at a family planning clinic

A small number of anti-abortion campaigners are present outside a family planning clinic with a temporary stall. They are handing out leaflets that contain graphic anti-abortion images, and are saying prayers. A couple of members of the public have complained to passing police officers about their presence.

Later in the day one or two of the campaign group's members are trying to stop women and members of staff from entering the clinic, by walking alongside them as they approach the clinic building. They are trying to thrust leaflets into the staff/women's hands. They are saying things like 'God doesn't want you to kill your child, there are alternatives available' and 'this is murder, and murderers go to hell'. They are asked by the clinic's management to leave the grounds of the clinic. The group has refused to leave, citing their rights to freedom of conscience and expression. The group is continuing to harass and upset women approaching and leaving the clinic.

Considerations

In the first part of this scenario, the campaigners are on the pavement. This means that they cannot be committing aggravated trespass, as the pavement is not 'land' for the purposes of s 68 (see section 9.3.1 of this chapter). Police will need to consider whether the campaigners' activity amounts to an obstruction of the highway (see section 5.6 of this book) or whether it amounts to some other offence, such as s 5 of the Public Order Act 1986.

In the later part of the scenario, the campaigners are on the private land of the clinic, and they are clearly trespassing because the clinic's management have asked them to leave. The conditions for use of s 68 are fulfilled:

- They are trespassing on land.
- On the same land, the women and the clinic's staff are acting lawfully.
- The campaigners' aim is to disrupt the lawful activity of the clinic, and to prevent women from going ahead with terminations, as it is against their beliefs.

Given the disruption and upset that is being caused, use of a s 69 direction followed by arrest could be justified as a necessary and proportionate response. Police should carefully record the decision-making process and rationale and give thought to the evidence that can be obtained about the effect of the campaigners' activities on those attending the clinic.

9.3.3 **Adjoining land**

The persons must be on the same land as the trespassers, or on adjoining land. 'Adjoining land' is not defined in the Act. It needs to be given its ordinary meaning of adjacent, or touching, and whether land is adjoining will be a question to be answered on the particular facts of each case. If trespassers are in a field, the intended targets in another field, and between the two fields is a strip of land owned by a third party, then the two fields cannot be said to be adjoining. A hedge, footpath or small stream is unlikely to be sufficiently large to mean that two tracts of land are not adjoining. A dual carriageway probably would be large enough.

9.3.4 **The act intended to intimidate, obstruct or disrupt**

The s 68 offence is not made out unless the trespasser does an act which is 'a distinct and overt act beyond the trespass itself' (*Director of Public Prosecutions v Barnard* (2000) Crim LR 371). Note that the offence requires an **act** rather than an **omission**. The offence requires that the trespasser intends this act to have the effect, in relation to the lawful activity, of:

- intimidating those persons or any of them so as to deter them or any of them from engaging in that activity; or
- obstructing that activity; or
- disrupting that activity.

Intimidation, obstruction and disruption should be given their ordinary meanings.

The offence can be made out even if the trespasser's actions are solely preparatory in nature. In *Winder v DPP* (160 JP 713, *The Times*, 14 August 1996, CO/36/96) trespassers ran towards a hunt. They did not intend the running itself to be disruptive, but were simply running in order to get closer so that they could then use sticks, whistles, pepper, etc, to cause disruption. The Divisional Court decided that the offence was still proved because the running was sufficiently closely connected to the intended disruption. The court gave some hypothetical examples of situations where the trespassers' acts are solely preparatory, but where they are sufficiently closely connected to the intended final act that the offence is made out:

> Suppose a trespasser on open land says to a third party 'go over the brow of that hill and there throw some stink bombs so as to disrupt the lawful activity—be it a hunt, be it a concert, be it a birthday celebration for the farmer's daughter—which is going on there'. Is the trespasser guilty of the section 68 offence, whether or not the third party throws the stink bombs and whether or not the members of the hunt know of the trespasser's existence? Clearly the act of giving the instruction does not in itself disrupt but it is intended in due course to result in acts which have that effect. We think that such a trespasser is guilty.
>
> The same goes for a trespasser who, wishing to disrupt a lawful activity, but out of sight, picks up a stone with a view to throwing it in the midst of those carrying out the lawful activity. We do not consider that the drafting of the section would require a court to hold that since picking up a stone in itself harmed no-one no offence was committed and that nothing could be done under the act other than giving a direction under s 69 to leave the land.

KEY POINTS—SUMMARY OF THE OFFENCE OF AGGRAVATED TRESPASS

For the offence under s 68 CJPOA to be committed, the following elements must be present:

- Person(s) trespassing on land: a highway does not count as land, unless it is a highway in one of the excluded categories covered at 9.3.1 of this chapter;
- Others are present on the same land, or on adjoining land;

- Those others are engaged in lawful activity, or about to engage in it: minor breaches of the law in the way the activity is committed are not sufficient to make the activity unlawful *as a whole*, see 9.3.2;
- The trespassing person does something over and above the trespass, which is intended to **intimidate** or **obstruct** or **disrupt** that apparently lawful activity.

9.4 **Power to Remove Persons Committing or Participating in Aggravated Trespass**

Section 69 of CJPOA provides:

(1) If the senior police officer present at the scene reasonably believes—
  (a) that a person is committing, has committed or intends to commit the offence of aggravated trespass on land . . .; or
  (b) that two or more persons are trespassing on land . . . and are present there with the common purpose of intimidating persons so as to deter them from engaging in a lawful activity or of obstructing or disrupting a lawful activity,

  he may direct that person or (as the case may be) those persons (or any of them) to leave the land.

(2) A direction under subsection (1) above, if not communicated to the persons referred to in subsection (1) by the police officer giving the direction, may be communicated to them by any constable at the scene.

(3) If a person knowing that a direction under subsection (1) above has been given which applies to him—
  (a) fails to leave the land as soon as practicable, or
  (b) having left again enters the land as a trespasser within the period of three months beginning with the day on which the direction was given,

  he commits an offence . . .

  . . .

(6) In this section 'lawful activity' and 'land' have the same meaning as in section 68.

9.4.1 **'Senior police officer'**

The power can be exercised by the senior police officer who is present at the scene. 'Senior' is not defined in the statute but it can be assumed that the seniority of police officers is determined by rank. In a situation where there are two officers of the same rank the 'senior' officer will probably be the one who has served longest in that rank.

Where police become aware in advance of an event where aggravated trespass may be committed, such as a protest, it is important that those in overall command consider, identify and make clear *who* will be the officer at the scene responsible for undertaking this role.

9.4.2 'Reasonable belief'

The requirement of reasonable belief means that the senior police officer does not have to be certain that the offence of aggravated trespass is taking place (or has taken place, or is about to take place). It involves the usual test of reasonable belief, formed on reasonable grounds. It is good practice for the senior officer to record *at the time* the reason(s) for his belief.

9.4.3 'Giving directions to leave'

The direction to leave can be communicated to the trespassers by the senior officer, or, under s 69(2), by any constable at the scene.

There is no requirement that the directions be in writing—a loudhailer or similar could be used. In practice, however, pro forma sheets are used by many forces. If those are used, they must be completed so that the directions are tailored to the individual event. Whatever method is preferred, it is vital that the reasons *why* the direction is being given and *to whom* it applies are clearly conveyed—see 9.4.4 of this chapter.

9.4.4 Offence of failing to comply with a direction

Section 69(3) creates an offence which is committed by a trespasser if he:

- **knows** that a direction has been given, and
- **knows** that that direction applies to him.

and he either:

- **fails to leave the land** as soon as reasonably practicable, or
- he **re-enters the land within three months** of the direction being given.

To prove the offence at court, it will have to be demonstrated that the person actually knew that the direction had been given, not merely that he ought to have known. This is why the direction must be given clearly. If a large number of people are present, the use of loudhailers or vehicle mounted loudspeakers will be necessary. The directions can be distributed in writing, and attached to gates, lampposts, walls, etc. The instruction must be given as a mandatory direction, rather than a request.

In *Capon v DPP* (*The Independent*, 23 March 1998) the High Court held that a police officer's direction was sufficient to comply with s 69, even though it did not refer to the statute and was posed to two of the three trespassers as a question 'Are you leaving the land?' rather than an order (though he had said 'You either leave the land or you're arrested' to the first trespasser), and it did not identify the land which the trespassers were being asked to leave. However, the trespassers in *Capon* were seasoned campaigners who were fully aware of the provisions of s 68 and s 69. The High Court referred to the Crown Court's judgment:

> Each of the appellants said that there was no intention at any point in time to disrupt or obstruct or indeed to intimidate. Each of the appellants was interested in taking a film of the fox being killed as part of the campaign against hunting . . . this became, so to speak, part of the policy of campaigners when they reviewed the legal position of campaigners following the introduction of the aggravated trespass provisions. We incline to the view, in so far as they could, the appellants were deliberately avoiding committing the offence of aggravated trespass. It seems to us it would be in their interests to avoid committing an aggravated trespass.

Lord Bingham, giving judgment, said that:

> it is true that no reference was made to the 1994 Act or to the section, or to the fact that the direction was being given (if it was being given) pursuant to a statutory power. It is also however true that the appellants were far from ill-informed about the effect of the Act.

The case therefore turned very tightly on its facts.

Often, events where aggravated trespass is being committed will be attended by a mixture of individuals, some of whom are likely to be less well-informed about the provisions of the law. A s 69 direction should therefore refer to the CJPOA and s 69 itself, include reasons why it is being given and specify to whom it applies.

'As soon as reasonably practicable' should be given a commonsense interpretation, taking into account all the circumstances. Section 69(4) provides a defence of 'reasonable excuse' for failing to leave as soon as reasonably practicable or re-entering again as a trespasser.

Use of section 68 or section 69?

The choice that exists between the giving of a direction under s 69, or the option of arresting trespassers immediately for a s 68 offence, will be governed to an extent by the conduct of the trespassers. Where the trespassers' activity amounts to a demonstration involving the exercise of their rights to freedom of expression and where the degree of damage or disruption to the land is minimal, or is not imminent, it would normally be a proportionate measure under Article 10(2) to first give a direction under s 69, allowing the trespassers the opportunity to leave without being arrested. See chapter 2, particularly section 2.7, of this book.

9.5 Removal of Trespassers who are on Land for the Purpose of Residing

Sections 61–62D of the CJPOA were introduced to address the perceived increasing problems of travelling groups setting up camps as trespassers and refusing to move when asked, frequently leaving behind damage to property or the environment.

Section 61 provides:

(1) If the senior police officer present at the scene reasonably believes that two or more persons are trespassing on land and are present there with the common purpose of residing there for any period, that reasonable steps have been taken by or on behalf of the occupier to ask them to leave and—

    (a) that any of those persons has caused damage to the land or to property on the land or used threatening, abusive or insulting words or behaviour towards the occupier, a member of his family or an employee or agent of his, or

    (b) that those persons have between them six or more vehicles on the land,

    he may direct those persons, or any of them, to leave the land.

(2) Where the persons in question are reasonably believed by the senior police officer to be persons who were not originally trespassers but have become trespassers on the land, the officer must reasonably believe that the other conditions specified in subsection (1) are satisfied after those persons became trespassers before he can exercise the power conferred by that subsection.

(3) A direction under subsection (1) above, if not communicated to the persons referred to in subsection (1) by the police officer giving the direction, may be communicated to them by any constable at the scene.

(4) If a person knowing that a direction under subsection (1) above has been given which applies to him—

    (a) fails to leave the land as soon as reasonably practicable, or

    (b) having left again enters the land as a trespasser within the period of three months beginning with the day on which the direction was given,

    he commits an offence . . .

    . . .

(7) In its application in England and Wales to common land this section has effect as if in the preceding subsections of it—

    (a) references to trespassing or trespassers were references to acts and persons doing acts which constitute either a trespass as against the occupier or an infringement of the commoners' rights; and

    (b) references to 'the occupier' included the commoners or any of them or, in the case of common land to which the public has access, the local authority as well as any commoner.

(8) Subsection (7) above does not—

    (a) require action by more than one occupier; or

    (b) constitute persons trespassers as against any commoner or the local authority if they are permitted to be there by the other occupier.

In essence this section provides the senior police officer present at the scene (for deciding on who is the senior officer, see 9.4.1 of this chapter) with a power to direct residing trespassers to leave land if the occupier has taken reasonable steps to ask them to leave and they have either caused damage to land, used threatening, abusive or insulting words or behaviour, or have six or more vehicles between them. There must be at least two trespassers present and residing in order for the section to apply, though only one of them needs to have done an act that falls within s 61(1)(a), if indeed it is that subsection rather than s 61(1)(b) being relied upon.

'Trespassing' should be understood to include trespass within the ordinary, civil meaning of the word—explained at the outset and at 9.3 of this chapter— but s 61(7) widens the definition somewhat to take into account activity on certain types of 'common land'. This is explained in later at 9.5.7.

In the case of persons who were originally on the land with permission, who became trespassers only at some later point in time (such as if the landowner withdrew his permission for them to be present), s 61(2) provides that before a s 61 direction can be given the senior police officer must hold a 'reasonable belief' that the conditions in s 61(1)(b) have been fulfilled *since* the persons became trespassers.

The same requirements and good practice recommendations for the senior officer's reasonable belief apply (as at 9.4.2 of this chapter).

9.5.1 Common purpose of residing for any period

This is not defined by the section, although s 61(9) provides that a person may be regarded as having a purpose of residing notwithstanding that he has a home elsewhere. It should be understood as having its ordinary meaning, ie a common purpose of staying there. The trespassers do not actually have to have this common purpose: it just has to appear to the senior officer that they do.

As the standard is the reasonable belief of the senior police officer at the scene, a note should be made *at the time* of the reasons for his belief. In many cases the presence of tents or caravans will in itself be an obvious indicator that the trespassers intend to stay. So too might be supplies such as bottled water, food, fire-making facilities, etc. The senior officer does not have to have heard the trespassers discussing and reaching a decision about staying and he does not have to have had a discussion with them in which they confirm to him that they intend to stay.

9.5.2 Steps taken by or on behalf of the occupier to ask them to leave

A s 61 direction can only be used where the trespassers have not complied with the occupier's request for them to leave: *R (Fuller) v Chief Constable of Dorset*

Police (2003) QB 480. This means that time must be given for them to comply with the request. 'Occupier' is defined by s 61(9) CJPOA as:

(a) in England and Wales, the person entitled to possession of the land by virtue of an estate or interest held by him;

But see 9.5.7 for the expanded definition of 'occupier' that applies in the case of common land.

In *Fuller*, a group of travellers had set up camp on a borough council-owned rubbish tip. After an initial period of tolerance, it was decided by the borough and county councils that they should be given 48 hours to leave. The police attended with a representative of the borough council who effected the 48-hour notice and at the same time the police inspector gave a s 61 direction. The Administrative Court held that on a true construction of s 61, a s 61 direction was an order to leave immediately. Therefore, the travellers had not been given an opportunity to comply with the borough council's request that they leave within 48 hours: the direction was unlawful.

As a matter of good practice it makes sense for occupiers' requests to specify a time and date by which they wish the trespassers to leave. This enables the police to know for certain the point at which they can use a s 61 direction.

If the occupier cannot be found, or does not want the travellers to leave, the power in this section is not available to police—no matter how disruptive their presence is to other members of the community.

9.5.3 **Land**

As with s 68, 'land' is not explicitly defined in s 61 CJPOA. The section does however specify that the following do *not* count as land for the purposes of s 61:

- Buildings, other than:
  - Agricultural buildings within the meaning of paragraphs 3–8 of Schedule 5 of the Local Government Finance Act 1988.
  - Scheduled monuments within the meaning of the Ancient Monuments and Archaeological Areas Act 1979. Section 1(11) of the 1979 Act defines a scheduled monument as any monument contained in the list of such monuments maintained by the Secretary of State.
- Land forming part of a highway, other than footpaths, bridleways, or byways open to all traffic within the meaning of Part III of the Wildlife and Countryside Act 1981, a restricted byway within the meaning of Part II of the Countryside and Rights of Way Act 2000, or cycle tracks under the Highways Act 1980 or Cycle Tracks Act 1984. See 9.3.1 for these definitions.

9.5.4 **Caused damage**

This should be given its ordinary meaning. Section 69(9) specifies that damage under s 61 can include any 'the deposit of any substance capable of polluting the land'. Thus the leaving of significant quantities of oil, ash or human/animal waste on the land would all constitute damage to the land.

9.5.5 **Threatening, abusive or insulting words or behaviour**

These words are not defined in CJPOA, but they should be understood consistently with their use in the Public Order Act 1986: see section 4.6.1 of this book.

Section 61 specifies that the words or behaviour cannot be directed against just anyone. In order for the s 61 powers to arise, the words or behaviour must be directed against the occupier, his employee or an agent of his, or a member of his family.

9.5.6 **Six or more vehicles**

'Vehicle' is defined by s 61(9). The vehicles do not have to be roadworthy. They do not even have to be whole vehicles: the definition includes the framework of a vehicle even if the wheels are missing, as long as it looks as though it did once form part of a vehicle. It also includes 'any load carried by, and anything attached to' a vehicle defined this way.

POINT TO NOTE

Consideration should be given to proving the threatening, abusive or insulting words or behaviour; the presence of the vehicles; or the damage. Consider witness statement from those involved and photographic or video evidence. Independent witnesses are also a good source of evidence.

9.5.7 **Trespass as infringement of the commoners' rights: section 61(7)**

The effect of s 61(7) is that if the land is common land, 'trespassing' includes acts which constitute a trespass against, or infringement of, commoners' rights.

Common land (defined by s 22(1) and s 22(1A) of the Commons Registration Act 1965) means:

1. Land which is subject to 'rights of common', whether those rights are exercisable at all times or only during limited periods. Such rights include cattle gates and beast gates, and certain rights of sole or several vesture or herbage or of sole or several pasture, not including rights held for a term of years or from year to year. In essence, these are different types of grazing rights.

2. Land which is the waste land of a manor not subject to rights of common. In essence, this means land which is open, uncultivated and unoccupied surrounding a manor: *Lewis and others v Mid Glamorgan County Council and others* [1995] 1 All ER 760.
3. Land on which a significant number of the local inhabitants have, for not less than twenty years, indulged in lawful sports and pastimes as of right. 'As of right' means not by force, nor stealth, nor the licence of the owner: *R (Lewis) v Redcar and Cleveland Borough Council and another* (2010) 2 AC 70.

The definition does *not* include town or village greens, or any land that forms part of a highway. These are often owned by the local authority. In practice, the local authority for the area will be able to assist with the issue of whether or not a particular piece of land is common land.

Where land is excluded from the application of s 61 (or s 62A, below), but where there are reasons why eviction is desirable, police may want to consider the use of arrests for breach of any applicable byelaws: see section 9.1.1 of chapter 9.

'Commoner' means a person with rights of common (defined by s 22 of the Commons Registration Act 1965), ie the 'grazing' rights mentioned above—cattle gate, beast gate, and certain rights of sole or several vesture or herbage or of sole or several pasture.

Whilst these definitions appear technical on paper, in practice it may be quite apparent if trespassers are doing something which infringes commoners' rights. If trespassers—whether members of the travelling community or a large protest camp—are present on common land and spread over the area in such a way that they are preventing others from effectively using the land, then it is likely that commoners' rights will be infringed simply by virtue of the fact that they are prevented from gaining access to, or using, the land.

If the land which the trespassers are on is common land as defined above, any of the commoners (or, if it is common land to which the public have access, the local authority *or* any of the commoners) can make the request to the trespassers to leave.

9.5.8 Giving a s 61 direction to leave

The senior officer gives the direction, and it may be communicated by him or any constable at the scene (s 61(3)). The direction should refer to the CJPOA and s 61 itself, include the reason why it is being given, and specify to whom it applies.

9.5.9 Offence of failing to comply with a s 61 direction

Section 61(4) creates an offence which is committed by a trespasser if he:

• **knows** that a direction has been given, and
• **knows** that that direction applies to him

and he either:

- **fails to leave the land** as soon as reasonably practicable, or
- he **re-enters the land as a trespasser within three months** of the direction being given.

To prove the offence at court, it will have to be demonstrated that the person actually knew that the direction had been given, not merely that he ought to have known. The direction must be given clearly: see 9.4.4 of this chapter. A similar defence of reasonable excuse is available under s 61(6), as there is for s 69.

POINT TO NOTE

Directions to leave under s 69 or s 61 CJPOA

It is essential that a record is kept of **who** is directed to leave under s 69 or s 61 CJPOA (or 62A CJPOA, below), and the **terms** of the direction. Bear in mind that it may well be necessary to prove, perhaps several months later, that a particular person has been directed to leave. Consider written records of directions given, signed acknowledgements, photographic and video evidence.

9.5.10 Supplementary power of seizure where a s 61 direction has been given

Section 62 CJPOA provides:

(1) If a direction has been given under section 61 and a constable reasonably suspects that any person to whom the direction applies has, without reasonable excuse—

(a) failed to remove any vehicle on the land which appears to the constable to belong to him or to be in his possession or under his control; or

(b) entered the land as a trespasser with a vehicle within the period of three months beginning with the day on which the direction was given,

the constable may seize and remove that vehicle.

The section is self-explanatory. 'Trespasser' and 'vehicle' have the same meaning as in s 61, above. This power enables the police to seize vehicles left behind by trespassers who have left following the making of a s 61 direction. The Police (Retention and Disposal of Vehicles) Regulations 1995 (SI 723/1995) apply to vehicles seized under this section, and make provision for retention, disposal and information to be given to the vehicle owner.

POINT TO NOTE

Human rights considerations for evictions under CJPOA ss 61, 62A and 77

Where the use of CJPOA eviction powers is considered, police should bear in mind that eviction of travellers in particular may, in some circumstances, engage the travellers' Article 8 rights. Consideration may be required as to whether the evictions or arrests are a necessary and proportionate response to the situation. Section 2.9 of chapter 2 gives an overview of the kinds of questions police need to consider before exercising these powers.

In some circumstances, swift eviction will be the most appropriate response and clearly justified, such as where travellers have settled on a school playing field during term time, or somewhere that similarly causes a high degree of inconvenience and disruption to the lives of others. In other circumstances it may be possible and appropriate to address local concerns through the use of other powers (such as individual arrests for offences such as criminal damage, or the use of Anti-social Behaviour Orders (ASBOs) or Acceptable Behaviour Contracts to tackle anti-social behaviour), or through higher-profile police patrols.

Police (as well as local authorities, under s 77 and s 78) also need to consider whether it is necessary and proportionate to evict the *whole* of an unauthorized encampment. If it is a minority who are causing distress, or if there is a traveller who is seriously ill, a proportionate use of powers may be to evict only named individuals.

The kinds of questions that police need to consider when questioning whether to use CJPOA powers to arrest and/or evict are:

- What is the impact of the settlement on the local community? For example, is it causing serious disruption or nuisance? Is it in a particularly inconvenient place such as a public car park or school playing field? Or is the disruption very minor?
- Is there somewhere more appropriate nearby where the trespassers could be persuaded to move, by consent?
- Is it the settlement itself, or the behaviour of a few of the trespassers, that is causing the problem?
- Is there any prior intelligence on the trespassers that suggests they are persistently anti-social, or on the other hand particularly cooperative?
- What other powers are available to police deal with the situation, short of eviction?

Where travellers are trespassing in opposition to the occupier's wishes it is nearly always likely to be proportionate and necessary to remove them, and particularly so where they have only been present on the land for a short time. However, the decision-making process and justification for doing so should be carefully recorded.

9.6 **Power to Remove Trespassers where there is an Alternative Site Available**

Section 62A of CJPOA provides a lower threshold for the removal of trespassers if there is an identifiable, suitable alternative site available for them nearby. Section 62A states:

(1) If the senior police officer present at a scene reasonably believes that the conditions in subsection (2) are satisfied in relation to a person and land, he may direct the person—
    (a) to leave the land;
    (b) to remove any vehicle and other property he has with him on the land.

(2) The conditions are—
    (a) that the person and one or more others ('the trespassers') are trespassing on the land;
    (b) that the trespassers have between them at least one vehicle on the land;
    (c) that the trespassers are present on the land with the common purpose of residing there for any period;
    (d) if it appears to the officer that the person has one or more caravans in his possession or under his control on the land, that there is a suitable pitch on a relevant caravan site for that caravan or each of those caravans;
    (e) that the occupier of the land or a person acting on his behalf has asked the police to remove the trespassers from the land.

(3) A direction under subsection (1) may be communicated to the person to whom it applies by any constable at the scene.

(4) Subsection (5) applies if—
    (a) a police officer proposes to give a direction under subsection (1) in relation to a person and land, and
    (b) it appears to him that the person has one or more caravans in his possession or under his control on the land.

(5) The officer must consult every local authority within whose area the land is situated as to whether there is a suitable pitch for the caravan or each of the caravans on a relevant caravan site which is situated in the local authority's area.

In essence, s 62A enables the senior police officer present at the scene to direct trespassers to leave the land, and to remove any vehicles or property, if he holds a reasonable belief that each of the following conditions are satisfied:

• the person and at least one other person is trespassing;
• between them they have at least one vehicle;
• the persons have a common purpose to reside there for any period;

- the persons have at least one vehicle in their possession;
- the occupier of the land (or someone acting on his behalf) has asked the police to remove the trespassers from the land;
- in respect of any person who has one or more caravans in his possession or under his control on the land, that there is a suitable pitch on a relevant caravan site for that caravan or each of those caravans.

As to senior police officer and reasonable belief, see 9.4.1 and 9.4.2 of this chapter. For common purpose to reside, see 9.5.1.

'Land' is defined so that it does not include buildings, other than agricultural buildings and scheduled monuments, as per the definitions given to those words at 9.5.3. Importantly, unlike s 61, highways are *not* excluded from the meaning of land in s 62A.

9.6.1 Caravans, caravan sites, relevant caravan sites and site managers

In s 62A, 'caravan' and 'caravan site' mean what they would be expected to mean, though they are actually defined by sections 29 and 1(4) of the Caravan Sites and Control of Development Act 1960.

'Caravan' means:

any structure designed or adapted for human habitation which is capable of being moved from one place to another (whether by being towed, or by being transported on a motor vehicle or trailer) and any motor vehicle so designed or adapted, but does not include—

(a) any railway rolling stock which is for the time being on rails forming part of a railway system, or

(b) any tent.

'Caravan site' means:

land on which a caravan is stationed for the purposes of human habitation and land which is used in conjunction with land on which a caravan is so stationed.

'Relevant caravan site' is defined by s 62(6), below, as:

. . . a caravan site which is

(a) situated in the area of the local authority within whose area the land is situated; and

(b) managed by a relevant site manager.

A 'relevant site manager' can be the local authority, a private registered provider of social housing, or a registered social landlord.

9.6.2 **Differences between s 61 and s 62A CJPOA powers**

The two sections are superficially similar, but contain important differences:

- Section 62A can apply to only one person. For s 61 powers to arise, there must be at least two trespassers.
- The presence of only one vehicle is required before a s 62A direction can be given, while under s 61 there must be six or more.
- Highways are included in the definition of land under s 62A (s 62E(2)).
- If there is one or more caravans present, the power under s 62A cannot be used unless the police have consulted all the local authorities on whose land the trespassers are, to see if there is a suitable pitch for each of those caravans within the local authority area: and there must be a suitable pitch available for each caravan.
- Under s 62A the occupier must have asked the police to remove the trespassers rather than asking the trespassers to leave (though it is submitted that in almost every conceivable case, they will have asked the trespassers to leave first).
- Under s 62A there is no need to show threatening, abusive or insulting words or behaviour towards the occupier, a member of his family or an employee or agent of his.

9.6.3 **Offence of failing to comply with a s 62A direction**

The offence created by s 62B is very similar to that created by s 61(4). See 9.5.9 of this chapter. Section 62B provides:

(1) A person commits an offence if he knows that a direction under section 62A(1) has been given which applies to him and—
   (a) he fails to leave the relevant land as soon as reasonably practicable, or
   (b) he enters any land in the area of the relevant local authority as a trespasser before the end of the relevant period with the intention of residing there.

(2) The relevant period is the period of 3 months starting with the day on which the direction is given.

An offence under s 62B is therefore committed if either the direction is not complied with as soon as reasonably practicable, or if within three months from the date of direction the trespasser enters **any** land in the area of the relevant local authority (as a trespasser), with the intention of residing there.

Section 62B(5) provides the same defence of reasonable excuse as for ss 69 and 61. However, there is a further defence which does not exist for the other sections, which is that the trespasser in question was, at the time of the direction, under the age of 18 and resident with his parent or guardian.

9.6.4 **Supplementary power of seizure where a s 62A direction has been given**

Section 62C provides:

(1) This section applies if a direction has been given under section 62A(1) and a constable reasonably suspects that a person to whom the direction applies has, without reasonable excuse—

    (a) failed to remove any vehicle on the relevant land which appears to the constable to belong to him or to be in his possession or under his control; or

    (b) entered any land in the area of the relevant local authority as a trespasser with a vehicle before the end of the relevant period with the intention of residing there.

(2) The relevant period is the period of 3 months starting with the day on which the direction is given.

(3) The constable may seize and remove the vehicle.

The section is self-explanatory. 'Trespasser', 'occupier' and 'vehicle' have the same meanings as given by s 61 CJPOA. This power also enables the police to seize vehicles left behind by trespassers who have left following the making of a s 62A direction. The Police (Retention and Disposal of Vehicles) Regulations 1995 (SI 723/1995) do not apply to vehicles seized under this section.

9.7 **Sections 61, 62, and 62A CJPOA and the Right to a Private and Family Life**

The combination of:

- the creation of an offence if a person fails to comply with a direction to leave (or returns within the relevant period), coupled with the power of arrest, and
- the power to seize and remove vehicles, and
- the power to remove trespassers

means that the exercise by the police of powers under ss 61, 62 and 62A CJPOA may constitute, in effect, summary eviction of trespassers without the legal procedures and safeguards that arise in court proceedings. Given the absence of an order for possession, are the travellers' rights under Article 6 (to a fair trial of his civil rights) or Article 8 (to a home life) engaged?

A similar question was considered by the House of Lords in *Leeds City Council v Price*, reported sub nom. *Kay v London Borough of Lambeth* [2006] 2 AC 465. The Maloney family were travellers, one of a number of families of travellers who parked their caravans on a recreation ground owned by Leeds City Council.

Two days after the Maloneys arrived, the Council started possession proceedings and an order for possession was eventually granted. The Maloney family appealed against the granting of the possession order, relying on Article 8 and stating that their personal circumstances were 'exceptional' in that several members of the family suffered from medical and psychiatric problems, three members of the family were school-aged children, and in the twelve months preceding their entry onto the recreation ground the family had been evicted or forced to move under threat of eviction more than 50 times. They also alleged that the Council was in breach of its statutory obligations to provide suitable sites where travellers could park their caravans.

In upholding the order for possession, the House of Lords unanimously agreed that Article 8 was *not* violated. Lord Scott stated, in paragraph 128, that Article 8:

> ... does not give any protection to the occupation of land or a building unless the land or building is the occupier's 'home'. If a traveller with his caravan enters as a trespasser upon a piece of land, by what process does the small area of land on which he happens to station his caravan and, presumably, a few square yards surrounding that small area of land, become identified as his 'home'? If a homeless person enters an unoccupied building, places his few possessions in one of the rooms and spends the next night or two there, does the room become his 'home' in relation to which he is entitled to an Article 8 'right of respect'? The answer must, I think, be 'No'. It is clearly possible for a trespasser to establish a 'home' in property that belongs to someone else but whether and when he has done so must be matters of degree.

A traveller, newly arrived, who parks his caravan in a place where he is trespassing, and declares that this is now his home, does not acquire any Article 8 right preventing the removal of himself, his family or his vehicles—provided there is a legal power to act. As the *exercise* of any legal power must in itself be lawful, it is still necessary to consider whether the use of eviction powers is a necessary and proportionate response.

In *R (Fuller) v Chief Constable of Dorset Police* (2001) 1 Pol LR 434 the court confirmed that Article 6 was satisfied by the ability to challenge an arrest or prosecution after the event (in that case, under s 61) before a court. The fact that under s 61 and s 62A CJPOA travellers can be directed to leave without court proceedings was not an Article 6 violation.

Case study

Case study C: Travellers in Quietshire and Reasonableshire

Quietshire Part 1

In Quietshire, a group of travellers turn up overnight in about 40 caravans. They move onto land in the park near the children's play area and where the annual community fête is due to be held in a fortnight's time. Several villagers call the local police station and dial 999, asking for the police to attend and remove the travellers. They complain that children are running around making noise and that there are dogs barking. The villagers are upset because the park is a central feature of the village and is where the weekly farmers' market is held, as well as regular events such as school cricket matches. The travellers tell the police that they intend to stay, as they have nowhere else to go. By the next morning a complaint has been received from the management of a nursing home bordering the park about the level of noise coming from the camp, which is upsetting the elderly residents. Further, villagers who have been out to walk their dogs have complained about being on the receiving end of unpleasant and racist abuse.

Considerations

Police are faced with a camp which is inconveniently located, which will cause a significant amount of disruption to the local community simply by virtue of its placement: it will affect the ability to hold cricket matches, the weekly farmers' market and the upcoming community fête.

Some of the conditions for the use of s 61 CJPOA appear to be met immediately:

- There are more than two persons trespassing.
- The travellers have confirmed that they intend to stay for as long as they can.
- There are more than six vehicles present. This satisfies 61(1)(b), so there is no need to show that the s 61(1)(a) criteria (damage to land, or threatening/abusive/insulting words or behaviour) are met. This means that if it transpired that the abuse directed at the villagers walking their dogs turned out to be a false allegation, s 61 could still be used.

In practice, if there is evidence of damage or words or behaviour that might fall under s 61(1)(a) this should still be recorded as it is possible to rely on the criteria in s 61(1)(a) **and** (b).

However, have the travellers been asked to leave? Immediate steps must be taken by the police to identify the occupier and verify he has indeed taken reasonable steps to ask the travellers to leave. The local authority should be able to assist. It may be that the local authority itself owns the park land, or in this scenario it may be common land (see 9.5.2 and 9.5.7).

Assuming that such a request *has* been made, the police can use s 61 to direct the travellers to leave. The travellers' Article 8 rights are highly unlikely to be engaged, as they have not been present on the land long enough to plausibly claim it as their 'home' (see *Leeds v Price; Kay and others v Lambeth London Borough Council* (2006) 2 WLR 570). Even if Article 8 were engaged, the exercise of s 61 could be justified as necessary and proportionate because of the serious impact that the encampment will have on the villagers' ability to use their park facilities.

Note that s 62A powers could also be used here if there was a suitable pitch on a relevant caravan site available for each of the caravans present (see 9.6) and if the occupier asks the police to remove the travellers. In practice this is something that the police should liaise with the local authority about. The local authority is under various duties beyond the scope of this book to consider the welfare and housing needs of the travellers. Where there is a pressing need to remove the travellers quickly, or where there is a pressing need to remove them but there simply are no relevant caravan sites with spaces available, and where the travellers cannot be persuaded to move by consent, **the use of s 61 can be justified**. The decision-making process and the rationale for the use of the section should be carefully recorded.

Quietshire Part 2

A s 61 direction has been given. Two weeks later one family of travellers from the same group, who have just bought two new caravans, return to the park and camp in a slightly different area in those new caravans.

Considerations

This fulfils the conditions for use of s 61(4):

- The family know that the direction was given, and that it applied to them.
- They have re-entered as trespassers within the three-month period.
- It is the re-entry of the same *persons*, not the same vehicles, that triggers the section.

The police can also use their powers under s 62(1) to seize and remove their caravans, even though they are not the same caravans that were on the site previously. Given that the vehicles are different, it will be necessary to prove that the same family members now on the land were previously directed to leave.

Reasonableshire

In the next town, Reasonableshire, a different group of travellers are present. They have moved overnight onto a largely disused industrial site, next to an existing caravan site. Part of their chosen camp area spills onto the local supermarket car park, though only by a few metres. Only two vehicles are on the supermarket's land. The site can be seen from the houses on that street, and several residents have made phone calls to the local station and to 999 asking for the police to remove the travellers. One resident has said that there is a traveller in his back garden stealing wood. The industrial site is owned by a private company, who confirm that they are happy for the travellers to stay, for the time being. The supermarket owns the car park and they say that they want their parking spaces back. The travellers have ignored the supermarket's request that they leave, and the supermarket is looking to the police to assist.

Considerations

Here, the owner of the industrial site has not asked the travellers to leave nor asked the police to remove them. This means that neither s 61 nor s 62A powers are available to police in respect of the travellers on *that* land, even though there have been complaints from members of the local community. The single incident of alleged theft should be dealt with in the same way that the police would deal with an allegation of theft outside of this context.

The part of the camp that spills onto the supermarket must be considered separately. There, the owner of the land objects to the presence of the travellers. Section 61 is probably not available to the police, because there are only two vehicles, and there has been no damage or threatening/abusive/insulting words or behaviour. Here, the police need to consider liaising with the local authority to verify that there are two spaces available on a relevant caravan site. If there are two sites available, the s 62A powers can be used to direct that minority of the travellers away from the supermarket land. Alternatively, the police may facilitate if the supermarket decide to exercise their right to self-help.

9.8 **Powers of Local Authorities to Direct Unauthorized Campers to Leave Land**

Section 77(1) CJPOA provides:

(1) If it appears to a local authority that persons are for the time being residing in a vehicle or vehicles within that authority's area—
   (a) on any land forming part of a highway;
   (b) on any other unoccupied land; or
   (c) on any occupied land without the consent of the occupier,
   the authority may give a direction that those persons and any others with them are to leave the land and remove the vehicle or vehicles and any other property they have with them on the land.

(2) Notice of a direction under subsection (1) must be served on the persons to whom the direction applies, but it shall be sufficient for this purpose for the direction to specify the land and (except where the direction applies to only one person) to be addressed to all occupants of the vehicles on the land, without naming them.

This section provides the local authority, rather than police, with a power to direct trespassers to leave. In practice, it provides powers for use against travellers rather than other types of trespassers—such as those engaged in protest camps—because of the requirement that the persons be 'residing in a vehicle or vehicles'. The word 'residing' should be given its ordinary meaning of staying, and vehicle is defined as per s 61—see 9.5.6—and to include caravans, defined at 9.6.1.

Section 79 provides that, if it is impracticable to serve a s 77 direction on a person named in it, the local authority can serve it if a copy of it is fixed in 'a prominent place on the vehicle concerned'. If the s 77 direction is directed towards the unnamed occupants of vehicles (ie if it has not been possible, as is likely, to get the names of all of the travellers) then under s 79 the direction will be treated as served if a copy of it has been fixed in a prominent place on *every* vehicle which is on the land at the time of service.

The local authority also has to inform or attempt to inform the owner and any occupier of the land (s 79(4)), and take reasonable steps to display a copy of the direction on the land in question other than on the vehicles, 'in a manner designed to ensure that it is likely to be seen by any person camping on the land'. In practice this may mean fixing copies of the s 77 direction to gate posts near the entrance/exit routes, or by water taps, or on nearby trees, etc, as well as making sure that it is headed appropriately and in a suitably eye-catching fashion.

9.8.1 Land—a broader definition than ss 61, 62A, 68 and 69

The definition of land in s 77 CJPOA is simply 'land in the open air': s 77(6). It can therefore be used against trespassers in more places than the sections covered above, and would include highways, and town and village greens. It does not need to be land owned by the local authority.

9.8.2 Offence of failing to comply with a s 77 direction

Section 77(3) provides:

> (3) If a person knowing that a direction under subsection (1) above has been given which applies to him—
>   (a) fails, as soon as practicable, to leave the land or remove from the land any vehicle or other property which is the subject of the direction, or
>   (b) having removed any such vehicle or property again enters the land with a vehicle within the period of three months beginning with the day on which the direction was given,
>   he commits an offence . . .
>
> (4) A direction under subsection (1) operates to require persons who re-enter the land within the said period with vehicles or other property to leave and remove the vehicles or other property as it operates in relation to the persons and vehicles or other property on the land when the direction was given.

The s 77(3) offence is extremely similar to those contained in ss 69, 61 and 62B. There is a defence provided by s 77(5) if the accused can show that his failure to leave or to remove the vehicle or other property as soon as practicable, or his re-entry with a vehicle, was due to:

- illness,
- mechanical breakdown, or
- other immediate emergency.

Section 77(4) ensures that a s 77 direction is effective for three months from the date on which it was given and does not need to be re-issued if one of the trespassers re-enters the land. The direction is also effective against those who were not themselves present on the land at the time it was given, but who re-enter within the three-month period.

Once a s 77 direction has been given and contravened by trespassers, it would be possible at that point for the police to begin arresting for s 77(3) offences. In practice, where the direction applies to a large group, arrest may be a less attractive option, in terms of resources, than following the s 78 route described in 9.8.3.

9.8.3 Orders made by magistrates for removal of persons and their vehicles

Section 78 CJPOA provides that where persons are in contravention of a s 77 direction, a magistrates court may 'make an order requiring the removal of any vehicle or other property which is so present on the land and any person residing in it'. By s 78(2), the order may authorize the local authority to take such steps as are reasonably necessary to ensure compliance with the order. This includes entering onto the land and removing vehicles.

The advantage of this approach from a policing perspective is that, through a s 78 order, the local authority can get authorization to use private contractors to assist with removal. Where the encampment is large, this is likely to be more pragmatic than trying to rely on police resources alone.

The application to the court must be made on complaint by the local authority, and so a detailed examination of s 78 is beyond the scope of this book. However, s 78(4) specifies that 'a person who wilfully obstructs any person in the exercise of any power conferred on him by an order under this section commits an offence'.

Police who attend the scene of an eviction under s 77/s 78 should be briefed on this beforehand and be aware of the provisions of the order, and who will be present: eg if a private security firm is being used to assist the eviction, how to identify the employees of that firm.

POINTS TO NOTE

Police involvement where s 77/s 78 is being used

There is benefit to be had from the police working together with a local authority who is considering using their s 77 CJPOA power, to plan **in advance** for an effective operation. For example, if the local authority issues inadequate or unclear s 77 directions, any arrests which are made for s 77(3) offences may later be successfully challenged. Police presence at the scene is likely to be necessary, not just because of the possibility of arrest for s 77(3) or s 78(4) offences, but generally to keep the peace.

Police and local authorities will also need to decide in advance whether or not to pursue a s 78 application after the initial s 77 direction has been given (if it is anticipated that the s 77 direction might not be followed), and to be clear on the timing of the operation, as well as the role the police will play as against the role of any private contractors the local authority will employ.

> In any decision over whether to use s 77/s 78, the reasons why the decision is being taken, including why it is deemed a necessary and proportionate measure, need to be carefully recorded.

9.9 Power to Remove Persons Attending or Preparing for Raves

Section 63 CJPOA confers similar powers to the sections discussed above, ie to give directions to leave which if not complied with mean an offence is committed. The section applies in relation to those who are preparing to attend, or are attending, a rave. It provides:

(1) This section applies to a gathering on land in the open air of 20 or more persons (whether or not trespassers) at which amplified music is played during the night (with or without intermissions) and is such as, by reason of its loudness and duration and the time at which it is played, likely to cause serious distress to the inhabitants of the locality; and for this purpose:

(a) such a gathering continues during intermissions in the music and, where the gathering extends over several days, throughout the period during which amplified music is played at night (with or without intermissions); and

(b) 'music' includes sounds wholly or predominantly characterized by the emission of a succession of repetitive beats.

(1A) This section also applies to a gathering if—

(a) it is a gathering on land of 20 or more persons who are trespassing on the land; and

(b) it would be a gathering of a kind mentioned in subsection (1) above if it took place on land in the open air.

(2) If, as respects any land, a police officer of at least the rank of superintendent reasonably believes that—

(a) two or more persons are making preparations for the holding there of a gathering to which this section applies,

(b) ten or more persons are waiting for such a gathering to begin there, or

(c) ten or more persons are attending such a gathering which is in progress,

he may give a direction that those persons and any other persons who come to prepare or wait for or to attend the gathering are to leave the land and remove any vehicles or other property which they have with them on the land.

(3) A direction under subsection (2) above, if not communicated to the persons referred to in subsection (2) by the police officer giving the direction, may be communicated to them by any constable at the scene.

(4) Persons shall be treated as having had a direction under subsection (2) above communicated to them if reasonable steps have been taken to bring it to their attention.

In essence, this section enables an officer of at least superintendent rank, who holds a reasonable belief that there is going to be a rave-type event which more than 20 people will attend, to give preventative directions either before the event starts or before an unmanageable number of people arrive. He can do this if:

- at least two people are preparing for a gathering on the land; or
- at least 10 people are waiting for a gathering on that land; or
- at least 10 people are attending a gathering which is in progress.

It can be indoors or outdoors, though if indoors there is a requirement that the persons be trespassing, which does not pertain to outdoor gatherings. This means that this section *cannot* be used against indoor raves where the occupier has given permission.

In either case, the section does not apply to an event which has been licensed by the local authority under the Licensing Act 2003, provided it is carried out in accordance with that licence: s 63(9). In such cases the consultation process will have provided the police, as well as the local community, with the opportunity to raise valid concerns by reference to the licensing objectives under the Licensing Act 2003.

The section specifically includes music 'wholly or predominantly characterised by the emission of a succession of repetitive beats'—in practical terms, to the types of electronic dance music that are likely to be played at raves. However, although the word rave is used in the title to the section, *any* musical genre might be covered, if reason of its loudness and duration and the time at which it is played, it is likely to cause serious distress to the inhabitants of the locality.

'Trespasser' has the same meaning as in s 61—see section 9.5 of this chapter.

In addition to the power to give directions, s 64(1)–(3) provides a power to enter the land without a warrant. This power can be used to establish that the suspected circumstances do in fact exist:

(1) If a police officer of at least the rank of superintendent reasonably believes that circumstances exist in relation to any land which would justify the giving of a direction under section 63 in relation to a gathering to which that section applies he may authorise any constable to enter the land for any of the purposes specified in subsection (2) below.

(2) Those purposes are—
   (a) to ascertain whether such circumstances exist; and
   (b) to exercise any power conferred on a constable by section 63 or subsection (4) below.

(3) A constable who is so authorised to enter land for any purpose may enter the land without a warrant.

Effectively, under this section, where the superintendent (or officer of higher rank) believes circumstances to exist which would justify the giving of a direction he can authorize his officers to enter the land to:

- ascertain whether such circumstances do in fact exist, and
- exercise s 63 powers (ie give directions), and
- seize and remove sound equipment and vehicles, under s 64(4) (covered at 9.9.7 of this chapter).

No warrant is required.

9.9.1 **Land**

This is not explicitly defined in the section and so it is submitted that any land will fall within the meaning of 'land' in the section. Section 63(10) specifies that 'land in the open air' includes land which is partly open to the air.

9.9.2 **Likely to cause serious distress to the inhabitants of the locality**

This requires that it is *likely* serious distress will be caused, not that it actually be caused. Police should record the reasons why it is thought likely. Evidence from police officers or local authority staff at the scene as to the volume should be gathered, as too should witness evidence from anybody who is living nearby who is actually affected.

9.9.3 **Reasonable belief of an officer of at least the rank of superintendent**

This is largely self-explanatory. It involves the usual test of reasonable belief, formed on reasonable grounds. It is good practice for the officer to record *at the time* the reason(s) for his belief.

9.9.4 **Giving a direction**

The direction can be communicated by any officer at the scene.

Under s 63(4), a direction will still apply to persons even if they have not actually seen or heard of it, provided that 'reasonable steps' have been taken to bring it to their attention. Reasonable steps that the police might take include large signs en route and at entrance points, speaking to people, loudspeakers and leaflets; also identifying organizers and speaking to them.

If a direction is being given, it will not apply to 'exempt persons'. These are the occupier of the land, any member of his family, any person who is an employee or agent of his, or any person whose home is situated on the land: s 63(5); s 63(1). 'Occupier' is defined in the same way as s 61—see 9.5.2 of this chapter.

9.9.5 **Offence of failing to comply with a direction**

Section 63(6) provides:

(6) If a person knowing that a direction has been given which applies to him—
   (a) fails to leave the land as soon as reasonably practicable, or
   (b) having left again enters the land within the period of 7 days begin-
       ning with the day on which the direction was given,
   he commits an offence . . .

Section 63(7) provides:

(7) In proceedings for an offence under subsection (6) above it is a defence for
    the accused to show that he had a reasonable excuse for failing to leave
    the land as soon as reasonably practicable or, as the case may be, for again
    entering the land.

'As soon as reasonably practicable' will depend on the circumstances of the
situation.
   Section 63(7A) provides:

(7A) A person commits an offence if—
   (a) he knows that a direction under subsection (2) above has been given
       which applies to him, and
   (b) he makes preparations for or attends a gathering to which this sec-
       tion applies within the period of 24 hours starting when the direction
       was given.

This covers a person who knows that a direction applies to him, who either
prepares for or attends another gathering, as defined by s 63, within 24 hours of
the direction being given.

9.9.6 **Power to turn people away, and the related offence under s 65(4)**

Section 65 CJPOA provides:

(1) If a constable in uniform reasonably believes that a person is on his way
    to a gathering to which section 63 applies in relation to which a direction
    under section 63(2) is in force, he may, subject to subsections (2) and
    (3) below—
   (a) stop that person, and
   (b) direct him not to proceed in the direction of the gathering.
(2) The power conferred by subsection (1) above may only be exercised at a
    place within 5 miles of the boundary of the site of the gathering.
(3) No direction may be given under subsection (1) above to an exempt
    person.
(4) If a person knowing that a direction under subsection (1) above has
    been given to him fails to comply with that direction, he commits an
    offence . . .

This section is self-explanatory. Note that the power can only be used by a uniformed officer, who is within five miles of the boundary site. A direction under this section could be given in writing and/or orally, as the officer will be face to face with the person he believes attending the rave. Police should keep a record of who has been given is such a direction, so that it is possible to later identify those who have disobeyed a direction.

'Exempt persons' are defined at 9.9.4 of this chapter.

9.9.7 Supplementary power of seizure for vehicles and sound equipment

Section 64(4) CJPOA provides:

(4) If a direction has been given under section 63 and a constable reasonably suspects that any person to whom the direction applies has, without reasonable excuse—

(a) failed to remove any vehicle or sound equipment on the land which appears to the constable to belong to him or to be in his possession or under his control; or

(b) entered the land as a trespasser with a vehicle or sound equipment within the period of 7 days beginning with the day on which the direction was given,

the constable may seize and remove that vehicle or sound equipment.

'Vehicle' has the same meaning as in s 61 (see section 9.5.6). The Police (Retention and Disposal of Vehicles) Regulations 1995 apply.

'Sound equipment' means equipment designed for or adapted for amplifying music, and it includes equipment suitable for use with such equipment. That means that electric cables, laptops and other electronic equipment that might form part of a sound set-up can potentially be seized.

Vehicles or property belonging to an exempt person, as defined at 9.9.4, cannot be seized.

The conditions for exercise of this power are:

- A reasonable suspicion on the part of the constable that a person to whom a s 63 direction applies has, without reasonable excuse, either
  - failed to remove any vehicle or sound equipment that is in his possession or control, or
  - entered the land as a trespasser with a vehicle or sound equipment within seven days.

The seven-day period begins with the day the direction was given: ie if the direction was given on a Sunday, the offence can be committed up to and including the following Saturday.

Where somebody is convicted of a s 63 offence, the court can order forfeiture of his sound equipment under s 66. An examination of that section is beyond the scope of this book.

9.10 **Other Miscellaneous Land-related Offences Relevant to Public Order Policing**

There are numerous other parts of our law that in certain circumstances *may* be of relevance to those involved in public order policing. Below are two further land-related matters and offences that are likely to be of most relevance.

9.10.1 **By-laws**

By-laws are:

> Ordinances affecting the public, or some portion of the public, imposed by some authority clothed with statutory powers, ordering something to be done or not to be done, and accompanied by some sanction or penalty for its non-observance.
>
> *Kruse v Johnson* [1898] 2 QB 91

In essence, they are 'local' laws made by local authorities and by other organizations who have statutory authority. They have the force of law within the area that they apply to, and they can create criminal offences for their breach. By-laws frequently exist to prohibit certain types of activity on land such as camping, lighting fires, attaching things to trees or walls or fences, or other activities which may be very relevant in relation to both traveller encampments and protest camps.

In practice, by-laws have sometimes been used to challenge the activity of protest groups and encampments in particular. In deciding whether or not to use by-laws as a means of policing a public order event involving protest, police should consider whether it amounts to a proportionate response to the situation (see chapter 2 on human rights). In *Tabernacle v Secretary of State for Defence* (*The Times*, 25 February 2009) the long-term 'peace' camp run by the anti-nuclear Aldermaston Women's Peace Camp was challenged on the basis that camping (and certain other activity) was prohibited by by-laws which applied to that land. One of women sought to challenge the legality of the byelaws by judicial review. On appeal, the Court of Appeal held, inter alia, that the prohibition on camping was a substantial interference with the appellant's Article 10 and 11 rights, which on the facts (which included the fact that the camp had run on a regular basis for over two decades without causing much interference to the Atomic Weapons Establishment, and the fact that the camp itself was an inherent part of the protest rather than just the 'mode' of protest) was not justified. Successful challenges have also been brought against byelaws on the basis that they are *ultra vires*, badly drafted, unreasonable or inconsistent with the general law.

The lawfulness of a particular byelaw is specific to that byelaw and if in doubt this is something on which the police should seek advice.

9.10.2 **Trespass on premises of foreign missions, etc**

Section 9 of the Criminal Law Act 1977 creates an offence of entering as a trespasser, or being present as a trespasser on, land such as foreign missions and diplomatic premises. 'Trespassing' should be understood to have the meaning that is ascribed to it throughout this chapter.

Section 9(2) sets out the different categories of premises that fall within the ambit of the offence. Typically, these will be:

• Foreign embassies
• Consulates
• Ambassadorial residences or official residences of foreign diplomats.

Section 9(3) provides a defence to an accused who can prove that he believed the premises were not covered by the 1977 Act.

Further reading

• *Guide to Effective Use of Enforcement Powers: Part 1, Unauthorised Encampments*, Office of the Deputy Prime Minister, 2006
• *ACPO Guidance on Unauthorised Encampments*, Association of Chief Police Officers, revised November 2009

NOTES

NOTES

NOTES

10

Football Violence

10.1 **Introduction**

The policing of football violence has certain unique features:

- the determination of some 'prominents' to indulge in pre-planned football violence;
- the existence and sophistication of coordinators, who use modern technology to arrange confrontations between rival supporters;
- the propensity for normally law-abiding, 'genuine' football fans to join in or follow (to a greater or lesser extent) a hardcore of violent supporters;
- the concurrent need to keep to a minimum the disruption of the football match, and inconvenience to the law-abiding football fans attending;
- as in many aspects of public disorder, alcohol plays a major part in football violence.

The majority of offences committed in association with football matches are fairly typical public order offences or offences against the person. However, there are a number of specific offences particular to football matches.

This chapter deals with the legislation specific to football disorder:

- Designated matches and stadiums;
- Restrictions on alcohol in and near football stadiums, and offences relating to alcohol and drunkenness;
- Criminal offences specific to football matches: racist chanting, pitch invasions, the throwing of missiles; illegal ticket sales and alcohol;
- Football Banning Orders in both the criminal and civil courts, and declarations of relevant offences.

10.1.1 **Hillsborough and the Taylor Reports**

The approach to the policing of football matches underwent a fundamental change following the tragic events at Hillsborough on 15 April 1989, which led to the deaths of 95 football supporters during a Football Association (FA) cup semi-final match at Sheffield Wednesday's football ground. In the aftermath an interim, then final, Taylor Report was produced. The reports recognized that, although the immediate cause of the tragedy was overcrowding and crushing rather than deliberate crowd violence, the conditions that led to the disaster had come about in part because of the hostile, aggressive and confrontational atmosphere that surrounded a large number of professional football matches in the United Kingdom and how this had affected the treatment of supporters both by the clubs and the police (see paragraph 26 of the report). A major theme of the final Taylor Report was that football violence could no longer be tolerated, or viewed as a problem mainly confined to those who choose voluntarily to attend football matches.

As well as investigating the events of the day that led to the disaster, the Hillsborough Inquiry looked at stadium design, crowd safety, ticketing, crowd control, the relationship between supporters, clubs, stewards and police, as well as the coordination of emergency services. Many of the 43 recommendations of the interim report and 76 recommendations in the final report were implemented. They now form a large part of the basis of stadium design (such as all-seater stadiums), crowd control, crowd safety and the policing of football matches today.

Over the last 15 years, considerable expertise has developed within dedicated police football intelligence and public order units. At times (such as in the season leading up to major international tournaments in the United Kingdom and Western Europe) the Home Office has provided funding ring-fenced for action against football hooliganism.

Perhaps due in part to these initiatives, arrests for football violence dropped significantly between 2001 and 2010. The extent to which these figures accurately reflect the reality of match day violence has been questioned. Nevertheless, it does appear that pro-active, diligent policing, engagement with football supporters and close liaison with football clubs, have reduced the frequency and seriousness of football violence and made the environment less intimidating (and, it is hoped, safer) for the peaceful spectator.

10.2 **Legislation**

Much of the legislation is restricted to particular matches or football grounds. Slightly confusingly, there are three different systems for categorizing matches and/or stadiums:

- 'designated' football matches or grounds for alcohol-related offences under the Sports Grounds and Sporting Events (Designation) Order 2005;
- 'designated' matches for offences under the Football (Offences) Act 1991; or
- 'regulated' matches for Football Banning Orders (FBOs) imposed under the Football Spectators Act 1989.

10.2.1 **Designated matches and grounds for alcohol**

Sports grounds are defined within s 9 of the Sporting Events (Control of Alcohol etc) Act 1985 (SECAA) as any place used (wholly or partly) for sporting events where accommodation is provided for spectators. Under the Sports Grounds and Sporting Events (Designation) Order 2005 (SI 2005/3204), all sports grounds are now 'designated grounds'.

Inside England and Wales, designated sporting events include all association football matches in which in which at least one team is from the Football League, the FA Premier League, the Football Conference National Division, the Scottish Football League or Welsh Premier League, or represents a country or territory, and all FA Cup matches (other than a preliminary or qualifying rounds).

If the sports ground is outside England and Wales, designated sporting events include all association football matches in which in which at least one team represents one of the domestic clubs referred to above, or represents the Football Association (FA) or the Football Association of Wales.

10.2.2 Regulated matches for Football Banning Orders

Regulated matches, for the purposes of the Football Spectators Act 1989 (FSA), include:

- Inside England and Wales, association football matches in which one or both participating teams represent:
  - a club which is a member of the Football League, FA Premier League, Football Conference or League of Wales;
  - a club whose home is outside England and Wales; or
  - a country or territory.
- Outside England and Wales, a match involving:
  - a national team appointed by the Football Association to represent England or appointed by the Football Association of Wales to represent Wales;
  - a team representing a club team from the Football League, the FA Premier League, the Football Conference or the League of Wales;
  - a national (or equivalent) team from a FIFA country, provided the match is part of an official FIFA/UEFA competition in which an English or Welsh team is eligible to participate or has participated;
  - an overseas club affiliated to FIFA, provided the match is part of a FIFA/UEFA competition and an English or Welsh club (from one of the leagues described above) is eligible to participate or has participated.

10.2.3 Restrictions on alcohol

SECAA sets out the specific offences connected with alcohol and football matches. Many of the offences can only be committed during a specific period spanning the match and a short period before and after it.

Definition of period

For the purposes of SECAA, the 'period' of a designated match is the period:

- beginning two hours before the start of the match or (if earlier) two hours before the time at which it is advertised to start, and
- ending one hour after the end of the match.

Where a match advertised to start at a particular time on a particular day is postponed to a later day, or does not take place, the restriction period, over two hours before scheduled kick-off to one hour after, still applies.

Transport to and from designated matches

One method of tackling football violence has been to focus on the transport that takes supporters to and from football matches. Increasing numbers of fans now drive to football matches. However, the sight of large numbers of coaches decked out in club scarves, making their way up and down the M1 on a Saturday morning, remains a common sight. 'Football specials', the chartered trains to football matches, became a focus for disorder, particularly after matches, and were phased out in the 1980s. However, the strain on public transport shortly before and after a well-attended football match has been experienced by many people, and trains and stations remain a flashpoint.

As a result, there are a number of specific prohibitions on alcohol in vehicles or trains in association with football matches, set out below.

(1) Sale of Alcohol on Public or Commercial Transport

Section 1(2) of SECAA 1985 creates the offence of permitting alcohol to be carried on coaches and trains. It provides that it is an offence for the operator of a train or a public service vehicle which is being used for the principal purpose of carrying passengers to or from a designated match to knowingly cause or permit alcohol to be carried on the vehicle. This offence is committed by the operator of the vehicle, and the servant or agent of the operator. It also applies to public service vehicles that have been hired privately.

A public service vehicle is defined by the Public Passenger Vehicles Act 1981, and includes those vehicles adapting to carry more than eight passengers which is being used to carry passengers for hire or reward. The passengers on such a vehicle may commit offences relating to drunkenness/possession of alcohol, even though the operator, servant or agent was unaware of the intention to use the service to attend (or return from) a designated match:

- Under s 1(3) of SECAA, a person is guilty of an offence if he has alcohol in his possession while on such a vehicle.
- Under s 1(4) of SECAA, a person is guilty of an offence if he is drunk while on such a vehicle.

It is not necessary to establish that every passenger on the coach is planning to attend a designated football match, provided the principal *purpose* (regardless of numbers) was to take spectators to the match. The passengers on such a vehicle may commit offences relating to drunkenness/possession of alcohol, even though the operator, servant or agent was unaware of the intention to use the service to attend (or return from) a designated match: see the case study *The Wives' Shopping Day Out* in this chapter.

(2) Private vehicles

Section 1A of SECAA applies to a vehicle which is adapted to carry more than eight passengers, but is not a public service vehicle, and is being used for the principal purpose of carrying two or more passengers for the whole, or even part of, a journey to or from a designated sporting event.

If this can be proved, then the following parties may commit an offence:

- the driver or keeper (or servant or agent of the driver or keeper), or someone to whom the vehicle has been made available by these people, if he knowingly causes or permits alcohol to be carried on the vehicle;
- a person who has alcohol in his possession while on such a motor vehicle;
- someone who is drunk while on the motor vehicle.

For the offence to be made out, it is not necessary that the transport be for the exclusive use of spectators attending the football match. The defence that the private coach has in fact been chartered for a 'shopping trip' should be carefully examined.

Case study

The Wives' Shopping Day Out

A coach chartered from London is stopped on match day, just a few miles from a football ground in Manchester, where a rival team from London is due to play a fixture. There are a large number of women on the coach, and a minority of men. Many of the passengers have been drinking alcohol, and several of them are drunk. There is alcohol on the coach.

The women claim they are on a shopping trip, and the men are their husbands who are coming along to keep their wives company. However, ten of the men have tickets for the football match.

The coach driver says that he has been chartered to take the coach to the car park of a nearby shopping centre, and no one—either from his employer or in the group—has mentioned the football match to him in any way.

- If the coach driver is telling the truth, it appears that neither he nor his employer (the owners of the coach who allowed the charter) is guilty of an offence.
- However, it appears that the shopping trip is, at least in part, a ruse. The principal purpose of the trip appears to be to ferry the football supporters to the match, giving the timing, distance of the 'shopping' trip, proximity of the shopping centre to the stadium and tickets possessed by a significant number (albeit not the majority) of passengers.
- Accordingly, those who were either drunk or in possession of alcohol have committed an offence under s 1A of SECAA.

Alcohol and containers at sports grounds

Alcohol

Section 2 of SECAA provides that a person is guilty of an offence if he is either drunk in a sports ground during the period of a designated match at that ground, or is drunk while entering or trying to enter a ground during the period of a designated match.

Under s 2, a person who is in possession of alcohol, at any time during the period of a designated match:

- when he is in any area of a designated sports ground from which the event may be directly viewed, or
- while he is entering or trying to enter a designated sports ground during the period of a designated sporting event at that ground,

is guilty of an offence.

A person who is drunk in a designated sports ground during the period of the match, or who is drunk while entering (or trying to enter) such ground during the period of the match, also commits an offence under s 2 of SECAA.

Containers

Section 2 also prohibits the possession of any drinks container (or fragment of a container) that is capable of causing injury to a person struck by it. A person is guilty of this offence if they are in possession of such an article at any time during the period of a designated match, (1) when at or near the designated sports ground, or (2) while entering or trying to enter the designated sports ground during the period of the match. This section is intended to prohibit the carrying of (primarily) glass bottles. However, it is not limited to glass containers.

10.2.4 **Fireworks**

Section 2A of the Act prohibits the possession or use of fireworks or flares. The section applies to any article or substance 'whose main purpose is the emission of a flare for purposes of illuminating or signalling (as opposed to igniting or heating) or the emission of smoke or a visible gas'. It expressly applies to distress flares, fog signals, and pellets and capsules intended to be used as fumigators or for testing pipes. Matches, cigarette lighters or heaters are expressly *excluded* from s 2A.

The section provides that a person is guilty of an offence if he or she has such an article in their possession during the period of a designated match when he is either (1) in any area of a sports ground from which the event may be directly viewed, or (2) entering or trying to enter a designated sports ground during the period of a designated match at that ground. If there is any doubt about the precise offence which has or may be committed, the officer also should consider whether they have the grounds to arrest to prevent a breach of the peace.

There is a defence where a person can establish that they had a lawful authority to be in possession of the item. However, it is difficult to imagine what the lawful authority might be for a supporter entering a ground with a flare, as opposed to a contractor arriving with fireworks for part of the official entertainment.

10.2.5 **Police powers under the Sporting Events (Control of Alcohol etc) Act 1985**

When policing football matches, the powers of stop and search granted to police officers under s 7 of SECAA have, if anything, a greater impact on the control of alcohol than the offences set out above. The regular, routine, searching of many—if not all—supporters upon their arrival has proved an effective deterrent to those who would previously have sought to bring alcohol into the ground.

Section 7 of SECAA entitles an officer to:

(1) enter any sports ground;
(2) search a person he has reasonable grounds to suspect is committing or has committed an offence under this Act;
(3) stop a public service vehicle (or a private vehicle carrying more than eight passengers—see 10.2.3 of this chapter) and may search such a vehicle, or any railway passenger vehicle, if he has reasonable grounds to suspect that one of the alcohol offences set out above has been committed in relation to that vehicle.

In addition to the statutory powers set out above, any football club or large sports stadium can, should, and in practice always does, impose the requirement that all people attending must consent to being searched (by either the police or stewards) as a condition of entry to the ground. This is one of the few exceptions to the general principle that officers should not seek to search people by consent where there is no power to do so.

10.3 **The Football (Offences) Act 1991**

The Football (Offences) Act 1991 ('the 1991 Act') creates a number of offences specific to football matches. In a similar way to the control of alcohol, the statute only applies to designated matches. However, the matches that are 'designated' for the purposes of the 1991 Act differ from those for the purposes of SECAA.

A 'designated match' within the meaning of the 1991 Act is a football match in which one or both of the teams represents a club in the Football League, the Football Association Premier League, the Football Conference or the League of Wales, or represents a country or territory, see s 1 of the 1991 Act.

10.3.1 **Throwing of missiles**

Under s 2 of the Football (Offences) Act 1991, it is an offence for a person at a designated football match to throw anything at or towards the playing area, or any area adjacent to the playing area to which spectators are not generally admitted, or any area in which spectators or other persons are or may be present.

The Act specifies that the throwing of any item towards the pitch is an offence. The article does not have to be one that might cause injury, alarm or fear.

There is a defence that the throwing of a missile was with lawful authority, or that the person throwing the missile had a lawful excuse. The burden is on the defendant to establish such an excuse. In practice, it is difficult to conceive what a lawful excuse might be.

10.3.2 **Racist or indecent chanting**

Under s 3 of the 1991 Act, it is an offence for any person to engage or take part in chanting of an 'indecent or racialist' nature at a designated football match.

'Chanting' means the repeated uttering of any words or sounds, whether alone or together with others. If a crowd is chanting a non-racialist chant, but within the group there is an individual using modified, racialist wording, that person would be regarded as chanting.

'Racialist nature' means consisting of or including matter which is threatening, abusive or insulting to a person by reason of his colour, race, nationality (including citizenship) or ethnic or national origins. 'Indecent' has its ordinary, everyday meaning: use of abusive words to describe players, managers or referees would qualify, such as, 'the referee's a wanker'. In *DPP v Stoke on Trent Magistrates Court* [2003] 3 All ER 1086 an accused had chanted the phrase, 'You're just a town full of Pakis'. The Divisional Court confirmed that this went beyond the taunt that 'Our town is better than your town'. Moreover, the word 'Paki' could not be dismissed as nothing more than a shortened form of 'Pakistani', and was not comparable to the phrase 'Brit' for 'Briton', as it was generally recognized as a racially offensive expression. The Divisional Court stated that there was 'no doubt' that behaviour fell squarely within the definition of the offence.

It follows that many of the chants used on a weekly basis by otherwise entirely law-abiding football supporters would qualify as 'indecent', and therefore expose those joining in to potential prosecution. In practice, a significant degree of latitude is allowed, and the offence of indecent, as opposed to racialist, chanting is rarely enforced.

There is no doubt that over recent years, clubs and police forces alike have taken a much tougher line with racist chanting as opposed to merely indecent and insulting songs. Provided that there is good quality evidence of a particular defendant participating in racist chanting—typically through CCTV or police camcorder footage—a decision to charge would rarely be controversial.

By contrast, there has been an extremely low incidence of arrest and prosecution for the singing of indecent, but otherwise non-threatening, football songs.

In many cases, it would be no more difficult to prove an individual was participating in an indecent chant than a racist one. The very low number of convictions suggests that there is a deliberate policy of tolerance towards relatively harmless, albeit indecent, chanting at football matches.

However, the crime of indecent chanting remains an offence that has significant potential to assist in combating football disorder. The offence was originally drafted so that it was not necessary to prove that the chanting was provocative, threatening or insulting, still less that the participant intended it to be so. Therefore, it is sensible and proportionate to consider arresting or charging for this offence, provided the chanting is more than mildly indecent, not intended to be good-natured, and is clearly likely to be intimidating or provocative, but where it might be difficult to prove that a specific public order offence has been committed by that individual. For indecent rather than racist chanting, if this line is to be taken, it would be important that it were enforced consistently.

The principle of proportionality would also require (1) that the individual or group were warned to stop prior to their arrest, and (2) that the prosecution of the defendant was *necessary* in order to achieve the goal of reducing the incidence of disorder and/or intimidation at football matches.

10.3.3 **Pitch invasions**

Section 4 of the 1991 Act, 'Going onto the Playing Area', provides that it is an offence for a person at a designated football match to go onto the playing area, or any area adjacent to the playing area to which spectators are not generally admitted, without lawful authority or lawful excuse. The burden is on a defendant to prove the lawful authority or excuse.

Following the Hillsborough disaster and Taylor Report, the barriers preventing pitch invasions were removed from all sports grounds. The pitch invasion (particularly by away fans) remained an incident likely to provoke hostility from rival fans. After the 1991 Act was passed, there was an initial reluctance to prosecute for the mere act of pitch invasion. However, it is now well recognized by football supporters that pitch invasions are unlawful. They are not tolerated by clubs, and are likely to lead to lengthy bans of supporters by the club.

Where someone is identified as having been involved in a pitch invasion, consideration should be given to whether or not to charge the person involved, or simply to use the incident as evidence in support of a football banning order (see 10.5 of this chapter).

10.4 **Ticket Touts**

The prevention of sale of tickets by touts is of real assistance in the policing of football disorder. It is well recognized that the scope for a small number of rival fans to antagonize and provoke each other is greatly increased if segregated areas are compromised by the unofficial sale of tickets to fans to whom the tickets were not originally allocated.

Section 166 of the Criminal Justice and Public Order Act 1994 (as amended by the Violent Crime Reduction Act 2006) makes it an offence for an unauthorized person to sell, offer for sale, advertise or otherwise dispose of a ticket for a designated football match.

'Designated football matches' for the purpose of s 166 are very similar to those designated for restrictions on alcohol—see section 10.2.1 of this chapter. A person is unauthorized to sell a ticket unless they have written authorization from the organisers of a match to sell (or otherwise dispose of) the ticket.

In addition to the criminal offence, on arresting a person for unauthorized sale of tickets, police officers have the power under s 166(5) of the Criminal Justice and Public Order Act 1994 to enter and search any vehicle which the officer has reasonable grounds for believing was being used for any purpose connected with the offence. An officer would therefore be entitled to search the vehicle of an arrested suspected ticket tout.

Professional ticket touts are often in possession of large amounts of cash. In many cases it will be appropriate to consider seizing cash and submitting an application for the forfeiture of seized cash under the Proceeds of Crime Act 2005 (POCA). Most police forces now have a financial crime unit, or similar, which would be able to assist in the necessary legal procedures. The most important features to be noted at the outset are:

- Forfeiture is a civil process in the magistrates' court, distinct from a confiscation order following conviction in the Crown Court;
- The minimum amount in a person's possession required to trigger the power to seize is triggered is £1,000;
- There are three stages: seizure, detention and forfeiture;
- Seized cash may not be detained for more than 48 hours (excluding weekends, Christmas Day, Good Friday and official bank holidays) except by order of a magistrate. The application for continued detention (s 298 POCA) must therefore be made immediately.

The court may order the forfeiture of the cash if satisfied that the cash is recoverable property (ie obtained through unlawful conduct) or is intended by any person for use in unlawful conduct.

10.5 **Football Banning Orders**

Football Banning Orders are governed by Part 2 of the FSA. They have proved to be a valuable tool in the fight against football hooliganism. Their widespread use has been coincided with a significant decrease in football related violence in and around football grounds. During the 2009–2010 season, 1,025 FBOs were issued across England and Wales.

FBOs can be imposed following either a criminal conviction for a relevant offence (s 14A FSA) or on a civil complaint in the magistrates' court (s 14B FSA).

The FSA is concerned with behaviour at or surrounding 'regulated' matches. A regulated match is defined by the Football Spectators (Prescription) Order (2004) (SI 2004/2409). It is any match in which either team is a club from the Football League, the FA Premier League, the Football Conference or the League of Wales; a club whose home ground is outside England and Wales, or any a country or territory.

10.5.1 Orders made on conviction

Section 14A FSA allows FBOs to be imposed by the magistrates' court or Crown Court on conviction for a relevant offence. The official Association of Chief Police Officers/Crown Prosecution Service policy is that 'there will be a presumption of prosecution whenever there is sufficient evidence to bring offenders before a court on appropriate criminal charges and where a Football Banning Order is considered necessary'. When an application is made following a conviction, if the court is satisfied that there are reasonable grounds to believe that making a banning order would help to prevent violence or disorder at or in connection with any regulated football matches, it *must* make an FBO. Prior to reaching the court making this decision:

- The prosecution must notify the defendant that in the event of conviction, it intends to seek a declaration that the offence is a relevant offence, and to seek an FBO;
- The prosecution must apply for an FBO;
- Both the prosecution and defence may submit evidence and/or make representations;
- An adjournment may be sought in relation to the banning order, even after sentence.

In order for an offence to be a 'relevant offence' it must be included in Schedule 1 of the Football (Disorder) Act 2000. Schedule 1 includes a wide variety of offences relating to violence, threats, and alcohol (including SECAA) either at or in the vicinity of a regulated football match, or those where the court makes a declaration at the time of the conviction that the offence related to football matches. A defendant may appeal against the declaration that the offence is a relevant offence.

The requirement of declaring at the time of the conviction that the offence was football related was considered in *R v Parkes* [2010] EWCA Crim 2803, (2011) 175 JP 33. The Court of Appeal upheld two FBOs imposed on Wolverhampton Wanderers ('Wolves') supporters, following a convictions for public order offences arising out of a confrontation between them and supporters from

West Bromwich Albion. The two sides were not playing each other that day, as West Bromwich Albion were playing Peterborough United. This was a regulated football match. Although the judge had not specified which regulated match the violence related to, he had found that it was abundantly clear that the violence was football related. The Court of Appeal confirmed that the West Bromwich Albion fans were together because of the match that their team had played, the Wolves supporters knew they would be together because of that match, where they would be and sought them out to cause trouble based on the rivalry between the clubs. The Court of Appeal confirmed that in these circumstances, the offences related to the match.

If the court is not satisfied that the making of a banning order would help to prevent violence or disorder at or in connection with any regulated football matches, it must state this in open court and give its reasons. Unusually, the prosecution has the right of appeal against a refusal of the court to impose an FBO. This right of appeal only arises where a person has been convicted but not banned.

In many cases, the connection with football and the grounds to believe that making an order would be help reduce help to prevent violence or disorder will be obvious. However, the court's power to adjourn is potentially extremely helpful: it may be that the police or prosecutor become aware of further material that is relevant to this question, such as information in relation to other incidents held by the dedicated football officers.

The opportunity should not be lost to obtain a FBO on conviction. The focus on any additional evidence, beyond that of the conviction, should focus on the prevention of violence or disorder at football matches by the defendant. In practice this is likely to require demonstration that the defendant has been involved in, or associated with, football related disorder on other occasions. If the defendant is, or may be, convicted in a court that is some distance from his home football club, the football intelligence unit for his home club should be contacted as a matter of routine. This is to ensure that the opportunity is not lost to put evidence before the court about the defendant's conduct at other matches.

There is a right of appeal to the Crown Court from magistrates, or to the Court of Appeal from the Crown Court.

10.5.2 **Convictions outside England and Wales**

Under s 22 of the FSA, where it is learned that a person had committed a 'relevant offence' (under Schedule 1 of the Football (Disorder) Act 2000) in other specific jurisdictions, a FBO can be sought on a similar basis to that following conviction in the UK.

The outline of the procedure is:

- An information is laid before magistrates that a person has been convicted of a corresponding offence in a country outside England and Wales. There is a specific format in which this information is to be provided, set out in the schedules to the orders relating to specific countries (see below);

- The magistrates issue a summons or warrant;
- Thereafter the procedure follows that of a summary trial (adjournments, etc);
- Upon the person attending, unless he has an appeal pending overseas, the magistrates may consider imposing a FBO;
- The test the court will apply is it is satisfied that there are reasonable grounds to believe that making the order would help to prevent violence or disorder at or in connection with regulated football matches: this is the same test as following a domestic conviction;
- Where the court refuses to make an order, the magistrates must state in open court that it is not satisfied that the reasonable grounds test is not satisfied, and why it is not satisfied.

An FBO imposed in this way takes effect as if it were imposed following a domestic conviction.

The only countries to which this provision currently applies are Scotland, Ireland, France, Italy, Belgium, the Netherlands, Sweden and Norway. There are a number of notable countries where overseas troubles have occurred in the past that are not included, such as Germany, Spain and Turkey. For these countries, the overseas conviction (and circumstances surrounding it) can still be relied upon in a s 14B application.

10.5.3 **Orders made in civil proceedings in the magistrates' courts**

While the majority of FBOs are made following conviction, they can also be made following a complaint to the magistrates' courts. These are civil proceedings. They are of particular assistance in cases where a person has not been convicted recently of violence or disorder, but there is evidence that they are associated with football violence. It has a real benefit in banning the organizers of confrontations who may remain in the background while the actual violence unfolds.

The complaint is made on behalf of the chief officer, so it must be ensured or verified that the necessary delegation of authority has been given to bring the proceedings. There is also the scope for the Director of Public Prosecutions (DPP) to bring the complaint. The complaint may only be brought if it appears to the police or the DPP that the person has at any time caused or contributed to any violence or disorder in the United Kingdom or elsewhere. There is no limitation period.

Although these are civil proceedings, in the leading case of *Gough v Chief Constable of the Derbyshire Constabulary* [2002] QB 1213, the Court of Appeal confirmed that the standard of proof was akin to the criminal standard. Subsequent legal authorities relating to the standard of proof in other civil proceedings (such as police misconduct matters) do *not* affect the decision in *Gough*.

It should not be thought that it will necessarily be 'easier' to obtain a FBO under section 14B rather than section 14A.

Under s 14B, the magistrates must consider a two-limbed test:

(1) Whether it is indeed proved that respondent has at any time caused or contributed to any violence or disorder in the United Kingdom or elsewhere; and if so

(2) Whether the court is satisfied that there are reasonable grounds to believe that making a banning order would help to prevent violence or disorder at or in connection with any regulated football matches.

If the court is satisfied of both these matters, it *must* impose a ban.

In most cases, the first stage of the test will be met by providing evidence of previous convictions, although the violence or disorder can also be proved using primary evidence. In proving that the respondent has in the past contributed to any violence or disorder, there is an historical limit of ten years prior to the date of the complaint. Conduct before this time cannot be considered, except circumstances relating to a conviction where the conviction is less than ten years old. There is no requirement that the violence or disorder be football related—it is no more than a 'threshold' test to be passed. However, the older the incident or incidents relied upon and the weaker their connection with football, the more cogent the evidence will have to be for the second stage of the test.

Although the second stage is described in terms of 'reasonable grounds', this must also be proved to the criminal standard. The evidence must either give 'rise to the likelihood that, if the respondent is not banned from attending prescribed football matches, he will attend such matches, or the environs of them, and take part in violence or disorder' (*Gough* paragraph 92), or demonstrate that if he is not banned, the respondent will attend at or near such matches and will encourage or assist in others taking part in violence or disorder.

It has been recognized that the second stage test will often be satisfied by building a profile of the respondent, using the football intelligence unit and by proving evidence of association with other problem supporters and presence at scenes of violent confrontation with other supporters or the police.

Case study

Football Banning Orders brought by civil proceedings: Case comparison

Case 1

The respondent has recently been convicted of an offence of violence during a fight between two groups of rival fans inside the stadium at an international match in Germany. His defence in the German trial was self-defence, but this was rejected by the court. An application for a FBO is made to the magistrate.

The first stage test is met, and can be proved by the conviction for violence. It should be straightforward to prove the second stage, subject to any evidence the respondent may wish to adduce.

Case 2

The respondent is 27. He has a conviction for street robbery from when he was 19 years old, unconnected with football. However, over the past three seasons, he has been seen repeatedly associating with problem supporters. He has been seen by officers in the vicinity of fights between rival supporters in locations that strongly suggest pre-planned confrontations. He has also been captured on CCTV apparently 'directing' supporters down a street towards a fight.

- The first stage is met by the fact of the conviction, but the conviction will provide the court *no assistance at all* in its decision whether or not to make a FBO.
- The evidence at the second stage must cogently and reliably establish, to the criminal standard, that the respondent is involved in football violence and that if a ban is not made, it is likely he will continue to attend at or near matches and participate in or otherwise contribute to disorder or violence.

Violence in this context has the straightforward definition of 'violence against persons or property' and includes 'threatening violence and doing anything which endangers the life of any person'. 'Disorder' includes:

(a) stirring up hatred against a group of persons defined by reference to colour, race, nationality (including citizenship) or ethnic or national origins, or against an individual as a member of such a group;

(b) using threatening, abusive or insulting words or behaviour or disorderly behaviour;

(c) displaying any writing or other thing which is threatening, abusive or insulting.

Technically, all that would be required to satisfy 'disorder' is insulting chanting. If all those supporters who joined in with insulting football chants inside stadiums faced the prospect of a FBO, the whole system would be discredited. It is important that the Act is applied in a proportionate way. and the behaviour subject to applications for FBOs does amount, in practical terms, to conduct properly characterized as 'criminal'. If an FBO is imposed, the respondent has right of appeal to the Crown Court.

10.5.4 **Evidence in support of FBOs**

The presentation of evidence in support of FBOs must be focused on the two-limbed test set out in 10.5.3. The evidential requirements are likely to be different on the two different limbs, although evidence relevant to the first limb may form an important part of the court's consideration at stage 2. It is desirable that the chief officer who applies for the FBO will have responsibility for the club the respondent supports. The local Football Intelligence Unit (FIU) should be in a position to provide the best evidence of the history of the respondent's conduct.

Section 14C(4) confirms that the magistrates may consider, among other things:

- any decision of a court or tribunal outside the United Kingdom,
- deportation or exclusion from a country outside the United Kingdom,
- removal or exclusion from premises used for playing football matches, whether in the United Kingdom or elsewhere,
- conduct recorded on video or by any other means.

The threshold test can often be satisfied by the production of certificates of conviction. However, there are other sources of information, such as police officers' witness evidence, that could establish either participation in, or contribution to, violence or disorder. This is particularly true if the respondent has been identified as encouraging or assisting others to participate in disorder. It may therefore be that in some cases it is the same evidence goes to the first and second stage.

The second stage of the test will often involve the presentation of compilation evidence by an officer of the FIU. This profile will be supported by video footage, both of incidents of disorder and association with other problem supporters, together with witness statements of other officers relating to previous incidents.

This distillation of evidence from numerous different sources to produce a profile raises potential problems in relation to the scope of the duty to disclose of the underlying material. Following the decision in *Newman v Commissioner of Police for the Metropolis* [2009] EWHC 1642 the following general principles apply to the preparation for a FBO hearing:

- There is no automatic duty of disclosure: the principle of fairness applies;
- Fairness does not require the routine disclosure of either the source material for the principal officer's statement, or the entirety of the footage on which the compilation video was based;
- The applicant is under a duty to disclose all material that might undermine the applicant's case or to assist the respondent's case. This does not normally require the routine disclosure of footage in which the respondent can be seen behaving responsibly (even the most hardened of football hooligans is not continuously rioting, so such footage is of minimal relevance);
- Applications for specific disclosure (for example relating to a specific incident where identification was dispute) are a potential exception: fairness would almost have certainly require that the appellant or his advisers be given an opportunity to view the full video before any reliance could be placed on the related clip;

- The admission of hearsay evidence is covered by the rules relating to hearsay in the civil context. If these rules are not followed, this may affect the weight which the court will attach to that evidence.

10.5.5 **Duration, terms and effect of FBOs**

The duration of an FBO is:

- 6–10 years if a sentence of immediate imprisonment or detention is imposed on conviction (either domestically or overseas): ss 14A, 14F(3), 22;
- In other s 14A/s 22 cases: 3–5 years;
- In s 14B cases: 3–5 years.

On making an FBO, a court must explain, in ordinary language, the effect to the person subject to the order (s 14E). Section 14E contains general terms that are automatically imposed as part of an FBO. In addition, specific additional restrictions relating to the individual may be sought under s 14. The court may impose these if it thinks fit, provided the restrictions are in relation to any regulated football matches. Under s 19 there are a number of requirements and restrictions on travel that arise during the 'control period' of overseas international tournaments. Once a ban has been imposed, the Football Banning Orders Authority (FBOA) is responsible for monitoring and enforcing FBOs and travel restrictions.

The general terms imposed under s 14E are that the person must report to a police station within five days of receiving the FBO. Thereafter he must report to the FBOA any changes in his name, address or passport, or if he either appeals against, or applies for a variation of, or early termination of the FBO. It will also require the claimant to surrender his passport when required to do so by the FBOA during the control period of an overseas tournament (see below).

The additional, specific terms that are sought will often relate to geographical exclusions at certain times of the week. For example, the FBO may prevent the defendant/respondent from being within one mile of any football stadium between midday and 5pm on Saturdays, or being prevented from entering a specific town centre during or within two hours either side of a home match. Careful thought must be given to specific restrictions to ensure that they are:

- Clearly worded, and easy to understand;
- Specific rather than ambiguous;
- Relevant to, and directed towards, the particular supporter's pattern of behaviour (eg the public houses where the 'risk supporters' for the home club generally congregate);
- Proportionate;
- Do not impact adversely on supporter, given his personal circumstances (work/home address, genuine family care requirements, etc).

The FBOA is responsible for enforcing travel bans on supporters subject to FBOs. On the supporter's initial attendance at his local police station after the imposition of an FBO, the police officer responsible for the police station will impose certain requirements on the banned supporter, as determined by the FBOA. Provided it is satisfied that it is necessary or expedient in order to reduce the likelihood of violence or disorder at or in connection with an overseas match, the FBOA may also require a person to report at a police station at a specified time (or between specified times) and to surrender his passport at a police station at or between specified times. These requirements arise when the government specifies a control period in relation to particular international tournaments, such as the World Cup or European Cup.

A person subject to a FBO may apply to the officer responsible for a police station for an exemption from the usual terms of his FBO. He must demonstrate that there are special circumstances which justify his being so exempted, and that as a result, if the exemption is allowed, he would not attend the match or matches. He may appeal to the magistrates' court against the refusal to allow an exemption.

10.5.6 **Offences**

A person who fails to comply with any requirement imposed by the FBO, or the travel restrictions under section 19, commits an offence under s 14J of the FSA. The punishment is imprisonment for a period up to six months, or a fine not exceeding level 5 on the standard scale, or both.

Further reading

- Interim Taylor Report, at <http://www.southyorks.police.uk/sites/default/files/foi/significantpublicinterest/interim%20report%20hillsborough.zip>
- Final Taylor Report, at <http://www.southyorks.police.uk/sites/default/files/foi/significantpublicinterest/interim%20report%20hillsborough.zip>
- The Association of Chief Police Officers and Crown Prosecution Service Prosecution Policy for Football Related Offences, at <http://www.cps.gov.uk/publications/prosecution/football_offences_policy.html>

NOTES

NOTES

Index

Printed and bound by CPI Group (UK) Ltd, Croydon, CR0 4YY